CCE edition

8

# LIVING SCIENCE

A C SAHGAL ◆ MUKUL SAHGAL

*Cover:* JAIKRIT RAWAT

Ratna Sagar

enriched & updated

# LIVING SCIENCE 6, 7, 8 at a glance

CCE edition

## WHAT DOES LIVING SCIENCE 6, 7, 8 CONSIST OF?

SUPPORT FOR THE TEACHER

**TEXTBOOKS**
a skill-based set of books that emphasize thinking skills, research skills, experimental skills and application skills, and go a long way in developing a scientific temper

**WORKBOOKS**
offer a wide variety of questions that can be used for both formative and summative assessment.

**TEACHER'S COMPANIONS**
consist of more tasks for formative assessment, guidelines for evaluation and answers to textbook questions.

**EDUCATOR SITE**
has more worksheets and interesting science-based information at science.ratnasagar.co.in

## STRUCTURE OF THE BOOK

The main book is divided into units according to the themes as per the NCERT syllabus. → The units are divided into chapters that follow the known-to-unknown approach. → There are 3–5 sets of tasks for formative assessment after every 4 or 5 chapters. → There are 2 test papers for summative assessment dividing the course into 2 terms as per the new CBSE pattern.

## STRUCTURE OF EACH CHAPTER

The TEXT conforms to the NCERT syllabus. The explanation of concepts is supported by photographs, diagrams and tables. → **ORAL QUESTIONS** after every main section are an important tool for formative assessment. They will strengthen the student's understanding of the concept. → **NOW YOU KNOW** includes a brief summary of the chapter. → **NEW WORDS** reiterates the meaning of the key concept words of the chapter.

## EXERCISES FOR FORMATIVE & SUMMATIVE ASSESSMENT

- MULTIPLE-CHOICE QUESTIONS
- VERY SHORT-ANSWER QUESTIONS
- SHORT-ANSWER QUESTIONS (TYPE I)
- SHORT-ANSWER QUESTIONS (TYPE II)
- LONG-ANSWER QUESTIONS
- HOTS QUESTIONS

## TASKS FOR FORMATIVE ASSESSMENT

- RESEARCH PROJECTS
- INTERNET-LINKED RESEARCH/ ACTIVITIES
- INFORMATION GATHERING
- PRESENTATIONS
- EXPERIMENTS/ MAKING MODELS/ DESIGNING EXPERIMENTS
- FIELD TRIPS

## THERE'S MORE . . .

- **IN-TEXT ACTIVITIES** in each chapter reinforce the concepts learnt
- **IT'S A FACT** gives snippets of interesting information that broaden and update knowledge.
- **LIFE SKILLS** link science with the day-to-day life of the child and his/ her surroundings.
- **TEACHER'S NOTES** have suggestions on a particular topic/concept or a chapter in general.

## science.ratnasagar.co.in

- **TEACHER'S ZONE** provides classwise worksheets for chapters.
- **MORE RESOURCES** provides information of the syllabus pertaining to different boards and interesting facts.
- **SCIENCE CALENDAR** highlights important events in science.
- **FAMOUS SCIENTISTS** gives a synopsis of famous scientists and their contributions.
- **ASK THE EXPERTS** lets user ask subject related queries and get satisfactory answers.

# CONTENTS

with extensive CCE support


CCE AND LIVING SCIENCE 8 6

## UNIT 1: Food

1. CROP PRODUCTION 7

◆ Crop plants ◆ Methods of crop production ◆ Nitrogen cycle ◆ Food from animals

FOR FORMATIVE ASSESSMENT
RESEARCH PROJECT; INTERNET-LINKED RESEARCH/ACTIVITIES; INFORMATION GATHERING; EXPERIMENTAL PROJECT; FIELD TRIP; PRESENTATION
LIFE SKILL

2. MICROORGANISMS 24

◆ Types of microorganisms ◆ Useful microorganisms ◆ Harmful microorganisms ◆ Food preservation

FOR FORMATIVE ASSESSMENT
RESEARCH PROJECT; INTERNET-LINKED RESEARCH/ACTIVITIES; EXPERIMENTAL PROJECT/MAKING A MODEL

## UNIT 2: Materials

3. SYNTHETIC FIBRES AND PLASTICS 37

◆ Polymers ◆ Synthetic fibres ◆ Plastics

FOR FORMATIVE ASSESSMENT
RESEARCH PROJECT; PRESENTATION; INTERNET-LINKED RESEARCH/ACTIVITIES; INFORMATION GATHERING; FIELD TRIP

4. METALS AND NON-METALS 47

◆ Occurrence of metals and non-metals ◆ Properties of metals and non-metals ◆ The reactivity series of metals ◆ Uses of common metals and non-metals ◆ Noble metals ◆ Corrosion of metals ◆ Alloys

FOR FORMATIVE ASSESSMENT
RESEARCH PROJECT; INTERNET-LINKED RESEARCH/ACTIVITIES; EXPERIMENTAL PROJECT; FIELD TRIP; PRESENTATION
LIFE SKILL

5. COAL AND PETROLEUM 65

◆ Natural resources ◆ Fossil fuels—coal, petroleum, natural gas ◆ Preventing an energy crisis

FOR FORMATIVE ASSESSMENT
RESEARCH PROJECT; INTERNET-LINKED RESEARCH/ACTIVITIES; INFORMATION GATHERING; PRESENTATION

MORE TASKS FOR FA 1 77

6. COMBUSTION AND FLAME 78

◆ Combustion ◆ Extinguishing a fire ◆ Flame ◆ Fuels ◆ Impact of burning fuels on the environment

FOR FORMATIVE ASSESSMENT
RESEARCH PROJECT; PRESENTATION; INTERNET-LINKED RESEARCH/ACTIVITIES; INFORMATION GATHERING; EXPERIMENTAL PROJECT
LIFE SKILL

## UNIT 3: The World of the Living

7. CONSERVATION OF PLANTS AND ANIMALS 91

◆ Biodiversity ◆ Flora and fauna ◆ Conservation of forests and wildlife ◆ Biosphere reserves ◆ Red data book

FOR FORMATIVE ASSESSMENT
RESEARCH PROJECTS; PRESENTATION; INTERNET-LINKED RESEARCH/ACTIVITIES; INFORMATION GATHERING; FIELD TRIP

8. CELL—STRUCTURE AND FUNCTIONS 102

◆ The cell theory ◆ Unicellular and multicellular organisms ◆ Plant and animal cells ◆ Growth and division

FOR FORMATIVE ASSESSMENT
RESEARCH PROJECT; INTERNET-LINKED RESEARCH/ACTIVITIES; EXPERIMENTAL PROJECT/DESIGNING A MODEL

9. REPRODUCTION 112

◆ Sexual reproduction ◆ Internal and external fertilization ◆ Reproduction in humans ◆ Metamorphosis ◆ Asexual reproduction

FOR FORMATIVE ASSESSMENT
RESEARCH PROJECTS; INTERNET-LINKED RESEARCH/ACTIVITIES; EXPERIMENTAL PROJECT

10. REACHING THE AGE OF ADOLESCENCE 123
◆ The endocrine system ◆ Puberty and adolescence ◆ Determining the sex of the baby ◆ Health for adolescents
FOR FORMATIVE ASSESSMENT
RESEARCH PROJECTS; INTERNET-LINKED RESEARCH/ACTIVITIES; EXPERIMENTAL PROJECT

MORE TASKS FOR FA 2 132
TEST PAPER 1 FOR SA 1 133

UNIT 4: Moving Things, People, and Ideas

11. FORCE AND PRESSURE 135
◆ Types of force and its effects ◆ Pressure and its applications in daily life ◆ Pressure exerted by liquids ◆ Atmospheric pressure
FOR FORMATIVE ASSESSMENT
RESEARCH PROJECT; INTERNET-LINKED RESEARCH/ACTIVITIES; INFORMATION GATHERING; PRESENTATION
LIFE SKILL

12. FRICTION 150
◆ What is friction? ◆ What causes friction? ◆ Advantages and disadvantages of friction ◆ Minimizing and increasing friction ◆ Fluid friction
FOR FORMATIVE ASSESSMENT
RESEARCH PROJECT; INTERNET-LINKED RESEARCH/ACTIVITIES; DESIGNING AN EXPERIMENT
LIFE SKILL

13. SOUND 158
◆ How sound is produced and its characteristics ◆ How sound travels ◆ Functioning of the human ear ◆ Reflection and absorption of sound ◆ Musical sound and noise
FOR FORMATIVE ASSESSMENT
RESEARCH PROJECTS; INTERNET-LINKED RESEARCH/ACTIVITIES; INFORMATION GATHERING; MAKING A MODEL

UNIT 5: Natural Phenomena & UNIT 6: How Things Work

14. SOME NATURAL PHENOMENA 173
◆ Concept of charge and its types ◆ Attraction and repulsion of charges ◆ Detection and measurement of charge ◆ Flow of charge ◆ Lightning ◆ Safety during lightning ◆ Richter scale ◆ Causes and effects of earthquakes ◆ Protection against earthquakes
FOR FORMATIVE ASSESSMENT
RESEARCH PROJECTS; INTERNET-LINKED RESEARCH/ACTIVITIES; MAKING A MODEL

15. CHEMICAL EFFECTS OF ELECTRIC CURRENT 190
◆ Electric current ◆ Conduction of electricity through liquids ◆ Electrolysis ◆ Electroplating
FOR FORMATIVE ASSESSMENT
RESEARCH PROJECTS; INTERNET-LINKED RESEARCH/ACTIVITIES; INFORMATION GATHERING; DESIGNING MODELS
LIFE SKILL

MORE TASKS FOR FA 3 200

16. LIGHT 201
◆ Regular and diffused reflection ◆ Laws of reflection ◆ Characteristics of image formed with a plane mirror ◆ Multiple reflection
FOR FORMATIVE ASSESSMENT
INTERNET-LINKED RESEARCH/ACTIVITIES; MAKING A MODEL
LIFE SKILL

17. REFRACTION AND DISPERSION OF LIGHT 211
◆ Refraction of light ◆ Dispersion of light ◆ Lenses ◆ Structure of the eye ◆ Visually impaired
FOR FORMATIVE ASSESSMENT
RESEARCH PROJECT; INTERNET-LINKED RESEARCH/ACTIVITIES; DESIGNING AN EXPERIMENT

18. THE UNIVERSE 229
◆ The universe, galaxies, stars, planets, satellites and constellations ◆ Measuring distances in the universe ◆ The solar system ◆ The origin of the universe
FOR FORMATIVE ASSESSMENT
RESEARCH PROJECTS; INTERNET-LINKED RESEARCH/ACTIVITIES; INFORMATION GATHERING; FIELD TRIP

UNIT 7: Natural Resources

19. POLLUTION OF WATER AND AIR 246
◆ Pollution and conservation of water ◆ Pollution and conservation of air
FOR FORMATIVE ASSESSMENT
RESEARCH PROJECTS; INTERNET-LINKED RESEARCH/ACTIVITIES; INFORMATION GATHERING; FIELD TRIP

MORE TASKS FOR FA 4 257
TEST PAPER 2 FOR SA 2 258

NCERT SYLLABUS 260

# CCE and Living Science 8

Living Science 6–8 was planned as a skill-based series of books that emphasize on **thinking skills**, **experimental skills**, **research skills** and **application skills**. Over the years, this emphasis has been continuously strengthened by including new features such as **HOTS Questions**, **My Virtual Library** and additional activities and projects.

This **edition of Living Science 6–8** incorporates CCE by introducing **oral questions**, **written assignments based on the pattern of the CBSE sample paper**, more skill-based projects and **life skill tasks**.

Given below are some examples to illustrate how the **Living Science 8 CCE edition** lends itself to tools suggested by the CBSE for assessment under CCE in science.

## Formative Assessment with Living Science 8

| | |
|---|---|
| Oral questions (for class response) | p. 10, p. 16, p. 19, p. 27, p. 32 and so on |
| Written assignments | p. 20–22, p. 33–35 and so on |
| Experimental work | p. 10–11 Activity 1–2, p. 24 Activity 1 and so on |
| Planning/designing experiment | p. 157 Investigate friction<br>p. 228 Observing a spectrum and detecting infrared rays |
| Deduction based on investigative research and information gathering | p. 22 Research on millets;<br>Research on Green Revolution—My Virtual Library gives sites for research project on Green Revolution<br>p. 110 Research on cancer<br>p. 121 Research on twins and on reproduction in honeybees<br>p. 122 My Virtual Library gives sites for research on cloning |
| Contextual (text-based) research projects | p. 35 Research on microorganisms<br>p. 100 Research on biosphere reserves, national parks and wildlife sanctuaries in India |
| Presentations including the use of IT | p. 23, p. 46, p. 64, p. 76, p. 100 and so on |
| Field tour | p. 23, p. 46, p. 64, p. 77, p. 101 and so on |
| Making models | p. 189—Leyden jar<br>p. 198 & 199—Current tester & electric pen<br>p. 210—Periscope |

## Life skills & Living Science 8

The HOTS questions included in the scholastic curriculum are designed to enhance the students' creative and thinking skills.

In some chapters, a **life skill task** has been given to develop the students' social skills, organizational skills and so on. See p. 23, p. 64, p. 90, p. 149, p. 210

1

# Crop Production

You know that all living organisms get their energy and nutrition mainly from food. You also know that we get food from plants and animals. The science that deals with the growth of plants and animals for human use is called **agriculture**. Agriculture is the world's largest and most important industry. It is thought to have begun 10,000 years ago. Before that, humans were wandering food-gatherers, ate raw fruits and vegetables and hunted animals for food. Then they discovered that by planting seeds, they could grow plants that gave them food. This was the beginning of crop production. Humans no longer had to wander around to search for food. They became farmers and settled in farming communities. They also started domesticating animals for food and other purposes.

Today nearly half of the world's workforce is employed in growing crops or looking after farm animals. In India, nearly 70 per cent of the population works in the agricultural sector. However, agriculture changed very slowly until about a hundred years ago. But since then, there have been tremendous advances in agriculture, such as development of new varieties of plants and animals, use of fertilizers for better produce, use of pesticides for protection of crops, and use of machines, such as tractors and harvesters, which are labour-saving devices. This has led to better crops and

**IN THIS CHAPTER**

CROP PLANTS ◆ METHODS OF CROP PRODUCTION ◆ NITROGEN CYCLE ◆ FOOD FROM ANIMALS

higher yields. In India, this **agricultural revolution** (or **green revolution** as we call it) began in 1960. As a result, production of foodgrains has increased several fold.

## CROP PLANTS

When a large number of plants are grown at the same place for food, it is called a **crop**. A large number of wheat plants grown in a field make up a crop of wheat. Cereals were the first crop known to be cultivated. Cereals are tall grasses which are cultivated for their nutritious seeds called **grains**. They provide the staple food for people in nearly every part of the world. Grains are rich in starch and also contain proteins, vitamins, minerals and fibre. Wheat is the most important cereal in the world, followed by paddy (rice) and maize.

Now many different kinds of crops are grown for food. Table 1.1 lists some common crop plants grown in India.

Horticulture is a branch of agriculture that deals with the production of vegetables, fruits, flowers and decorative plants. It is similar to agriculture in many ways, but is usually carried out on a smaller scale. Vegetables and fruits are rich sources of minerals and vitamins.

**Kharif and rabi crops:** In India, there are two main seasons for cultivating crops—the kharif and the rabi seasons. Accordingly, the crops grown in these seasons are known as **kharif** and **rabi** crops.

- Kharif crops, such as paddy, require a lot of water. They are sown at the beginning of the south-west monsoon, during June or July. They are harvested after the monsoon, in September or October. Some other kharif crops are maize, soya bean and cotton.
- Rabi crops, such as wheat, are sown at the beginning of the winter season (October to December) and harvested by March or April. Some other rabi crops are gram, pea, mustard and linseed.

TABLE 1.1 Some common crop plants grown in India

| CROP PLANTS | EXAMPLES |
|---|---|
| cereals | wheat, paddy (rice), maize, barley, ragi |
| pulses | gram, peas, beans |
| oil seeds | mustard, groundnut, sunflower |
| root crops | sweet potato |
| tuber crops | potato, tapioca |
| sugar crops | sugarcane, beetroot |
| plantation crops | tea, coffee, rubber, coconut |
| fibre crops | cotton, jute |

## METHODS OF CROP PRODUCTION

Modern agriculture is carried out in a scientific and systematic way. It recognizes that for healthy growth and good output, crops require oxygen, sunlight, water, nutrients from the soil, protection from weeds and pests, and proper storage after harvesting. It also recognizes that the needs of crops, such as soil type, nutrients, water, etc. are different for different crops.

Sunlight and air are abundantly available in the open crop fields. For other requirements, however, the farmer has to make special efforts. The step-by-step methods of agriculture that take care of these requirements are as follows.

Preparation of soil → Seed selection and sowing
→ Manuring → Irrigation → Weeding
→ Protection from pests and diseases
→ Harvesting, threshing and winnowing
→ Storage

### Preparation of soil

Soil anchors the roots of plants, provides nutrients and water to them, and also provides oxygen to the roots. The microbes and other organisms, such as earthworms in the soil, help to keep it fertile.

Preparation of the soil involves **loosening** and **turning** it. This has the following advantages:

- Loose soil has a lot of air trapped in it, which is used by the roots to breathe easily.
- Loose soil allows the roots to penetrate deeper, thus securing the plant more firmly.
- Loose soil helps the growth of earthworms and microbes in the soil. They provide nutrients to the soil and aid in further loosening of the soil.
- Turning and loosening of soil brings nutrient-rich soil to the top. Plants can then absorb these nutrients more efficiently.
- Loose soil mixes more uniformly with fertilizers.

The process of loosening and turning the soil is called **tilling** or **ploughing**. It is carried out by using a wooden or iron plough which is pulled either by animals or by tractors. Iron ploughs are more popular these days.

Tilled soil may have big lumps of soil. These need to be crushed and the soil **levelled**. This is done with the help of a wooden or iron leveller. Levelling also prevents erosion of soil by wind or water.

Table 1.2 lists some common implements used in agriculture.

### Seed selection and sowing

Once the soil is prepared, seeds are sown in it.

TABLE 1.2 Common implements used in agriculture

| STEPS | IMPLEMENTS |
|---|---|
| soil preparation | |
| ◆ ploughing | wooden or iron ploughs |
| ◆ levelling | wooden or iron levellers |
| sowing | ploughs, hand sowing, seed drills |
| manuring | manually or with drills |
| irrigation | tubewells, sprinklers |
| weeding | trowel (*khurpa*) |
| crop protection | knapsack sprayer, aerial spray |
| harvesting | sickle, harvesting machine |
| threshing | animals, threshers, combines |
| storage | jute bags, wooden, clay or metal containers |

While sowing, the following points need to be kept in mind:

- Seeds should be of **good quality**, **healthy** and **free from diseases**.
- They must be planted at the **proper depth** in the soil. If planted deep in the soil, they cannot respire, and their shoots may not be able to push through the soil. If planted on the surface, they will be eaten by birds.
- Seeds require **water** for germination. The soil should, therefore, have water in it. However, if there is too much water, seeds will not germinate properly.
- Seeds should be sown at **proper distances**. If they are too close they will not get enough water, sunlight and nutrients. If they are too far apart, there is wastage of field space.

Seeds can be sown manually or by seed drills. They are sown manually by sprinkling

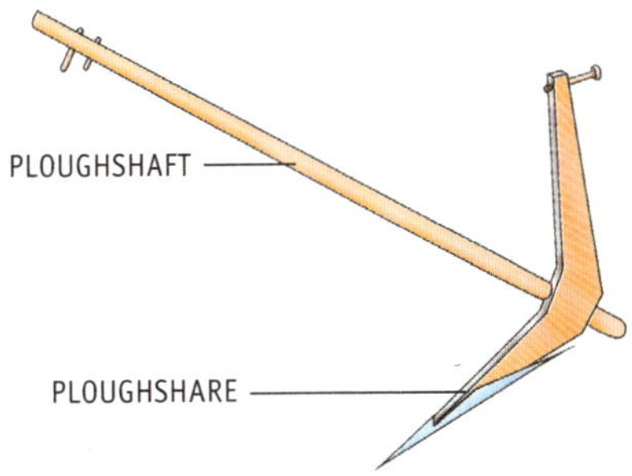


FIG. 1.1 A plough

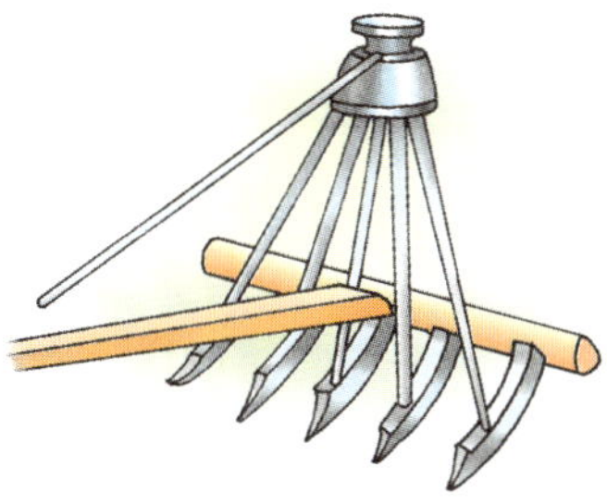

FIG. 1.2 A seed drill

FIG. 1.3 Sowing seeds using a seed drill

**ACTIVITY 1 (Experimental investigation): To separate healthy seeds from unhealthy ones**

Half-fill a beaker with water. Put some wheat seeds in it and stir. Wait for some time. Do some of the seeds settle down and others float in the water?

Damaged seeds become lighter and hence float on water. This is a good method of separating healthy seeds from the damaged ones.

them into the soil by hand. This process is called **broadcasting**. It has the disadvantage that seeds are unevenly distributed in the field.

A **seed drill** has a funnel-shaped opening leading to long tubes (Fig. 1.2). It is attached to a plough. Seeds are put into the funnel. As the plough makes furrows in the soil, the seeds are deposited in the soil by the drill. The seed drill sows the seeds at equal distances and proper depth. This ensures that the seeds also get covered by soil after sowing. This saves them from being eaten by birds.

Sometimes, as in rice, tomato, onion, chilli and brinjal, seeds are not directly planted in the fields. Instead, they are planted in seed beds called **nurseries**. After they have grown into small plantlets, they are called **seedlings**. The seedlings are then transferred and **transplanted** in the field. This helps the farmers select only the healthy seedlings and to space them properly while planting. This increases crop production.

## ORAL QUESTIONS FOR FORMATIVE ASSESSMENT

1. Agriculture deals with plants and not with animals. Do you agree? Give reasons.
2. Name three crops that are classified as cereals and three that are classified as pulses.
3. If a crop is sown in June and harvested in October, what will it be classified as—*rabi* or *kharif*?
4. It is necessary to loosen the soil by ploughing before sowing seeds. Why is it necessary to level the soil after ploughing?
5. Seeds are often grown in nurseries and then transplanted to the fields. What is the advantage of this?

### Manuring

Plants require nutrients for growth. They get these nutrients from the soil. Therefore, by the time a crop is harvested, it has taken away some of the nutrients present in the soil. This way, the nutrients get used up if land is cultivated for a long time. This causes the crop yield to start falling. Therefore, these nutrients need to be replenished from time to time. This can be done either by natural methods or by adding manures and fertilizers to the soil.

**Natural methods**

- **Field fallow:** One way of allowing land to naturally regain the nutrients is to leave it free (or fallow) for one or more season. Dead plants, animals and other organic matter that collect on the land are decomposed by microbes. Thus, the nutrients are returned to the soil.
- **Crop rotation:** Each crop uses more of some nutrients and less of others. Farmers, therefore, change their crop in each season so that the soil is not depleted of any particular nutrient. This is called **crop rotation**. For example, wheat or rice uses up large amounts of nitrogen from the soil. This nitrogen can be naturally replenished if the next crop grown is that of a legume, like pea or groundnut. You have read in Class 7 that bacteria called *rhizobium* are present

in the nodules of roots of leguminous plants. They can fix atmospheric nitrogen to form water-soluble nitrogen compounds. The soil is then ready for the next wheat or rice crop.

- **Mixed cropping:** Sometimes two or more crops are grown together in the same field. The crops are chosen in such a way that the nutrients needs of one crop are fulfilled by the other. Any leguminous crop, such as peas, soya beans or green beans, and a cereal crop, like wheat or rice, can be grown together in the same field for this reason. Cotton and groundnut crops are also often grown together.

However, these natural methods alone are not enough to maintain the fertility of the soil, and farmers have to add manures and fertilizers from time to time.

**Using fertilizers and manures**

- **Manures:** Manures are organic substances obtained from dead plants and animal wastes. Green manure is made from crops grown specifically to be ploughed into the soil while still green, i.e. legumes, rye grass, fenugreek, etc., to improve the fertility of the soil.

  Animal manure consists of animal wastes. **Compost** is a manure obtained by the decomposition of dead plants and animal waste. Compost is made by burying all available organic materials in a pit with alternating layers of soil, and leaving it to rot. Bacteria and fungi in the layers of soil speed up the decomposition. Compost is rich in organic nutrients but not in some important nutrients like nitrogen, phosphorus and potassium.
- **Fertilizers:** Fertilizers are human-made chemical substances that contain one or more nutrients essential for plant growth. The most widely used fertilizers are **NPK fertilizers** that are rich in nitrogen (N), phosphorus (P) and potassium (K) salts. They are easy to store and handle. Since they are soluble in water, they are directly absorbed by plants and greatly increase crop yields.

  However, if overused, fertilizers harm the soil by making it porous. Excess fertilizers get washed into water bodies and harm aquatic animals.

Fertilizers are prepared in factories but manure can be prepared in fields. Farmers normally use a combination of manures and fertilizers.

**Activity 2 (Experimental investigation): Nutrients and plant growth**

Germinate some *moong* seeds for 12–18 hours. Let them grow into seedlings. This may take 1–2 days more.

Collect some soil, compost and NPK fertilizers. These will have to be mixed as explained below.

Take four empty glasses. In the first glass, put some soil mixed with compost. In the second glass, put soil mixed with NPK fertilizer. In the third glass, put some soil mixed with both compost and NPK fertilizer. In the fourth glass, put some soil with no manure or fertilizer mixed with it.

Select some equal-sized seedlings, and plant two seedlings in the soil mixture in each glass. Pour the same amount of water in each glass. Keep the seedlings in the sun. Water them regularly and observe their growth for about 10 days. Note your observations.

In which glass was the growth fastest, i.e. in which glass did the seedlings become tallest? Which glass showed better growth of seedlings, i.e. which glass showed healthier seedlings?

TABLE 1.3 Differences between manures and fertilizers

| MANURES | FERTILIZERS |
|---|---|
| These are natural organic substances. | These are inorganic salts made by humans. |
| These are rich in humus but not in inorganic nutrients. | These are rich in inorganic nutrients but do not contain humus. |
| These are prepared in fields. | These are prepared in factories. |

## Irrigation

**Irrigation** means supplying water to crops in the field. Irrigated land in India gives several times more yield than non-irrigated land. In our country, a large number of farmers depend on rain for irrigation. However, rain varies and does not always supply the right amount of water at the right time. Therefore, it is important for farmers to supply water regularly to the crops.

Water required for irrigation can be taken from rivers, reservoirs, lakes, ponds, wells and tubewells. It is delivered to the fields by irrigation canals, or pumped up from a tubewell which is operated by using electric or diesel pumps, and then guided to the fields through channels (Fig. 1.4).

Modern methods of irrigation help to use water economically.

- In the **sprinkler system**, water escapes from revolving nozzles and is sprinkled like rain on the crops (Fig. 1.4). This system is useful for sandy soil and uneven land.
- In **drip irrigation**, water is allowed to fall drop by drop from a pipe, just near the roots of plants (Fig. 1.4). This minimizes wastage of water. However, it is very expensive. It is useful in areas where there is water shortage.

Crops need water at the right time and in the correct quantity. This quantity varies from crop to crop. For example, rice plants are transplanted into fields full of water and need continuous irrigation. However, wheat does not require so much water. It requires water at specific times during its growth.

Besides providing the right amount of water, it is necessary to have adequate drainage in irrigated fields. If a field is supplied with excess water it is said to be **waterlogged**. Waterlogging replaces the air in the soil with water, which reduces the supply of air to the roots of plants. This stops the growth of the plants. It also increases the amount of salt in the soil which is harmful for the crops.

## Weeding

Weeds are unwanted plants that grow along with the crops. They compete with the crops for water, minerals and sunlight and, therefore, reduce crop yield. They spread very fast. It is, therefore, necessary to remove them from time

a. Tubewell b. Sprinkler system c. Drip irrigation

FIG. 1.4 Some methods of irrigation

FIG. 1.5 Some common weeds

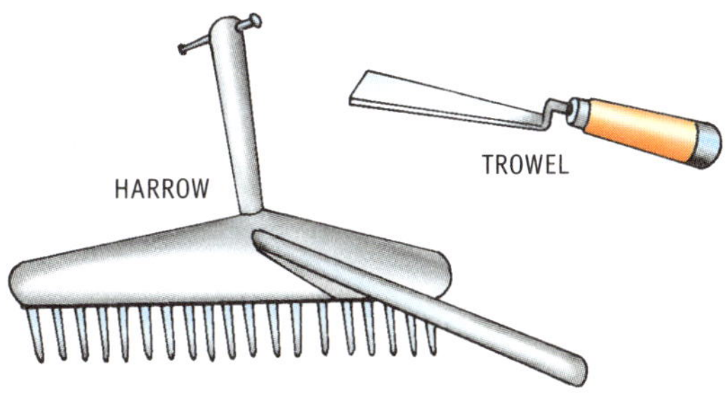


FIG. 1.6 Implements used for weeding

to time. Different types of weeds grow with different crops. They also vary from place to place and from season to season. *Amaranthus* is a very common weed which grows with almost every crop (Fig. 1.5).

The process of removing weeds from a field is called **weeding**. Weeding can be done manually by pulling the weeds out by hand or by using a trowel or a harrow to uproot them (Fig. 1.6). Weeding is also done by spraying special chemicals called **herbicides** or **weedicides**, with the help of a sprayer. They destroy the weeds but do not affect the main crop. Some common weedicides are dalapon, metachlor and siniazine. However, weedicides are poisonous and the grains must be properly washed before being consumed. Since weedicides are poisonous, spraying may affect the health of farmers. They should be careful while using weedicides. It is advised that they should cover their mouths and noses with cloth while spraying.

Research for evolving safer methods to kill weeds is going on. For example, insects that attack only specific weeds have been used to control those weeds. However, it is necessary to check the reproduction of these insects. Experiments have been conducted to attract and trap the male population of the insects, in order to check their reproduction.

### Protection from pests and diseases

Pests are organisms that attack and damage crops. They may be rodents (like rats) or insects (like locusts, weevils or termites). Rats eat the grains produced, whereas insects damage crops as well as grains.

Pests can be controlled by pesticides which are poisonous chemicals. Pesticides kill pests as well as their eggs and larvae but do not affect the plant. These include **insecticides** which are used to kill insects, and **rodenticides** which are used to kill rodents. Insecticides are sprayed by hand-operated machines or by low-flying aircraft if fields are large (Fig. 1.7). They must be sprayed at appropriate times in the correct dosage, otherwise pests might become resistant to them. Some common insecticides are BHC (commonly known as gammaxane), malathion and disyston.

a. Using a hand sprayer

b. By an aircraft

FIG. 1.7 Spraying pesticides

Plants are also damaged by diseases caused by fungi, bacteria or viruses. These diseases are transmitted through seeds, air, soil or through insects.

- Rust and smut are fungal diseases of wheat.
- Blight of potatoes is also a fungal disease.
- Wilt is a disease caused by a bacterium. The xylem tissue of the plant gets blocked and the plant wilts and dies as water cannot be conducted up.

Spraying of chemicals of various kinds gives protection to crops against these diseases. For example, a group of pesticides called **fungicides** are used to destroy fungi.

Pesticides must be used with caution, otherwise they can cause damage. These kill useful insects as well, such as honeybees. In humans, these cause irritation of skin and respiratory problems. The worst thing is that these get mixed up with the soil and water and are absorbed by the plants. These then enter our bodies through fruits and vegetables which we eat and cause us harm.

Fruits and vegetables bought from the market often have a coating of pesticides on them. They must be washed off carefully before eating as these are harmful for our health.

**IT'S A FACT!**

Organic farming of crop cultivation employs biological methods of fertilization and pest control as substitutes for chemical fertilizers and pesticides. It was started in the 1930s by **Sir Albert Howard**, a British agricultural scientist who came to India at that time. He considered fertilizers and pesticides as being injurious to health and the environment, and unnecessary for successful cultivation. He learned the processes of organic farming from Indian peasants, whom he treated with respect as his professors.

a. Sickle is used for harvesting.

b. A thresher

c. Combine is used for both harvesting and threshing.

FIG. 1.8 Harvesting and threshing

### Harvesting, threshing and winnowing

Once the crop matures, it is harvested, i.e. cut and gathered. This may be done manually by using a **sickle** (Fig. 1.8), or by using a machine called a **harvester**.

Next, the grain is separated from the cut crop. This process is called **threshing**. Threshing can be done manually by making oxen or buffaloes trample over the cut crop. Or it can be done by a machine called **thresher**. A farm machine called **combine** (Fig. 1.8) is used for both harvesting and threshing.

After threshing, the grain has to be separated from the chaff. This can be done manually with the help of the wind and is called **winnowing**. In this process, the mixture is dropped on the ground from a height. The heavier seeds fall almost vertically down, whereas the lighter chaff gets blown away by the wind and falls at a distance (Fig. 1.9).

a. Manually with the help of wind

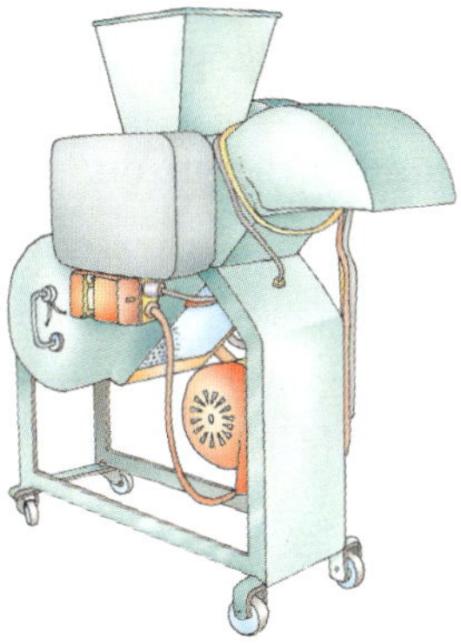

b. A winnowing machine

FIG. 1.9 Separation of grain from chaff

FIG. 1.10 Silos for storing grains

The stem of the crop is cut into small pieces and used as cattle fodder.

After harvesting the crop, often stubs are left in the fields which are then burnt by the farmers. This causes pollution in the atmosphere. Therefore, farmers are advised not to burn the stubs in the fields. Do you know of a safe way these stubs can be removed?

**IT'S A FACT!**

A study shows that stubs should be retained in the field after harvest and eventually returned to the soil. Retaining crop stubs minimizes erosion, returns nutrients, increases soil organic matter content, increases soil water-holding capacity, suppresses weeds and minimizes soil water evaporation.

Also technology is being developed for using the stubs to make ethanol, which is used as a biofuel—as a substitute of petrol.

### Storage

Harvested foodgrains normally contain more moisture than required for storage. The excess moisture is removed by drying the foodgrains in the sun. You will read in Chapter 2 that this is necessary to prevent the grains from getting spoilt by microbes. How does drying in the sun prevent the growth of microbes?

The grains can now be packed in bags or bins and stored. Large scale storage of grains is done in **silos** or **granaries**. These must be made free of microbes, insects and rodents by spraying chemicals, before storing the grains. The grains should be periodically inspected to ensure that they are not attacked by rodents, insects or microbes. Since grains are harvested once a year they need to be stored safely so that they last till at least the next harvest season. In practice, however, an extra stock called **buffer stock** is always maintained so that grains are available in plenty even if there is a shortfall in production in a particular year, for example, due to monsoon failure.

**IT'S A FACT!**

A new method of grain storage involves the use of nitrogen gas. Nitrogen gas is circulated through the grain piles in silos. It replaces air and hence oxygen in the silos. This kills all pests and microorganisms. The method is simple and easy to implement, and grain can be stored for much longer periods of time.

**IT'S A FACT!**

Do you know what is common in the festivals of Pongal, Holi, Diwali, Baisakhi and Bihu? These are all harvest festivals of India, celebrated at the time of harvesting of crops. At this time farmers get the fruits of their hard labour of the past few months. Men and women celebrate these festivals with great enthusiasm.

## ORAL QUESTIONS FOR FORMATIVE ASSESSMENT

1. Which of these are organic substances—manures or fertilizers?
2. Drip irrigation saves wastage of water because it supplies water directly to the roots. Why is drip irrigation not used by all farmers?
3. Some fruits such as grapes are not peeled before eating. You are advised to be extra careful in cleaning such fruits. Why?
4. After harvesting his bountiful crop, a farmer was so happy that he forgot to dry the crop before storing it. What problems can he face?

## INCREASING CROP PRODUCE

To feed the ever increasing population in our country, we need to constantly increase the foodgrain production. One method of doing this is by increasing the land under cultivation. While this has happened in the past few decades, we cannot indefinitely go on increasing farmland, as this leads to environmental problems, such as soil erosion. Also, if forests are cut down to get more land for farming, it leads to even greater environmental problems.

Improvement in the methods of agriculture which we have discussed till now, is the most suitable alternative to increase crop produce. Providing better irrigation facilities, proper use of manures and fertilizers, use of natural methods of replenishing nutrients in the soil, using better methods of protection from weeds, pests and diseases, and increasing the use of modern agricultural implements, etc., will help in improving the crop produce. By providing better storage methods, we can reduce wastage of foodgrain.

Recently, however, a substantial increase in crop produce has come about from using better varieties of crops which have higher yield and more resistance to disease. In the future also, development of still better varieties is expected to be the main method of increasing crop output. This is done by a process called **plant breeding**.

Breeding means producing offspring. Scientists have controlled the reproduction in plants and animals so that they have the required characteristics which make them more useful.

### Hybridization

Hybridization is a technique used for developing new varieties of crops by cross breeding two different varieties. By cross breeding, a new variety can be made to have the desired characteristics from both parents.

Suppose scientists want to develop a new crop having some desired characteristics, for example, high yield and resistance to disease. They select two varieties, one having high yield and the other being more resistant to disease. Cross breeding between the two varieties is done in order to develop one variety which has both the desired characteristics.

To prevent self fertilization, anthers of one variety of plants are removed by a process called **emasculation**. Then pollens from the other variety of plants (with different characteristics) are transferred to the stigma of emasculated flowers of the first variety of plants. This process is repeated for several generations to get the desired characters in the seed. This seed is called **stock** of the new variety.

Once this is achieved, scientists may try to develop another useful characteristic like greater resistance to pests. Producing plant hybrids can be a long and tedious process.

The **green revolution** of the 1960s and

1970s in India was brought about by importing high yielding varieties of wheat from Mexico. Besides giving high yield, the plants were smaller and stronger and had better response to fertilizers. However, these varieties required more water and fertilizers, and also required frequent weeding.

The effect of the green revolution on production of foodgrains is clearly seen in Table 1.4.

TABLE 1.4 Production of foodgrains in India

| FOOD GRAINS | PRODUCTION (MILLION TONNES) | | | |
|---|---|---|---|---|
| | 1950–51 | 1983–84 | 1995–96 | 2007–08 |
| wheat | 6.8 | 45.0 | 62.6 | 78.4 |
| rice | 22.0 | 60.0 | 80.0 | 96.4 |

Considerable research is in progress in this field.

## NITROGEN CYCLE

Nitrogen is used by life forms to carry out many of the functions of life. For example, it is needed for the formation of proteins, amino acids and nucleic acids. It is especially important to plant life.

Air contains about 78 % nitrogen. Yet nitrogen in its gaseous form is almost entirely unusable to life forms. It must first be converted or 'fixed' into a more usable form—mainly soluble nitrates. The process of converting nitrogen into a form in which it can be used by plants is called **nitrogen fixation**.

In nature, nitrogen fixation is done by specialized bacteria in the soil. There are other bacteria that return nitrogen to its gaseous form.

After nitrogen is fixed, it can be absorbed, and used by plants, and subsequently by animals.

The cyclic process of nitrogen being fixed, used by plants and animals, and later returned to the atmosphere is referred to as the **nitrogen cycle** (Fig. 1.11).

Nitrogen cycle involves the following steps.

- Nitrogen fixation
- Nitrogen assimilation
- Ammonification
- Nitrification
- Denitrification

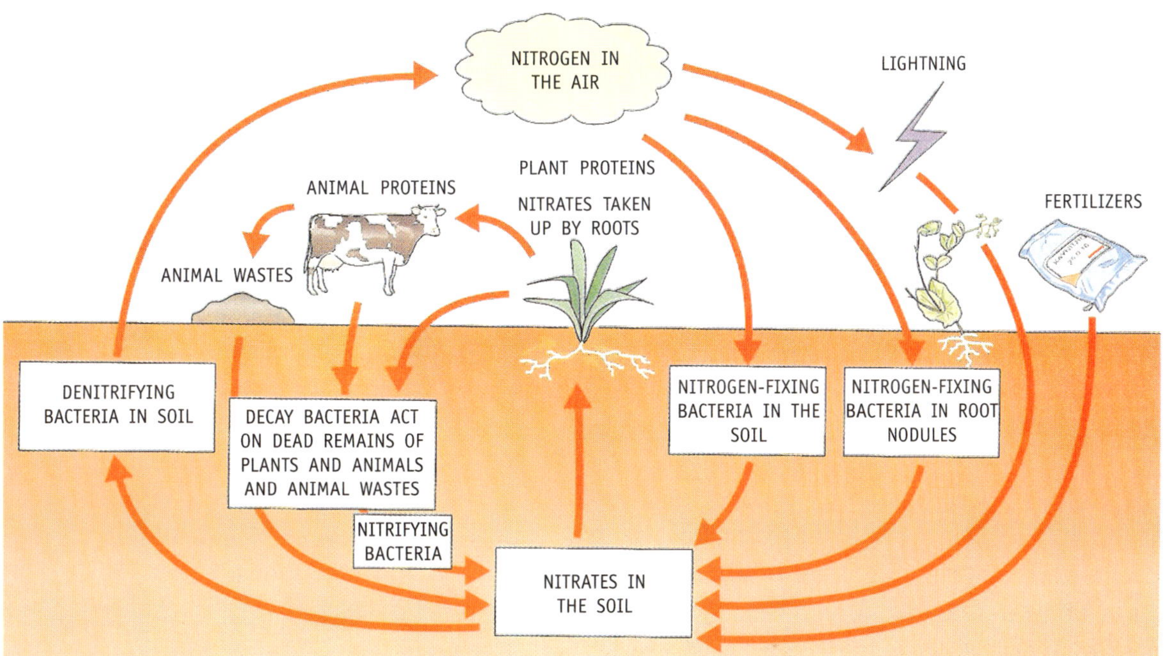


FIG. 1.11 The nitrogen cycle

### Nitrogen fixation

The process of converting free nitrogen gas of the atmosphere into nitrogen compounds is called **nitrogen fixation**. In nature it takes place in the following ways.

**Atmospheric nitrogen fixation:** Lightning causes high temperatures which results in a reaction between nitrogen and oxygen present in air to produce oxides of nitrogen. These dissolve in rainwater forming dilute nitric acid. This nitric acid reacts with the alkalis of the soil (like limestone) to turn into nitrates.

$$N_2 + O_2 \rightarrow 2NO$$

$$2NO + O_2 \rightarrow 2NO_2$$

$$4NO_2 + 2H_2O + O_2 \rightarrow 4HNO_3$$

$$CaCO_3 + 2HNO_3 \rightarrow Ca(NO_3)_2 + H_2O + CO_2$$

**Biological nitrogen fixation:** It is the conversion of atmospheric nitrogen into nitrogen compounds by living organisms. Nitrogen fixing bacteria, called *rhizobium* bacteria, are found in the soil. They are also found in the root nodules of leguminous plants like peas and beans. These bacteria can fix atmospheric nitrogen into nitrates.

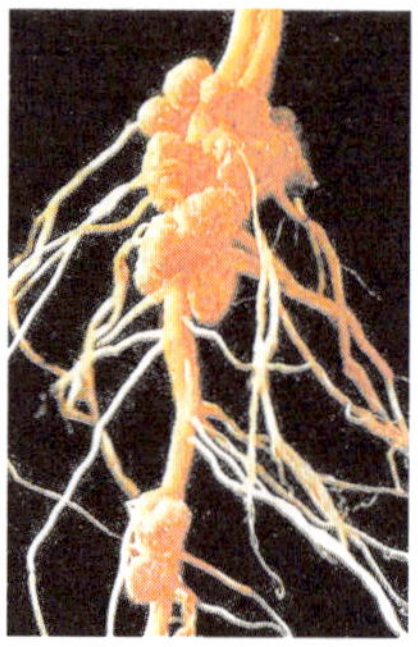

FIG. 1.12 Root nodules in a leguminous plant

### Nitrogen assimilation

The plants absorb these nitrates from the soil, and convert them into plant proteins. The nitrogen passes from plants to herbivores that eat them, and then to carnivores that eat the herbivores. This process of conversion of inorganic nitrogen compounds into organic compounds that become a part of living organisms is called **nitrogen assimilation**.

### Ammonification

When plants and animals die, their remains are converted into ammonia and ammonium compounds by decay bacteria and fungi (decomposers) present in the soil. This process of conversion of complex organic compounds like proteins into ammonia is called **ammonification**.

### Nitrification

Some of these compounds are taken up by plants and the rest are converted into nitrates by **nitrifying bacteria** present in the soil. The process of conversion of ammonia into nitrates is called **nitrification**.

### Denitrification

Some of these nitrates are absorbed by plants. The rest are converted to free nitrogen gas by **denitrifying bacteria**. This is called **denitrification**.

## FOOD FROM ANIMALS

Like plants, animals also provide us with different kinds of foods and other products. The breeding, feeding and caring of domestic animals for food and other purposes is called **animal husbandry**.

The kinds of animals that provide us with food are:

- **Meat and egg yielding animals** such as goat, poultry animals (e.g. chicken, duck and turkey), fish, sheep and pig. The large scale rearing of fish for food is known as **pisciculture**.
- **Milch** (or **milk yielding**) **animals** such as cow, buffalo, goat and camel. Milk is also used to prepare a large number of products such as butter, cheese, curd and *ghee*.
- Besides these, honeybees provide us with honey. Large scale rearing of honeybees is called **apiculture**.

## ORAL QUESTIONS FOR FORMATIVE ASSESSMENT

1. A farmer has two varieties of wheat in his field—one gives good yield but is prone to diseases; the other is resistant to diseases but does not give good yield. How can you help him as an agriculture scientist?
2. Which one of these add nitrogen in usable form to the soil—nitrifying bacteria or denitrifying bacteria?
3. If you are a pisciculturist, what do you do?
4. If you say that a certain process 'fixes nitrogen' what does this mean? Which natural process in the atmosphere fixes nitrogen?

## NOW YOU KNOW

- Agriculture began 10,000 years ago and enabled humans to settle down in one place.
- Horticulture deals with the production of vegetables, fruits, flowers and decorative plants.
- The step-by-step methods in modern agriculture are:
  - Preparation of the soil by ploughing and levelling it.
  - Sowing seeds or transplanting plants at correct depth and correct distances.
  - Manuring, either by natural methods (field fallow, crop rotation, mixed cropping), or by using manures and fertilizers.
  - Irrigation, i.e. supplying the right amount of water at the right time.
  - Weeding, which can be carried out manually or by using weedicides.
  - Protection from pests and diseases by spraying pesticides and other chemicals.
  - Harvesting, threshing and winnowing.
  - Storage after drying in the sun to get rid of excess moisture.
- Crop produce can be increased by increasing the land under cultivation, by improvement in the methods of agriculture, and by developing better varieties of crops by plant breeding.
- Hybridization is a technique used for plant breeding in which new varieties with desired characteristics of high yield and resistance to disease, are developed.
- The cyclic process by which nitrogen in the atmosphere enters the soil so that it can be used by plants and animals, and later returned to the atmosphere, is referred to as the nitrogen cycle.

## NEW WORDS

**HORTICULTURE**—branch of agriculture that deals with the production of vegetables, fruits, flowers and decorative plants

**BROADCASTING**—sowing of seeds manually or by seed drills

**WEED**—unwanted plants that grow along with crops

**HYBRIDIZATION**—technique used for developing new varieties of crops by cross breeding two different varieties

**NITROGEN FIXATION**—the process of converting free nitrogen gas of the atmosphere into nitrogen compounds

**AMMONIFICATION**—the process of conversion of complex organic compounds like proteins into ammonia

**NITRIFICATION**—the process of conversion of ammonia into nitrates

**DENITRIFICATION**—the process of conversion of nitrates into nitrogen gas

## FOR FORMATIVE AND SUMMATIVE ASSESSMENT

### A. MULTIPLE-CHOICE QUESTIONS: Choose the most appropriate answer.

1. Which of these is not a cereal?
   a. maize b. gram c. wheat d. rice
2. Which of these is not a kharif crop?
   a. wheat b. rice c. maize d. groundnut
3. Which of these nutrients is compost rich in?
   a. organic nutrients b. nitrogen c. phosphorus d. potassium
4. Which of these is not a fungal disease of plants?
   a. wilt b. rust c. smut d. blight (of potatoes)
5. Which one of the following is not true about ploughing?
   a. It loosens the soil. b. It aerates the soil.
   c. It prevents soil erosion. d. It allows easy penetration of roots into the soil.
6. Compost lacks which of the following nutrients?
   a. nitrogen b. phosphorous c. potassium d. all of these
7. Which one of the following does not add nutrients to the soil?
   a. crop rotation b. field fallow c. manures d. ploughing
8. Which of the following machines can be used to harvest a crop and also to beat out the grain from the chaff?
   a. harvester b. combine c. thresher d. harrow

### B. VERY SHORT-ANSWER QUESTIONS: Give one-word answers.

1. About how many years ago did agriculture begin?
2. Large grasses cultivated for their nutritious seeds are called __________
3. Preparation of the soil involves __________ and __________ it.
4. The agricultural implement used to sow seeds is called a seed __________
5. Allowing a field to remain free of crops for one or more seasons is called field __________ It allows the field to regain __________
6. All crops require approximately the same amount of water at roughly the same time periods of their growth. True or false?

7. Name one pesticide you will use to kill insects that harm crops.
8. Pesticides are used to kill small pests, but they are not strong enough to cause harm to humans. True or false?
9. Name the nitrogen fixing bacteria in root nodules of leguminous plants.
10. Conversion of proteins into ammonia is called ________
11. Some bacteria can convert nitrate salts in the soil to free nitrogen. True or false?
12. A milch animal is one that yields ________
13. Rearing honeybees for honey is called ________

## C. SHORT-ANSWER QUESTIONS (TYPE I): Answer in a sentence or two.

1. Name three natural methods of adding nutrients to soil.
2. What are weeds?
3. Why should grains be dried before storage?
4. Why does the government usually maintain a buffer stock of grains?
5. What is hybridization?
6. List the steps involved in the nitrogen cycle.
7. What do you mean by nitrogen fixation?
8. What is nitrogen assimilation?
9. What enables leguminous plants to fix nitrogen?
10. What is animal husbandry?

## D. SHORT-ANSWER QUESTIONS (TYPE II): Answer in about 30 words.

1. Distinguish between kharif and rabi crops, giving two examples of each.
2. List the steps involved in crop production, in sequential order.
3. Why is it important to plant seeds at the correct distances from each other?
4. Why do farmers normally use a mixture of manures and fertilizers in their fields?
5. What method of irrigation will you use if you live in a dry area with shortage of water? Explain the method.
6. What is waterlogging? How does it harm the crops? How can it be prevented?
7. Discuss two methods of weeding in which poisonous chemicals are not used.
8. Differentiate between insecticides, rodenticides and fungicides. Which of these are pesticides?
9. Discuss with an example how hybridization is used for developing new varieties of crops with desired characteristics.
10. Differentiate between nitrification and denitrification.

## E. LONG-ANSWER QUESTIONS: Answer in about 60 words.

1. What are the advantages of ploughing the soil before sowing seeds?
2. What precautions must be kept in mind while sowing seeds in a field?

3. Discuss two natural methods of manuring.
4. Draw a labelled diagram to illustrate the nitrogen cycle.

## HOTS QUESTIONS: Think and answer.

1. Which method, according to you, can bring about the maximum increase in crop produce in our country in future?
   a. increasing land under cultivation
   b. using more manures and fertilizers
   c. less wastage in storage
   d. using better varieties of crop plants
2. What do you think are the drawbacks of seeds being unevenly distributed in a field while sowing?
3. Do you expect to find fully-grown crop plants in a nursery? Why? Why not?
4. Crop rotation is practised by farmers so that they have different products to sell in the market in every season. Do you agree? Give reasons.
5. I have grown a few wheat plants in my garden because I like the plants. Am I growing a wheat crop? Give reasons.
6. It is observed that melon fruits growing in the fields sometimes crack, exposing the contents inside. What do you think can be the reason? (HINT: This generally happens in fields where drainage is not proper.)

## FOR FORMATIVE ASSESSMENT*

### In the Library—Research Project

Millets are grains that used to be popular in India years ago. However, after the Green Revolution, they gave way to wheat and rice. There is a growing understanding that overemphasis on wheat and rice and the extensive use of fertilizers and pesticides to increase their yield has damaged the soil and also affected the health of farmers using them. In this scenario, millets are poised to make a comeback due to their many advantages, for example, higher nutritional content than wheat and rice. Find out:

- Which grains are termed millets?
- What other advantages do they offer because of which they are set to replace wheat and rice in a big way?

### My Virtual Library—Research/Activities on the Internet

- Visit rsgr.in/lsc-cce-8 and click on LINK 1 and LINK 2 to find out more about the Green Revolution in India.
- Visit rsgr.in/lsc-cce-8 and click on LINK 3 to find about plant breeding—that brought about the Green Revolution.
- Visit rsgr.in/lsc-cce-8 and click on LINK 4 to find out about bio-fertilizers.

### To Meet—Research on Scientist

**Benjamin Peary Pal** (1906–1989) This Indian agricultural scientist worked on the development of disease-resistant varieties of wheat. He was the first Director of the Indian Council of Agricultural Research at New Delhi.

Find out more about his work on disease-resistant varieties of wheat.

*For more tasks see Page 77

### In the Laboratory—Experimental Project

**Study root nodules** Carefully uproot a legume plant such as a pea or a gram plant and study its roots. Can you see round structures on it? These are the root nodules.

### Beyond the Classroom—Field Trip

Visit a nearby farm.

- **Know the manures used in a farm** Ask the farmers which manures they prefer to use—chemical fertilizers or farm manures. Note down the reasons they give for their preference for various crops.

  Try to grow some vegetables in your backyard or school garden. Which one will you use—chemical fertilizer, farm manure or a mixture of both?

- **Know the tools used by women farmers** Talk to some men and women farmers about farming and farm practices. You can ask questions like:

  Which farm tools do they use? Do the male and female farmers prefer the same tools? If there is a difference in their preferences why is that so?

  Which irrigation method do they practise?

  Also, discuss with elders in the farm about the changes in agricultural practices over the last 50 years.

### Talk to the Class—Presentation

Make a presentation (preferably a PowerPoint presentation) on your findings in the above field trip.

## LIFE SKILL

**Weeding your way to a better garden**

Whether you have flower plants growing in pots or a flower/vegetable garden at home, weeding is essential to keep your plants grow well and healthy. While weeds can be identified and removed by hand or with a trowel, this is quite back-breaking work! Also, identifying the weeds is normally possible only after they have already grown.

**Mulching** is an extremely effective method of controlling weeds. **Mulch** is a material that is layered on the soil to lock in moisture and to stop weed growth. It prevents sunlight from reaching the weed seeds which are sprouting at soil level. This lack of sunlight prevents the seedlings from growing, and most of them die before they can reach sunlight.

Most mulch is organic matter such as grass clippings, shredded leaves, straw and bark. Shredded bark makes a good mulch for flower beds, and also makes the garden look good. Straw or organic material from the compost pile can be used in vegetable gardens—it not only helps to stop weeds but also supplies nutrients to the vegetables.

Mulching also provides the additional benefits of conserving soil moisture, preventing soil erosion, and keeping the soil at a more uniform temperature.

Synthetic mulch material is also available.

SKILLS INVOLVED: Thinking skill, Preservation of environment

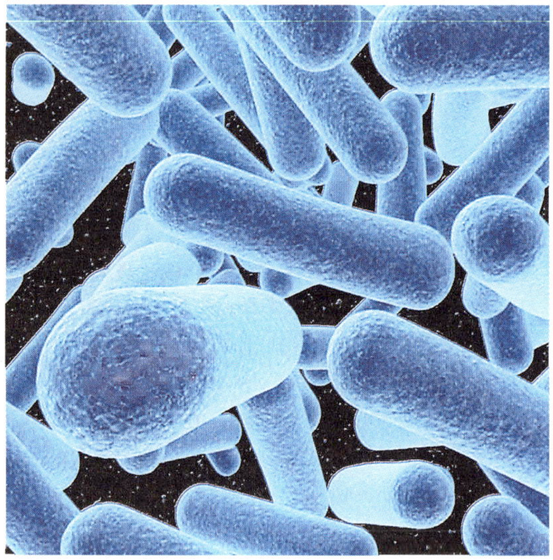

2

# Microorganisms

## WHAT ARE MICROORGANISMS?

You can see a large number of living organisms around you. However, do you know that there is a larger number of living organisms around you and inside your body that you cannot see with the naked eye?

**ACTIVITY 1 (Experimental investigation): To observe microorganisms**

Take a drop of pond water and look at it carefully. Can you see any living organisms in it? Now put this drop of water on a glass slide and examine it under a light microscope. Can you see many tiny one-celled organisms floating or moving about swiftly?

Collect some moist soil from a field. Put it into a beaker. Add some water to it and mix well. After the soil has settled down, observe a drop of water under a microscope. What do you see?

Scrape your tooth with a toothpick and observe the scraping under a microscope. Can you see tiny rod-like organisms in it?

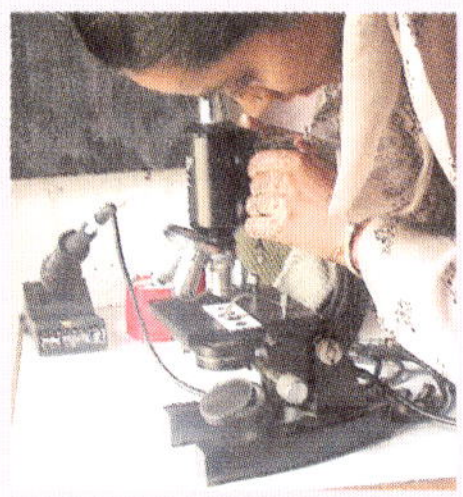

a. Looking through a microscope

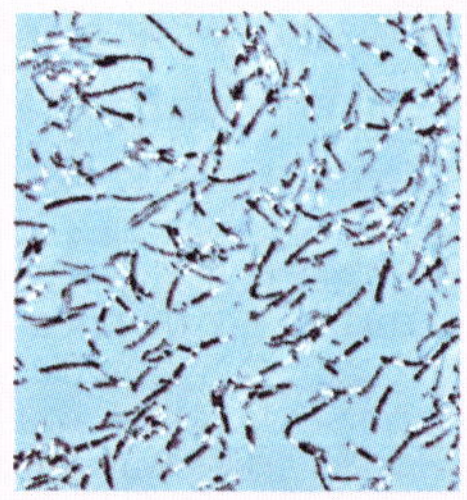

b. Microbes in pond water

FIG. 2.1

**IN THIS CHAPTER**

TYPES OF MICROORGANISMS ◆ USEFUL MICROORGANISMS ◆ HARMFUL MICROORGANISMS ◆ FOOD PRESERVATION

This activity shows that tiny organisms live in water, soil and even inside your body. These are so small that they cannot be seen with the naked eye. They are called microorganisms or microbes.

Organisms that are so small that they can only be seen through a microscope, are called **microorganisms** or **microbes**.

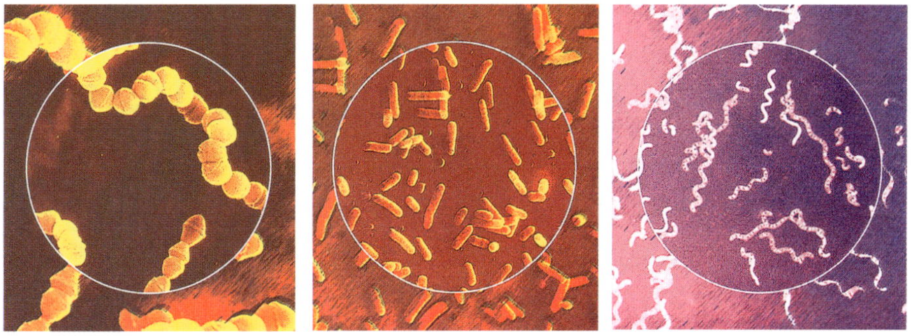

a. Cocci b. Bacilli c. Spirilla

FIG. 2.2 Different types of bacteria

These organisms have a great impact on humans in many ways. Some can cause illness, whereas others can cure diseases. Some supply us with food, whereas others spoil food.

The study of microorganisms is known as **microbiology**. Scientists who study microorganisms are known as **microbiologists**.

## WHERE ARE MICROBES FOUND?

Most microorganisms are hardy and can be found in almost any kind of environment. They are found in the hottest of deserts and in the coolest icy polar regions. Some microbes live in cracks in the sea floor. Some microorganisms can even survive a volcanic eruption. Microorganisms are found in salt water, in marshland and even inside our body.

Microorganisms are hardy because they form a hard outer covering called a **cyst** around themselves. They do this when conditions are not favourable, such as under extreme conditions of temperature and dryness. They survive by remaining inactive within the cyst until conditions are favourable again.

## TYPES OF MICROORGANISMS

There are five major groups of microorganisms. These are as follows:

- **bacteria** (singular: bacterium)
- **algae** (singular: alga)
- **protozoa** (singular: protozoan)
- **fungi** (singular: fungus)
- **viruses** (singular: virus)

### Bacteria

Bacteria are among the simplest and very small living things. They are single-celled organisms that can be found almost everywhere—in air, in water, in soil, and in bodies of most other organisms, including human beings.

Nearly 2,50,00,00,000 bacteria are present in one gram of garden soil. Each bacterial cell can exist singly, but sometimes they cling together to form chains or groups.

Bacteria are found in three different shapes (Fig. 2.2):

- **rod-shaped**, called **bacilli**
- **spherical**, called **cocci**
- **spiral**, called **spirilla**

### Algae

The term **algae** refers to simple plant-like organisms that have cell walls and chlorophyll within the cells. They make their own food by photosynthesis. They have no roots, stems or leaves.

Almost all algae live in water—in ponds, lakes and seawater. Some algae are found in snow and some in hot springs. They also grow in moist soil, barks of trees and rock surfaces. Algae can be unicellular or multicellular.

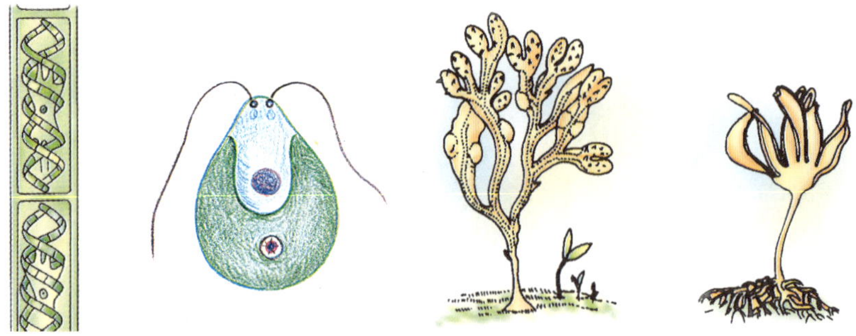

a. *Spirogyra* (filamentous algae) b. *Chlamydomonas* c. *Fucus* d. *Laminaria*

FIG. 2.3 Different types of algae

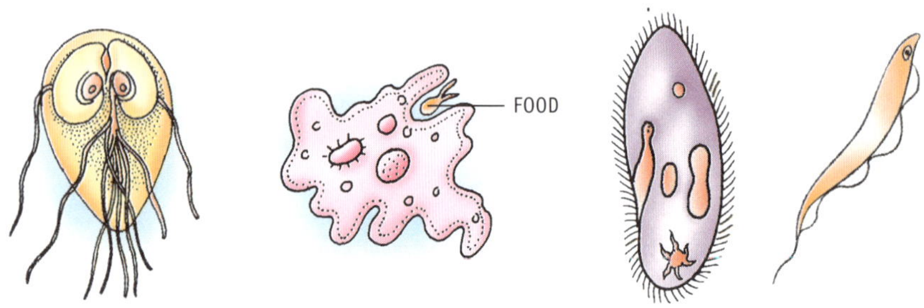


a. *Giardia* b. *Amoeba* engulfing food c. *Paramecium* d. *Trypanosoma*

FIG. 2.4 Some protozoa

## Protozoa

Protozoa are unicellular organisms that have animal-like characteristics. They can move from place to place. They capture and eat food. Some protozoa live in fresh or salt water. Others live in soil. Some are parasites that live in the bodies of other organisms, including human beings. *Amoeba*, *Giardia* and *Paramecium* are some examples of protozoa (Fig. 2.4).

## Fungi

Plant-like organisms that do not contain chlorophyll are called **fungi**. Fungi may be unicellular or multicellular. Yeasts are unicellular. Bread mould is multicellular (Fig. 2.5). Though fungi are present everywhere, from deserts to very cold regions, they grow best in dark, warm, moist places.

## Viruses

Viruses are smaller than any known cell. They are so small that they cannot be seen by a light microscope. To observe viruses, scientists use an electron microscope, which magnifies an object to more than 2,00,000 times. Viruses do not have a cellular structure like other microorganisms.

Viruses cannot reproduce by themselves, respond to changes or use energy or grow. This seems to indicate that viruses are not living organisms. However, when a virus enters the living cell of an organism, say a human, it is able to reproduce. It uses the energy of the host cells for this purpose. After the formation of thousands of viruses, the host cell often dies.

a. *Penicillium* b. Yeast c. *Agaricus* (mushroom) d. *Rhizopus* (bread mould)

FIG. 2.5 Some fungi

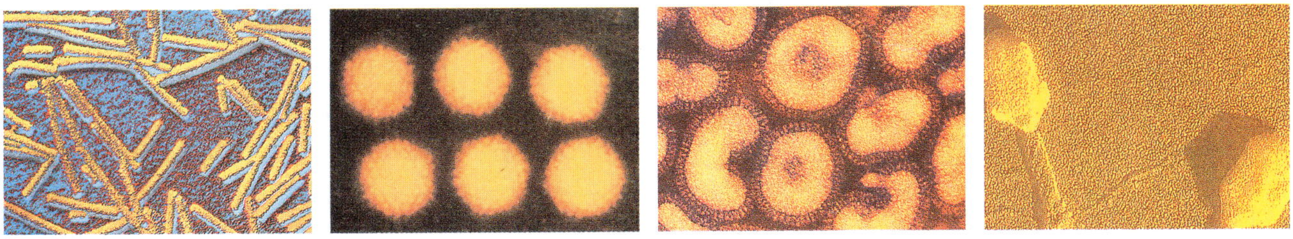

a. Tobacco mosaic virus b. Adeno virus c. Influenza virus d. Bacteriophage

FIG. 2.6 Some viruses

It bursts and the new viruses spread and invade other cells. As a large number of host cells die, the person falls ill.

Since reproduction is a very important characteristic of life, scientists regard viruses as a link between living and non-living. They have been placed on the dividing line between the living and the non-living.

## ORAL QUESTIONS FOR FORMATIVE ASSESSMENT

1. All microbes are harmful. Do you agree? Give reasons.
2. Name the types of microorganism that:

   a. have chlorophyll: ______ b. do not have a cellular structure: ______
3. Give one property because of which viruses are regarded as being on the borderline of living and non-living.
4. Which of these are closer to plants—algae or protozoa? In what aspect?
5. Where do you normally expect to find algae—in the soil, in a pond or in the air?

## USEFUL MICROORGANISMS

Microorganisms are useful in the following ways.

- In food and beverage industry
- In making medicines and vaccines
- In agriculture
- In cleaning the environment

### Food and beverage industry

Bacteria help us in making certain foods. *Lactobacillus* is a bacterium that sours milk and is used to make curd from milk. Cheese is also made by the action of bacteria on milk. Vinegar is produced by the action of bacteria. Bacteria are also used in the production of tea, coffee and cocoa.

- **Making curd and cheese:** Bacteria is used in preparation of some of our most common foods, as we see in Activity 2.

**ACTIVITY 2 (Experimental investigation): Making curd**

Heat some milk in a pan until it is lukewarm (40–45 °C). Add a teaspoon of curd to it and stir. Cover and leave it for 6–8 hours. The milk in the pan will get converted to curd. If you live in a cold place, preheat an oven to about 80 °C; switch it off and keep the milk-curd mixture in it for 6–8 hours.

Curd contains a bacterium called *Lactobacillus*. When a little curd (called the starter) is added to milk, it multiplies and converts the milk into curd.

Curd or *dahi* is known as plain yogurt in

**IT'S A FACT!**

Curd is a nutritious food. It also aids in digestion. *Lactobacillus* bacteria inhibit the growth of illness-causing bacteria inside the intestinal tract and promote beneficial bacteria needed for digestion. These friendly bacteria help in the absorption of minerals and aid in the synthesis of vitamins of B group.

many countries. It also is available in many flavours such as fruit and chocolate. Industrially also, yogurt is prepared by adding *Lactobacillus* bacteria to milk.

The production of cheese also starts by curdling of milk using *Lactobacillus* bacteria. Different bacteria are then added, depending on the type of cheese being made.

- **Making bread:** Yeast plays an important role in preparation of food. You may be familiar with Activity 3.

**ACTIVITY 3 (Experimental investigation):**
**Effect of yeast on dough**

Take about $1/2$ kg flour (*atta* or *maida*). Put warm water in a cup so that the cup is $1/3$ full. Add 2–3 teaspoons of sugar to the warm water and mix well. Now, add half teaspoon of yeast powder to the warm water. Cover the cup and leave for $1/2$ hour. Then add this sugar-and-yeast solution to the flour. Add more warm water to the flour and knead to form a dough. Cover the dough and keep in a warm place for 2–3 hours. Does the dough rise?

You will see that the dough has risen and its volume has increased.

The yeast uses sugar for food. In the process of breaking down of sugar, alcohol is formed and carbon dioxide is given off. This process is known as **fermentation**. The bubbles of carbon dioxide given off cause the dough to rise. This dough can be used to make bread. When this dough is baked, more bubbles of gas are formed due to the heat. As the gas escapes, the bread rises and becomes soft and fluffy. The heat during the baking process also evaporates the alcohol.

- **Making *idli, dosa* and *dhokla*:** *Idli* and *dosa* are prepared from a mixture of *dal* and rice, which has been ground to a fine paste. The mixture is allowed to stand for a few hours. As fermentation occurs naturally (due to bacteria present in the mixture), the mixture rises and becomes sour. *Dhokla*, a popular food item in Gujarat, requires yeast to be added to its mixture, to make it soft and fluffy. In this case, fermentation may not take place naturally.

FIG. 2.7 The fluffy texture of bread and *dhokla*

- **Manufacture of alcohol and alcoholic drinks:** You have seen that during fermentation of sugar by yeast, alcohol is produced as a result.

**ACTIVITY 4 (Experimental investigation): Fermentation of sugar by yeast**

Take some warm water in a cup so that it is $1/3$ full. Add 2–3 teaspoons of sugar to it and mix well. Now add half a teaspoon of yeast to it. Cover the cup and keep in a warm place for 4–5 hours. Now smell the solution. Can you smell alcohol in it?

The process of fermentation of sugar by yeast is used in the manufacture of alcohol and alcoholic drinks such as beer and wine. One of the main differences between wine and beer production is the source of the sugars. Wine is prepared by fermentation of sugar in grapes, and beer by fermentation of sugar in germinating barley.

- **Other uses of microorganisms in the food industry:** Some seaweeds are used as food in China and Japan. Some substances obtained from algae are used to thicken foods, such as ice creams and jellies. Algae are important as food for animals, such as fish or snails. Scientists believe that in future some algae can be important sources of food for all humans. They are experimenting on ways to make algae tastier.

### Making medicines and vaccines

- Bacteria and fungi are used to make medicines called **antibiotics**. These medicines kill or stop the growth of disease-causing microorganisms, and hence are used to cure diseases. Penicillin comes from a species of mould called *Penicillium*. Streptomycin, tetracycline and erythromycin are some other common antibiotics made from bacteria or fungi. Antibiotics are also used to control some diseases of animals and plants.

**IT'S A FACT!**

Some bacteria develop resistance to antibiotics. In a population of bacteria, there are some hardy ones that are not killed by the antibiotic. These bacteria reproduce very quickly, and soon most of the bacteria become resistant. It is therefore advisable that antibiotics should not be taken unless prescribed by a doctor. They should always be taken in proper doses and the course prescribed by the doctor should be completed.

- Microorganisms are used to make **vaccines**, which protect humans and other animals from several diseases. Diseases such as cholera, typhoid, tuberculosis, hepatitis, chickenpox, measles, polio and smallpox can be prevented by vaccination. Vaccines consist of dead or weakened microbes. When these are swallowed or injected into the body of a patient, the body produces **antibodies** to fight them. The antibodies remain in the body and protect it from any future attack of the disease germs. The body is then said to have developed **immunity** against that disease. Vaccination is therefore called **immunization**.

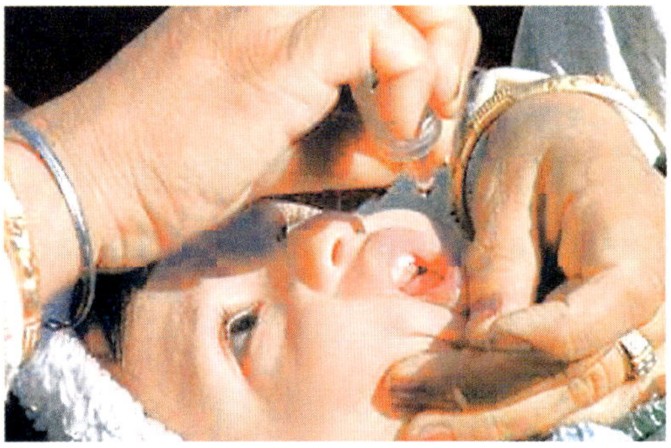

FIG. 2.8 A child being vaccinated against polio

- Bacteria and yeast are used in making vitamin B complex tablets.
- The human hormone called **insulin** can also be obtained from bacteria. Insulin obtained from bacteria is used to help diabetic patients whose body produces little or no insulin.

### In agriculture

Some bacteria live in the root nodules of plants, such as gram, pea, bean, etc. These bacteria absorb the nitrogen of the atmosphere and convert it into nitrates which serve as natural fertilizers for plants. You have read about these in Chapter 1. Some blue-green algae can also fix atmospheric nitrogen.

### In cleaning the environment

- Microorganisms such as bacteria, fungi and protozoa help by decomposing the tissues of dead organisms to get their food. Without bacteria, piles of dead organisms would cover the earth.
- When microorganisms decompose organic

matter, they break down plant and animal tissues into simple substances, which are restored to the soil. Thus, the nutrients that were taken from the soil by plants and animals are restored and are used again by living organisms.

- Some bacteria decompose sewage and other wastes in water. This is nature's method of keeping the environment free from pollution.
- Since algae can photosynthesize, they give off oxygen. It is thought that most of the oxygen that we have on the earth was initially produced by algae in the oceans.

**IT'S A FACT!**

*According to scientists, if dead tissues were not decomposed, they would have formed a heap on this earth about 20 km high!*

### Some other uses of microorganisms

- Certain bacteria and protozoa normally live in the digestive systems of some animals, such as cows, goats and sheep. They help the animals digest grass and plants by breaking down cellulose which the animals themselves cannot do.
- Bacteria are useful in tobacco, leather and jute industries. **Tanning** (to make animal skin into leather by treating it with chemicals) is done with the help of bacteria. In the jute industry, jute plants are submerged in water, where bacterial action separates the fibres from the rest of the tissues. The fibres are then woven into jute cloth.
- In the villages, animal waste, leafy waste from crops, etc., is decomposed by bacteria in the absence of oxygen to produce **methane**, which is used as a fuel. It is one of the chief constituents of **biogas**.

## HARMFUL MICROORGANISMS

### Microorganisms cause diseases

The microorganisms that cause diseases are known as **pathogens** or **germs**. To cause disease the germs have to first enter our body. They can enter in the following ways.

- **Through air:** When a person suffering from common cold or flu sneezes, coughs or spits, germs are released in the air. A healthy person breathing this air can get infected. Some diseases that spread through air are common cold, flu, chickenpox, mumps, tuberculosis, measles and polio.
- **Through food and water**, e.g. cholera, typhoid, hepatitis.
- **Through direct contact** with a sick person, e.g. ringworm, common cold, flu, chickenpox.
- **Through insects** such as mosquitoes, flies and fleas. These are **carriers** of germs. For example, the female *Anopheles* mosquito carries the malaria germs. When it bites a healthy person, he/she can get infected with malaria. When houseflies sit on dirt, germs stick to their bodies. When they sit on food, they transfer the germs to the food. The person consuming the food can become sick. The female *Aedes* mosquito acts as carrier for the dengue virus.

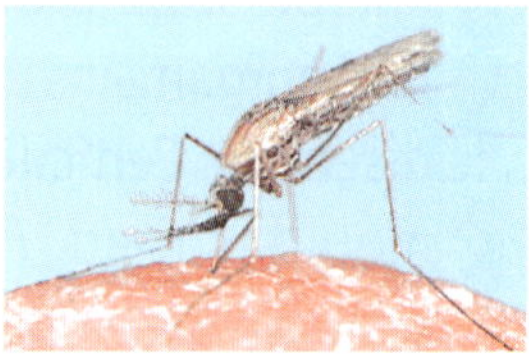

FIG. 2.9 The *Anopheles* mosquito spreads malaria.

- **Through cuts and wounds**, e.g. tetanus.

Microorganisms also cause diseases in animals and plants. For example:

- **Anthrax** is a disease that affects humans and cattle. It is caused by a bacterium.
- A virus causes the dangerous **foot and mouth disease** in cattle.
- **Citrus canker** is a bacterial disease that affects trees of citrus fruits and is spread by air.
- **Yellow vein mosaic** which affects vegetables like *bhindi* is a viral disease spread by insects.

* **Rust of wheat** is a fungal disease spread by air and seeds.

FIG. 2.10 Rust of wheat

**IT'S A FACT!**

During 1845–1847 in Ireland, the potato crop was destroyed by the potato blight fungus, causing many people to starve.

### Preventing the spread of communicable diseases

Diseases spread by microorganisms that can spread from an infected person to a healthy person through air, food, water and direct contact are called **communicable diseases**. Some simple methods of limiting the spread of communicable diseases are to keep the infected person separated from others and to advice him/her to keep a handkerchief on the nose and mouth while sneezing. Diseases spread by insects such as mosquitoes can be contained by not allowing them to breed. To prevent mosquitoes from breeding we should not allow water to collect anywhere in our neighbourhood.

### Microorganisms spoil food

Bacteria are responsible for spoilage of food. The souring of milk, putrefaction of meat, rotting of potatoes, vegetables and fruits are due to the action of bacteria.

Growth of mould can make food unfit for consumption.

Yeast can also make fruit juices, tomato juice, etc., unfit for consumption due to fermentation.

Microorganisms growing on food sometimes produce toxic substances. These make the food poisonous. Consuming such food can cause a serious illness called **food poisoning**.

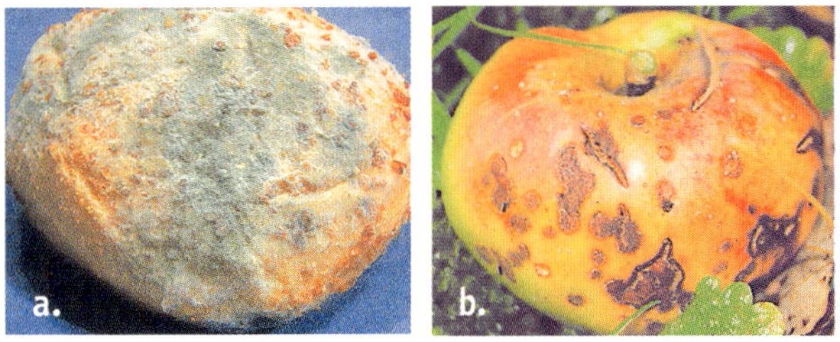


FIG. 2.11 **a.** A piece of bread, and **b.** an apple spoilt by growth of microorganisms

## FOOD PRESERVATION

How do we stop food from getting spoilt because of the growth of microorganisms on it? We can do this by:

* killing the microbes in the food, and
* stopping them from growing again.

These steps ensure that the food lasts a longer time without getting spoilt. This is known as food preservation.

The following are some common methods for food preservation.

* **Heating** food to a high temperature kills microbes. For example, milk and water are boiled to kill microbes. Ultra-heat treatment (UHT) is the partial sterilization of milk by heating it for a short time, around 1–2 seconds, at a temperature exceeding 135 °C. UHT milk available in tetrapacks has a shelf life of 6 months or more, until opened.

FIG. 2.12 UHT milk

* **Pasteurization of milk** consists of heating it to a high temperature of 70 °C for about half a minute and then cooling it quickly. This kills most of the bacteria without affecting the flavour. This method was invented by **Louis Pasteur**.
* **Cooling** food stops microbes from growing

and reproducing, and hence preserves food. A refrigerator keeps food at about 5 °C, and keeps it from spoiling for a few days. A deep freezer preserves food at below –18 °C, and can prevent it from getting spoilt for a few months. However, once the food is taken out of the freezer and warmed, microbes start growing again.

- **Chemical preservatives** such as sodium benzoate and sodium metabisulphite help control microbial growth. They are used to preserve jams, squashes and ketchups. Other preservatives that are commonly used are:
  - **Salt**, which checks the growth of bacteria by forcing microorganisms to lose water by a process called osmosis. It is used for preserving meat, fish, pickles, chips, etc.
  - **Sugar** inhibits the growth of bacteria and is used as a preservative in jams, jellies and squashes. It also makes microbes lose water by osmosis.
  - **Oil** and **vinegar** provide an environment in which microorganisms cannot grow. They are used to preserve vegetables, fruits, fish, meat and pickles.
- **Drying** or **dehydration** of food consists of removing water from it. This stops microorganisms from growing as they cannot grow without water. Cereals, pulses, spices and dry fruits are preserved by this method.
- **Canning:** After sterilizing the food, it is canned in airtight containers. Many canned food items are available in the market.

FIG. 2.13 Canned food

## ORAL QUESTIONS FOR FORMATIVE ASSESSMENT

1. While making cake or *dhokla*, the dough rises because of a substance that is produced during fermentation. What substance is this? Why does it cause the dough to rise?
2. To prevent a disease caused by a certain microbe, doctors inject the same microbes in a person's blood. How is it ensured that this **prevents** the disease instead of **causing** it? What is this process of injecting microbes called?
3. Microbes that live inside the bodies of animals normally cause diseases. However, some of them also help animals. Give an example to prove this point.
4. Pasteurization means boiling the milk to kill germs. Do you agree? Give reasons.

## NOW YOU KNOW

- Organisms that are small and can be seen only through a microscope are called microorganisms or microbes. They are present all around us and also inside our bodies.
- Microorganisms belong to five major groups—bacteria, algae, protozoa, fungi and viruses.
- Bacteria are single-celled organisms. They may be rod-shaped, spherical or spiral.
- Algae are simple plant-like organisms with chlorophyll in their cells. They may be unicellular or multicellular.
- Protozoans are unicellular animal-like organisms.

- Fungi are plant-like organisms that do not contain chlorophyll. They may be unicellular or multicellular.
- Viruses are very small and do not have a cellular structure. They are regarded as being on the dividing line between the living and the non-living.
- Microorganisms are used in the food and beverage industry, in making medicines and vaccines, in agriculture and in cleaning the environment.
- Yeast ferments sugar to produce alcohol and gives out carbon dioxide. This is used to make bread and alcoholic beverages.
- Microorganisms cause diseases in humans, other animals and plants, and spoil food.
- Food can be preserved by killing microbes in food and stopping them from growing again.
- Some methods of food preservation are: heating, cooling, pasteurization (of milk), adding chemical preservatives, drying and canning.

## NEW WORDS

**MICROBES**—tiny organisms that can only be seen through a microscope

**MICROBIOLOGY**—study of microorganisms

**MICROBIOLOGISTS**—scientists who study microorganisms

**VACCINE**—dead or weakened germs that help protect the body against future attack by the germs

**PASTEURIZATION (OF MILK)**—a method of preserving milk by heating it to a high temperature for half a minute and then cooling it quickly

## FOR FORMATIVE AND SUMMATIVE ASSESSMENT

### A. MULTIPLE-CHOICE QUESTIONS: Choose the most appropriate answer.

1. Which of the following cannot be classified as either living or non-living?
   a. fungi  b. bacteria  c. viruses  d. protozoa
2. *Amoeba* is a
   a. bacterium.  b. virus.  c. fungus.  d. protozoa.
3. Which of the following make their own food by photosynthesis?
   a. algae  b. viruses  c. fungi  d. protozoa
4. The unicellular organisms that sour milk to make curd are
   a. bacteria.  b. viruses.  c. fungi.  d. protozoa.
5. Which of the following is responsible for making bread soft and fluffy?
   a. finely ground flour
   b. sugar
   c. alcohol given off during fermentation of sugar
   d. carbon dioxide gas given off during fermentation of sugar
6. Which of these do not have a regular cell structure?
   a. bacteria  b. viruses  c. algae  d. protozoa

7. Which of these are found as both unicellular and multicellular organisms?
   a. bacteria b. viruses c. algae d. protozoa
8. The bacterium *Lactobacillus* is useful in making
   a. cheese. b. cake. c. alcohol. d. all of these
9. Microorganisms spread through
   a. air. b. cuts. c. water. d. all of these
10. Which of these does not prevent growth of bacteria?
   a. salt b. sugar c. water d. oil

## B. VERY SHORT-ANSWER QUESTIONS: Give one-word answers.

1. What is the study of microorganisms known as?
2. Microbes are disease-causing microorganisms. True or false?
3. All fungi are unicellular. True or false?
4. Under unfavourable conditions, microorganisms form a ________ around themselves.
5. What are spherical bacteria called?
6. A virus can reproduce on its own. True or false?
7. Where are algae mostly found—in water or on land?
8. Is the decomposition of the bodies of dead plants and animals by microorganisms desirable or undesirable?
9. Name the class of medicines usually made from fungi or bacteria that can cure dangerous diseases.
10. Is yeast a bacterium or a fungus?
11. The female *Aedes* mosquito is a carrier of the ________ virus.
12. The foot and mouth disease is caused by a ________
13. Food poisoning is caused by a toxin getting accidentally mixed with food. True or false?
14. What is heating milk to a high temperature and then cooling it quickly called?
15. Salt forces microbes to lose water. True or false?

## C. SHORT-ANSWER QUESTIONS (TYPE I): Answer in a sentence or two.

1. What is a microorganism?
2. Name the five groups into which microorganisms are divided. Which of these have only unicellular organisms?
3. Name the three types of bacteria shown in this figure.
4. What kinds of living organisms are classified under algae? Give two examples.

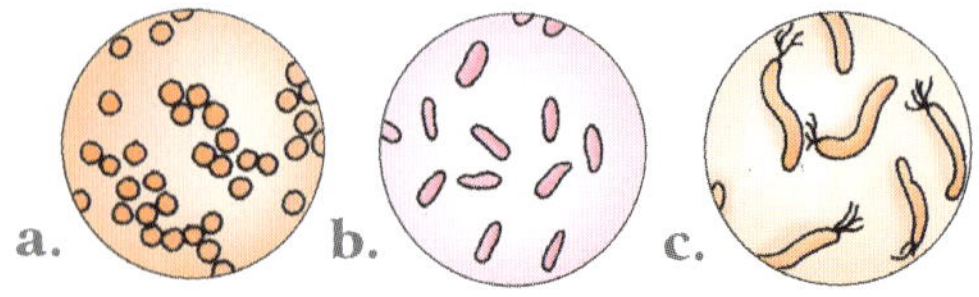


5. Under what circumstances can viruses reproduce?
6. Give one important use of algae.
7. How does cooling help in food preservation?

8. What causes food poisoning?
9. What is pasteurization?

**D. SHORT-ANSWER QUESTIONS (TYPE II): Answer in about 30 words.**

1. How does mosquito help in spreading viruses/microorganisms?
2. Microorganisms are found even in places where no other life forms can exist. What makes microorganisms so hardy?
3. Which microorganism is used to make bread soft and fluffy? Discuss how this happens.
4. What is fermentation? Discuss its use in making alcoholic beverages.
5. How do viruses cause diseases?
6. How does a vaccine work?
7. How does salt prevent food spoilage?
8. What is 'dehydration' of food? In what way is this technique useful?
9. Which microorganisms act as decomposers? How is this activity useful to us?

**E. LONG-ANSWER QUESTIONS: Answer in about 60 words.**

1. Why are viruses considered to be on the borderline of living and non-living?
2. Discuss three important ways in which bacteria are useful to us and two ways in which they are harmful.
3. Discuss the different ways in which communicable diseases spread from person to person.
4. Discuss five methods of food preservation.

**HOTS QUESTIONS: Think and answer.**

1. Why do you think:
   a. curd sets faster in summer than in winter?
   b. curd turns sour faster in summer than in winter?
2. The sealed packets in which food items such as chips are sold are usually filled with nitrogen. How do you think that helps?
3. Why should you always wash your hands before handling food and after coming from the toilet?
4. Evolution, i.e. changes in an organism to adjust to the environment, as suggested by Charles Darwin, is a very slow process that takes place over tens of thousands of generations, over millions of years. However, in bacteria, developing resistance to antibiotic, which is a type of evolution, takes place within our own lifetime. Can you say why it occurs so quickly in bacteria?

## FOR FORMATIVE ASSESSMENT*

### In the Library—Research Project

Here are some important milestones in the discovery of microorganisms. In each case, find out the name of the scientist.

*For more tasks see Page 77

This Dutch scientist (1632–1723) improved the microscope and first saw microorganisms with its help.

This French scientist (1822–1895) is considered to be the father of bacteriology—the study of bacteria. He discovered that bacteria in the air spoil food and also cause diseases.

This English surgeon (1827–1912) first used an antiseptic to kill bacteria while operating on his patients. He used carbolic acid as an antiseptic to disinfect the operation theatre, the surgical tools and surgical cuts. Within five years, he was able to bring down the death rate in major operations from 45 per cent to 12 per cent.

## My Virtual Library—Research/Activities on the Internet

- Visit rsgr.in/lsc-cce-8 and click on LINK 5 to explore on microorganisms.
- Visit rsgr.in/lsc-cce-8 and click on LINK 6 to find about microorganisms and diseases.
- Visit rsgr.in/lsc-cce-8 and click on LINK 7 to watch an animated movie on germs.

## In the Laboratory—Experimental Project / Making a Model

- **To make a carbon dioxide balloon** You have seen that yeast is used for fermentation. Yeast ferments sugar by feeding on the sugar and expelling carbon dioxide in the process. To fill a balloon with carbon dioxide given off during fermentation, proceed as follows. Then, also test the gas to prove that it is carbon dioxide.

  **You will need** ◆ a packet of dry yeast ◆ half litre of warm water (40 °C –50 °C) ◆ two tablespoons sugar ◆ a large rubber balloon ◆ a one-litre empty water bottle

  **Procedure:**

  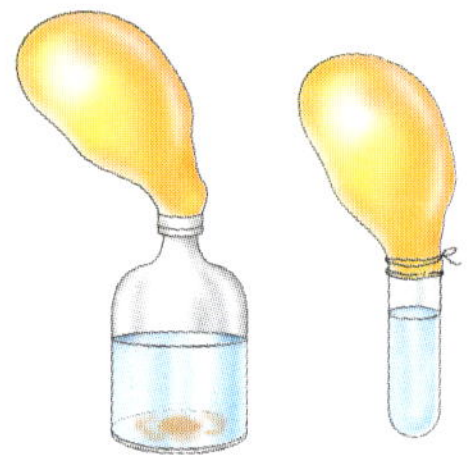

  - Loosen out the balloon by blowing it up repeatedly.
  - Add the packet of yeast and the sugar to the cup of warm water and stir.
  - Once the yeast and sugar have dissolved, pour the mixture into the bottle. You'll notice the water bubbling as the yeast produces a gas.
  - Attach the balloon to the mouth of the bottle.
  - After several minutes, you'll notice that the balloon blows up.
  - Now fill another test tube about ¼ with lime water. Carefully remove the filled balloon so that the gas inside does not escape. Fit the balloon on the test tube with lime water and shake it well.
  - Did the lime water turn milky? What does this show?

  As the yeast feeds on the sugar, it produces carbon dioxide. This gas slowly fills the balloon.

  A very similar process happens when bread is baked. Carbon dioxide from yeast forms thousands of tiny balloon-like bubbles in the dough. These cause the dough to rise and give the loaf its airy texture.

- **Make your own lens**

  **You will need** ◆ a glass tumbler ◆ water ◆ some old newspaper

  **Procedure:**

  - Take a glass tumbler with smooth straight walls. Fill it with water.
  - Place a piece of newspaper on one side of the tumbler and look from the other side.
  - Can you see a magnified image of the print in the newspaper?

  This is your own home-made magnifying lens. Experiment with glass vessels of different shapes and sizes. Which shape and size gives the most magnification?

3

# Synthetic Fibres and Plastics

We use a number of materials in our daily life. Some of these such as wood, cotton, stones and clay are **natural materials**. However, most of the materials we see around us do not occur as such in nature. They have been changed from their natural state by chemical processes. Plastics, paints, medicines, cement, fertilizers and synthetic fibres are some such **human-made materials**. These materials are made from **raw materials** such as coal, crude oil, natural gas, air, water, salt and limestone. Chemical processes are used to change these raw materials into materials with special properties which we can use for specific purposes.

Human-made materials are made in factories called industrial plants. Raw materials are converted into useful materials by chemical reactions. The human-made materials industry is one of the largest industries in the world today.

## WHAT ARE POLYMERS?

Synthetic fibres and plastics are made up of molecules called **polymers**. Polymers are huge molecules—usually consisting of long chains made from thousands of similar small molecules called **monomers**. The name polymer is derived from two Greek words—'*poly*' meaning many and '*mer*' meaning part or unit. As the name implies, a polymer is made up of many repeating units.

**IN THIS CHAPTER**

POLYMERS ◆ SYNTHETIC FIBRES ◆ PLASTICS

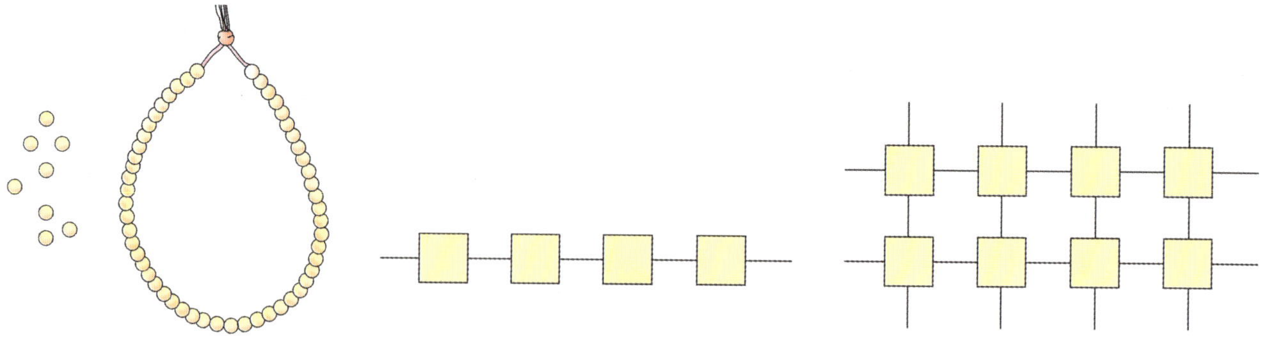

a. Beads to necklace b. Monomers to polymers (linear) c. Cross-linked structure

FIG. 3.1 The structure of a polymer can be compared with that of a bead necklace.

The structure of a polymer can be compared to that of a bead necklace—with the beads being the monomers.

All polymers are not linear in structure. In some the structure is cross-linked, as shown in Figure 3.1c.

Most polymers are light, strong, long-lasting, easy to form into shapes, and cheap. This is what makes them so useful.

## SYNTHETIC FIBRES

The common natural fibres used for making cloth are wool, cotton and silk. They are obtained from plants and animals. They are natural polymers. Other fibres are man-made. They are polymers, many of which are obtained from petroleum. They are called **synthetic fibres**. Rayon, nylon, polyester and acrylic are some synthetic fibres.

### Rayon

Silk is a natural fibre with a beautiful texture. However, it is expensive. Attempts at making a synthetic fibre with similar texture succeeded towards the end of the nineteenth century, when scientists made **rayon**. Rayon is also called **artificial silk**. It is cheaper than silk and can be woven like silk fibres.

Rayon is made from wood pulp. Wood pulp is first dissolved in an alkaline solution. The thick liquid produced is then passed through tiny holes to make fibres. The fibres are hardened by passing them into a bath of sulphuric acid. The fibres are then spun into yarn and woven into cloth.

Rayon is called a **regenerated fibre** because the original raw material, cellulose, is broken down and then reformed. This makes it stronger and easier to dye in a variety of colours. Another useful property of rayon is that it absorbs sweat. Rayon clothes are therefore comfortable to wear in summers.

### Uses of rayon

- It is used to make apparel, such as suits, ties, blouses, jackets, stockings, slacks, sportswear, etc.
- Home furnishings, such as bedspreads, bedsheets, blankets, curtains, tablecloths, upholstery, carpets, etc., are made from rayon fibre, as it has a silky lustre.

### Nylon

Nylon was the first synthetic fibre to be made entirely of chemicals. It derives its name from the cities of **N**ew **Y**ork and **Lon**don, where it was first marketed.

Nylon fibre is very **strong** and **elastic**; in fact, nylon thread is stronger than steel wire. It is **light** and **wrinkle-resistant**. It is also **wear-resistant**; that is why nylon garments last for a long time. It is **easy to wash** and **absorbs** very little water; therefore, garments made from nylon dry quickly. It is lustrous in appearance.

**Activity 1 (Experimental investigation): Tensile strength of fibres**

Take threads of cotton, wool, silk and nylon of about the same length and thickness. Hang one of them from a stand. Attach a pan at the other end of the thread. Add weights, one by one, to the pan until the thread breaks. Note the total weight required to break the thread. This gives a measure of the tensile strength of the thread. Repeat with the other threads. Tabulate your results and compare the strengths of the threads.

Table 3.1

| THREAD | WEIGHT REQUIRED TO BREAK THE THREAD |
|---|---|
| Cotton | |
| Wool | |
| Silk | |
| Nylon | |

### Uses of nylon

- Garments such as saris are made from nylon. Since it is wear-resistant, garments made from it last for a long time.
- Being very strong, nylon fibre is used to make ropes (including ropes used during rock-climbing), tents, fishing nets and parachutes.
- It has good elasticity and is, therefore, useful for making socks and stockings.
- Nylon is also used to make toothbrushes, combs, zip fasteners and machine parts.

NYLON STOCKINGS

NYLON TOOTHBRUSH

Fig. 3.2 Some uses of nylon

### Polyester

Polyester is manufactured from petroleum. Polyester (poly + ester) is made by repeating units of a chemical called an ester. It has properties similar to those of nylon. It is very strong, crease-resistant, light, elastic and absorbs very little water. It is often mixed with natural fibres to make clothes. With cotton it makes **polycot**, and with wool it forms **polywool**. Clothes made of these mixed fibres are more comfortable to wear than those made of pure polyester.

Terylene, terene and dacron are different types of polyester fibres.

### Uses of polyester

Because of many desirable qualities, polyester has many uses.

- Polyester is used to make pants, shirts, suits, and bedsheets either by itself or as a blend.
- Its water-resistant property makes it ideal for garments and jackets that are to be used in wet or damp environments.
- It is used to make jackets and quilted garments.
- PET is a form of polyester used to make bottles, films, utensils, wires, etc.

POLYESTER BAG

POLYESTER PANTS

POLYESTER COAT

Fig. 3.3 Some uses of polyester

### Acrylic

Acrylic is a type of synthetic fibre that resembles wool in its properties. It is lightweight, soft and warm, with a wool-like feel. It resists shrinkage and wrinkles. It can also be dyed very well in a variety of colours. Clothes made from acrylic are cheaper than wool.

**Activity 2 (Experimental investigation): Absorption of water by fibres**

Take two pieces of cloth of same size, each about half metre square, but made of different fibres. Let one piece be of a natural fibre, such as cotton, and the other of a synthetic fibre, such as nylon. Take two beakers, both containing the same amount of water. Soak each piece in different beakers. After ten minutes, take the pieces out of water. Put them in the sun to dry. Which piece dries first? Compare the amount of water left behind in each beaker. Which beaker has lost more water?

### Characteristics of synthetic fibres

Synthetic fibres have become very popular due to the many advantages that they have over natural fibres. They are strong, crease-resistant, elastic (ability to regain original shape after being stretched), mothproof, easy to wash and last for a long time. However, since they **do not absorb water** or sweat, clothes made of synthetic fibres are not very comfortable to wear. In hot and humid weather, these clothes stick to the body and make us feel uncomfortable.

Some synthetic fibres catch fire very readily. They are easily **inflammable**. Also, they melt on heating and stick to the body of the person wearing them. Therefore, they cause severe burn injuries. Synthetic clothes should not be worn in the kitchen or in the laboratory.

## ORAL QUESTIONS FOR FORMATIVE ASSESSMENT

1. There is a difference between the raw materials used in rayon and other synthetic fibres like nylon or polyester. What is the difference?
2. The prefix 'poly' means 'many' for example, 'polygon' means a figure with many sides. What is the significance of the prefix 'poly' in 'polyester'?
3. Synthetic fibres are strong, elastic, light, wrinkle-resistant, and easy to wash and dry. Even with so many advantages, we do not wear clothes made of pure synthetic fibres, but a mixture of synthetic and natural fibres. Why is this necessary?

## PLASTICS

A material is said to be 'plastic' if it can be moulded or formed into different shapes. Thus, dough and plasticine are plastics; so is clay and heated glass. However, the word plastics is now commonly used for several human-made materials that can be moulded into desired shapes or drawn into fibres. All these materials have one common property—they are made of polymers. Scientists have created an enormous range of human-made plastics with different properties. The main source of these plastics is **crude oil**.

Plastics can be classified into two groups, depending on their reaction to heat.

- Thermoplastics, and
- Thermosetting plastics.

In thermoplastics, the process of softening by heating and hardening on cooling can be repeated again and again to soften the plastic to get different shapes. However, thermosetting plastics can be softened by heating only once. Once they are put into a mould and allowed to harden on cooling, they cannot be softened again on heating, e.g. bakelite and melamine. They can maintain their shape and size even at very high temperatures.

### Common uses of plastics

Today, plastics play an important part in our lives. It is the versatility of plastics that is responsible for their many uses. Carry bags, toys, soft drink bottles, car parts, computer parts, refrigerator parts, telephones and many other things around us are made of plastics. Such variety of uses is possible because plastics can be manufactured to have a variety of properties. They can be thin and flexible as well as thick and tough; transparent or coloured; soft or hard; smooth or rough. They are inexpensive, lightweight, resistant to corrosion and action by bacteria, and last much longer than any other material.

TABLE 3.2 Some common man-made plastics and their uses

| MAN-MADE PLASTIC | TYPE OF PLASTIC | PROPERTY | USES |
|---|---|---|---|
| 1. polythene (or polyethylene) | thermoplastic | strong but flexible; can be rolled into sheets or moulded into any shape; water resistant | sheets of polythene are used to pack liquids such as milk; polythene pipes are used to transport liquids such as oil or water; polythene containers are used to store liquids |
| 2. polyvinyl chloride (PVC) | thermoplastic | tougher than polythene; insulator | used as a covering for electric wires; used to make shoes, handbags, furniture, upholstery, floor coverings, raincoats and bottles |
| 3. polystyrene | thermoplastic | easily moulded | used as a packaging material for delicate objects like electronic items and to make thermocol; used to insulate the hollow walls of refrigerators |
| 4. perspex | thermoplastic | transparent like glass, but much stronger | used as a substitute for glass, for making windows in aeroplanes and windscreens of cars |
| 5. teflon or PTFE (polytetra-fluoroethene) | thermoplastic | slippery, not affected by heat and does not react chemically with other substances | used as a non-stick coating on pans and other cooking utensils |
| 6. bakelite | thermosetting | harder than other plastics and a good electrical insulator | used for making buttons, plugs, switches and other electrical fittings |
| 7. formica and melamine | thermosetting | hard and smooth surface | used as table-tops, and for making crockery |

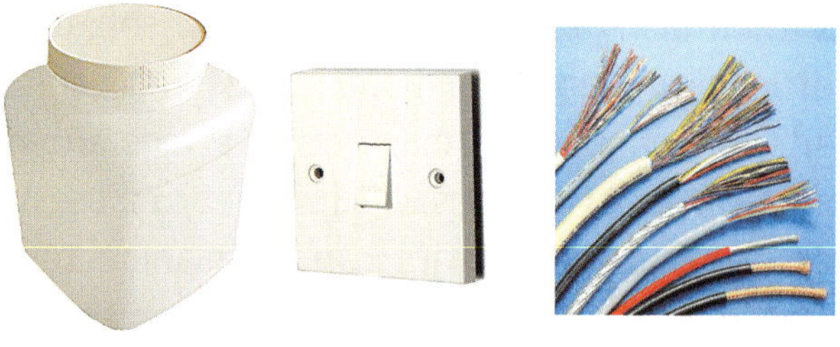

FOOD CONTAINER BAKELITE SWITCH ELECTRIC WIRE COVERING

FIG. 3.4 Some common plastic articles

FIG. 3.5 Plastic waste materials needs to be properly managed.

## Characteristics of plastics

- **Thermal conductivity:** Plastics are poor conductors of heat ('thermal' means 'heat'). Therefore, they are used to make handles of cooking utensils, and as insulating wool used in refrigerators to prevent heat from outside to enter inside it.
- **Electrical conductivity:** Plastics are poor conductors of electricity. This is the reason why electric wires, cords of electrical appliances and cables have a plastic coating.
- **Solubility in water:** Plastics are insoluble in water; that is why buckets to store water and glasses to drink water are made from plastics.
- **Effect of flame:** Plastics are inflammable, that is, they burn easily. This explains why a polythene bag burns so easily.
- **Reactivity:** Plastics have no reaction with water and air. They are non-reactive and do not corrode easily. That is why they are used to store chemicals and other materials.

## Problems with plastics

When plastics were introduced, they were hailed as a wonder material. However, today plastics have become a serious worldwide environmental and health concern. This is because of their non-biodegradable nature and widespread use.

One of the most significant environmental problems associated with plastics is the improper disposal of plastic goods by people. Do you know that plastic bags and bottles thrown on the roadside could stay in the ground or soil for years? This is because plastics are non-biodegradable, i.e. they cannot be decomposed by the microorganisms in the soil. Careless disposal of plastic bags chokes drains, chokes the soil and hinders the absorption of water by the soil. If eaten by animals such as cows, it can kill them. Plastic bags can also contaminate foodstuffs because of poisonous dyes getting absorbed into food. If burnt, they release poisonous fumes and pollute the air.

Thankfully over the last decade or so, a countrywide network for collection of plastic waste through rag pickers, waste collectors and waste dealers, and recycling enterprises has sprung up all over the country.

Because of this, approximately 60–80 % of the plastic bags generated as waste are collected to be recycled. You must have seen the rest strewn on the ground, littered around in open drains, or in garbage dumps. It is this portion that is of concern as it causes extensive damage to the environment.

In India, some municipal areas have banned the use of plastics and they seem to have achieved success, for example, in Ladakh and Sikkim. Several other states have followed suit but the implementation of the ban is still not satisfactory everywhere.

### Conservation action

The problem of plastic pollution is serious and immediate action is required, such as:

- Reduction of the amount of plastic used in packaging that is usually immediately thrown away.
- Recycling and reuse of plastic should be encouraged.
- Plastic wrappings and bags should carry a warning label stating the dangers of plastic pollution and shoppers should be encouraged to use their own bags or recycled paper bags.

### What you can do

- Buy products with less plastic packaging.
- Shoppers should use their own bags or recycled paper bags.
- Support recycling schemes and promote support for one in your local area.
- Practise and promote proper disposal of plastics in your home. Never dispose off plastics in the sewage system.
- Pick up any plastic litter that you see in the vicinity and dispose it off in a proper place. Encourage others to do likewise.
- Never throw plastic litter in the streets, on the pavement or in drains.
- Set an example to others and encourage them to help.

As a responsible citizen, always remember the 4R principle—Refuse, Reduce, Reuse and Recycle.

## ORAL QUESTIONS FOR FORMATIVE ASSESSMENT

1. The molecular structures of synthetic fibres and plastics have one common feature. What is it?
2. Bakelite and polythene are both plastics. However, there is one major difference in their nature. What is the difference?
3. Can bacteria break down plastics?

## NOW YOU KNOW

- Human-made materials are obtained from natural raw materials by chemical processes.
- Polymers are materials with long chain molecules containing thousands of smaller molecules called monomers.
- Synthetic fibres are made of polymers, many of them obtained from petroleum. They are cheaper and stronger than natural fibres.
- Rayon is made from cellulose obtained from wood pulp. Nylon, polyester and acrylic are made entirely of chemicals and are strong, crease-resistant and absorb very little water.
- Human-made plastics can be classified as thermoplastics and thermosetting plastics depending on their behaviour on heating.
- Polythene, polyvinyl chloride (PVC), polystyrene, perspex, teflon (PTFE), bakelite, formica and melamine are different types of plastics with properties suitable for specific uses.

## NEW WORDS

**POLYMER**—long chain of molecules containing thousands of similar smaller molecules called monomers

**SYNTHETIC FIBRES**—human-made fibres made from polymers

**PLASTIC**—a material that can be moulded or formed into different shapes

## FOR FORMATIVE AND SUMMATIVE ASSESSMENT

### A. MULTIPLE-CHOICE QUESTIONS: Choose the most appropriate answer.

1. Which of these is a natural fibre?
   a. rayon  b. cotton  c. nylon  d. polyester
2. Which of these is a fibre derived from chemicals?
   a. rayon  b. cotton  c. nylon  d. silk
3. Which of these fibres is made from a raw material obtained from plants?
   a. rayon  b. nylon  c. terylene  d. polyester
4. Which of these is a thermosetting plastic?
   a. polystyrene  b. bakelite  c. polythene  d. polyvinyl chloride
5. Which of these plastics is a polymer?
   a. bakelite  b. polystyrene  c. polythene  d. all of these
6. Which of these plastics can be repeatedly heated and moulded into any desired shape?
   a. bakelite  b. polythene  c. formica  d. melamine
7. Which of these can you use as a substitute for glass in windows?
   a. polythene  b. PVC  c. perspex  d. teflon
8. Which of these is not a property of plastics?
   a. bad conductor of heat  b. bad conductor of electricity
   c. inflammable  d. soluble in water

### B. VERY SHORT-ANSWER QUESTIONS: Give one-word answers.

1. What name is given to natural materials that are used to manufacture human-made materials?
2. What is the most common source for synthetic fibres?
3. Which artificial fibre is made from wood pulp?
4. Cotton and wool are natural polymers. True or false?
5. Which synthetic fibre is commonly used to make strong ropes?
6. Which synthetic fibre is also called artificial silk?
7. All plastics are made of long chain molecules called ______
8. Name the plastic whose sheets are used for packing liquids.
9. From which plastic material is thermocol made?
10. Which plastic material is used to make non-stick pans?

11. Name one thermosetting plastic which is a good insulator and is used to make plugs and switches.

## C. SHORT-ANSWER QUESTIONS (TYPE I): Answer in a sentence or two.

1. Give two examples each of natural and synthetic fibres.
2. What is a polymer?
3. Why is rayon called a regenerated fibre?
4. List two disadvantages of synthetic fibres.
5. What is a plastic? All plastics have one common property—what is it?
6. Why are plastic bottles commonly used to store chemicals in a chemistry laboratory?

## D. SHORT-ANSWER QUESTIONS (TYPE II): Answer in about 30 words.

1. List the important properties of nylon that make it a useful synthetic fibre. Give two important uses of nylon.
2. Give three uses of polyester, and explain the reason for each use.
3. These days clothes made out of a mixture of synthetic fibres and natural fibres are more popular than those made purely out of synthetic fibres. Discuss the reasons for this.
4. Differentiate between thermoplastics and thermosetting plastics. Give two examples of each.
5. Plastics are very useful materials. Why then is there concern today about their increasing use?
6. List three steps you can take to reduce the danger that plastics pose to the environment.

## E. LONG-ANSWER QUESTIONS: Answer in about 60 words.

1. How is rayon made? Why is it called artificial silk? List its important properties and uses.
2. List and explain four properties of plastics. Give one use of plastics linked to each of these properties.
3. Give the characteristic properties and important uses of the following:
   a. polythene  b. polystyrene  c. teflon  d. bakelite

## HOTS QUESTIONS: Think and answer.

1. Do you think rayon when burnt will stick to the body like other synthetic fibres?
2. Burning cotton smells like burning paper, whereas burning wool smells like burning hair. Why?
3. Which property of plastics makes them so useful but also makes them an environmental hazard?
4. Clay is a 'plastic' material. Does this imply that it is a polymer?
5. Ankit was learning how to cook. His father strictly told him not to wear nylon clothes in the kitchen. Why?

## FOR FORMATIVE ASSESSMENT*

### In the Library—Research Project

Plastics such as PVC or polythene do not react with chemicals. They are said to be chemically inert. This makes them useful for storing acids, alkalis and other corrosive chemicals. However, their

*For more tasks see Page 77

inertness, and also the fact that microbes cannot act on plastics and disintegrate them, creates a major problem. More and more plastics that degrade are now being designed. Chemists have worked out the following methods to make degradable plastics.

- **Plastics that absorb light:** The light breaks down the polymer chains. The plastics, therefore break down into small bits which degrade more quickly.
- **Plastics made by bacteria:** New plastics have been made by using bacteria. The bacteria are grown and they produce granules of a plastic. This plastic is totally biodegradable. It breaks down completely in about nine months. The problem however, is that it is very expensive.
- **Soluble in water:** A new plastic has been designed that is soluble in water.

Find out more about biodegradable plastics.

### Talk to the Class—Presentation

Make a presentation on your findings about biodegradable plastics.

### My Virtual Library—Research/Activities on the Internet

- Visit rsgr.in/lsc-cce-8 and click on LINK 8 to know more about the basics of polymers.
- Visit rsgr.in/lsc-cce-8 and click on LINK 9 for loads of information on fibres.
- Visit rsgr.in/lsc-cce-8 and click on LINK 10 to read about the history of plastics.

### To Meet—Research on Scientist

**Hermann Staudinger** (1881–1965) In 1920, this German chemist proposed for the first time that plastics were made of giant long chain molecules. This lead to a sudden burst of scientific investigations on plastics. As a consequence, a large number of new plastics were introduced in the 1920s and 1930s. This included PVC. Staudinger won the Nobel Prize in 1953 for his contribution to the development of plastics.

Find out more about the life and work of Hermann Staudinger and make a presentation based on your findings.

### Beyond the Classroom—Field Trip

**A group project** Make groups of 10. Visit shops and houses in your neighbourhood or in the vicinity of your school. Encourage shoppers, shopkeepers and the general public to use cloth bags or recycled paper bags. Also, discuss with them the proper ways of disposal of plastics.

You can take the help of organisations that carry out these kinds of awareness programmes.

TEACHER'S NOTES

- Bring different kinds of synthetic fibres and fabrics, and plastic materials to the class and let students examine them and study their properties.
- Create awareness about the problems with plastics and encourage them to organise campaigns against the use of plastic bags. This will involve them and help them imbibe the habit of saying no to plastics.

4

# Metals and Non-metals

Elements can be classified into the following two groups depending on their physical and chemical properties:

- **Metals** such as iron, copper, tin, silver and gold. In general, metals are hard and shiny in appearance.
- **Non-metals** such as sulphur and phosphorus. In general, they are not so hard and dull in appearance.

There are also certain elements, such as silicon, arsenic, antimony and germanium, which have some properties of metals and some properties of non-metals. They are known as **metalloids**.

From the electronic viewpoint, metals are defined as elements which form positive ions by losing electrons. They contain 1, 2 or 3 valence electrons. For example, a sodium atom loses 1 electron, a calcium atom loses 2 electrons and an aluminium atom loses 3 electrons, to form the respective positively-charged ions.

Non-metals are defined as elements which form negative ions by gaining electrons. They contain 5, 6 or 7 valence electrons. For example, chlorine contains 7 valence electrons and gains 1 electron to form a negatively-charged chlorine ion. Oxygen contains 6 valence electrons and gains 2 electrons to form the negatively-charged oxygen ion.

**IN THIS CHAPTER**

OCCURRENCE OF METALS AND NON-METALS ◆ PROPERTIES OF METALS AND NON-METALS ◆ THE REACTIVITY SERIES OF METALS ◆ USES OF COMMON METALS AND NON-METALS ◆ NOBLE METALS ◆ CORROSION OF METALS ◆ ALLOYS

Elements with 4 valence electrons are normally metalloids. The noble gases with 8 valence electrons do not form ions and cannot really be classified as metals or non-metals. However, since they are gases they show the physical characteristics of gases.

## OCCURRENCE OF METALS

In nature, most metals occur in the combined state as minerals. Nearly all rocks contain some metallic minerals. Often the amount of metal present in the rock is so little that it is too expensive to mine these rocks and extract the metal from them. If the amount of metal is more, it is profitable to mine the rocks and extract the metal. Such rocks are called **ores**.

In ores, the useful metallic mineral is mixed with other minerals which are not of much use. These minerals, present as impurities, are called **gangue** (pronounced as 'gang').

Some metals, such as silver, platinum and gold, are not very reactive. They occur in the free state in nature. Their ores contain particles of metals mixed with large quantities of impurities. They are known as **noble metals**.

The ores of very reactive metals, such as sodium or calcium, contain chlorides or carbonates of the metals, for example, rock salt (NaCl), dolomite ($CaCO_3 \cdot MgCO_3$).

The ores of other metals, such as aluminium, iron, copper or zinc, contain mostly oxides or sulphides, for example, bauxite ($Al_2O_3$), iron pyrites ($FeS_2$), haematite ($Fe_2O_3$), copper glance (CuS), and zinc blende (ZnS).

The series of processes carried out to extract pure metals from their ores is called **metallurgy**.

## OCCURRENCE OF METALLOIDS AND NON-METALS

### Hydrogen

Hydrogen is the most abundant element in the universe—it is the chief element that makes up the sun and other stars. On earth, hydrogen mainly occurs in combined form as a constituent of water (about 11% by weight of water is hydrogen), petroleum, natural gas, coal, clay, and all animals and plants.

### Nitrogen

Nitrogen mainly occurs in the free state in the atmosphere. About 76% by mass of air is nitrogen. In the combined state, it is a constituent of minerals such as chile saltpetre ($NaNO_3$) and nitre ($KNO_3$).

### Oxygen

Oxygen is the most abundant element in the earth's crust. It occurs in the free state in the atmosphere, forming about 23% by mass of the atmosphere. In the combined state, it constitutes about 89% by mass of water. It is also present in the combined state in the earth's crust as oxides, carbonates and silicates of metals.

### Carbon

In the free state, carbon occurs as graphite, diamond and coal. Diamond and graphite are pure forms of carbon. Coal contains 60–90% of carbon. In the combined state it occurs in the atmosphere as carbon dioxide. In the earth's crust, it occurs as carbonates of metals and as fossil fuels. Carbon is the central element of all living matter.

### Silicon

Silicon is the second most abundant element in the earth's crust. It does not occur in the free state. In the combined state, it occurs as silica ($SiO_2$) and silicates. The most common form of silica is sand.

### Sulphur

Sulphur occurs in the free state in the earth's

crust. In the combined state, it occurs in rocks as metal sulphates and sulphides. It also occurs as hydrogen sulphide ($H_2S$) which is present in petroleum and natural gas.

Noble gases, such as helium, neon, argon, krypton and xenon occur in elemental form in air.

Extraction of non-metals from their sources is equally important. Non-metals so obtained help in the production of many useful chemicals.

## PROPERTIES OF METALS AND NON-METALS

### Physical properties of metals and non-metals

**Physical state:** Metals are generally solid at room temperature. Mercury and gallium are exceptions—they are liquid at room temperature.

Non-metals occur as solids (carbon, sulphur), liquids (bromine) or gases (oxygen, nitrogen).

**Lustre:** Metals have a **metallic lustre**, i.e. they have a shiny appearance. Non-metals do not have a metallic lustre (graphite is an exception).

**Hardness and strength:** Metals are generally hard and strong. Exceptions are sodium, potassium and magnesium which are soft and can be easily cut with a knife. Non-metals are generally not so hard and strong. Diamond is an exception. It is the hardest substance known.

**Malleability and ductility:** Do Activity 1 to observe a well-known difference between metals and non-metals.

**ACTIVITY 1 (Experimental investigation):**
**Malleability of metals and non-metals**

Collect pieces of the following objects: thick copper wire, thick aluminium wire, iron nail, coal, 'lead' of pencil (graphite) (Note that both coal and graphite are forms of carbon.)

Beat each of them with the help of a hammer. Record what happens to their shape on beating. Do they break or not? Do they get flattened or not?

| OBJECT/MATERIAL | CHANGE IN SHAPE ON BEATING |
|---|---|
| Copper wire | |
| Aluminium wire | |
| Iron nail | |
| Coal | |
| Graphite | |

You will find that copper, aluminium and iron can be flattened on beating. Coal and graphite break on beating, i.e. they are brittle.

The property of metals by which they can be beaten into thin sheets is known as **malleability**.

You have seen wires of copper and aluminium. In general, metals can be drawn into wires. However, have you ever seen wires of coal or graphite? Non-metals cannot be drawn into wires.

The property of metals by which they can be drawn into thin wires is known as **ductility**. Gold and silver are the most malleable and ductile metals.

Non-metals are neither malleable nor ductile; they are **brittle**.

ANTIMONY CHROMIUM GOLD MERCURY SILVER

FIG. 4.1 Some metals

FIG. 4.2 Aluminium foil

**Conductivity:** The following activity demonstrates another property of metals and non-metals, on which various applications in our daily life are based.

**ACTIVITY 2 (Experimental investigation): Electrical conductivity of metals and non-metals**

Set up an electric circuit, as shown, by using copper wire. Test if the following conduct electricity or not, by putting them in the circuit, one at a time: aluminium foil, iron nail, coal, 'lead' of pencil (graphite). In which cases does the bulb light up? Tabulate your results.

| OBJECT/MATERIAL | CONDUCTING OR NOT |
|---|---|
| Aluminium foil | |
| Iron nail | |
| Coal | |
| Graphite | |

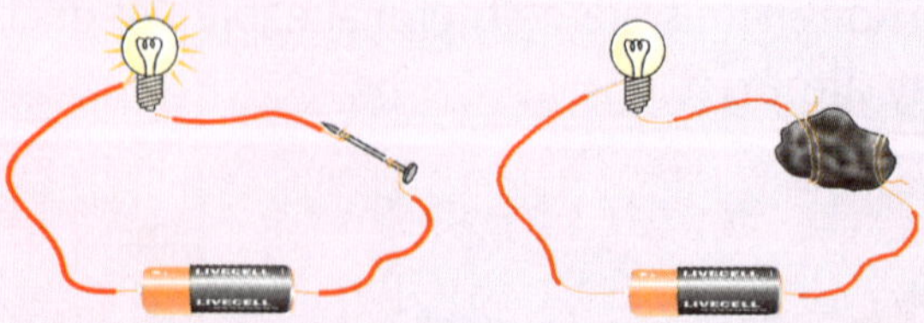


FIG. 4.3 Testing for electrical conductivity

What do you find?

Metals are good conductors of electricity. In general, non-metals are bad conductors of electricity. However, graphite is an exception. It is a good conductor of electricity.

Why are cooking utensils made of metals and not of non-metals? However, the handles of cooking utensils are not made of metals but of wood or plastic. Why?

Metals are good conductors of heat. Therefore, heat gets properly conducted from the fire into the food being cooked. However, if the handles of cooking utensils were made of metals, they would become very hot to hold. Therefore, handles are made of plastic or wood, which are bad conductors of heat.

In general, **metals are good conductors of heat and electricity**. Silver and copper are the best conductors of electricity, followed by gold and aluminium. If you examine electric wires, you will find that they are made of copper or aluminium.

Non-metals are bad conductors of heat and electricity. Graphite is an exception. It is a good conductor of heat and electricity.

**Sonorous:** When wood is struck, does it produce a ringing sound? Do the following activity to listen to sounds produced by different materials.

**ACTIVITY 3 (Experimental investigation): Sound produced by metals and non-metals when struck**

Strike a metal utensil with a metal spoon. Note the kind of sound emitted. Now strike a piece of coal with the same spoon. Do you find a difference in the kind of sound produced?

Most metals produce a ringing sound when struck, i.e. they are **sonorous**. Non-metals are not sonorous.

**Melting and boiling points:** Metals generally have higher melting and boiling points than non-metals. Exceptions are sodium and potassium, which have low melting and boiling points.

Non-metals have low melting and boiling points. The exception is graphite which has very high melting and boiling points.

### Specific gravity

Most metals have high specific gravities, for example, iron 7.8, copper 8.7, lead 11.3, mercury 13.6, gold 19.3. Exceptions are sodium and potassium, both of which have specific gravity less than 1. Non-metals generally have low specific gravities.

### Chemical properties of metals and non-metals

As in the case of physical properties, metals and non-metals differ in their ability to chemically combine with other elements and compounds.

**Reaction with oxygen:** Oxygen reacts with metals and non-metals to produce oxides.

**ACTIVITY 4 (Experimental investigation): Reaction of metals with oxygen**

Hold a piece of magnesium wire with a pair of tongs over a flame. After some time the magnesium burns with a dazzling flame. Collect the white ash of magnesium oxide thus formed in a glass dish.

$$\underset{\text{magnesium}}{2Mg} + \underset{\text{oxygen}}{O_2} \longrightarrow \underset{\text{magnesium oxide}}{2MgO}$$

Dissolve a little of the magnesium oxide in water taken in a test tube. Test it with red litmus.

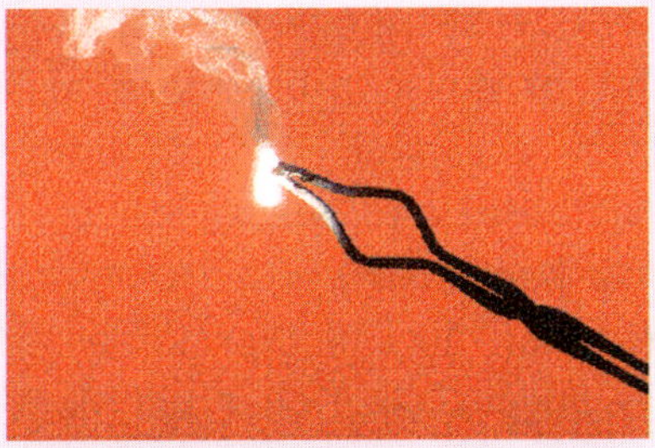

FIG. 4.4 Magnesium burning

The litmus will turn blue, showing that the solution is a base. Thus, magnesium burns in air to produce a basic oxide.

Similar experiments with other metals show that **most metals react with oxygen to give basic oxides.**

Some metals, such as sodium and potassium, react with oxygen even at room temperature and catch fire while reacting.

$$\underset{\text{sodium}}{4Na} + \underset{\text{oxygen}}{O_2} \longrightarrow \underset{\text{sodium oxide}}{2Na_2O}$$

To prevent this reaction, these metals are stored in kerosene.

Others, such as iron and copper, react only on heating at very high temperatures and do not burn while reacting.

$$\underset{\text{copper}}{2Cu} + \underset{\text{oxygen}}{O_2} \xrightarrow{\text{heat}} \underset{\text{copper oxide}}{2CuO}$$

**ACTIVITY 5 (Experimental investigation): Reaction of non-metals with oxygen**

Take a small amount of sulphur in a deflagrating spoon. Heat it over a Bunsen burner flame. As soon as it starts burning, introduce it into a gas jar and cover it with a lid. After the sulphur stops burning, remove the spoon. Add a small amount of water into the gas jar, quickly replace the lid and shake the jar so that the gas formed dissolves in the water.

Test the solution with blue litmus papers. Does it turn red?

FIG. 4.5 Sulphur burns in air to make an acidic oxide.

The litmus turns red, showing that the solution is an acid. Thus, sulphur burns in air to produce an acidic oxide.

| S | + | $O_2$ | $\longrightarrow$ | $SO_2$ |
|---|---|---|---|---|
| sulphur | | oxygen | | sulphur dioxide |

When the sulphur dioxide is dissolved in water, it forms sulphurous acid.

| $SO_2$ | + | $H_2O$ | $\longrightarrow$ | $H_2SO_3$ |
|---|---|---|---|---|
| sulphur dioxide | | water | | sulphurous acid |

When phosphorous burns in air, it forms phosphorous pentoxide, which is also an acidic oxide.

| 4P | + | $5O_2$ | $\longrightarrow$ | $2P_2O_5$ |
|---|---|---|---|---|
| phosphorus | | oxygen | | phosphorus pentoxide |

In general, **non-metals react with oxygen to give acidic oxides.**

**Reaction with water:** Metals react with water to form oxides or hydroxides, and hydrogen.

**Activity 6 (Experimental investigation): Reaction of sodium with water**

(Note: This activity should be demonstrated by the teacher as it is dangerous.)

Half-fill a beaker with water. Cut a small piece of sodium, about the size of a wheat grain. Dry it with a filter paper. Hold it with a pair of tongs and gently drop it in the beaker. Note your observations.

Touch the beaker after the reaction is over. Is it hot? Test the water with red and blue litmus paper. Is the solution acidic or basic?

Sodium, potassium and calcium react vigorously with water, giving off a lot of heat.

| 2Na | + | $2H_2O$ | $\longrightarrow$ | 2NaOH | + | $H_2\uparrow$ |
|---|---|---|---|---|---|---|
| sodium | | water | | sodium hydroxide | | hydrogen |

Magnesium reacts with hot water or steam.

| Mg | + | $H_2O$ | $\longrightarrow$ | MgO | + | $H_2\uparrow$ |
|---|---|---|---|---|---|---|
| magnesium | | hot water | | magnesium oxide | | hydrogen |

The reaction of aluminium with water is interesting. It reacts with water to form aluminium oxide which gets deposited as a thin layer on aluminium and prevents further reaction from taking place.

| 2Al | + | $3H_2O$ | $\longrightarrow$ | $Al_2O_3$ | + | $3H_2\uparrow$ |
|---|---|---|---|---|---|---|
| aluminium | | water | | aluminium oxide | | hydrogen |

Zinc reacts only with steam.

| Zn | + | $H_2O$ | $\longrightarrow$ | ZnO | + | $H_2\uparrow$ |
|---|---|---|---|---|---|---|
| zinc | | steam | | zinc oxide | | hydrogen |

Iron reacts with steam when it is heated strongly.

Copper, gold or platinum do not react with water or steam.

The reaction of metals with water show that different metals have different reactivities.

Non-metals do not react with water. Very reactive non-metals such as phosphorous, which catch fire when exposed to air, are therefore stored in water.

**Reaction with dilute acids:** Let us observe how dilute acids react with metals and non-metals.

**Activity 7 (Experimental investigation): Reaction of dilute acids with metals and non-metals**

Take samples of the following metals and non-metals: magnesium ribbon, aluminium foil, iron filings, copper wire, charcoal powder, sulphur powder. Keep the samples in separate test tubes. To each test tube, add about 5 mL of dilute hydrochloric acid. Note if a reaction occurs. If it does, bring a burning matchstick to the mouth of the test tube. What happens?

If a reaction does not occur, heat the test tube. Does a reaction occur now? Test with a lighted matchstick.

Now try the same with dilute sulphuric acid instead of hydrochloric acid.

Which metals and non-metals did not react with dilute acids at all?

Metals react with dilute hydrochloric and sulphuric acids to form the corresponding salt and to liberate hydrogen. The hydrogen formed burns with a pop sound when a lighted matchstick is brought near it.

$$\text{Metal} + \text{Acid} \longrightarrow \text{Salt} + \text{Hydrogen}\uparrow$$

The more reactive metals, sodium and potassium react violently with dilute acids. The reaction is slower for less reactive metals. Copper, silver and gold do not react with acids.

$$\underset{\text{sodium}}{2Na} + \underset{\text{hydrochloric acid}}{2HCl} \longrightarrow \underset{\text{sodium chloride}}{2NaCl} + \underset{\text{hydrogen}}{H_2\uparrow}$$

$$\underset{\text{iron}}{Fe} + \underset{\text{hydrochloric acid}}{2HCl} \longrightarrow \underset{\text{ferrous chloride}}{FeCl_2} + \underset{\text{hydrogen}}{H_2\uparrow}$$

$$\underset{\text{aluminium}}{2Al} + \underset{\text{hydrochloric acid}}{6HCl} \longrightarrow \underset{\text{aluminium chloride}}{2AlCl_3} + \underset{\text{hydrogen}}{3H_2\uparrow}$$

$$\underset{\text{magnesium}}{Mg} + \underset{\text{sulphuric acid}}{H_2SO_4} \longrightarrow \underset{\text{magnesium sulphate}}{MgSO_4} + \underset{\text{hydrogen}}{H_2\uparrow}$$

This is the reason why certain food items which contain acids, like pickles and curd should not be stored in metallic utensils made of iron and aluminium. As there is a reaction between the acid and the metal, it may result in the formation of a poisonous substance.

Non-metals do not react with dilute acids.

**Reaction with bases:** Only some metals such as aluminium, zinc and lead react with strong bases such as sodium hydroxide to release hydrogen gas.

The reaction of non-metals with sodium hydroxide is complex.

### Displacement reactions—the reactivity series of metals

The reaction of metals with oxygen, water and acids shows that metals have different reactivities. Potassium and sodium are the most reactive, whereas silver and gold are the least reactive. We can arrange the common metals in order of decreasing reactivity as shown in Table 4.2.

Such an arrangement of metals in decreasing order of reactivity is called the reactivity series of metals.

TABLE 4.1 Comparison of properties of metals and non-metals

| PROPERTIES | METALS | NON-METALS |
|---|---|---|
| Physical | generally solid at room temperature (except mercury) | solid, liquid or gas at room temperature |
| | lustrous | not lustrous (except graphite) |
| | generally hard | comparatively soft (except diamond) |
| | generally have high density | generally have low density |
| | malleable and ductile | generally brittle when solid |
| | good conductors of heat and electricity | bad conductors of heat and electricity (except graphite) |
| | generally have high melting and boiling points | generally have low melting and boiling points |
| | sonorous | not sonorous |
| Chemical | generally form basic oxides with oxygen | form acidic oxides with oxygen |
| | form oxides or hydroxides with water and hydrogen | do not react with water |
| | metals above hydrogen in the reactivity series displace hydrogen from dilute acids | do not react with acids |

TABLE 4.2 Reactivity series of metals

| ELEMENT | SYMBOL | REACTIVITY |
|---|---|---|
| potassium | K | most reactive |
| sodium | Na | ↓ |
| barium | Ba | |
| calcium | Ca | |
| magnesium | Mg | |
| aluminium | Al | |
| zinc | Zn | |
| iron | Fe | decreasing reactivity |
| nickel | Ni | |
| tin | Sn | |
| lead | Pb | |
| hydrogen | H | |
| copper | Cu | |
| mercury | Hg | |
| silver | Ag | ↓ |
| gold | Au | least reactive |

Hydrogen though a non-metal is also placed in the series because it also forms positive ions like metals.

You have read that some metals can replace other metals from their salt solutions. It has been observed that a more reactive metal can replace a less reactive metal. Thus, a metal can replace another metal placed below it in the reactivity series, but cannot replace a metal placed above it in the reactivity series. The reaction in which one metal replaces another from its salt solution is known as a **displacement reaction**.

**ACTIVITY 8 (Experimental investigation): Displacement reaction**

Take an iron nail and use sandpaper to remove dirt and rust from it. Place it in a test tube containing copper sulphate solution (Fig. 4.6). Remove the nail after five minutes. Is there a thin layer of copper on the nail? This shows that iron can displace copper from a solution of copper sulphate.

$$\underset{\text{iron}}{Fe} + \underset{\text{copper sulphate}}{CuSO_4} \longrightarrow \underset{\text{iron sulphate}}{FeSO_4} + \underset{\text{copper}}{Cu}$$

Now take a clean copper wire and put it in a solution of iron sulphate. Remove the copper wire after some time.

You will find that there is no deposit on the wire. This shows that copper cannot displace iron from its salt solution.

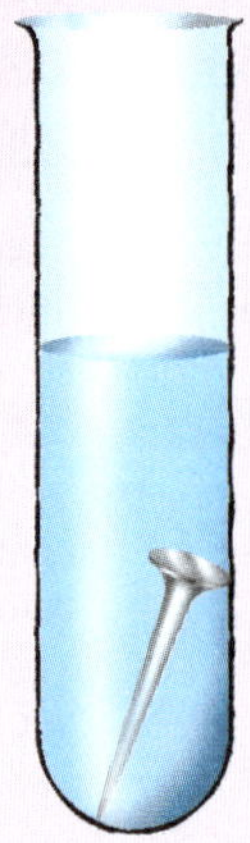

FIG. 4.6 Iron nail in copper sulphate solution

In the reactivity series, iron is placed above copper. Therefore, these observations prove that a metal can replace another metal placed below it in the reactivity series, but cannot replace a metal placed above it in the series.

Magnesium, zinc and aluminium, being above copper in the reactivity series, can replace copper from its salt solution.

$$\underset{\text{magnesium}}{Mg} + \underset{\text{copper sulphate}}{CuSO_4} \quad \underset{\text{magnesium sulphate}}{MgSO_4} + \underset{\text{copper}}{Cu}$$

$$\underset{\text{zinc}}{Zn} + \underset{\text{copper sulphate}}{CuSO_4} \longrightarrow \underset{\text{zinc sulphate}}{ZnSO_4} + \underset{\text{copper}}{Cu}$$

$$\underset{\text{aluminium}}{2Al} + \underset{\text{copper sulphate}}{3CuSO_4} \longrightarrow \underset{\text{aluminium sulphate}}{Al_2(SO_4)_3} + \underset{\text{copper}}{3Cu}$$

## ORAL QUESTIONS FOR FORMATIVE ASSESSMENT

1. A rock is found to have a very small amount of iron. Geologists thought it would be too expensive to extract iron from it. Would you call the rock an ore of iron?
2. An element is a metal or not is finally determined by whether it is hard and shiny or not. Do you agree? Give reasons.
3. Which property must a substance possess for it to be possible to make thin wires of the material?
4. A metal was burnt in air. The substance formed was dissolved in water and tested with blue and red litmus paper. What result do you expect?
5. Metal M1 is more reactive than metal M2. Which metal will be higher up in the reactivity series?
6. Metal M3 reacted with a salt of metal M4. The products were M4 and a salt of M3. However, metal M4 had no reaction with a salt of M3. What can you say about the reactivities of M3 and M4?

## USES OF SOME METALS

### Uses of iron

- Pig iron is a hard and brittle form of iron with a high carbon content. It is used to make pipes, sinks, storage tanks, railings, cylinders, etc., by the process of casting.
- Articles, such as nails, bolts, chains, wire nets, agricultural tools, etc., are made by hammering heated wrought iron. Wrought iron is a tough, malleable form of iron with very little carbon content.
- Steel (contains 0.5–1.5% carbon) is used in construction of buildings, ships, bridges, railway lines, etc. Stainless steel is used to make utensils, knives, etc.

### Uses of copper

- Copper is widely used to make electric wires and cables. Copper coils are used in several electrical appliances.
- It is also used to make heating utensils, car radiators and calorimeters.
- It forms useful alloys.

### Uses of aluminium

- Aluminium is increasingly replacing copper as an electric conductor, especially in overhead cables.
- It is used to make cooking utensils.
- Aluminium foil is used for packing food.
- Aluminium powder is used as paint to prevent rusting of iron.
- Aluminium alloys are light and strong. They are used to make bodies and engine parts of aircrafts and cars.

### Uses of zinc

- Zinc is used in dry cells.
- It is used in coating iron sheets to prevent rusting of iron. The process is known as **galvanizing of iron**.
- It is used in the preparation of useful alloys, such as brass, bronze and German silver.

### Other metals

**Lead** is mainly used for making electrodes for automobile batteries. It is also used for making alloys such as solder and type metals.

Steel or iron plates with a coating of **tin** are used to make food containers. Tin is also used to make alloys such as solder and bronze.

**Chromium** electroplated on iron gives it a corrosion resistant shining finish, for example, in handles of bicycles, car bumpers, etc.

## USES OF SOME METALLOIDS AND NON-METALS

### Uses of silicon

- Silicon is extensively used in the electronic and computer industries to make devices, such as transistors, microchips and solar cells.

- It is used to manufacture silicones, which are used for making waterproof clothes, greases and polishes, and insulating material for electrical appliances.

### Uses of sulphur

- Sulphur is used in the manufacture of sulphuric acid, which is used in several industrial processes.
- It is used in the vulcanization of rubber, which makes rubber hard enough to be used in tyres.
- It is used in skin ointments because of its fungicidal properties.
- Being an insecticide and fungicide, it is used to spray fruit trees against pests and diseases.

### Uses of phosphorus

- Phosphorus is used in making matchboxes and in the fireworks industries.
- It is used in the manufacture of phosphate fertilizers.

### Uses of graphite

- Graphite is used in making electrodes in dry cells and electric arcs. It is also used as a lubricant.
- It is used to make the 'lead' of pencils.

### Uses of hydrogen

- Hydrogen is used for the manufacture of ammonia gas, which is used to manufacture fertilizers such as urea and ammonium sulphate.
- It is used in the extraction of metals such as copper, lead and tin.
- Oxy-hydrogen flame, obtained by burning hydrogen in oxygen is used for cutting and welding metals.
- Hydrogen is considered to be a non-polluting fuel of the future. Considerable amount of research is being carried out to use it efficiently as a fuel.

## NOBLE METALS

Silver and gold are present at the bottom of the reactivity series of metals. They are unreactive metals and do not react with water, acids and alkalis. They, therefore, occur in the free state in nature. They are known as **noble metals**. Platinum has similar properties and is also a noble metal.

- The noble metals are mainly used to make ornaments. As they are unreactive, the ornaments made from them do not lose their shine easily.
- Gold and silver are also used to give a decorative and protective coating on other metals by the process of **electroplating**.
- Gold and silver are used for making high value coins.
- Platinum is used in electrical gadgets. The international standards of weight and measures are made of platinum-iridium alloys.
- Being highly priced, a number of people invest their money in noble metals or ornaments made from them especially in times when the economy is not doing well.

## CORROSION OF METALS

Corrosion is used to describe the process by which materials, such as metals, are slowly eaten away when exposed to air and moisture. Thus, rusting of iron which eats into the metal layer by layer, the conversion of the surface of copper into a greenish powder, or the turning black of the surface of silver ornaments, are all examples of corrosion of metals on exposure to air. The more moist the air, the faster is the

**FIG. 4.7** A rusted iron chain

corrosion. Corrosion causes heavy losses.

The rusting of iron is troublesome and wasteful. However, sometimes corrosion is useful. For example, a newly cut piece of aluminium corrodes to form a layer of aluminium oxide on its surface. This layer protects the aluminium from further corrosion.

## RUSTING OF IRON

To investigate the conditions under which iron rusts, perform the following activity.

### ACTIVITY 9 (Experimental investigation): Conditions for rusting

Take three clean iron nails without any rust on them and three test tubes with corks.

In test tube A, put a few lumps of anhydrous calcium chloride (a good drying agent which absorbs water vapour from the atmosphere). Put a layer of cotton wool and then the nail. Close the test tube with a cork (Fig. 4.8). In test tube B, take some pure (distilled) water. Boil it for one minute to drive off any dissolved air. Then drop in the nail. To keep the air out, seal the water surface in the test tube by pouring molten wax on it (wax will solidify on the cool water surface). Close the test tube with a cork. Half-fill test tube C with tap water and drop the nail in it. Close this test tube also with a cork. Leave the tubes for several days and then examine them. What do you observe?

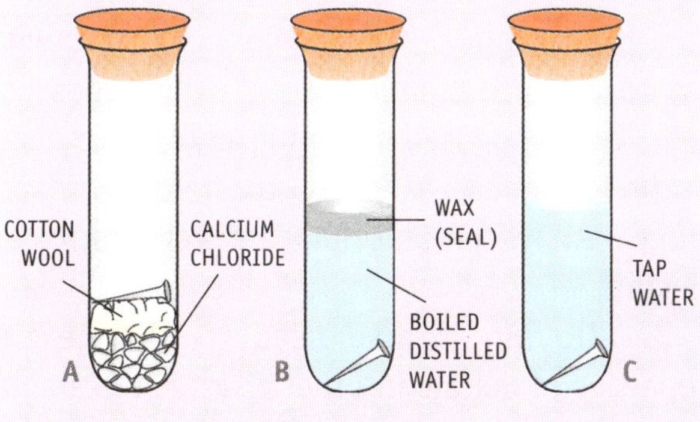


FIG. 4.8 Rusting of iron

You will find that the nails in test tubes A and B have not rusted, while that in test tube C has rusted. What do you conclude?

The experiment shows that for rusting to take place, both air (oxygen) and water are essential.

### ACTIVITY 10 (Experimental investigation): Nature of rust

To test the nature of rust, scrape off some rust from an old iron gate. Collect a spoonful of the rust and add a small amount of water to it. Shake it well and test with blue and red litmus. Is the solution acidic or basic?

Rust is iron oxide, that is, it is an oxide of a metal. Will it be acidic or basic?

### Corrosion of other metals

Copper gets corroded in the presence of carbon dioxide and water to form a green coating, which is a mixture of copper hydroxide [$Cu(OH)_2$] and copper carbonate ($CuCO_3$).

FIG. 4.9 A corroded copper coin

$$2Cu + H_2O + CO_2 + O_2 \rightarrow Cu(OH)_2 + CuCO_3$$

Silver does not get easily corroded in unpolluted air. However, if the air is polluted with sulphur compounds, such as hydrogen sulphide, silver reacts with it to form a black coating of silver sulphide.

Some metals, such as gold and platinum, do not corrode in air. That is why gold ornaments do not lose their shine even after several years.

### Prevention of corrosion

Rusting of iron, and corrosion of other metals can be prevented by not allowing air to come in contact with the metal. Some methods for doing this are as given below.

**Painting or applying oil:** Painting the surface of the metal after cleaning it thoroughly is the most common method of preventing corrosion. The paint keeps air away from the metal surface. Applying grease or oil on the surface has a similar effect. However, if there is a break in the layer of paint, grease or oil, the metal starts corroding at that point.

**Covering with another metal:** Depositing a layer of another metal which is more resistant to corrosion is another commonly used method for the prevention of corrosion of metals. The metals mostly used are tin and zinc. Covering a metal with another metal can be done by the following ways:

- **Galvanizing:** Clean iron sheets are dipped in molten zinc to deposit a layer of zinc on it. This process is called galvanization. The G.I. water pipes available in the market are made of galvanized iron. Galvanized iron does not rust even if there is a scratch on the zinc layer.
- **Electroplating:** The process of electroplating is also used to deposit a metallic layer to prevent corrosion. Tin is electroplated on iron to make food containers commonly called tin cans. However, if the tin layer gets scratched, the iron starts rusting at that place. The tin can is then no longer suitable for storing food. Chromium is electroplated on steel furniture and bicycle handles to prevent rusting. In addition, the chromium layer also gives steel an attractive shine.
- **Anodizing of aluminium:** A layer of aluminium oxide is formed on aluminium upon exposure to air. This prevents further corrosion of aluminium. If this layer is made more uniform, it protects the aluminium underneath more effectively. This is done by a process called anodizing. It consists of passing an electric current through sulphuric acid using aluminium as anode. Oxygen is evolved at the anode which reacts with aluminium to form a uniform protective layer of aluminium oxide.
- **Alloying:** Some metals become corrosion-resistant when alloyed with other metals. For example, stainless steel which is an alloy of iron, chromium and nickel, does not rust easily.

## ALLOYS

An alloy is a mixture of two or more metals, or one or more metals and a non-metal (usually carbon). Alloying is used to alter the properties of metals to suit certain applications. An alloy is usually made by mixing together metals in their molten form. They are also sometimes made by mixing metal powders together.

1. Alloying can be used to increase hardness of metals. Alloys are used because they have specific properties that are more desired than those of the pure elements. For example, pure aluminium, iron and copper are too soft for construction purposes. However, alloying them with small amounts of other metals or non-metals considerably increases their hardness. Nickel is alloyed with chromium and molybdenum to make alloys that are so hard and heat-resistant that they can be used to make the parts of jet engines that get heated up to extreme temperatures.

2. Alloying is used to make metals more resistant to attack by chemicals, and atmospheric corrosion. Chromium is alloyed with iron to produce stainless steel which does not rust. It is also used in lining containers used in the chemical industry to hold corrosive liquids. Alloys of platinum are very corrosion resistant.

3. Alloying is also used to change the properties of metals in other ways. For example, solder, an alloy of lead and tin, has a melting point which is much lower than that of lead or

TABLE 4.3 Alloys, their composition, properties and uses

| ALLOY | CONSTITUENTS PRESENT | PROPERTIES | USES |
|---|---|---|---|
| brass | copper, zinc | hard, corrosion-resistant | utensils, electrical goods, cartridge containers, parts of watches and musical instruments |
| bronze | copper, tin | hard, corrosion-resistant | statues, bearings |
| solder | lead, tin | low melting point | joining metals |
| steel | iron, carbon | very strong | bodies of ships and other vehicles, bridges, railway lines, construction of buildings |
| stainless steel | iron, chromium, nickel | very strong, does not rust | utensils, cutlery, surgical instruments |
| duralumin (or duralium) | aluminium, copper, magnesium, manganese | light and strong | bodies of aeroplanes and vehicles |
| magnalium | aluminium, magnesium | light and strong | balances and other light instruments, bodies of aeroplanes and vehicles |
| German silver | copper, zinc, nickel | high electrical resistance | utensils, electric heaters, resistors |

tin. This makes solder useful for joining copper wires in electric circuits. Superplastic, an alloy of aluminium can be stretched several times more than any metal or alloy.

Some common alloys, their composition, properties, and uses are given in Table 4.3.

## ORAL QUESTIONS FOR FORMATIVE ASSESSMENT

1. Which metalloid can be said to be the backbone of the electronics industry?
2. Steel is not a pure form of iron. What does it consist of? What is the advantage of adding another substance to iron?
3. Noble metals are used to make jewellery because they are very reactive. Do you agree? Give reasons.
4. Painting a metal prevents it from corroding. Why?

## NOW YOU KNOW

- Elements can be classified into metals and non-metals depending on their physical and chemical properties.
- The ore of a metal consists of rocks containing minerals of the metal in sufficient quantities, so that it is profitable to mine it and extract the metal from it.
- Metals are generally solid at room temperature, have a metallic lustre, are generally hard and strong with high specific gravities, melting and boiling points. They are malleable and ductile, good conductors of heat and electricity, and are sonorous.

- Non-metals are solid, liquid or in gaseous form at room temperature, are not lustrous, are comparatively soft and have low density. They are generally brittle when solid, are bad conductors of heat and electricity, have low melting and boiling points and are not sonorous.
- Metals react with oxygen to give basic oxides; non-metals react with oxygen to give acidic oxides.
- Metals react with water, and with dilute acids to displace hydrogen; non-metals do not react with water or acids.
- In the reactivity series of metals, the metals are arranged in decreasing order of their reactivity.
- A metal can displace another metal placed below it in the reactivity series from its salt solution, but cannot displace a metal placed above it in the series.
- Most metals, when exposed to moist air, get corroded. Corrosion can be prevented by not allowing air to come in contact with the metal by painting or applying oil, covering with another metal resistant to corrosion, or by making corrosion-resistant alloys.
- An alloy is a mixture of two or more metals, or one or more metals and a non-metal, which has properties to suit certain applications.
- Alloying can be used to increase hardness, increase corrosion resistance, or change the properties of metals in other ways.

## NEW WORDS

**METALLOIDS**—elements which have some properties of metals and some of non-metals

**NOBLE METALS**—metals which are not very reactive and occur in a free state in nature

## FOR FORMATIVE AND SUMMATIVE ASSESSMENT

### A. MULTIPLE-CHOICE QUESTIONS: Choose the most appropriate answer.

1. Which of the following is true for all metals?
   a. They are hard solids.  b. They have high melting and boiling points.
   c. They have 1–3 valence electrons.  d. They are malleable and ductile.
2. Gold normally occurs in nature
   a. in free state.  b. as carbonate ore.  c. as sulphate ore.  d. as sulphide ore.
3. Which of these is the most reactive metal?
   a. magnesium  b. gold  c. platinum  d. sodium
4. Which of these metals cannot displace hydrogen from a dilute acid?
   a. iron  b. zinc  c. silver  d. calcium
5. Which one of the following alloys is light and strong?
   a. brass  b. stainless steel  c. duralium  d. bronze

6. Which of these metals can displace all the other three metals from their salt solutions?
   a. copper  b. iron  c. silver  d. zinc
7. Metal A dipped in a salt of metal B displaces B from the solution. This shows that
   a. A is more reactive than B.
   b. B is more reactive than A.
   c. both A and B are equally reactive.
   d. no such conclusion can be drawn.
8. Metals react with oxygen to form
   a. acidic oxides.
   b. basic oxides.
   c. either acidic or basic oxide depending on the metal.
   d. there is no reaction
9. The metal most used in the construction industry is
   a. iron.  b. copper.  c. aluminium.  d. tin.
10. Pieces of copper, silver and gold are dropped into a solution of iron sulphate. The piece that will get a coating of copper is
   a. iron.  b. silver.  c. gold.  d. none of them

## B. VERY SHORT-ANSWER QUESTIONS: Give one-word answers.

1. Name a metal which is liquid at room temperature.
2. Metals generally have a low specific gravity. True or false?
3. If a material can be drawn into thin wires, it is said to be ________
4. Aluminium does not react with water. True or false?
5. $Zn + CuSO_4 \rightarrow ZnSO_4 + Cu$ is an example of a ________ reaction.
6. Which metal is higher up in the reactivity series—sodium or silver?
7. Any rock containing metallic mineral is called an ore. True or false?
8. ________ is the most abundant element in the universe, whereas ________ is the most abundant element in the earth's crust.
9. Sand contains the elements ________ and ________
10. Which non-metal has very high melting and boiling points?
11. Metal food containers have a coating of ________
12. Name a soft metal.
13. What is the black material inside a pencil?
14. Metals react with oxygen to produce ________ oxides, and non-metals react with oxygen to produce ________ oxides.
15. Do non-metals react with water?
16. A metal X can replace another metal Y from its metal salt. Is X above or below Y in the reactivity series?
17. The presence of air and ________ are necessary for iron to rust.
18. Galvanized iron starts rusting if there is a scratch on the zinc layer. True or false?
19. Copper corrodes in the presence of ________ and water.
20. Name a metal that does not corrode in air.

## C. SHORT-ANSWER QUESTIONS (TYPE I): Answer in a sentence or two.

1. What is the difference between the physical state of metals and non-metals at room temperature?
2. What do you mean by reactivity series of metals?
3. What is the advantage of galvanized iron over tin-plated iron?
4. What is an alloy? How are alloys generally made?
5. What are noble metals? Why are they used to make ornaments?
6. Can a wire be drawn out of wood. Why not?
7. Can alloying be used to lower the melting point? Give an example.
8. How is anodizing of aluminium carried out?

## D. SHORT-ANSWER QUESTIONS (TYPE II): Answer in about 30 words.

1. What do you mean by malleability and ductility? How are these properties different in metals and non-metals?
2. Give three examples of reactions between metals and water, to show that different metals have different reactivities.
3. Give the important uses of copper.
4. Aluminium protects itself against corrosion. Discuss why it is necessary to anodize aluminium to make it corrosion resistant.
5. List three important uses of hydrogen.
6. List three uses of silicon.

## E. LONG-ANSWER QUESTIONS: Answer in about 60 words.

1. State whether a displacement reaction will occur if the following are mixed. Give reasons. Give the reaction.
   a. copper sulphate and zinc
   b. copper sulphate and iron
   c. zinc sulphate and copper
   d. zinc sulphate and iron
   e. iron sulphate and zinc
   f. iron sulphate and copper
2. Describe an experiment to show the conditions necessary for rusting of iron.
3. Discuss briefly the different methods used for preventing corrosion of metals.
4. Give the names and composition of alloys that are used for the following.
   a. making statues
   b. joining wires in electronic equipments
   c. making surgical instruments
   d. making bodies of aircrafts
   e. making accurate laboratory balances
   f. making bodies of ships

## HOTS QUESTIONS: Think and answer.

1. Silver is the best conductor of electricity. Can you say why electric wires are not made of silver?
2. Why are bells made of metals and not from wood?
3. Suppose copper was high up in the reactivity series. Would it still have been such a useful metal? Give reasons.

4. It has been noticed that silverware becomes black faster today than it did fifty years ago. What can be the reason for this?
5. Aluminium is above iron in the reactivity series. However, its reactions with oxygen and water seem to indicate that it is less reactive than iron. Explain.
6. If you are an engineer constructing a multi-storey building, which alloy would you be extensively using and why?
7. A doctor diagnosed a patient with iron deficiency, and gave him tablets containing iron. But the tablets were not hard and did not look like iron at all. What do you think the tablets contained?

## FOR FORMATIVE ASSESSMENT*

### In the Library—Research Project

**Superconductors** When electricity flows through a metal, some of it is wasted in the form of heat generated. This happens because all metals offer resistance to the flow of electric current. Superconductors are metals, alloys or compounds that conduct electricity without offering any resistance. However, this happens only below a certain temperature. This phenomenon is known as **superconductivity**. This means that a current flowing in a closed loop of a superconducting material will continue to flow forever—much like an object moving on a frictionless surface will continue to move forever!

Research over the past few decades has focussed on producing superconductors at higher and higher temperatures so that they can be practically used.

On 10 October 2009, it was reported that a record high temperature of 254 K had been achieved. This is still 19 °C below freezing point.

Find out more about superconductors. What is the highest temperature achieved till date? Find out about the benefit if superconductors working at room temperature are discovered?

### My Virtual Library—Research/Activities on the Internet

- Visit rsgr.in/lsc-cce-8 and click on LINK 11. Now click on 'Activity' for a very interesting interactive presentation on atoms, periodic table, and metals and non-metals. Click on 'Test' to take a test.
- Visit rsgr.in/lsc-cce-8 and click on LINK 12. Now click on pages 5 and 6 for a discussion on reactivity series, and metal and non-metal oxides.
- Visit rsgr.in/lsc-cce-8 and click on LINK 13 to get an overview of the important alloys used in jewellery.

### In the Laboratory—Experimental Project

**Electroplate a metal object with copper**

**You will need** ◆ a plate of pure copper ◆ copper sulphate ◆ hydrochloric acid ◆ water ◆ metallic objects, such as keys, for electroplating ◆ battery/cells ◆ connecting wires

If a pure copper plate is not available, purchase thick copper wire and hammer to flatten it.

**Procedure:**

- Dissolve 70 g of copper sulphate in 500 mL water to make the electrolyte.
- Clean the object to be electroplated by first placing it in dilute hydrochloric acid, then washing it in running water, and finally scrubbing it with sandpaper.

*For more tasks see Page 77

- Put the electrolyte in a glass bowl. Connect one end of a wire to the copper plate and the other end to the positive end of a cell. Connect another wire to the object to be electroplated and the negative end of the cell through a switch (Fig. 1).
- Dip the copper plate and the object in the electrolyte. Put the switch ON and let current flow for 8–10 minutes. Does copper get electroplated on the object? Test the toughness of the copper layer by first rubbing with your hand and then with harder substances, like sandpaper, nail file, etc.

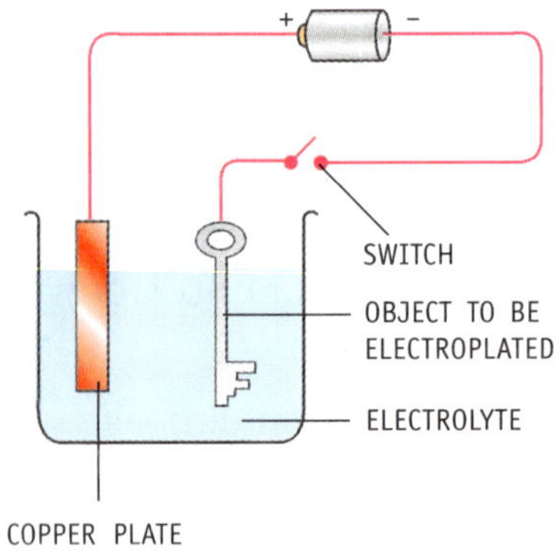


FIG. 1

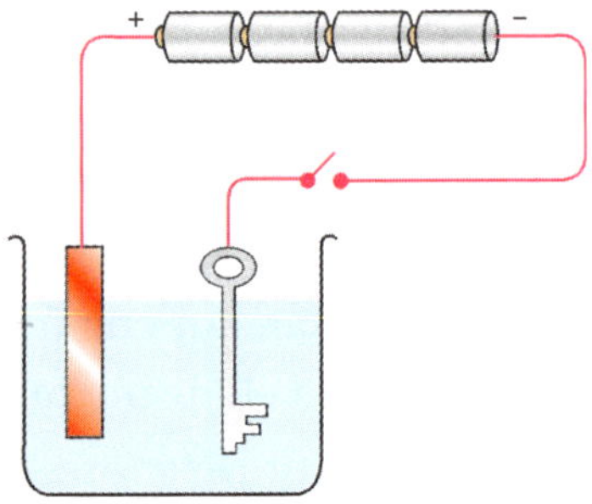


FIG. 2

- Now vary the conditions of electroplating, as explained below, to see their effect on the toughness of the electroplated layer.
  a. Increase the current by connecting four cells as shown in Figure 2. What effect does this have on the nature and toughness of the electroplated layer?
  b. Clean the object to be electroplated only with soap and water before electroplating. What effect does this have?
  c. Warm the electrolyte (only slightly, but do not boil) using a spirit lamp or Bunsen burner. Does this have any effect?

### Beyond the Classroom—Field Trip

Visit a blacksmith/coppersmith/goldsmith. Find out about (observe if possible) the handlings of various metals there.

### Talk to the Class—Presentation

Make a presentation (preferably a PowerPoint presentation) on your findings in the above field trip.

## LIFE SKILL

**Prevent rusting of your bicycle, two-wheeler or car**

Rust usually begins through the chips and nicks from small stones that hit your vehicle, and scratches due to minor brushing of the vehicle against a hard object. Even small nicks expose bare metal and rusting soon starts. If you leave it unchecked, very soon you may have a rust hole in the body of the vehicle. Here is what to do for preventing this.

- Carry out a thorough periodic checking of the body of the vehicle. Look for chips and nicks in the paint.
- If you find a chip, sand it with fine sandpaper until the bare metal can be seen. For tiny nicks wrap the sandpaper around the tip of a small screw driver and try not to affect the surrounding painted surface.
- Clean the dirt from the chips with a rag dampened with nail polish remover.
- After it has dried, use a touch-up brush to dab a little touch-up paint (touch-up paint is available in the market) on the nick, just enough to fill in the gap.
- If it looks clumsy, wipe it off with the rag dampened in nail polish remover and try again.
- For bigger chips and dents, it is best to go to a professional car painter.

SKILLS INVOLVED: Thinking skill, Preservation skill

5

# Coal and Petroleum

## NATURAL RESOURCES

Our earth is the only planet in the universe known to support life. Scientists believe that the earth was formed about 4500 million years ago, and that life first appeared on the earth about 3500 million years ago. The conditions that existed on the earth at that time enabled life to originate. It is believed that the first life forms that appeared on the earth were unicellular, i.e. they consisted of single cells. Over millions of years, higher forms of life slowly evolved from these simpler forms of life. This led to the millions of species of plants and animals that exist on the earth today.

Living things originated and survived on the earth because:

- All the materials required by living things, such as air, water, soil and minerals are present on the earth. These are the major **resources** of the earth.
- The earth is at the right distance from the sun and therefore has the right temperature range for life to exist. The light energy received from the sun plays an important role in the survival of life on the earth.

### Utilization of resources

Plants use carbon dioxide from the air, water and minerals from the soil to make food in the

**IN THIS CHAPTER**

NATURAL RESOURCES ◆ FOSSIL FUELS—COAL, PETROLEUM, NATURAL GAS ◆ PREVENTING AN ENERGY CRISIS

FIG. 5.1 We use natural resources in several ways.

presence of sunlight. You already know that this process is known as **photosynthesis**. It takes place in green leaves in the presence of the green pigment chlorophyll, present in these leaves.

Animals need oxygen, water and food to survive. They get oxygen from the air, water from water bodies such as ponds, lakes and rivers, and food from plants or other animals.

We humans also need food, air and water. We use the resources of the earth in several other ways also. For example:

- We use **rocks** and **soil** to construct houses, roads, dams, etc.

**ACTIVITY 1 (Observation and classification): To classify materials as natural or human-made**

Make a list of materials that you need and use in daily life. Classify them as natural or human-made.

| NATURAL | HUMAN-MADE |
|---|---|
| | |

- We use **metals** such as iron, aluminium, copper, etc., for constructing buildings and bridges, making machines, vehicles, aeroplanes, utensils and other household items, etc.
- We use **fuels**, such as coal, petroleum and natural gas for cooking, running vehicles, running machines in factories, producing electricity, etc.

Natural materials found on the earth that allow the existence of life and satisfy the needs of living organisms are called **natural resources**. Plants and animals are **living natural resources**. Air, water, soil and minerals are **non-living natural resources**. We get these natural resources from:

- the solid parts of the earth's crust.
- the water bodies, such as seas, rivers and lakes on the earth.
- the gases (air) surrounding the earth, known as the atmosphere.

## RENEWABLE AND NON-RENEWABLE RESOURCES

Our natural resources can be divided into two main groups:

- Renewable resources
- Non-renewable resources

Renewable resources are those that will either never run out, or those that are replaced within a reasonable period of time through natural processes. For example, sunlight is a resource which will never run out as the sun is expected to last for another 5 billion years. Oxygen is renewable because it is replaced in the atmosphere as plants release oxygen during photosynthesis.

However, most renewable resources are exhaustible if we use them faster than they are renewed, or if we disturb the natural method of their renewal. For example, groundwater is a renewable resource. However,

**Fig. 5.2a** Water and forests are renewable resources

**Fig. 5.2b** Topsoil and petroleum are non-renewable resources.

today we are using it faster than it is renewed. This is the reason why the level of groundwater is going down.

Non-renewable resources are those which once used up cannot be replaced within a reasonable period of time. For example, fuels like petroleum, natural gas or coal take millions of years to form. Hence, once used up, these resources cannot be renewed before million of years. Similarly, topsoil takes hundreds of years to form. Once topsoil is eroded, it cannot be replaced immediately.

However, some non-renewable resources such as metals can be used again and again. These non-renewable resources can be **recycled**.

## CONSERVATION OF RESOURCES

All life on earth depends on the earth's resources. Therefore, all resources, whether renewable or non-renewable, need to be conserved. Conservation is the wise and careful use of resources. It means not wasting the resources, and also maintaining their quality.

**Fig. 5.3** Cutting down of trees can deplete groundwater.

A few decades back, people did not give much attention to conservation. However, now it has become very important. Why?

There are two primary reasons for this:

- The population of the world has increased. There are more people on the earth, and they use more resources to feed, clothe and house themselves.
- As humans have progressed, their needs have increased. Their energy needs, for example, have increased several-fold. The average resources consumed per person have, therefore, increased considerably.

Because of these two factors, the natural resources today are getting used up and depleted much faster than a few decades back. This often leads to an imbalance in nature. A few forms in which these imbalances appear are pollution of air, water and soil, changes in climate, and decrease in animal and plant populations. Therefore, if we do not practice conservation, we will endanger our very survival.

In this chapter, we will learn about some non-renewable natural resources such as coal, petroleum and natural gas, which are used as fuels.

## ORAL QUESTIONS FOR FORMATIVE ASSESSMENT

1. Mention four natural resources that helped life to originate and survive on the earth.
2. Natural resources are both living and non-living. Do you agree? Give examples of each.
3. The amount of groundwater on the earth will always remain the same. Do you agree? Give reasons.
4. How has the increase in human population and its needs affected natural resources?
5. Sunlight and groundwater are both renewable resources. What is the difference between them?

## FUELS

Anything that burns gives off heat. Wood, paper, coal and LPG are combustible substances which produce heat on burning. However, all combustible substances cannot be called fuels.

A fuel is a substance that can be used to produce heat at a reasonable cost.

Fuels contain potential energy that is locked within the chemical bonds of their constituent molecules. When they are burnt, a large part of this energy is released as heat. This forms the basis of their use as fuels.

All common fuels contain carbon, either as a free element or in the combined state.

## FOSSIL FUELS

**Coal**, **petroleum** and **natural gas** are called **fossil fuels**, as they were naturally formed from the dead remains of living organisms. Coal was formed during a period of over millions of years from dead plants that got buried inside the earth. Petroleum and natural gas were formed from dead sea animals, the process again taking over millions of years.

Since all living plants and animals ultimately derive their energy from the sun, the energy of fossil fuels is also indirectly derived from the sun.

Fossil fuels are the most important source of energy for us today. They are concentrated stores of energy and give off heat and light on burning. The heat can be used to cook food or to run engines such as automobile engines. It can be used to generate electricity as in powerhouses where the most common fuel used is coal.

## COAL

FIG. 5.4 Coal

Coal is a fossil fuel. It is black in colour and hard as a stone. It has formed over a period of millions of years, by the gradual decay and compression of buried remains of ancient forests.

About 300 million years ago, there were dense forests in low-lying wetland areas on the earth. As the trees died, they got covered with sand and mud. More trees grew on this sand and mud. When these died, they too got covered. This process went on for centuries. Sometimes earthquakes and volcanoes buried entire forests deep down in the earth. The high temperature and high pressure inside the earth slowly converted the buried vegetation into coal. As coal contains mainly carbon, this slow process of conversion of wood into coal is called **carbonization**. The period during which this process of coal formation took place is called the **carboniferous age**.

Coal mainly consists of carbon. Hydrogen, oxygen and small amounts of nitrogen and sulphur are also present. There are three main varieties of coal. They vary in their carbon content.

- **Anthracite** has up to 96 per cent of carbon and is regarded as **the best variety of coal**.
- **Bituminous coal** has about 65 per cent carbon.

- **Lignite** has about 38 per cent carbon.

When coal is heated in air, it burns to produce mainly carbon dioxide gas.

$$C + O_2 \longrightarrow CO_2$$

Coal is used as a domestic and industrial fuel. It is widely used in thermal power plants to produce electricity.

In India, coal deposits are mainly found in Jharkhand, West Bengal, Odisha, Chhattisgarh, Madhya Pradesh and Tamil Nadu.

### Destructive distillation of coal

Destructive distillation of coal is carried out by heating coal strongly to 1000 °C in the absence of air. It yields various useful organic and inorganic products. These products are as follows:

- **Coke:** The residue left behind when destructive distillation of coal is carried out is coke. It is an almost pure form of carbon. It is a good fuel and burns with no smoke. It is also used to reduce metal oxides, such as iron and zinc oxides, to get the metals. Coke is also used to manufacture gaseous fuels—**producer gas** ($N_2$ + CO) by passing air through red hot coke, and **water gas** ($H_2$ + CO) by passing steam over white hot coke.
- **Coal gas:** It is a mixture of hydrogen, methane, carbon monoxide and other gases. It was earlier used for domestic cooking and lighting, but is not much used now.
- **Coal tar:** Coal tar contains several carbon compounds. On fractional distillation, it yields many important organic compounds such as benzene, toluene, naphthalene, phenol, etc. These compounds are used to make pesticides, explosives, synthetic fibres, perfumes, naphthalene balls to repel moths and insects, dyes and paints. However, today these compounds are mainly obtained from petroleum.
- **Ammonium compounds:** These are given off during the destructive distillation of coal. When dissolved in water, they give ammoniacal liquor. It is used for making nitrogenous fertilizers.

**ACTIVITY 2 (Experimental investigation):**

**To demonstrate destructive distillation of coal in the laboratory**

Take two boiling tubes, A and B. Put powdered coal in tube A and half-fill tube B with water and set them up as shown in Figure 5.5. Heat powdered coal strongly in boiling tube A. As the gases given off by heated coal pass through the water in tube B, you will see that black drops of coal tar collect at the bottom of tube B. The ammonium compounds will dissolve in the water in tube B. However, coal gas will pass through the water and rise up. It can be lighted at the end of the open tube.

The residue left behind in tube A after the gases have stopped being evolved is coke.

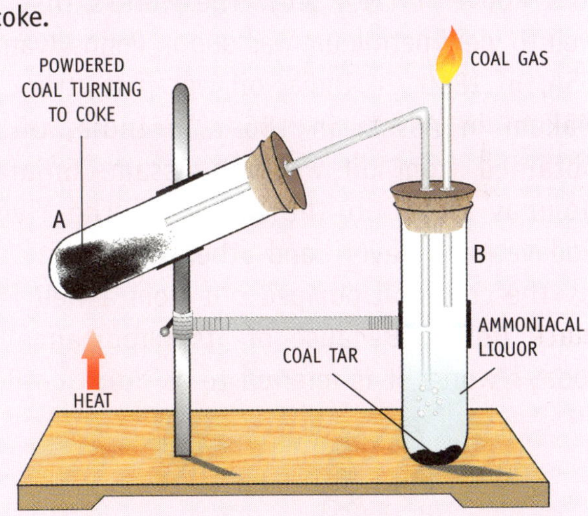


FIG. 5.5 Destructive distillation of coal

## PETROLEUM

Petroleum or crude oil is found trapped in underground rocks. This is why it is called petroleum (*'petra'* means rock, and *'oleum'* means oil). It is a mixture of several hydrocarbons, with the number of carbon atoms in the molecules varying from one to more than one hundred. The different components in petroleum are separated and used in various ways. Their most important use is as fuel. Petrol, diesel and kerosene are some of the fuels obtained from petroleum.

### Origin

Petroleum is believed to have formed, over a period of millions of years, from organisms that lived in the sea at that time. When these organisms died, their bodies settled on the seabed, and got covered with sand and clay. Over millions of years, heat and pressure changed the dead organisms into petroleum hydrocarbons.

### Occurrence

Petroleum and natural gas are often found together as large deposits deep inside the earth's crust. Petroleum is obtained by drilling through the earth and impervious (non-porous) rock above it (Fig. 5.6). The world's first oil well to yield petroleum was dug in Pennsylvania, USA, in 1859. In India, oil was first struck in Makum in Assam in 1867. In India, oil is obtained from oil wells in Assam, Gujarat, Bombay High, in the deltas of the rivers Godavari and Kaveri, and other places.

The crude oil pumped out from a well is a black liquid. Because of its importance in today's world, it is referred to as **black gold**.

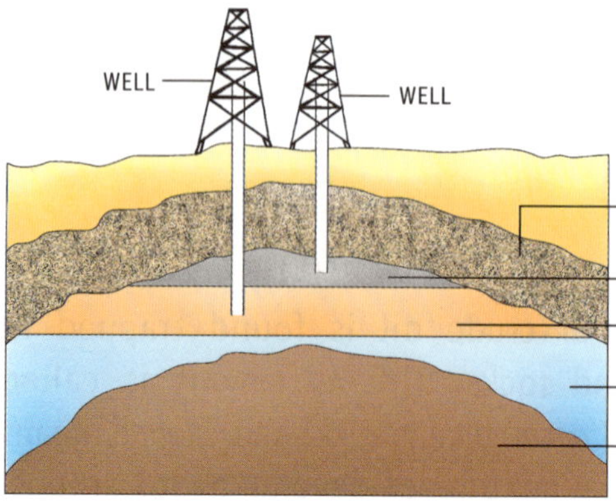


FIG. 5.6 Oil well

### Refining of petroleum

The various hydrocarbons present in petroleum have different boiling points. As the number of carbon atoms in a hydrocarbon increases, its boiling point also increases. This property is used to separate the different components of petroleum by **fractional distillation**. The components with different boiling points are known as **fractions**, and the process of separating the fractions by fractional distillation is known as **refining**. It is carried out in a petroleum refinery.

Crude oil is first heated to about 400 °C in a furnace. The vapours formed are passed into a tall **fractionating tower** (Fig. 5.7). The hydrocarbons with the highest boiling points condense first. They get collected near the base of the fractionating tower.

As the vapour rises, the hydrocarbons with lower boiling points condense at different heights. They get separated in the fractionating tower to form the different fractions. The hydrocarbons with 1–4 carbon atoms, which are gases, do not condense and escape from the top of the tower.

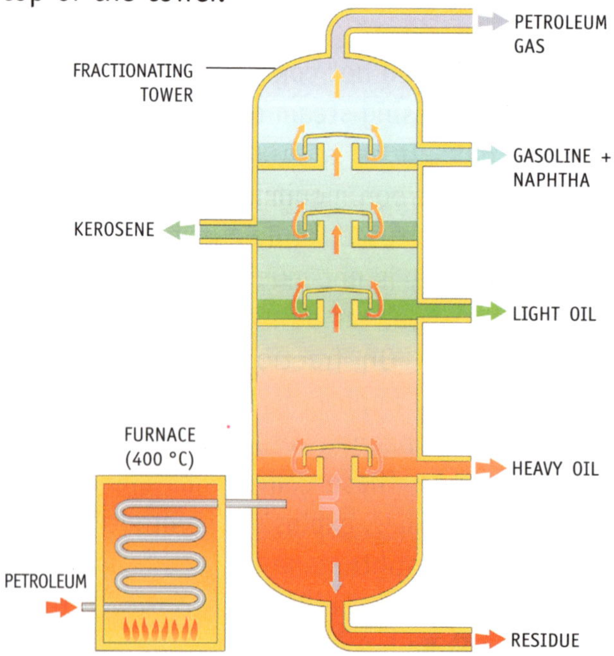


FIG. 5.7 Fractional distillation of petroleum

TABLE 5.1 Some important fractions of petroleum and their uses*

| FRACTION | BOILING POINT | NUMBER OF CARBON ATOMS | PRODUCTS OBTAINED/USES |
|---|---|---|---|
| Petroleum gas | below 40 °C | 1–4 | LPG (liquefied petroleum gas)—fuel for home and industry |
| Gasoline and naphtha | 90–165 °C | 4–10 | Petrol—motor fuel, aviation fuel, solvent for dry-cleaning |
| Kerosene | 150–245 °C | 10–16 | Kerosene—domestic fuel, jet engine fuel |
| Light oil | 215–315 °C | 16–20 | Diesel—fuel for motor vehicles (especially heavy vehicles), electric generators |
| Heavy oil | 285–370 °C | 20–25 | Useful organic chemicals |
| Residue | over 370 °C | over 25 | Lubricating oil—lubricating machinery; Paraffin wax—candles, vaseline, ointments, etc; Asphalt (bitumen)—paints, road surfaces |

* Petroleum extracted from different wells around the world is not uniform in composition. It varies not only in its composition of hydrocarbons but also in several other ways, for example density and presence of impurities such as sulphur, lead, arsenic, arene etc. This makes the composition and boiling points of the fractions differ considerably. The data regarding the composition and boiling points in Table 5.1 is only indicative and may vary considerably in different samples of petroleum.

Each fraction obtained is itself a mixture of several hydrocarbons. Some of these are used in the same form as obtained. Others are further separated by fractional distillation or other methods to give different products. Some important petroleum fractions and their uses are given in Table 5.1.

### Uses of petroleum

Table 5.1 lists the uses of the major products obtained from petroleum. As you can see, petroleum products are primarily used as **fuels**.

In addition, some chemicals obtained from petroleum are used to make medicines, ointments and cosmetics. Further fractional distillation of petroleum fractions yield chemicals that are used to manufacture materials such as plastics, synthetic rubber, synthetic fibres and explosives.

## NATURAL GAS

Natural gas is found along with petroleum in reservoirs under the ground. It is chiefly made up of methane, though butane and propane are also present in small proportions. It can be easily transported through pipes and is a clean non-polluting fuel. It is stored under high pressure as **compressed natural gas (CNG)**.

- CNG is used for power generation.
- In some parts of India, e.g. Vadodara, CNG is supplied to homes and factories through pipes and directly used as a fuel.
- CNG is also now being used as a non-polluting fuel for vehicles.
- Natural gas is used as a starting material for the manufacture of a number of chemicals and fertilizers.

Deposits of natural gas are found in India in Tripura, Rajasthan, Maharashtra and in the Krishna-Godavari delta.

## ENERGY AND TECHNOLOGICAL DEVELOPMENT

Our energy needs have been increasing at a tremendous pace due to two main reasons. One is the increase in population. The other more important reason is that as we progress and develop new technologies, we need more energy to run new factories, and to power the new gadgets made by the use of the new technologies. For example, the tremendous development in the field of computers in the last few years has meant that computers are now widely used in factories, offices, shops and homes. Manufacturing and using these billions of computers uses up huge amounts of electrical energy.

Some areas in which energy consumption has increased several times are as follows:

- Manufacturing goods in factories uses up huge amounts of energy.
- In agriculture, energy is needed for running tube-wells, tractors and other machines.
- Food processing and storage of food in cold storage houses uses up huge amounts of energy.
- Means of transportation require large amounts of energy in the form of fuels or electricity.
- We use much more energy at home today due to the increased number of electrical gadgets, such as refrigerators, air conditioners, washing machines, etc.

Electricity is the major source of energy today. The use of electrical energy has shown a tremendous surge in the past few decades. However, electrical energy is not a natural source of energy and, as we have seen in this chapter, is produced in many ways—both by conventional and by non-conventional sources of energy. Setting up new generation plants is very expensive and time consuming.

In India today, the supply of electrical energy is far lower than our requirements. That is why we suffer power cuts. Several of our villages do not have access to electricity. In several other villages where electricity is available, the supply is insufficient and unreliable. This affects us in several ways. Our food production suffers, as sufficient electricity for proper irrigation is not available. Our industrial production suffers, as factories cannot run full time. Shortage of electricity also limits the use of new technologies for development. All this affects the development of our country.

## PREVENTING ENERGY CRISIS

As our energy needs increase at a tremendous pace, an energy crisis in the near future is a distinct possibility. The steps we need to take to prevent this are as follows:

### Using energy judiciously

Judicious use of energy implies that we do not waste energy and that we use energy-efficient methods.

**Not wasting energy:**

- Switching off lights, fans, etc., when not in use. Using air coolers, air conditioners, room heaters, geysers, etc., only when needed.
- Reducing the flame while cooking and when the water starts boiling to save fuel.

**Using methods where energy spent is less:**

- Using CFLs and tubelights, (or better LEDs which are now available, though still expensive. CFLs have toxic mercury in them which LEDs do not have.) which use less energy, instead of bulbs.
- Using public transport instead of private vehicles as much as possible; walking or cycling along small distances.
- Using pressure cookers for cooking.
- Using efficient smokeless *chulhas* in houses instead of kerosene, coal or wood for cooking.
- Reducing cooking time by soaking pulses for some time before cooking, and keeping vessels covered while cooking.

Judicious use of energy has two main advantages:

- It will delay the energy crisis, and
- It will give our scientists more time to develop more efficient alternate sources of energy.

## CONSERVATION OF FOSSIL FUELS

India produces only about thirty per cent of the petroleum that we need. We import the rest. The exhaustible resources like coal and petroleum will be finished soon if we do not manage them properly. We can also use natural gas as a substitute. The reserves of natural gas discovered by us have gone up ten times within 20 years. Alternative sources of energy such as solar, wind, and biomass should be used in place of fossil fuels.

Biogas is a cheap and convenient fuel for our rural population. It is produced from waste products like human waste, cattle dung, garbage, etc. Effective use of biomass to derive many products of industrial and commercial importance has increased with the progress in biotechnology.

## ORAL QUESTIONS FOR FORMATIVE ASSESSMENT

1. Name three fuels we get by digging into the earth. What is the common name given to them? Why is this name given?
2. All fossil fuels are made up of compounds of carbon and hydrogen. Do you agree? Give reasons.
3. Which is a better fuel—coal or coke? Why?
4. While refining petroleum, which property is used to separate petroleum into its various fractions?
5. Nowadays, a number of vehicles run on CNG. What is the full form of CNG? What is the advantage of using CNG over petrol or diesel?

## NOW YOU KNOW

- Materials found on the earth that allow the existence of life and satisfy the needs of living organisms are called natural resources.
- Renewable resources are those that will either never run out, or those that are replaced within a reasonable period of time through natural processes.
- Non-renewable resources are those which once used up cannot be replaced within a reasonable period of time.
- Conservation is the wise and careful use of resources. It means not wasting the resources, and also maintaining their quality.
- A fuel is a substance that can be used to produce heat at a reasonable cost.
- A fuel produced naturally from the remains of plants and animals buried in soil and rocks is known as a fossil fuel.
- Coal is a fossil fuel formed over millions of years from wood buried under high pressure.
- The process of conversion of wood into coal is called carbonization.
- The process of heating coal in the absence of air is called destructive distillation of coal. It gives useful products such as coke, coal tar, coal gas and ammonium compounds.
- Petroleum is a fossil fuel formed over millions of years from the bodies of dead sea organisms.
- Natural gas is chiefly made up of methane, though butane and propane are also present in small proportions. Compressed natural gas (CNG) is a clean non-polluting fuel.
- We can prevent an energy crisis by using energy judiciously. Solar energy, wind and biomass are some of the alternative sources of energy which can be used in place of fossil fuels.

## NEW WORDS

**FRACTIONS**—components with different boiling point which are obtained during fractional distillation

**REFINING**—process of separating the fractions by fractional distillation

## FOR FORMATIVE AND SUMMATIVE ASSESSMENT

### A. MULTIPLE-CHOICE QUESTIONS: Choose the most appropriate answer.

1. Renewable resources need to be conserved because
   a. we are using them faster than they are replenished by nature.
   b. they are slowly disappearing from the earth.
   c. if we overuse them nature will stop replacing them.
   d. all of these
2. It is an important fraction of petroleum. It is further distilled to get lubricating oil and paraffin wax.
   a. petroleum gas  b. heavy oil  c. anthracite  d. residue
3. Coal mainly contains
   a. carbon.  b. carbon and hydrogen.
   c. carbon, hydrogen and nitrogen.  d. carbon, nitrogen and oxygen.
4. Which of the following is regarded as the best variety of coal?
   a. bituminous  b. lignite  c. anthracite  d. peat
5. Which of the following is a non-polluting fuel for vehicles?
   a. petrol  b. diesel  c. kerosene  d. CNG
6. In destructive distillation, coal is heated strongly to about
   a. 5000 °C.  b. 1000 °C.  c. 100 °C.  d. 10,000 °C.
7. Which of these is not a natural source of energy?
   a. coal  b. petroleum  c. electricity  d. sun
8. Fossil fuels are
   a. renewable but exhaustible.  b. renewable and inexhaustible.
   c. non-renewable but can be recycled.  d. non-renewable and cannot be recycled.
9. Which of these is not a fossil fuel?
   a. CNG  b. LPG  c. petrol  d. hydrogen
10. Which of these is obtained by destructive distillation of coal?
    a. LPG  b. coal gas  c. CNG  d. methane

### B. VERY SHORT-ANSWER QUESTIONS: Give one-word answers.

1. Are natural resources living, non-living or both?
2. Petroleum is a renewable resource, as it is naturally renewed in a million years. True or false?
3. The process of conversion of wood into coal is called ________
4. ________ is the variety of coal with maximum carbon content.

5. Petroleum and natural gas were formed from dead ________
6. In fractional distillation, hydrocarbons with the ________ (highest / lowest) boiling points condense first.
7. Name two fuels obtained from petroleum, which can be used as domestic fuels.
8. Which fuel is used in jet aeroplanes?
9. Name one non-polluting fuel for vehicles.
10. What is the colour of the crude oil pumped out from a well?
11. Which petroleum product is used for surfacing roads?
12. Name the petroleum product used to manufacture candles, vaseline, grease, polish, etc.
13. Which is the ultimate source of the energy of fossil fuels?
14. The fuel obtained from coal that is almost pure form of carbon is ________

## C. SHORT-ANSWER QUESTIONS (TYPE I): Answer in a sentence or two.

1. Differentiate between renewable and non-renewable resources, giving two examples of each.
2. What are fossil fuels?
3. Why should fossil fuels not be wasted?
4. How is coke obtained?
5. What are the advantages of using natural gas as a fuel?
6. Why is there a rapid increase in our energy consumption?
7. Why are fossil fuels our most important source of energy today?
8. What is the main purpose of petroleum refining?

## D. SHORT-ANSWER QUESTIONS (TYPE II): Answer in about 30 words.

1. If a resource is renewable, it can still get exhausted. Discuss with two examples.
2. Why is topsoil considered a non-renewable resource eventhough it is constantly being formed by weathering of rocks?
3. Why do we feel the need for conservation more today than our ancestors did?
4. How was coal formed?
5. What are the important uses of coke?
6. How was petroleum formed?
7. Name four important products of petroleum and give their uses.
8. What are the advantages of using energy judiciously?

## E. LONG-ANSWER QUESTIONS: Answer in about 60 words.

1. How is destructive distillation of coal carried out? What are the products obtained and their main uses?
2. How is refining of petroleum carried out? Name the important products obtained.
3. List five things that you can do to help in preventing an energy crisis.
4. How is CNG obtained? What are its main uses?

## HOTS Questions: Think and answer.

1. If a resource can be replaced within ten years by natural processes, would you classify it as renewable or non-renewable?
2. All renewable resources are inexhaustible. Do you agree? Give reasons.
3. All combustible substances are not fuels. Why?
4. Can fossil fuels be made in the laboratory?
5. Conservation of resources means avoiding their wasteful use. Does this definition cover all aspects of conservation? Explain.
6. In a petroleum well, crude oil is found above water. Which two properties of petroleum make it possible to form a layer of it above water?

## FOR FORMATIVE ASSESSMENT*

### In the Library—Research Project

Biofuel is any fuel that is derived from biomass, that is, from living organisms or their metabolic by-products. Agricultural products and waste from industry, agriculture, forestry and households such as straw, sawdust, manure, sewage, garbage and food leftovers can be used as biofuels. It is a renewable energy source, unlike other natural resources such as petroleum, coal and natural gas. Biofuels can be used for the production of bioenergy. Bioenergy contributes to about 15 % of the world's energy consumption.

Find out about the main biofuels in use today and how they are made.

### My Virtual Library—Research/Activities on the Internet

- ❒ Energy explained simply! Visit rsgr.in/lsc-cce-8 and click on LINK 14 to find out.
- ❒ Visit rsgr.in/lsc-cce-8 and click on LINK 15 for games and activities on climate change.
- ❒ Visit rsgr.in/lsc-cce-8 and ◆ click on LINK 16 to read about petroleum ◆ click on LINK 17 to read about coal ◆ click on LINK 18 to read about renewable resources.

### To Meet—Research on Scientist

**Edwin Laurentine Drake** (1819–1880) The petroleum industry was born when Edwin L Drake drilled a successful oil well at Titusville Pennsylvania in USA in 1859. Initially, the wells that he dug kept getting filled with water. Then he had a bright idea. He bought some pipe sections made out of cast-iron. Each one was ten feet long. He joined the sections together and drove the joined pipe 32 feet into the ground using a battering ram. This way the water could not seep into the oil. He drilled inside the pipe and ultimately struck oil at a depth of 69 feet. The well produced about 10 barrels of oil each day.

Find out more about Edwin Drake and his contribution in the field of petroleum.

### Talk to the Class—Presentation

Study the history of the petroleum industry, and make a PowerPoint presentation on your findings.

*For more tasks see Page 77

# MORE TASKS for FORMATIVE ASSESSMENT (FA 1)

## for Chapters 1–5

In addition to the activities and projects given in the respective chapters, the following tasks can also be used for formative assessment.

### RESEARCH PROJECTS

- The Iron Pillar at Mehrauli, in Delhi, was constructed over 1600 years ago, during the reign of the Gupta rulers. The pillar is 7.2 metres high and weighs around 6.5 tonnes. It is known as the 'rustless wonder' because despite remaining exposed to sun and rain for all these centuries, it has not rusted. Try to find out why. Also, find out about the advances India had made in metallurgy and metal technology as early as 1600 years ago.
- **A group project** Find out about the measures to conserve energy in your home. If possible do the same for 1–2 more households in your locality. Make groups of 5. Prepare a group report listing these measures and discuss in Class.

### INTERNET-LINKED RESEARCH/ACTIVITY

- Visit rsgr.in/lsc-cce-8 and click on LINK 19 to take an energy quiz.
- How energy efficient are you? Visit rsgr.in/lsc-cce-8 and click on LINK 20 to find out.

### DEBATE

Conduct a debate on 'Plastic bags are a boon to society' with one team speaking for manufacturers of plastic bags and the other for concerned citizens opposing the use of plastic bags.

### EXPERIMENTAL PROJECT

**To observe orange mould under a microscope** Carefully pick up a small amount of mould growing on an orange or bread with forceps. Keep it on a glass slide. Put a drop of water over the mould and cover with a coverslip. Observe the mould under a microscope. Draw its diagram.

### FIELD TRIP

**Do you know the similarities/differences between a cold storage and a granary which stores grain?** Make a visit to a cold storage in or near your town or city. Make a list of the vegetables/fruits you see being stored there. Have these vegetables been grown locally in farms near your town or city? Or have they been grown far away, but transported there for storage? Ask the owner or the manager of the cold storage to tell you more about the vegetables/fruits being stored there. You can ask about the conditions required to keep the vegetables fresh, and for how long they can remain fresh in the cold storage.

Next, visit a granary which stores grain. What are the similarities/differences between a cold storage and a granary?

6

# Combustion and Flame

## COMBUSTION

You read in the last chapter that we use fuels for various purposes, at home, in public places and in industry. Energy is provided when fuels burn. But do all materials burn? Do they all burn in the same way? We will learn more about how substances burn in this chapter.

### ACTIVITY 1 (Experimental investigation): Combustion

**(Note: Teacher's supervision required)**

Hold a piece of coal with a pair of tongs in a Bunsen burner flame. Does the coal start glowing after some time? Can you also see a flame?

Now collect some materials such as paper, wood, iron nails, dried leaf, cloth, stone, kerosene, cooking oil, etc. Try to burn each of these materials one by one. Record your results in Table 6.1.

TABLE 6.1

| MATERIAL | BURNS OR NOT |
|---|---|
| Paper | |
| Wood | |
| Iron nails | |
| Dried leaf | |
| Cloth | |
| Stone | |
| Kerosene | |
| Cooking oil | |

**IN THIS CHAPTER**

COMBUSTION ◆ EXTINGUISHING A FIRE ◆ FLAME ◆ FUELS ◆ IMPACT OF BURNING FUELS ON THE ENVIRONMENT

The process of burning of substances in air or oxygen with the evolution of heat and light is known as **combustion**.

A substance that burns in air or oxygen to produce heat and light is called a **combustible substance**, e.g. paper, wood, kerosene, LPG.

A substance that does not burn in air or oxygen is called a **non-combustible substance**, e.g. stone, metal.

You have seen that a combustible substance that can be used to produce heat at a reasonable cost is called a fuel.

### Products of combustion

Fuels are mostly made up of hydrocarbons, i.e. substances made up of carbon and hydrogen only. When a hydrocarbon burns completely, the products formed are carbon dioxide and water. Heat and light energy are released.

Complete combustion takes place when a fuel burns with enough oxygen to support the burning process. For instance, when methane burns in sufficient supply of oxygen, carbon dioxide and water are formed and energy is given out.

| $CH_4$ | + | $2O_2$ | $\rightarrow$ | $CO_2$ | + | $2H_2O$ | + | energy |
|---|---|---|---|---|---|---|---|---|
| methane | | oxygen | | carbon dioxide | | water | | |

On the other hand, when sufficient oxygen is not available, incomplete combustion occurs.

The resulting products in the case of incomplete combustion of methane are carbon monoxide, water and energy.

| $2CH_4$ | + | $3O_2$ | $\rightarrow$ | $2CO$ | + | $4H_2O$ | + | energy |
|---|---|---|---|---|---|---|---|---|
| methane | | oxygen | | carbon monoxide | | water | | |

### Conditions necessary for combustion

For combustion to take place, we need a combustible substance. What else do we need?

**ACTIVITY 2 (Experimental investigation): Conditions needed for combustion (Note: Teacher's supervision required)**

- Burn two candles and fix them on a table. Cover one of them with a glass tumbler. Does it get extinguished after some time? Does the uncovered candle continue burning? Why?
- Strike a match and try to burn a piece of paper with it. Does the paper start burning? Next, strike the match to light the LPG gas stove in the kitchen. Is the flame instantaneous? Now try burning a piece of wood and a piece of coal with a burning matchstick. Do they start burning?

a. Air is needed for combustion.

b. Paper burns at its ignition temperature.

FIG. 6.1

The first observation shows that burning does not take place in the absence of air. Oxygen (a supporter of combustion) is necessary for combustion.

The second observation shows that to start burning, the combustible substance must be heated to above a certain temperature.

The lowest temperature at which a

combustible substance starts burning in the presence of air is called its **ignition temperature**. A substance does not catch fire until its temperature is raised to its ignition temperature. Different substances have different ignition temperatures.

A matchstick, a piece of wood or a can full of kerosene do not catch fire on their own. This is because the temperature of the matchstick, wood and kerosene are lower than their ignition temperatures.

Thus, the conditions necessary for combustion to take place are as follows:

- Presence of a combustible substance
- Presence of supporter of combustion
- Heating the combustible substance to its ignition temperature

Combustion will not occur in the absence of any one of these.

Let us perform the following activity.

### ACTIVITY 3
### (Experimental investigation): Combustion and ignition temperature (Note: Teacher's supervision required)

Make two paper cups by folding sheets of paper. Half-fill one of the cups with water. Fix two burning candles on a table. Heat the two cups above the candle flames. Which cup starts burning? Why does the cup with water in it not start burning? Does the water in it become hot?

FIG. 6.2

Paper cup with water in it does not burn. This is because the paper cup with water loses its heat to the water by conduction. Hence, its temperature does not rise above its ignition temperature, even when held above the candle flame. The temperature of the water rises due to the heat transferred.

### Inflammable substances

Substances that have a very low ignition temperature and hence can catch fire easily are called **inflammable substances**. Examples are petrol, kerosene, alcohol and LPG. Care has to be taken while storing such substances as even a small spark can ignite them and cause a major fire.

### Types of combustion

In Activity 2, a matchstick, a piece of paper or the LPG in the kitchen burn rapidly to produce heat and light. Such combustion is called **rapid combustion**.

The ignition temperature of white phosphorous is 35 °C. What will happen to it if the room temperature, it is kept in, rises to more than 35 °C in summer? It will burst into flames. This type of combustion in which a material bursts into flame without the application of heat is called **spontaneous combustion**.

When you light a firecracker, it explodes, giving out heat, light and sound. This is a

FIG. 6.3 Explosion

combustion reaction that occurs suddenly with the evolution of a large amount of gas. Such a reaction is called an **explosion** (Fig. 6.3).

## EXTINGUISHING A FIRE

A fire can be disastrous if not controlled in time. Every city has a fire station equipped with fire-fighting equipment. You may have seen that water is normally used to extinguish fire. However, water does not extinguish all kinds of fires.

You have seen that the three conditions necessary for a fire are: presence of a combustible substance, presence of a supporter of combustion and heating the combustible substance above its ignition temperature. Therefore, the methods of extinguishing a fire involve the following:

- **Removing the combustible substance:** However, this is not possible in case of say a building on fire, as the entire building is the combustible substance.
- **Cooling the substance to below its ignition temperature:** This is normally done with the help of water. But water works only when wood or paper are on fire. Fire in electrical equipments cannot be controlled with water as water conducts electricity. Hence the person trying to extinguish the fire can get an electric shock. Also, oil or petrol fires cannot be put out by water as oil and petrol are lighter than water. They float on water and keep burning.
- **Cutting off the supply of air:** This can be done with the help of carbon dioxide gas, which is not a supporter of combustion. Besides, it is heavier than air and forms a blanket around the fire. **Fire extinguishers** that give off carbon dioxide are used for this purpose. These are available in smaller sizes for household purposes. This method works well for electrical and petrol fires.

### Fire extinguishers

The simplest fire extinguisher is the **soda-acid type fire extinguisher**. In this, the property of acids to liberate carbon dioxide on reacting with carbonates and bicarbonates of metals is utilized. As the gas carbon dioxide is evolved with brisk effervescence, it extinguishes the fire when released over it (Fig. 6.4).

There are three parts in a fire extinguisher:

- Container
- Bottle
- Knob

The container of a fire extinguisher is cylindrical in shape. It contains sodium bicarbonate solution. The small bottle contains concentrated sulphuric acid. This bottle is attached to the knob.

For the chemical reaction to take place, the knob is struck. The bottle breaks and sulphuric acid reacts with sodium bicarbonate liberating large amount of $CO_2$ gas with great force. It forms a blanket around the fire, cutting off the air supply, due to which the fire gets extinguished.

| $2NaHCO_3$ | + | $H_2SO_4$ | → | $Na_2SO_4$ | + | $2H_2O$ | + | $2CO_2$ |
|---|---|---|---|---|---|---|---|---|
| sodium bicarbonate | | sulphuric acid | | sodium sulphate | | water | | carbon dioxide |

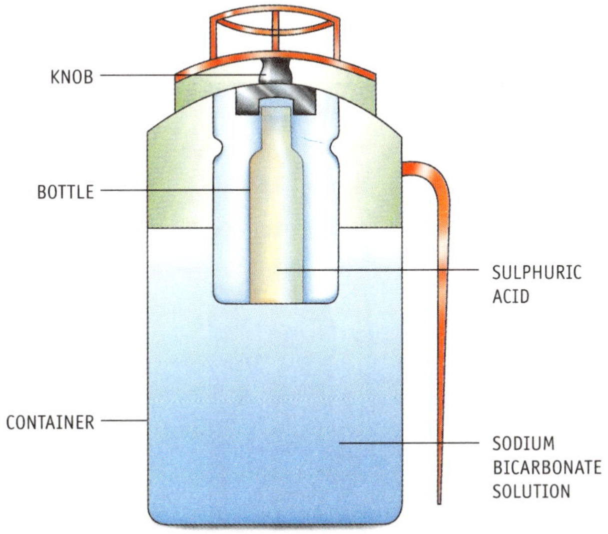


FIG. 6.4 A soda-acid type fire extinguisher

In another type of fire extinguisher, carbon dioxide is stored under great pressure in a cylinder. When released from the cylinder, it expands suddenly and cools down. Thus, besides cutting off the air supply, it also cools down the combustible substance. It is therefore very effective.

## FLAME

Do you know that everything that burns does not produce a flame? Only substances that vaporize burn with a flame. Kerosene rises up the wick of a stove and vaporizes before burning. The vapour burns with a flame. When a candle burns, hot molten wax rises up in the wick and vaporizes. The wax vapour burns with a flame.

Charcoal does not vaporize and burns without a flame, producing a glow.

When there is sufficient supply of oxygen, the substances burn completely producing a non-luminous or blue flame. You would have seen LPG burn with a blue flame. However, in an insufficient supply of oxygen, a flame of yellow colour is obtained. This is because of the glowing of unburnt carbon atoms.

The flame of a Bunsen burner is blue when the air hole is open and adjusted for the right amount of air. However, if the air hole is closed, the supply of air is insufficient and the flame becomes yellow (Fig. 6.5).

a. air hole closed

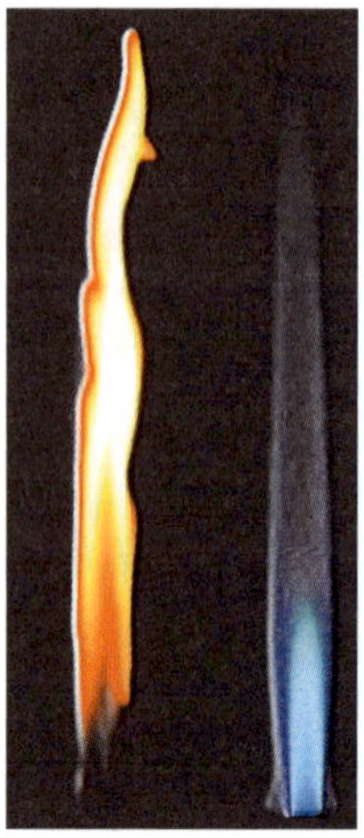

b. air hole open

FIG. 6.5 Bunsen burner flame

**IT'S A FACT!**

Wax is actually made up of compounds of hydrogen and carbon. Solid particles of carbon in the flame become incandescent when the candle burns, giving out light.

### Candle flame

Light a candle and observe its flame. You will find that it is spindle-shaped and has different colours in different regions. The flame has three main zones depending on the amount of air it receives (Fig. 6.6). The zones have different colours.

- **Non-luminous zone** or the zone of complete combustion is the hottest part of the candle flame. Because of adequate supply of oxygen, complete combustion occurs. Therefore, no residue is left on an object placed in this zone. The flame appears blue. It is the outermost zone of the flame.
- **Luminous zone** or the zone of incomplete combustion is moderately hot. The wax vapours do not burn completely as the supply of oxygen is inadequate. It leaves a

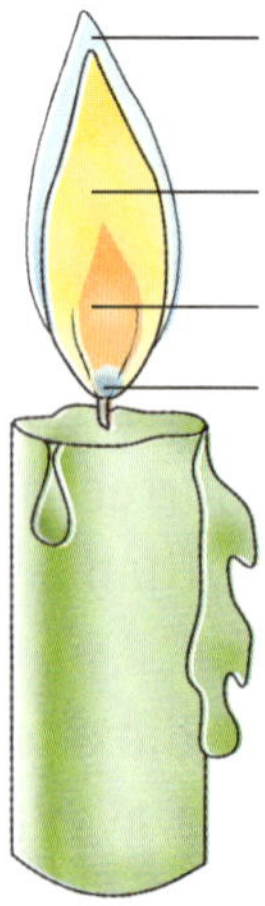


FIG. 6.6 Different zones of a candle flame

black soot and other residues on an object placed here. The carbon particles glow emitting a yellow light. It is the middle zone of the flame.

- **Dark zone** or the zone of no combustion is the least hot. It covers the area surrounding the wick containing unburnt vapours produced by the melting of wax. Here the wax vapours do not come in contact with oxygen, hence do not burn. It is the innermost zone of the flame.

There is also a small region at the base of the wick where carbon monoxide burns with a blue colour (called **blue zone**).

**What happens to the wax when a candle burns?**

A candle has two parts:

- The wax (paraffin wax) that serves as a fuel. It is a hydrocarbon made from crude oil.
- The wick, made of a material that absorbs liquids such as water or molten wax.

When a candle is lighted, the wax in and near the wick melts. The wick absorbs the liquid wax and pulls it upward. The heat of the flame vaporizes the wax—it is this wax vapour that burns.

Why does the wick not burn? This is because when the wax vaporizes, it takes heat from the wick and cools it. This is similar to the reason why the paper cup in Activity 3 does not burn.

The (innermost) dark zone consists of unburnt wax vapours. In Activity 4, it is these vapours which rise up the glass tube, and burst into flame when a lighted matchstick is brought near them.

**ACTIVITY 4 (Experimental investigation): Structure of a candle flame**
**(Note: Teacher's supervision required)**

Light a candle. Do not keep it in an airy place, as the flame should not flicker. Can you see the three zones clearly?

- Take a narrow glass tube. Hold it with a pair of tongs and introduce one of its ends in the dark zone of the flame. Bring a lighted matchstick near the other end of the tube. Do you see a flame at this end? What has produced a flame here?
- Now take a clean glass slide. Hold it with a pair of tongs and introduce it into the luminous zone of the flame. Has a circular black ring formed on the slide? What is the black deposit on the slide?
- Next, take a thin long copper wire. Hold it with a pair of tongs and introduce its tip just inside the outermost region of the flame. Notice that the wire tip becomes red hot and glows. Try the same in other parts of the flame. Does the wire tip take longer to become red hot in other parts? What do you conclude?

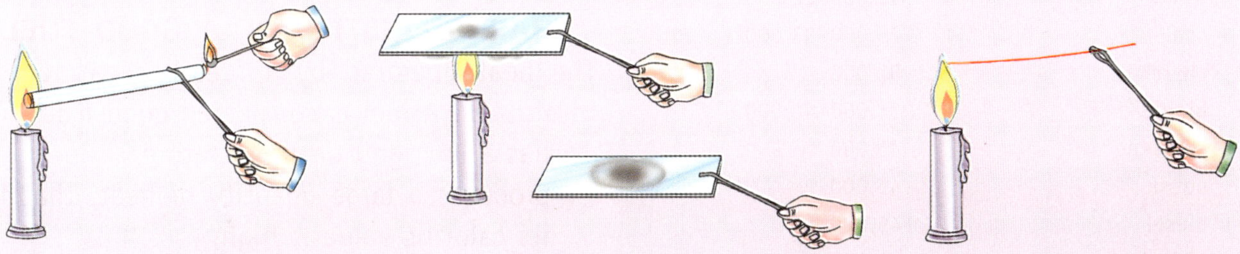

a. In dark zone　　b. In luminous zone　　c. In non-luminous zone

FIG. 6.7 Structure of a candle flame

The circular dark ring is formed on the slide by deposition of unburnt carbon particles present in the (middle) luminous zone of the candle.

The copper wire takes the least time to become red hot when introduced into the (outermost) non-luminous zone of the flame as this zone has the highest temperature.

## ORAL QUESTIONS FOR FORMATIVE ASSESSMENT

1. When a hydrocarbon fuel is burnt, it always gives out carbon dioxide and water vapour. Do you agree?
2. To set fire to a combustible substance, you have to heat it to a certain minimum temperature. What is this minimum temperature called? If this minimum temperature is very low for a certain substance, what is the substance called?
3. To extinguish a fire, you can remove the combustible substance. What other methods can you use?
4. Carbon dioxide is the most commonly used gas for extinguishing a fire. Which properties of carbon dioxide are used here?
5. The innermost part of a candle flame is the hottest. Do you agree? Give reasons.

## CALORIFIC VALUE OF A FUEL (FUEL EFFICIENCY)

All combustible substances liberate heat when they are burnt. The amount of heat liberated when unit mass of a combustible substance burns is different for different substances. This determines whether or not the substance is a good fuel. We refer to it as the calorific value of the fuel.

**Calorific value** of a fuel can be defined as the amount of heat liberated when one kilogram of the fuel is completely burnt in sufficient supply of oxygen.

TABLE 6.2 Calorific value of some common fuels

| FUEL | CALORIFIC VALUE (kJ/kg) |
|---|---|
| cowdung cake | 7000 |
| wood | 17,000–22,000 |
| coal | 25,000–33,000 |
| charcoal | 32,000 |
| biogas | 35,000–40,000 |
| kerosene | 45,000 |
| petrol | 45,000 |
| diesel | 45,000 |
| LPG | 50,000 |
| methane | 55,000 |
| hydrogen gas | 1,50,000 |

Higher the calorific value, better is the fuel. The calorific values of some common fuels are given in Table 6.2.

The SI unit of calorific value is joule per kilogram (J/kg), though commonly the unit kilojoule per kilogram (kJ/kg) is used.

Scientists are working on using hydrogen as a fuel, as it has the highest calorific value and creates no pollution after burning. Some success has been achieved and hydrogen is expected to be the fuel of the future.

LPG has a fairly high calorific value. Since it does not produce smoke when it burns, it is preferred for domestic use. Petrol and diesel are used in the transport sector. However, they release harmful gases in the atmosphere on combustion.

## CHARACTERISTICS OF A GOOD FUEL

The heat liberated by a fuel is measured in **kilojoules**. A fuel is considered good if it:

- has a low ignition temperature,
- produces a large quantity of heat, that is, its calorific value is high,
- has a moderate rate of combustion,
- is safe to store, handle and transport,
- does not cause pollution,

- leaves behind little or no residue after being burnt,
- is cheap and easily available.

Natural gas best meets all these conditions.

## TYPES OF FUELS

Fuels can be classified on the basis of their physical state—solid, liquid and gas. On this basis, fuels can be of the following types:

**Solid fuels:** Some solid fuels are wood, coal, cattle-dung cakes, bagasse (sugarcane from which juice has been extracted), etc.

**Liquid fuels:** Some liquid fuels are kerosene, liquefied petroleum gas (LPG), fuel oil, petrol, diesel, etc.

**Gaseous fuels:** Some gaseous fuels are natural gas, coal gas, water gas, producer gas, biogas, acetylene, etc.

### IT'S A FACT!

Food is fuel for the body. During cellular respiration the glucose obtained from food is 'burnt' to form carbon dioxide and water, and energy is given out. The reaction involved is similar to that in combustion. However, the two processes differ from each other in some ways. What are these differences? You have already read about them in the chapter on Respiration in Class VII.

## IMPACT OF BURNING FUELS ON THE ENVIRONMENT

The increasing energy consumption has a harmful impact on the environment. The main impact, due to the burning of fuels, is as follows:

- Burning of carbon-containing fuels releases ash and fine particles of unburnt carbon in the air. These fine particles, called **SPM (Suspended Particulate Matter)** are dangerous pollutants.
- Combustion of fuels adds **carbon dioxide** to the environment. A percentage increase in carbon dioxide in the air leads to the **greenhouse effect**, which can cause **global warming**. This can result in melting of the Polar ice caps and rise in sea levels, leading to flooding of large portions of land on the sea coasts.
- **Carbon monoxide** produced when fuels containing carbon burn in insufficient supply of air, is a very dangerous pollutant and can cause death if breathed in.
- Coal contains sulphur, which produces **sulphur dioxide** on burning. Besides being a poisonous gas, it dissolves in rain to form sulphuric acid. This gives rise to **acid rain**, which is very harmful for soil, crops, buildings, etc.
- The **oxides of nitrogen** given off from exhausts of engines of vehicles are poisonous gases. Many vehicles now use catalytic converters to convert these to harmless gases.
- **Lead compounds** are released in exhausts of vehicles. They are poisonous. Increasing use of unleaded petrol is expected to reduce lead pollution.

The other effects on the environment are as follows:

- **Oil spills** from oil tankers transporting petroleum have resulted in widespread pollution in the sea leading to the death of a large number of aquatic animals.
- **Dams** constructed over rivers to produce hydroelectricity cause large areas of land to get filled up with water. This displaces several people from their homes, and leads to the destruction of habitats of a large number of flora and fauna. Besides this, dams increase the chances of earthquakes.
- Extremely dangerous **radiation pollution** can be caused by nuclear power plants. An accident in such a plant can lead to radiation pollution over a vast area.

## ORAL QUESTIONS FOR FORMATIVE ASSESSMENT

1. Which fuel gives off the maximum heat when 1 kg of it is burnt? What is this amount of heat called?
2. A cheap non-polluting fuel with a very high calorific value was developed by a scientist. It had an ignition temperature of 20 °C. Is it a good fuel? Give reasons.
3. Which gas released during combustion is thought to cause global warming?
4. Which dangerous pollutant is given off if a fuel while burning does not get sufficient air?

## NOW YOU KNOW

- Combustion is the process in which a substance burns in air or oxygen to produce heat and light.
- When a hydrocarbon fuel is burnt in a sufficient supply of air, carbon dioxide and water are produced. If the supply of air is insufficient, carbon monoxide is produced instead of carbon dioxide.
- The lowest temperature at which a combustible substance starts burning in the presence of air is called its ignition temperature.
- Conditions necessary for combustion are: presence of a combustible substance, presence of a supporter of combustion and heating of the combustible substance to its ignition temperature.
- If the ignition temperature of a substance is less than the room temperature, it will undergo spontaneous combustion.
- Water extinguishes a fire by cooling down the combustible substance to below its ignition temperature; carbon dioxide extinguishes a fire by cutting off the air supply.
- In a soda-acid type fire extinguisher, the property of acids to liberate carbon dioxide on reacting with carbonates and bicarbonates of metals is utilized.
- A candle flame has three main zones—non-luminous, luminous, and dark zone.
- Calorific value of a fuel is the amount of heat produced when one kilogram of the fuel is burnt completely in a sufficient supply of air. It is expressed in J/kg or kJ/kg.
- A good fuel has low ignition temperature and high calorific value, besides satisfying other conditions.
- Burning of fuels releases various pollutants in the air.

## NEW WORDS

**COMBUSTION**—the process of burning of a substance in air or oxygen with the evolution of heat and light

**IGNITION TEMPERATURE**—the lowest temperature at which a combustible substance starts burning in the presence of air

**INFLAMMABLE SUBSTANCE**—a substance that has a very low ignition temperature and hence can catch fire easily

**SPONTANEOUS COMBUSTION**—type of combustion in which a material bursts into flame without the application of any heat

**CALORIFIC VALUE**—amount of heat liberated when one kilogram of a fuel is completely burnt in sufficient supply of oxygen

## FOR FORMATIVE AND SUMMATIVE ASSESSMENT

### A. MULTIPLE-CHOICE QUESTIONS: Choose the most appropriate answer.

1. Good fuels have
   a. low ignition temperature and high calorific value.
   b. low ignition temperature and low calorific value.
   c. high ignition temperature and high calorific value.
   d. high ignition temperature and low calorific value.
2. Calorific value of a fuel is the heat energy produced when
   a. any amount of the fuel is completely burnt.
   b. one kilogram of the fuel is completely burnt.
   c. one milligram of the fuel is completely burnt.
   d. hundred grams of the fuel are completely burnt.
3. Which poisonous gas is formed as a result of incomplete combustion?
   a. coal gas  b. carbon monoxide  c. carbon dioxide  d. nitrogen oxide
4. Acid rain can be caused by the burning of
   a. petrol.  b. CNG.  c. diesel.  d. coal.
5. To extinguish a flame, which of these methods can be used?
   a. reduce temperature to below ignition temperature
   b. remove combustible substance
   c. cut of air supply
   d. any one of these
6. The hottest zone of a candle flame is
   a. non-luminous zone.  b. luminous zone.
   c. dark zone.  d. blue zone at the base of the wick.
7. Which of these is a solid pollutant?
   a. SPM  b. carbon monoxide  c. nitrogen oxides  d. sulphur dioxide
8. Which of these fuels has the highest calorific value?
   a. CNG  b. coal  c. hydrogen  d. petrol

### B. VERY SHORT-ANSWER QUESTIONS: Give one-word answers.

1. What is the process of burning of substances with the evolution of heat and light called?
2. Most fuels are made up of __________ and __________

3. Which gas is produced when a fuel burns in a. sufficient supply of air b. insufficient supply of air.
4. All combustible substances must be heated to the same temperature to make them burn. True or false?
5. Any substance that can burn is an inflammable substance. True or false?
6. Spontaneous combustion starts at room temperature. True or false?
7. During an explosion, a large amount of __________ is given out.
8. Water is useful in putting out all fires. True or false?
9. In a soda-acid type fire extinguisher, __________ reacts with sulphuric acid to give out carbon dioxide.
10. The __________ zone in a candle flame is the zone of no combustion.
11. The amount of heat liberated when one kilogram of a fuel is completely burnt in sufficient supply of oxygen is called __________ __________ of the fuel.
12. Name one unit in which the heat liberated by a fuel is measured.
13. The lower the ignition temperature the better the fuel. True or false?
14. What are the fine particles released on burning carbon-containing fuels called?

## C. SHORT-ANSWER QUESTIONS (TYPE I): Answer in a sentence or two.

1. What is combustion?
2. Distinguish between combustible and non-combustible substances, giving three examples of each.
3. Why is it more difficult to burn some combustible substances than others?
4. State the conditions under which combustion occurs.
5. Why is more care needed to store kerosene than coal, though both are fuels?
6. What problem will arise if a fuel has an ignition temperature lower than the average room temperature? Name the type of combustion that will occur in such a case.
7. What is an explosion?
8. Why is water not suitable for extinguishing a fire in an electrical appliance?

## D. SHORT-ANSWER QUESTIONS (TYPE II): Answer in about 30 words.

1. Name and give chemical equations to show the products of the combustion reaction in
   a. a limited supply of air. b. sufficient supply of air.
2. List the different methods by which a fire can be extinguished.
3. What kind of fires can effectively be put out by water? What kind of fires is it not suitable for? Give reasons for both cases.
4. How does carbon dioxide extinguish a fire?
5. What is calorific value of a fuel? Why is hydrogen not used as a fuel though it has the highest calorific value?
6. How are fuels classified on the basis of their physical state? Give two examples of each.
7. How is burning of fossil fuels thought to be related to global warming?

## E. LONG-ANSWER QUESTIONS: Answer in about 60 words.

1. Explain, with the help of a labelled diagram, how a soda-acid type fire extinguisher works.
2. Name the different zones of a candle flame. Give details of the conditions in each zone.
3. What are the characteristics of a good fuel?
4. Discuss the impact of burning fuels on air.

## HOTS QUESTIONS: Think and answer.

1. Only gases burn with a flame. But when you burn wood, it initially burns with a flame. Later, it only glows without a flame. What do you think is the reason for this?
2. Would you consider coal as a good fuel? Give reasons.
3. When a fuel is burnt, carbon dioxide (or carbon monoxide) and water vapour are given out. Can you name one fuel which burns without giving off water vapour? Why does it not give out water?
4. Why does a matchstick burn on rubbing it on the side of the matchbox?
5. Your LPG gas stove at home is giving a yellow flame. What can this mean?
6. A flame always points upwards. Why do you think this is so?
   (**HINT**: Gases produced in a flame are hot, and hence lighter.)
7. When a candle burns, is it possible to get the wax back
   a. after the wax melts? b. after the wax burns?
   (**HINT**: Are these physical changes or chemical changes?)
8. Why do we wrap a blanket around a person whose clothes have caught fire?
9. Why do forest fires occur during hot summers?
10. Why is it easier to burn dry leaves but not green leaves?

## FOR FORMATIVE ASSESSMENT*

### In the Library—Research Project

Vehicles today use the internal combustion engine, in which combustion of fuel occurs inside the engine. Find out about:

- history of the internal combustion engine—who invented it and how it developed over the years
- how an internal combustion engine works

### Talk to the Class—Presentation

Make a presentation on the history of the internal combustion engine.

### My Virtual Library—Research/Activities on the Internet

- Visit rsgr.in/lsc-cce-8 and click on **LINK 21** for an interesting conversation on combustion.
- Visit rsgr.in/lsc-cce-8 and click on **LINK 22** for a discussion on fire.
- Visit rsgr.in/lsc-cce-8 and click on **LINK 23** for a discussion on fire extinguishers.
- Visit rsgr.in/lsc-cce-8 and click on **LINK 24** to learn how a candle works.
- Visit rsgr.in/lsc-cce-8 and click on **LINK 25** to see animated flames.

*For more tasks see Page 132

## To Meet—Research on Scientist

**Michael Faraday** (1791–1867) was an English chemist and physicist who contributed to the fields of electromagnetism and electrochemistry. Some historians refer to him as the best experimentalist in the history of science. He discovered a number of new organic compounds, including benzene, and was the first to liquefy a 'permanent gas' (one that was believed to be incapable of liquefaction).

**The Chemical History of a Candle** was the title of a series of lectures on the chemistry and physics of candle flame, given by Michael Faraday at the Royal Institution, UK. This was the origin of the Christmas lectures for young people that are still given every year and bear his name.

Visit rsgr.in/lsc-cce-8 and click on **LINK 26** to read the famous Faraday's Lectures on the history of the candle.

## In the Laboratory—Experimental Project

**To prove that burning of a candle is similar to respiration**

- To show that carbon dioxide is produced when candle wax is burnt
- To show that water vapour is produced on burning candle wax

**You will need** ◆ a glass beaker with a lid ◆ a small candle ◆ lime water solution ◆ a metal spoon

**Procedure:**

- Fix a small candle inside the glass beaker. Light the candle. Put the lid on the beaker to stop air supply to the burning candle. The candle will get extinguished. Gently remove the lid and the candle, and quickly pour a small amount of lime water solution into the beaker. Cover the beaker with the lid, and shake the beaker well. The lime water will turn milky. This shows that carbon dioxide was produced when the candle burned.

- Dip a metal spoon in ice-cold water. Dry it well. Hold it above the candle flame. Drops of water will be seen on the spoon. It is steam that has condensed on the cold metal spoon. (When the spoon becomes hot, condensation will not take place.) This is similar to when you breathe onto a cold window glass pane.

  Repeat this experiment with burning charcoal. Is burning of charcoal similar to respiration?

## LIFE SKILL

**Prevent fires at home—a few life-saving rules**

- Do not wear synthetic clothes or loose clothing in the kitchen. Do not leave frying pans unattended. Keep the stove area clear of clutter.
- Never leave candles unattended or let them burn near flammable materials such as curtains. Put them in a non-flammable container to protect the surface below them.
- Never store hazardous chemicals such as paint, kerosene or petrol inside the house.
- Inspect electrical appliances for frayed wiring. Replace all defective appliance cords.
- Matches should be blown out, never shaken, and never thrown into a basket of papers.
- Small fire extinguishers are not expensive. All households should have at least one in the kitchen. It should be periodically inspected.

SKILLS INVOLVED: Thinking skill, Social skill, Self-preservation

7

# Conservation of Plants and Animals

Living things do not live in isolation. All organisms, both plants and animals, need food and other materials from their surrounding in order to survive. Air, water and soil form an essential part of our surrounding. The life of an organism is, thus, affected by the living and non-living things around it. An **ecosystem** is made up of all the plants, animals and microorganisms in an area, along with all the non-living components, such as climate, soil, rivers, deltas, etc.

## BIODIVERSITY

You know that all living organisms are made up of elements and molecules. They possess cells as their structural units. Though all living organisms have some fundamental similarities, yet nature is full of fascinating diverse forms of living organisms. A wide range of different types of organisms which grow, multiply and thrive naturally, are found at any given time in a particular habitat. In a tropical rainforest habitat, there live tens of thousands of different species of plants, animals and microorganisms. Even in a desolate habitat like a desert where we may see very few plants and animals, there will be thousands of different types of microorganisms. This wide range of different types of organisms in an area constitute the biodiversity (or biological diversity) of the area.

**IN THIS CHAPTER**

BIODIVERSITY ◆ FLORA AND FAUNA ◆ CONSERVATION OF FORESTS AND WILDLIFE ◆ BIOSPHERE RESERVES ◆ RED DATA BOOK

Biodiversity can be defined as the variety of plants, animals and microorganisms generally found in an area.

India has a rich biodiversity as we have a variety of habitats ranging from tropical rainforests to alpine vegetation and from temperate forests to coastal wetlands.

The plants and animals found in a particular region are known as flora and fauna respectively, of that region. They together form the biodiversity of the area. India is very rich in flora and fauna.

The flora and fauna of a country are very important renewable natural resources. The management of forests and wildlife resources is therefore an important task.

**ACTIVITY 1 (Research)**

Try to identify the flora and fauna in your region. Take the help of teachers to make a list.

## FOREST WEALTH

About one-fifth of the area of our country is under forest cover. This is estimated to be 67.71 million hectares, which is 20.6 % of the total area of India. You have already read in Class VII that forests are useful to us because of the following reasons.

- They yield valuable products, such as timber (for construction and furniture), wood (for fuel), wood pulp (for making paper), latex (for the manufacture of rubber), turpentine, resin, gum, lac, and medicinal plants.
- They protect wildlife, since wildlife depends on forests for food and shelter.
- They help in maintaining the balance between carbon dioxide and oxygen in the atmosphere, as plants take in carbon dioxide and give out oxygen during photosynthesis.
- They regulate the temperature of the earth; you may have noticed that forest areas near a city are cooler than the city.
- They maintain the water cycle in nature, by releasing water during transpiration, which cools the atmosphere.
- They maintain the water table by slowing down the flow of rainwater, which results in increased absorption of water by the soil. This also helps in checking floods.
- They prevent soil erosion, as the roots of trees bind the soil and prevent soil erosion by wind and water.

## DEFORESTATION

**ACTIVITY 2 (Information gathering and deducing)**

Ask your elders how big your city was when they were children. Compare it with the situation now. What do you find? Hasn't the city grown considerably? Why has it grown?

A major portion of the land needed for growth of cities comes from cutting down forests. Cutting down forests and using the land for other purposes is known as deforestation. Deforestation is done for the following reasons.

- To build homes, factories, roads and dams
- For farming, as more food is needed to feed the growing population
- For mining of minerals such as coal, petroleum and ores
- To get wood, which is used in construction, for making furniture and as fuel

Overgrazing by cattle, sheep, horses, etc. is another cause of deforestation. Overgrazing not only destroys grasslands but also trees in forests. The young trees get eaten or killed by trampling. The lower leaves are eaten up and the roots and trunks are injured.

Sometimes, deforestation also occurs due to natural causes such as drought, forest fires,

FIG. 7.1 Deforestation

tsunamis, diseases, and attack by insects and pests.

### Consequences of deforestation

Deforestation has an adverse effect on the environment. It has the following consequences.

- It causes an increase in soil erosion. As the top soil gets eroded, the lower hard and rocky soil with less humus gets exposed. This soil is less fertile. Over time, continued soil erosion can convert the land into a desert. This is called **desertification**.
- It causes an increase in carbon dioxide in the atmosphere. A possible consequence of this is **global warming** as carbon dioxide traps the heat rays reflected by the surface of the earth. The consequent increase in the atmospheric temperature can affect the water cycle and may result in lower rainfall. This can cause droughts.
- It causes reduction in groundwater due to decreased water absorption capacity of the soil. The reduction in absorption of water into the soil can result in floods.
- It causes shortage of products we get from forests.

## WILDLIFE

In recent years, the population of many wildlife species has been decreasing, mainly due to changes in the environment brought about by humans. We have cleared forests, converted grasslands into farmlands, flooded large areas by constructing dams, drained swamps and polluted the air and water. This has destroyed the habitats of wildlife and has disturbed the delicate balance of nature.

### Endangered and extinct animals

Animals that cannot adjust to the environmental changes begin to die, and some species become **endangered** as their population becomes very small. If such species are not protected, they may become **extinct**, i.e. disappear from the earth. Dodo and dinosaur are two animal species that have become extinct in the past years.

The mountain quail of western Himalayas, pink-hued duck and Sikkim stag are some animals that have become extinct in the recent past. The bison, beaver, pronghorn antelope, tiger, Asiatic lion and leopard are some of the endangered species.

Smaller animals are also facing the danger of becoming extinct. An example is the ruthless killing of snakes by humans. If we were to kill all snakes in a region, the rat population would increase as there would be no more snakes to eat the rats. The rats would eat more grain, which may result in a food shortage. Thus, killing snakes disturbs the food chains and food webs of which they form a part. This ultimately harms us.

FIG. 7.2 Dodo: An extinct species

## ORAL QUESTIONS FOR FORMATIVE ASSESSMENT

1. What are you referring to when you talk about the flora and fauna of a place?
2. Give one word for 'variety of all forms of life found in a region'.
3. You would have read that trees take water from the soil and lose it by transpiration. This implies that in a forest, trees will reduce groundwater by losing it in transpiration. Do you agree? Give reasons.
4. If you cut down all trees in a place, what effect could this have on the land?
5. Which species of animals cannot be found on the earth—extinct or endangered?

## CONSERVATION OF FORESTS AND WILDLIFE

You studied about methods to conserve forests in Class VII. In brief, some of these methods of conservation are as follows.

- **Planned harvesting**, i.e. cutting only some of the trees in an area. The uncut trees prevent erosion and produce seeds so that new trees can grow.
- **Afforestation** (or **Reforestation**), which means renewing a forest by planting seedlings or small trees of the same species as found in the forest. At least as many trees as we cut should be planted. Afforestation takes place naturally also—if we let the area remain undisturbed, the trees grow back and the forest gets re-established.
- **Protection from forest fires** by spraying fire extinguishing solutions from aircrafts or by changing the direction of the wind by using strong blowers.
- **Protection from insects and pests** by using insecticides and fungicides and removing infected trees.
- **Protection from overgrazing** to protect growing plants, by providing pastures which can be used by rotation.

FIG. 7.3 Afforestation

Wildlife conservation is closely related to forest conservation. When a forest is destroyed, a large number of animals become extinct or endangered. So, to conserve the habitat of endangered animals, it is necessary to protect the forests.

The following steps need to be taken to conserve wildlife.

**Habitat preservation:** Preserving the habitat of wildlife helps in their conservation. Preventing deforestation is an important method of habitat preservation. Afforestation provides shelter and food for the wildlife.

**Hunting regulations:** Government regulations related to hunting and their effective implementation is very important for wildlife conservation. The hunting of endangered species is completely banned. Illegal hunting of animals is called poaching.

In India, though the hunting of tigers is banned, they are being regularly killed as their skin and bones fetch large amounts of money. Effective implementation of such laws is, therefore, of extreme importance.

Fig. 7.4 Wildlife reserves in India

## Biosphere Reserves, Wildlife Sanctuaries and National Parks

To effectively implement the methods of conserving forests and wildlife, the Government has set aside permanent protected areas for conservation of biodiversity in that area. These are known as **biosphere reserves.**

A biosphere reserve is a large protected area set aside for conservation of wildlife, plant, animal and microorganism resources, and the traditional life of the tribals living in that area.

**National parks** and **wildlife sanctuaries** are protected forests to preserve wildlife. They provide protection and suitable living conditions for wild animals. The animals can breed and multiply in these areas.

A biosphere reserve may have national parks and wildlife sanctuaries within it. For example, the Pachmarhi Biosphere Reserve in Madhya Pradesh contains one national park (Satpura National Park) and two wildlife sanctuaries (Bori, Pachmarhi) within it.

**ACTIVITY 3 (Research)**

Find out all you can about the flora and fauna of the Pachmarhi Biosphere Reserve.

In India, there are a large number of wildlife sanctuaries and national parks managed by the Government (Fig. 7.4). Cutting down trees, and hunting (poaching) or capturing of animals in these reserves is strictly prohibited. The Indian Government launched **Project Tiger** in 1973 to protect the tiger, which had become an endangered species. It started with 9 tiger reserves. By 2010, this number has risen to 'about 40'. The project aims to maintain a suitable tiger population in the natural environment.

The Forest (Conservation) Act in India aims at reservation and conservation of natural forests. However, in spite of such laws, poachers do kill animals for their body parts, such as ivory or tiger skin, which fetch high prices. People living in the neighbourhood also encroach upon the forests and destroy them.

World Wide Fund for Nature (WWF) and International Union for Conservation of Nature and Natural Resources (IUCN) are international organizations that work towards wildlife conservation.

### Forests and paper

Paper is made from wood pulp. Roughly, seventeen full grown trees are required to make one ton of paper. Saving paper therefore means saving trees. It also means saving energy and water needed to manufacture paper, as well as reduction in pollution, by reducing use of harmful chemicals required in making paper.

## ENDEMIC SPECIES

Plants and animals are distributed non-uniformly on the globe. Some, like humans, dogs and cats, are widespread and inhabit most regions. However, others have very restricted distributions and may be found only in a limited region such as a particular forest, on a single island, or in a single river or lake. These highly restricted organisms are known as **endemic species** because they are unique to a specific region.

Endemic species are those species of plants and animals that are found exclusively in a particular area and are not naturally found anywhere else. They may be endemic to a restricted region, a state or a country. For example:

- The Indian giant squirrel and flying squirrel are endemic to the Pachmarhi Biosphere Reserve area.

FIG. 7.5 The royal Bengal tiger

FIG. 7.6 The Asiatic lion

- The Asiatic lion is now believed to reside only in the Gir National Park in Gujarat.

**ACTIVITY 4 (Research)**

Find out if there are any endemic plants and animals in your region or state. Take the help of your teachers.

## RED DATA BOOK

The IUCN (International Union for Conservation of Nature and Natural Resources) assesses the conservation status of species around the world. This is done to highlight those threatened with extinction, with the aim of promoting their conservation. The IUCN maintains a **Red List**, which is a compilation of endangered wildlife species. It also maintains a **Red Data Book**, which provides data on population status of the species included in the Red List. Both the Red List and the Red Data Book show the risk of extinction of various species.

The Red Data Book species are classified into different categories depending on the risk of extinction, for example, 'extinct', 'critically endangered', 'endangered', and 'vulnerable'.

The Red List and the Red Data Book are revised periodically. According to the 2004 IUCN Red List of Threatened Species, a total of 15,589 species face extinction. One in four mammals, one in eight birds, one in three amphibians, and almost half of all freshwater turtles are threatened.

**IT'S A FACT!**

The **Arctic Tern** is called the champion of migration. It makes the longest migration by any living creature. This seabird breeds in the northern hemisphere, as far north as the Arctic, and spends winter in the southern hemisphere, as far south as the Antarctic. This means a round trip of up to 35,000 km each year. By moving continually between the Arctic summer and the Antarctic summer, it sees more daylight than any other animal on the earth.

## ORAL QUESTIONS FOR FORMATIVE ASSESSMENT

1. Harvesting of a crop means cutting down all the plants of the crop in the field. Similarly, planned harvesting of trees means cutting down all trees in a forest. Do you agree? Give reasons.
2. An animal species that is widely distributed over the earth is said to be endemic. Do you agree? Give reasons.
3. Saving paper means saving trees. Why?
4. What is the purpose of producing the Red List and the Red Data Book?

## NOW YOU KNOW

- Ecosystem consists of all the plants, animals and microorganisms in an area, along with all the non-living components, such as climate, soil, rivers, deltas.
- Biodiversity is the variety of plants, animals and microorganisms generally found in an area.
- Species of plants found in a particular region are known as flora, whereas those of animals are known as fauna.
- Forests are useful to us in many ways.
- Deforestation is the cutting down of forests and using the land for other purposes.

- Deforestation can result in desertification, global warming, droughts, reduction in groundwater, shortage of forest products.
- Endangered animals are those that begin to die as they cannot adjust to environmental changes, resulting in their population becoming very small.
- Forests can be conserved by planned harvesting of trees, afforestation, protection from fire, insects and pests and protection from overgrazing.
- Wildlife can be conserved by habitat preservation, building wildlife sanctuaries and by implementing hunting regulations.
- A biosphere reserve is a large protected area set aside for conservation of wildlife, plant and animal resources, and the traditional life of the tribals living in that area.
- National parks and wildlife sanctuaries are protected forests to preserve wildlife. They provide protection and suitable living conditions for wild animals.
- Endemic species are those species of plants and animals that are found exclusively in a particular area and are not naturally found anywhere else.
- The Red List and the Red Data Book show species at the risk of extinction.

## NEW WORDS

**FLORA**—species of all plants found in a particular area
**FAUNA**—species of all animals found in a particular area

## FOR FORMATIVE AND SUMMATIVE ASSESSMENT

### A. MULTIPLE-CHOICE QUESTIONS: Choose the most appropriate answer.

1. The plants found in a particular region are known as the
   a. fauna. b. flora.
   c. endangered species. d. endemic species of that region.
2. Which one of the following is not a conservation category of wildlife?
   a. extinct b. endangered c. endemic d. vulnerable
3. Which of these is not caused by deforestation?
   a. desertification b. global warming
   c. reduction in groundwater d. storms
4. Dodo is a/an
   a. critically endangered species. b. extinct species.
   c. endangered species. d. vulnerable species.
5. Different species are classified into different threat categories in the
   a. Blue Data Book. b. Yellow Data Book.
   c. Black Data Book. d. Red Data Book.
6. WWF works in the field of
   a. wildlife conservation. b. child labour.
   c. forest conservation. d. water conservation.

7. Which of these is extinct?
   a. Asiatic lion   b. leopard   c. dodo   d. tiger
8. Which of these is endangered?
   a. dodo   b. Asiatic lion   c. dinosaur   d. Sikkim stag

**B. VERY SHORT-ANSWER QUESTIONS: Give one-word answers.**

1. What do you mean by biodiversity of an area?
2. What does 'fauna' refer to—plants or animals?
3. Forests are helpful in checking floods. Do you agree?
4. Endangered animals no longer exist on the earth. True or false?
5. If all trees in a forest are cut, it will lead to __________ of soil.
6. __________ by cattle should be controlled for forest conservation.
7. Soil erosion can finally lead to desertification. True or false?
8. The flora and fauna of a country are among the most important __________ (renewable / non-renewable) natural resources.
9. Are the dinosaurs endangered or extinct?
10. Wildlife conservation and __________ conservation are closely related.
11. A tiger reserve can be called a biosphere reserve. True or false?
12. Saving paper means saving __________
13. Species which are confined to a restricted area on the earth are known as __________ species.
14. The Red List is a list of __________ animals.

**C. SHORT-ANSWER QUESTIONS (TYPE I): Answer in a sentence or two.**

1. What is biodiversity?
2. What do you mean by flora and fauna?
3. What is deforestation?
4. Why do some animals become endangered?
5. What is a biosphere reserve?
6. What are endemic species?
7. Why did IUCN prepare the Red Data Book?
8. Into what categories are the species listed in the Red List and Red Data Book classified?

**D. SHORT-ANSWER QUESTIONS (TYPE II): Answer in about 30 words.**

1. List four ways in which forests are useful to us.
2. List three main causes of deforestation.
3. 'Deforestation can lead to desertification'. How?
4. What effect can deforestation have on groundwater? Give reasons.
5. What do you mean by planned harvesting of forests? How does it help in their conservation?

6. In what ways are wildlife conservation and forest conservation related?
7. What is the difference between a wildlife sanctuary and a biosphere reserve?

## E. LONG-ANSWER QUESTIONS: Answer in about 60 words.

1. Discuss five methods of forest conservation.
2. What are the consequences of deforestation?
3. Discuss the steps necessary for wildlife conservation.

## HOTS QUESTIONS: Think and answer.

1. To conserve forests we should ban cutting down of trees completely. Do you agree? Give reasons.
2. Animals are protected in a zoo (zoological gardens) also. What is the difference between a zoo and a wildlife sanctuary? Where do you think animals will be happier?
3. When you plant saplings in a forest for afforestation, it takes several years for them to grow into big trees. A construction company thought of doing planned harvesting in a forest. They cut 10 trees every month and planted 10 new saplings every month as replacement. Do you think they will be successful in maintaining the number of trees in the forest? What change in strategy can you suggest?
4. Tribals depend on forests for food and livelihood. Is it fair to prevent them from entering the forests? How can their symbiotic relationship be maintained?

## FOR FORMATIVE ASSESSMENT*

### In the Library—Research Projects

- **Ornithology** is the branch of zoology concerned with the scientific study of birds. It involves observation of the structure and classification of birds, their habits, singing and migratory flights. Find out the name of the most famous ornithologist of India. Find out which books he has written.
- **A group project** From among the biosphere reserves, national parks and wildlife sanctuaries in India, select five. Divide the class into five groups. Let each group study one of these. Collect information such as the year of establishment, location, area, types of animals conserved, successes and failures in their objectives.

### Talk to the Class—Presentation

Let each group make a presentation (preferably a PowerPoint one) on its findings.

### My Virtual Library—Research/Activities on the Internet

- Visit rsgr.in/lsc-cce-8 and click on LINK 27 to find what Project Tiger is all about.
- Visit rsgr.in/lsc-cce-8 and click on LINK 28 to investigate the IUCN Red List.
- Visit rsgr.in/lsc-cce-8 and click on LINK 29 to explore the environment including biodiversity, play games and lots more.
- Visit rsgr.in/lsc-cce-8 and click on LINK 30 to find out about biodiversity hotspots—select the hotspot, for example, 'Himalayas' and learn about it.
- Visit rsgr.in/lsc-cce-8 and click on LINK 31 to learn about Project Elephant—when did it commence and which states does it cover.

*For more tasks see Page 132

### To Meet—Research on Scientist

**Valerie Jane Morris Goodall** (b. 1934) is an English primatologist, who works for protection of wildlife, especially the primates of Africa, and their habitats. Although she was interested in animals since her youth, it was her association with anthropologist Louis Leakey that prompted her to study about chimpanzees in 1960. She is best known for her 40-year-long study of chimpanzees in the **Gombe Stream National Park** in Tanzania. In 1977, she founded the Jane Goodall Institute to support the conservation efforts at the Gombe Park.

Find out more about Goodall and the work she has done.

### Beyond the Classroom—Field Trip

Visit a biosphere reserve, national park or a wildlife sanctuary in your district or state. Find out:

- which animals are protected
- steps taken to protect them
- their past and present population

TEACHER'S NOTES

An often asked question is why we should spend money on protecting the tiger when so many humans are dying of hunger. One who asks this question has not understood the real meaning of conservation, especially tiger conservation. Children should be clear why protecting the tiger is important.

Explain to them the importance of the tiger being at the top of all food chains and webs. To conserve tigers, we have to make sure that all animals the tiger eats should be preserved—deer, antelope and other herbivores. To make these herbivores live, we have to make sure that all the trees, grasses and other plants that they eat are protected. In this way, saving the tiger means saving the entire forest with all the flora and fauna in it. The tiger is therefore the symbol for the protection of all species on our earth and an indicator of our ecosystem's health.

8

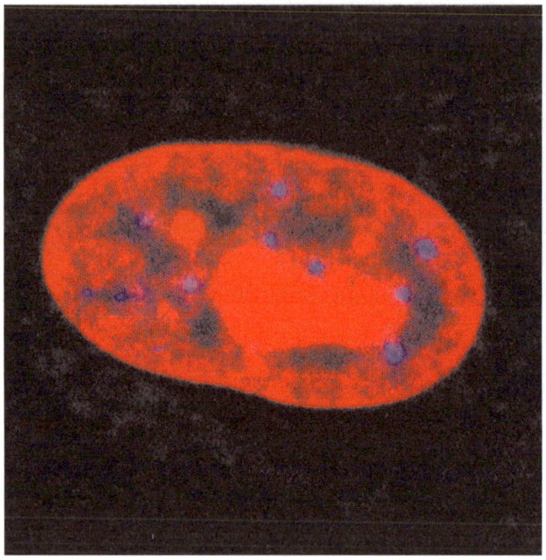

# Cell—Structure and Functions

## DISCOVERY OF THE CELL

You already know that all living things are made up of one or more cells. For this reason, cells are known as the building blocks of life. Cells were discovered by **Robert Hooke** in 1665. He looked at a thin slice of cork under the microscope that he had discovered, and saw that it was made up of many small box-like structures. The boxes were separated from each other by a partition. He called these boxes, **cells**. What Hooke actually observed were dead cells in the cork.

However, even 150 years after Robert Hooke's discovery, not much was known about the cell, until improved microscopes with high magnifications were made. Today, scientists use high magnification microscopes to study cells. They use stains (dyes) to colour parts of the cell to study their detailed structure.

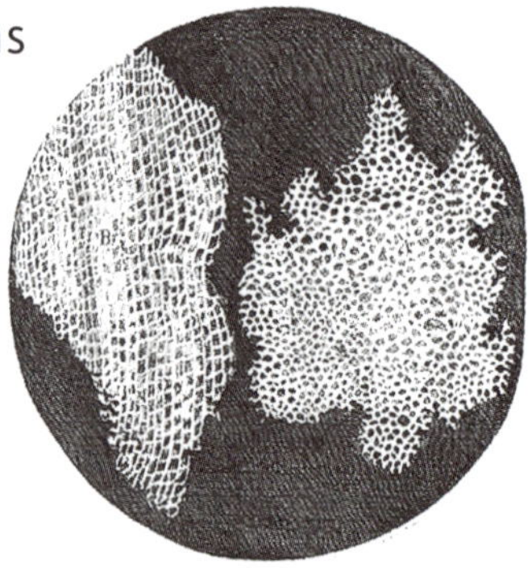

FIG. 8.1 Cells in cork as seen by Robert Hooke

## THE CELL THEORY

In 1838, two German biologists **Mathias Schleiden** and **Theodor Schwann** put forward

**IN THIS CHAPTER**

THE CELL THEORY ◆ UNICELLULAR AND MULTICELLULAR ORGANISMS ◆ PLANT AND ANIMAL CELLS ◆ GROWTH AND DIVISION

the cell theory of life. The main points of this theory are as follows:

- All living things are made up of cells, much as a wall is made up of bricks. Hence, cells are the **basic structural units** of living organisms. They are complex living structures.
- All cells are similar in their basic structure and function but are not identical. They differ in size and structure.
- New cells are formed due to division in old cells.
- The organization of cells in the body of a living organism determines its structure.
- The way an organism functions depends on the way the cells work.

## UNICELLULAR AND MULTICELLULAR ORGANISMS

You are aware that organisms, such as *Amoeba*, *Paramecium*, *Euglena* and bacteria are made up of one cell each. These are examples of **unicellular organisms**. Although made up of a single cell, they perform all the activities necessary for life. They grow, move, digest food, give out wastes and reproduce. All these activities are carried out by a single cell.

Plants and animals that you can see around you with the naked eye are made up of many cells. They are **multicellular organisms**. It is estimated that a fully grown human has about 100 trillion cells. (A trillion is 1000 billion; a billion is 1000 million; so 1 trillion = $10^{12}$.) All multicellular organisms begin life as a single cell, which is the fertilized egg. The fertilized egg cell multiplies and the number of cells increase as the organism develops.

You know that in a multicellular organism, the lower levels of organization are as follows:

Cells → Tissues → Organs
Organism ← Organ systems ←

In the organization of the living world, cells represent the lowest level called cellular level. Life activities in a multicellular organism are performed by groups of specialized cells forming different tissues, which in turn form organs.

## SHAPES AND SIZES

In multicellular organisms, cells have special jobs to do. So, they have different shapes and sizes (Fig. 8.2). Nerve cells, for example, have fibres that may be more than one metre long. Messages pass from one nerve cell to another along these fibres.

Muscle cells expand and contract. Their long, thin shape helps them do this. The outer layer of skin forms a protective cover over your body. Their flat shape helps them to cover a large area. White blood cells (WBC) present in the blood can change their shape. This helps them to destroy germs.

Plant cells located on the outer part of the stem give strength to a plant. These cells have thick cell walls for support. Some cells in plants are used to store food. These cells are larger than other cells.

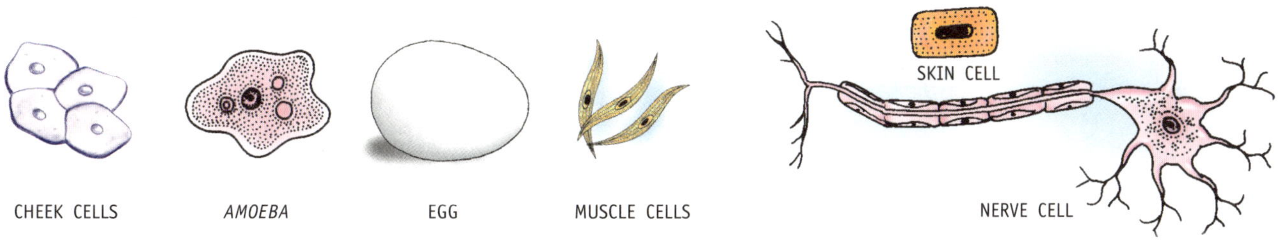


**FIG. 8.2** Cells have different shapes and sizes.

The egg of a bird is only a single cell. An ostrich egg measuring 170 mm × 130 mm is the largest single cell. The smallest cell which measures 0.0001 mm × 0.0005 mm is found in bacteria. The smallest cells in the human body are the red blood cells. They are about 0.007 mm in diameter. A typical cell is about 0.02 mm in diameter. It can only be seen through a powerful microscope. In plants like jute and hemp, the fibre cells are few centimetres long.

An *Amoeba* is a unicellular organism with no definite shape. Its pseudopodia, which help it to move and feed, keep appearing and disappearing.

**ACTIVITY 1 (Experimental investigation): To observe an egg cell**

Boil the egg of a hen. Peel the shell and observe the albumin (white part) and the yolk (yellow part). These are parts of a single egg cell.

**IT'S A FACT!**

A bigger organism has a larger number of cells than a smaller one—but the size of cells has no relation to the size of the organism.

## ORAL QUESTIONS FOR FORMATIVE ASSESSMENT

1. In a unicellular organism, one cell performs all life activities. Do you agree?
2. In a multicellular organism, all cells have the capability to perform all life functions. Do you agree? Give reasons.
3. The cell is the basic structural unit of living organisms. What does this statement mean?

## STRUCTURE

Though cells vary so much in their size and shape, they have a number of things in common. The basic components of a cell are cytoplasm, cell membrane, nucleus and organelles. Figure 8.3 shows the general structure of a cell.

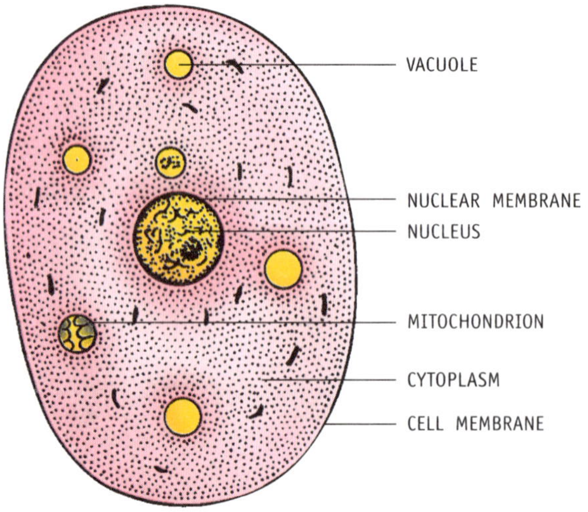


FIG. 8.3 A typical cell

### Cytoplasm

The cytoplasm is a jelly-like substance that makes up most of the inside of a cell. All life functions take place in the cytoplasm (*kytos* means hollow and *plasma* means liquid).

### Cell membrane and cell wall

Surrounding the cytoplasm is a thin covering called the **cell membrane** or **plasma membrane**. The cell membrane separates the cell from its surroundings. It protects the cell and gives it a shape. However, it allows water, minerals and some other necessary substances to pass through it. In addition, plant cells have a **cell wall** which is absent in animal cells. The cell wall supports and protects the plant cell since plants do not have skeletons for support. Present in the cytoplasm are small structures called **organelles**.

### Nucleus

Floating within the cytoplasm in the centre is

a small spherical body called the **nucleus** (plural: nuclei). The liquid in the nucleus is called **nucleoplasm**. It is separated from the cytoplasm by a thin **nuclear membrane**. The nuclear membrane is porous and allows the movement of materials between the cytoplasm and the nucleus.

Present inside the nucleus is a smaller spherical body called the **nucleolus**. Also present in the nucleus are thread-like structures called **chromosomes**. These carry **genes** which contain all the information needed by the cell to function and to reproduce further cells of the next generation. Thus, genes are responsible for inheritance, i.e. transfer of characteristics from the parent to the offspring.

The nucleus is the control centre of the cell. It directs the growth of the cell and controls all the activities that go on within the cell. It can, therefore, be compared to the brain in animals.

The nucleus and the cytoplasm together make up the **protoplasm** (*proto* means first and *plasma* means liquid), which is called the living substance of the cell. The main constituent elements of protoplasm are carbon, hydrogen, oxygen and nitrogen but it contains other elements also.

## Organelles

Scattered in the cytoplasm are small structures called **organelles**. There are various types of organelles that perform different functions. Some of these are as follows:

- **Mitochondria** are small rod-like structures. They oxidize food to provide energy. They are, therefore, often called the powerhouses of the cell.
- **Vacuoles** are sac-like structures. They store food, water and wastes. Plant cells have large vacuoles as compared to animal cells.
- Plant cells have organelles called **plastids** present in the cytoplasm. They are of different colours and types. Green coloured plastids are called **chloroplasts**. They contain the green coloured pigment **chlorophyll** which provides green colour to the leaves. You know that chlorophyll is essential for photosynthesis. Animal cells do not have chloroplasts.

In addition, there are **golgi bodies** that secrete substances, such as enzymes, **endoplasmic reticulum** that help transport substances within the cell, **ribosomes** that make proteins, **lysosomes** that help destroy old cell structures, and **centrosomes** that regulate cell division.

**ACTIVITY 2 (Experimental investigation): To observe the basic components of a cell**

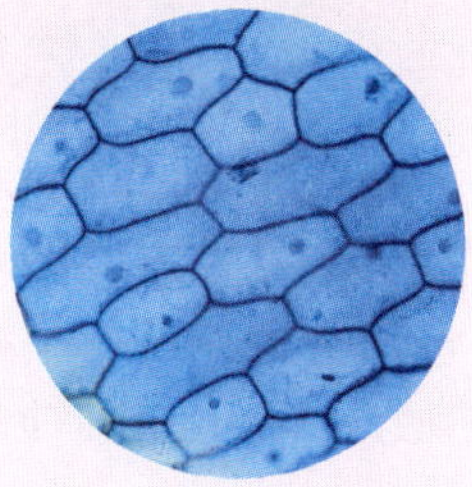

FIG. 8.4 Onion cells

Slice an onion and take out one of the thick leaves from inside. Use forceps to pull away the thin lining from the inner surface of the leaf. Use a blade to cut a small piece from it. Place it flat in a drop of water on a glass slide. Add a drop of methylene blue solution and place a coverslip on it, ensuring that no air bubbles are trapped under the coverslip. Observe the slide under a microscope. Draw what you see and label the parts.

In many unicellular organisms, cells have projections on their outer surface which help in the movement of the cells or the organisms. They are called **cilia** as in *Paramecium* or **flagella** as in *Euglena*.

Generally, cells are similar in basic structure, but attain different shapes in different organs. Figure 8.5 gives us an idea how the cells of different organs appear different. A group of similar cells that combine together to perform a special function are called **tissue**. For example,

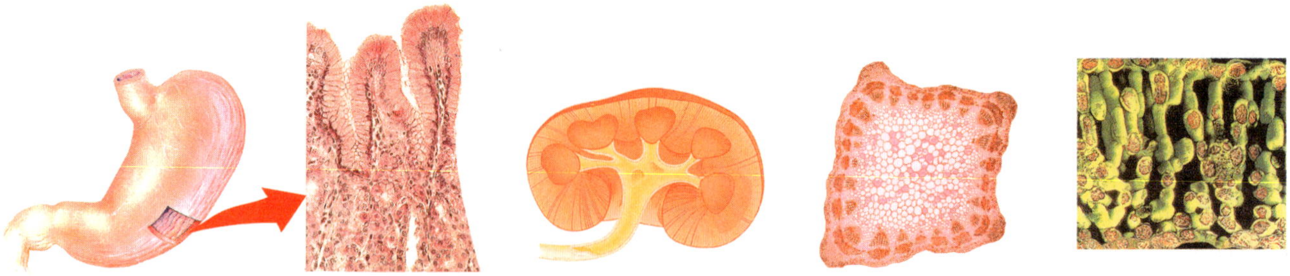

FIG. 8.5 Cross section of stomach, kidney, stem and leaf

a plant leaf is made up of different tissues like dermal tissue, vascular tissue and ground tissue. Different types of tissues combine together to form an **organ**. Group of organs join to form the **organ system** to carry on life activities. For example, the digestive system in an animal digests and absorbs food.

**IT'S A FACT!**

Chromosomes in the nucleus occur in matching pairs. There are 23 pairs of chromosomes in every normal human cell. In each pair, one chromosome comes from the father and one from the mother. Each chromosome in the nucleus has thousands of tiny genes along its length—like the beads of a necklace. The gene is the unit of inheritance in the living organism—it controls the transfer of hereditary characteristics from parents to offspring. Each gene carries information about a specific trait of an organism, for example, colour of eyes or the type of hair (curly or straight). What characteristics you end up with depends on the combination of genes that you get from your parents.

**IT'S A FACT!**

Cells which have a well organized nucleus with a nuclear membrane are called **eukaryotic cells**. Organisms with such cells are called **eukaryotes** (*eu* = true; *karyon* = nucleus). However, the nucleus of a bacterial cell or that of blue-green algae is not well organized and does not have a nuclear membrane. Cells with such nuclei are called **prokaryotic cells**. Bacteria and blue-green algae are called **prokaryotes** (*pro* = primitive; *karyon* = nucleus).

## PLANT AND ANIMAL CELLS

Let us now observe how animal cells are different from plant cells.

**ACTIVITY 3 (Experimental investigation): To study a plant cell**

Put a single leaf of moss in a drop of water on a slide. Place a coverslip on it and examine it under a microscope. Draw the plant cell and label it.

**ACTIVITY 4 (Experimental investigation): To study an animal cell**

Gently scrape the inside of your cheek with a toothpick. Put the scraping on a glass slide. Add a drop of methylene blue. This makes it easier to see the cells under the microscope. Place a coverslip on it and examine the slide under a microscope. Draw the diagram of a cheek cell as seen under the microscope and label it.

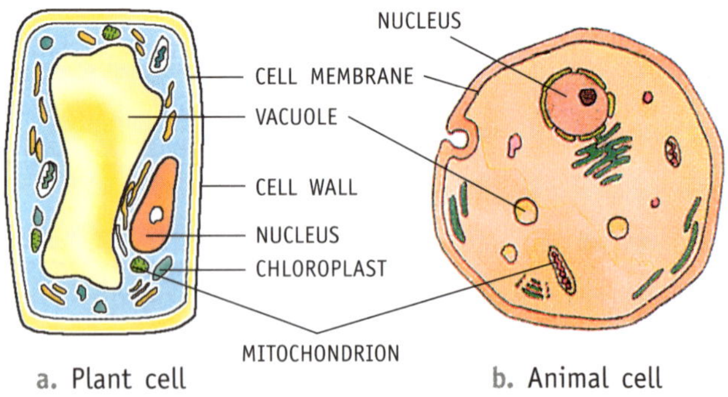


FIG. 8.6 A plant cell has a rigid cell wall while an animal cell has only a cell membrane.

In general, plant cells are larger than animal cells. The major differences between a plant cell and an animal cell are given in Table 8.1.

TABLE 8.1 Differences between a plant cell and an animal cell

| PLANT CELL | ANIMAL CELL |
|---|---|
| It is surrounded by a cell wall, in addition to the cell membrane (Fig. 8.6a). | It only has an outer cell membrane. There is no cell wall (Fig. 8.6b). |
| It usually has one or two large vacuoles. | Vacuoles are either absent, or they are very small. |
| It has chlorophyll present in organelles called chloroplasts. | Chloroplasts are absent. |

### IT'S A FACT!

Cells can be seen through a powerful optical microscope, which magnifies objects a few hundred times. An **electron microscope**, however, magnifies objects over 50,000 times. The image produced by the electron microscope is projected onto a fluorescent screen or recorded on film. The first commercial electron microscopes were built in the 1930s. With its help, scientists could see structures inside a cell that could not be seen with an optical microscope.

## GROWTH AND DIVISION

When a cell is formed, it is small. After digesting food, it grows in size. However, its growth is limited. After reaching a certain critical size, it divides to form two cells. The process by which new cells are formed is known as **cell division** (Fig. 8.7). The new cells formed in this way are known as **daughter cells**. New cells are needed for the growth of an organism and to replace cells that die.

Some cells in our body keep on dividing throughout our life. In a human body, millions of blood cells die and are replaced each second. The skin cells also keep dividing. However, nerve cells of the brain cannot be replaced once they die. This is why the body can heal injuries in all parts of the body except to the nervous system.

### IT'S A FACT!

The cell wall in plants contains **cellulose**. This cellulose acts as roughage in our diet and therefore is very important for us.

We cannot get roughage from animal foods, as animal cells do not contain a cell wall.

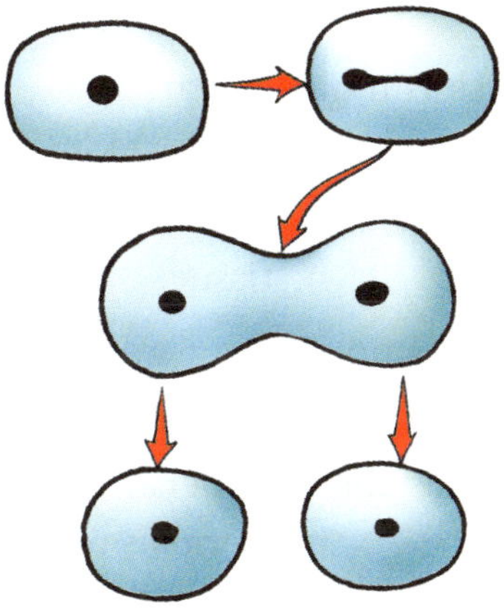


FIG. 8.7 Cell division

## ORAL QUESTIONS FOR FORMATIVE ASSESSMENT

1. What part of the cell can be called the 'brain' of the cell? Why?
2. A cell requires water, minerals and other substances to stay alive. But the cell is covered with a cell membrane. How do these things reach inside the cell?
3. The cells in a tissue have identical shapes and perform identical functions. Do you agree? Give reasons.
4. How does growth in an organism occur—by growth in the size of cells or by growth in the number of cells?
5. Organelles that contain a green pigment are only found in plants and not in animals. What are the organelles and the green pigment called?

## NOW YOU KNOW

- All living organisms are made up of one or more cells. In unicellular organisms, a single cell performs all life functions. In multicellular organisms, the cells are specialized to perform certain functions.
- Cells consist of the jelly-like cytoplasm surrounded by the cell membrane. Within the cytoplasm is the nucleus. It is the control centre of the cell and is surrounded by the nuclear membrane.
- Organelles, such as mitochondria and vacuoles, are also present in the cytoplasm.
- A plant cell has a cell wall and organelles called chloroplasts which contain chlorophyll. Animal cells do not have a cell wall or chloroplasts. Also, the vacuoles in a plant cell are large.
- New cells for growth and repair are formed by cell division.

## NEW WORDS

**CHLOROPLAST**—cell organelle that contains chlorophyll and is present in plant cells

**MITOCHONDRIA**—small rod-like organelle present in the cell which helps to get energy from food

**VACUOLE**—sac-like organelle present in cells which store food, water or wastes

## FOR FORMATIVE AND SUMMATIVE ASSESSMENT

### A. MULTIPLE-CHOICE QUESTIONS: Choose the most appropriate answer.

1. Which of these is multicellular?
   a. *Paramecium* b. *Amoeba* c. bacteria d. mushroom
2. The egg of a hen is a
   a. cell. b. tissue. c. organ. d. organ system.
3. Which of these is not present in an animal cell?
   a. mitochondria b. nucleus c. cell membrane d. chloroplasts
4. Which of these is the control centre of the cell?
   a. nucleus b. cytoplasm c. mitochondria d. protoplasm
5. Which organelles are responsible for energy production in a cell?
   a. vacuoles b. chloroplasts c. mitochondria d. golgi bodies
6. Which of these is not stated by the cell theory?
   a. Cells are the basic structural units of living organisms.
   b. All cells are identical.
   c. New cells are formed due to division in old cells.
   d. The way an organism functions depends on the way the cells work.
7. In which of these does a single cell NOT perform all life functions?
   a. *Amoeba* b. mosquito c. bacteria d. *Euglena*
8. Which of these unicellular organisms has no definite shape?
   a. *Amoeba* b. *Paramecium* c. *Euglena* d. bacteria

## B. VERY SHORT-ANSWER QUESTIONS: Give one-word answers.

1. All living organisms are made up of one or more ________
2. Which is the largest known single cell?
3. What is the jelly-like substance present in cells called?
4. The cell membrane which surrounds the cell does not allow anything to pass through it. True or false?
5. The cytoplasm and the nucleus together make up the ________
6. Name the cell organelles that help to get energy from food.
7. Which of these has a cell wall—plant cell or animal cell?
8. Name the process by which new cells are formed.
9. Which structure in the nucleus is a storehouse for information needed by the cell to function?
10. Plant cells have large vacuoles as compared to animal cells. True or false?

## C. SHORT-ANSWER QUESTIONS (TYPE I): Answer in a sentence or two.

1. What are the 'building blocks of life'? Why are they so called?
2. Differentiate between unicellular and multicellular organisms.
3. What is cytoplasm?
4. What do you mean by protoplasm?
5. What is a tissue?
6. What are organelles?

## D. SHORT-ANSWER QUESTIONS (TYPE II): Answer in about 30 words.

1. What are the lower levels of organization in a multicellular organism? Are these levels also present in unicellular organisms?
2. Draw a labelled diagram to show the general structure of a cell.
3. What are the differences between plant and animal cells?
4. What is meant by the term cell division? Why is cell division necessary?

## E. LONG-ANSWER QUESTIONS: Answer in about 60 words.

1. What are the main points of the cell theory of life?
2. What are the functions of the following in a cell?
   a. cell membrane b. cytoplasm c. nucleus d. chromosomes
   e. mitochondria f. vacuoles
3. With the help of examples, show the variation in shapes and sizes of cells.

## HOTS Questions: Think and answer.

1. In general, cell sizes are not related to the size of an organism. However, will there be a difference in the length of the nerve cells in a rat and a giraffe?

2. White Blood Cells can squeeze through walls of blood vessels and get into intercellular spaces to fight against germs. Which property of WBCs allows them to do this?
3. Why do plant cells need a cell wall, and animal cells do not?
4. Why do you think parents and doctors get very worried if a child gets a head or spinal injury?
5. Living things are made up of cells while non-living things are made up of atoms and molecules. Do you agree? Give reasons.

## FOR FORMATIVE ASSESSMENT*

### In the Library—Research Project

You have seen that cells increase in number by dividing. The development of these new cells is controlled so that the new cells are identical to the old ones. Sometimes, however, some defective cells in the body keep on dividing in an uncontrolled manner and start interfering with normal body functions. This is a dangerous disease of the cells and can occur in any part of the body—even in the brain. It sometimes causes a large number of such diseased cells to collect in some part of the body as a mass of tissue.

Find out the name of the disease. What is the mass of tissue made out of the diseased cells called? What methods are available for treating this disease?

### My Virtual Library—Research/Activities on the Internet

- Visit rsgr.in/lsc-cce-8 and click on LINK 32 to learn a lot more about cells—click on the topic you want to read about.
- Visit rsgr.in/lsc-cce-8 and click on LINK 33 for a detailed discussion on cells and click on LINK 34 for information and interactive diagrams of cells.
- Visit rsgr.in/lsc-cce-8 and click on LINK 35 for interesting animations.

### In the Laboratory—Experimental Project / Designing a Model

- **Diffusion of water in cells** The diffusion of water into and out of a cell occurs by a process called **osmosis**. The cytoplasm in a cell largely consists of water with other materials dissolved in it. If the cell is put in pure water, there are more water molecules per unit volume outside the cell than inside. In such a case, osmosis causes water to enter the cell, and the cell swells. However, if the cell is put in a concentrated solution of salt in water, the number of water molecules per unit volume are more inside the cell than outside. Which way will osmosis cause the water to flow now?

  You can test this out by using a large cell, such as the yolk of an egg. The yolk consists of one cell only.

  **You will need** ◆ two egg yolks ◆ two bowls ◆ salt

  **Procedure:**

  - Put the yolks in two separate bowls. To the first bowl, add tap water. To the second bowl, add a saturated salt solution. Observe both yolks after some time. Which yolk has swollen up and which has shrunk? Why?
  - Try the experiment with salt solutions containing different amounts of salt dissolved in the same volume of water. Is there a relation between the amount of salt dissolved and the swelling up or shrinking of the egg yolk?

*For more tasks see Page 132

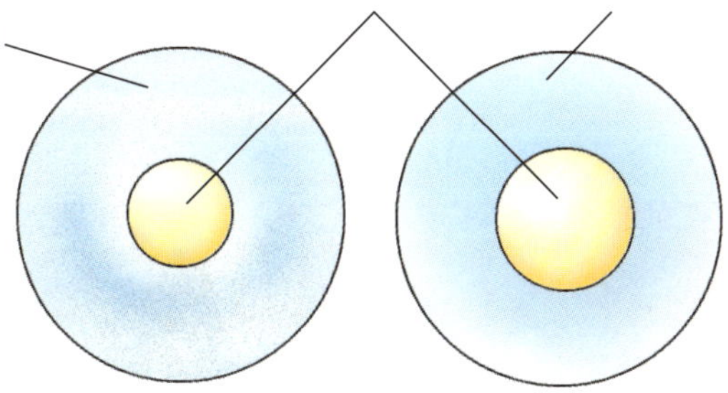


- Put your hands in salt water for some time. Does your skin shrivel up? Can you now explain why this happens?

❐ **Designing a model of a plant or animal cell**

- Take a 'zip lock' bag which will represent the cell membrane.
- Put oil or clear detergent liquid in the bag to represent the cytoplasm.
- You can use either thermocol or other materials to represent different cell parts. For example, you can use:
  - a nut for nucleus
  - cooked noodles for endoplasmic reticulum
  - pasta of different colours for mitochondria

Think of other materials you can use—be innovative! Put the cell parts in the bag.

TEACHER'S NOTES

- The important part of this chapter is for children to comprehend life at the microscopic level, and understand the large variety of microscopic living things and cells that exist. This can only be done by making them look at various unicellular organisms and different plant and animal cells under a microscope.
- Try to make fresh slides (for example, of a drop of dirty pond water) where children can actually see unicellular organisms alive and moving.
- If possible, take children to an institution with an electron microscope so that they can see the structures inside a cell.

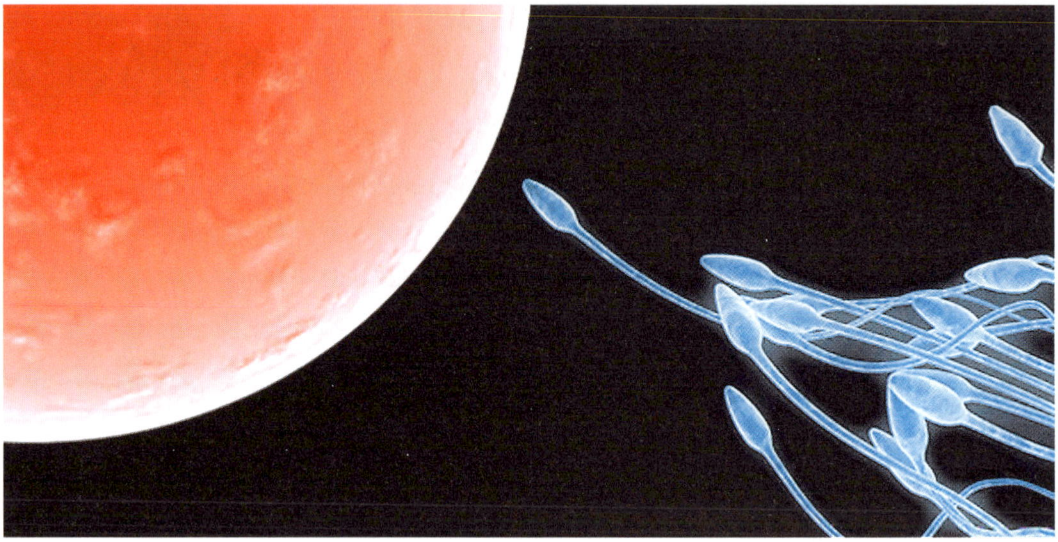

# 9 Reproduction

All living things ultimately die. Many of them produce young ones of their own kind. This is known as **reproduction**. It is because of reproduction that life continues from generation to generation.

All other systems of living organisms are essential for life. If one of them were to stop working, the organism would die. But the reproductive system is not needed for the organism to stay alive. However, without it, the organism cannot produce offsprings and, therefore, cannot continue its species.

There are several methods of reproduction in animals. Some of these are:

- Some animals reproduce by giving birth to babies, e.g. humans and cows.
- Some animals lay eggs from which their young ones are hatched, e.g. birds and snakes.
- In *Hydra*, the offspring grows out of the parent's body.
- An *Amoeba* simply splits into two.

Like plants, there are two modes of reproduction in animals—sexual and asexual.

## SEXUAL REPRODUCTION

Most animals and plants reproduce by the method of sexual reproduction. For sexual

**IN THIS CHAPTER**

SEXUAL REPRODUCTION ◆ INTERNAL AND EXTERNAL FERTILIZATION ◆ REPRODUCTION IN HUMANS ◆ METAMORPHOSIS ◆ ASEXUAL REPRODUCTION

reproduction to occur, two parents, one male and the other female, are required. Males and females have different reproductive organs. Each parent produces one reproductive cell or **gamete**. The male parent produces the **sperm** and the female parent produces the egg or **ovum**. When the sperm and ovum fuse together, they form a third cell known as the **zygote**. This process of fusion of the sperm and ovum is called **fertilization**. The zygote is the first cell of the new organism. It changes over a period of time to form the new organism.

In animals, such as frogs, fishes, birds, reptiles and humans, an individual carries only one kind of gamete—either sperm (in the male) or the ovum (in the female). However, in some organisms, both male and female gametes are present in the same individual. Such organisms are called **hermaphrodites**. Earthworms and leeches are hermaphrodites. This means that each earthworm or leech is both male and female.

You already know that in flowering plants, the flower is the reproductive organ. Flowers of most plants are hermaphrodites. They have the pistil which produces the egg cell and the stamen which produces the male gamete, in the same flower.

### Fertilization

There are various methods by which fertilization takes place in the living world.

**External fertilization:** Sea animals, such as starfish and jellyfish, gather in large groups in water. They lay their eggs and sperms together on the surface of the water. The sperms fuse with the eggs on the water to form zygotes. The zygotes develop into new individuals in the water. This type of fertilization is known as external fertilization as it occurs outside the animal's body. Animals living in or near ponds and lakes also have external fertilization.

During spring and the rainy season, frogs and toads move to ponds and slow-moving streams. The male and female clasp each other in water. The female lays hundreds of eggs. The eggs are delicate and do not have a shell. A layer of a jelly-like substance holds them together and provides protection to them. The male ejects sperms directly on the cluster of floating eggs. The sperms swim in water with the help of their long tail, and fertilize the eggs.

In fishes too, the fertilization is external.

**ACTIVITY 1 (Field investigation)**

Visit a pond during the rainy season. Try to locate clusters of frog's eggs floating in water. Study them. Note their colour, size and structure.

FIG. 9.1 Frog's eggs floating in water

**Internal fertilization:** In birds, reptiles and mammals, including humans, fertilization occurs inside the female's body. This is known as **internal fertilization**. In earthworms also, fertilization is internal. An earthworm, though a hermaphrodite, does not fertilize itself. Two earthworms come in contact with each other and exchange sperms. The eggs are fertilized internally with the sperms received from the partners.

## REPRODUCTION IN HUMANS

Human reproduction involves two sexes—male and female. Each sex has a different reproductive system. Fertilization is internal, and the development of the zygote into a fully

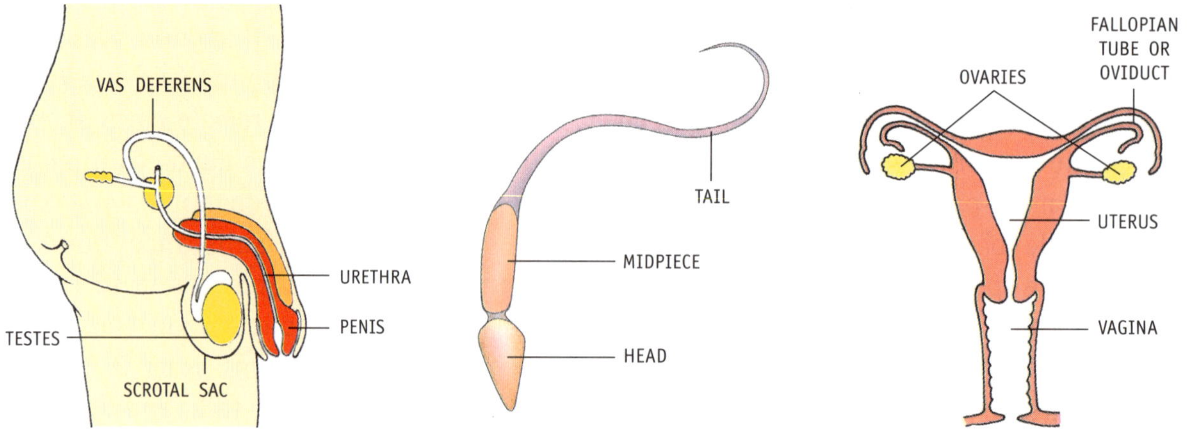


a. The male reproductive system b. Human sperm c. The female reproductive system

FIG. 9.2 Reproductive system in humans

formed individual also occurs inside the body of the female.

### Puberty

The onset of sexual maturity occurs in boys at the age of 11–16 years, and in girls at the age of 10–15 years. This is known as **puberty**. In boys, puberty is marked by the voice becoming deeper, growth of hair on the face and body, development of muscles and production of sperms by the testes. In girls, breasts become bigger and hips get more rounded. These changes are caused by hormones that are different in girls and boys.

### The male reproductive system

In males, the reproductive organs are a pair of **testes** (singular 'testis') (Fig. 9.2a). They are located outside the abdominal cavity in a sac called the **scrotal sac**. The testes produce the male gametes or **sperms** in millions. Each sperm is a single cell with all the usual cell components. Each sperm has a head, a middle piece and a tail (Fig. 9.2b). The sperms leave each testis through a sperm duct or **vas deferens**. As the sperms move through sperm ducts, fluids from three glands pour their secretions into the ducts. The mixture of fluids and sperms is called **semen**. The sperms swim in it and reach the urethra which lies inside the **penis**. The penis is the organ that transfers sperms into the **vagina** of the female's body.

### The female reproductive system

The female reproductive organs are a pair of **ovaries**, the **oviduct** (fallopian tubes) and the **uterus**. These are located in the lower part of the abdomen (Fig. 9.2c). The ovaries produce the egg or **ovum** (plural 'ova') when a female reaches puberty. Usually one ovum is released from one of the ovaries every month. The ovum is also a single cell. The ovum passes into the oviduct.

### Fertilization

It is in the oviduct that the sperms and the ovum meet. One of the sperms may fuse with the ovum and fertilization takes place. During fertilization, the nuclei of the sperm and the ovum fuse together to form a single nucleus. This results in the formation of the fertilized

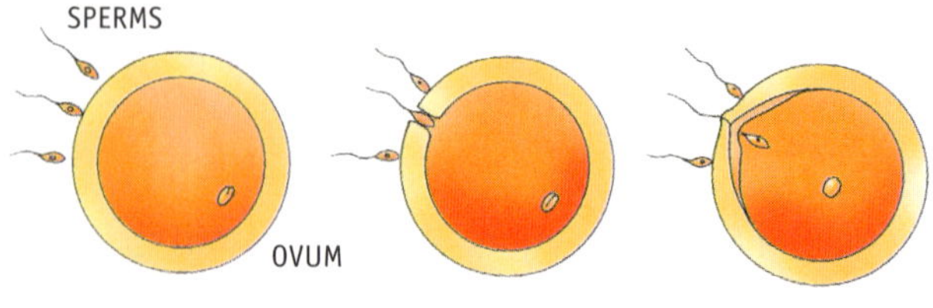


FIG. 9.3 The process of fertilization in human beings

egg or zygote (Fig. 9.4). The formation of the zygote marks the beginning of a new individual.

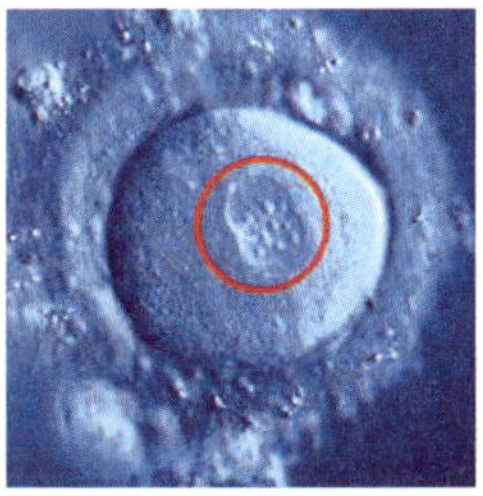

FIG. 9.4 Fusing nuclei in a zygote

If the ovum is not fertilized by a sperm, it is expelled from the uterus along with some uterine muscles and blood. This is known as **menstruation**.

The number of eggs produced at a time is different for different mammals. Humans, elephants and cows usually produce one egg at a time. Cats, dogs and rabbits produce more than one egg at a time. Hence, more babies are born to them at the same time.

The zygote results from the fusion of the sperm cell from the father and the egg cell from the mother. Hence, it has the chromosomes and genes from both mother and father. Thus, the new individual inherits characteristics from both mother and father. Can you recognize some of the characteristics that you have inherited from your parents?

**IT'S A FACT!**

Some women are unable to have babies because their fallopian tubes are blocked. This prevents the ova being fertilized as the male gametes from the father cannot come in contact with female gametes of mother. This problem can be overcome through **test tube baby technology**. In this technique, freshly matured ova collected from a woman's ovaries by using a special syringe and semen from the man are kept in an incubator (*in vitro*). The sperms fertilize the ova to form an embryo. After a week, the embryo thus formed is then inserted into the woman's womb where the embryo gets implanted and develops into a baby in about nine months. The baby thus produced is called a **test tube baby**. This technique was first successfully introduced in humans in 1978 and is called ***in vitro* fertilization (IVF)**.

### Development of embryo

After fertilization, the zygote travels down the oviduct and divides over and over again, to form a ball of cells. This is known as **cell division** (Fig. 9.5a). The cells then begin to form different groups that finally develop into different tissues and organs of the body. This developing structure is called the **embryo**. It gets embedded in the wall of the uterus, where further development occurs (Fig. 9.5a).

During the development, the different groups of cells change their size and shape, and turn into particular types of cells performing specific functions, such as muscle cells, nerve cells and blood cells. This is called **cell differentiation** or **cell maturation**. It is from these differentiated cells that different tissues and organs develop.

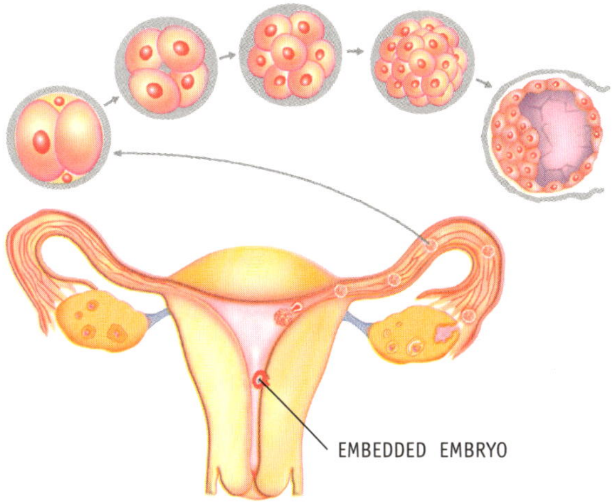


a. Cell division and zygote development

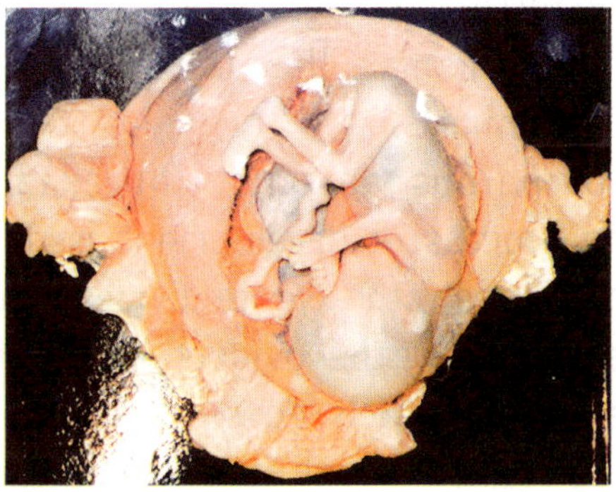

b. The foetus

FIG. 9.5

Gradually the different body parts such as head, hands, legs, etc. develop. The stage at which all the body parts of the embryo could be recognized is called the **foetus** (Fig. 9.5b). In humans, this stage is reached after about eight weeks of fertilization. The foetus keeps developing further. When all body parts assume the right size and forms, the development is complete and the individual is born. A single cell ultimately gives rise to trillions of cells in the body of the individual.

### ORAL QUESTIONS FOR FORMATIVE ASSESSMENT

1. Suppose a disease affecting the reproductive system, strikes all individuals of a species. What will happen to the species? Give reasons.
2. In what kind of animals does fertilization normally occur outside the body? Where does it occur in the case of humans?
3. In humans, which organ produces the egg, and which organ produces the sperms? How many of each are produced at a time?
4. During the reproduction process in humans, after which process does a new individual start getting formed?
5. Which two processes are responsible for the development of embryo in multicellular organisms?

## VIVIPAROUS AND OVIPAROUS ANIMALS

In animals where the fertilization is internal, there are different ways in which the fertilized egg develops into a new organism.

Other than humans, most other mammals such as cows, goats, dogs and tigers give birth to fully formed young ones. The animals that give birth to young ones are called **viviparous** animals.

Birds lay fertilized eggs and keep them warm by sitting on them. A chick comes out of the egg in due course of time. Snakes and crocodiles also lay fertilized eggs which develop into young ones. Animals that lay eggs are called **oviparous** animals.

In oviparous animals, for example, a hen, the process of development is different. After fertilization, the zygote divides repeatedly and travels down the oviduct as in humans. However, as it travels down, many protective layers are formed around it. The hard shell of a hen's egg is one such layer. After the hard shell is formed around the embryo, the hen lays the egg. The hen then sits on the egg to keep it warm. Development of the chick takes place inside the shell. It takes about 3 weeks for the embryo to develop into a chick. After its development is complete, the chick comes out by bursting open the egg shell.

**ACTIVITY 2 (Experimental investigation)**

Collect the eggs of as many oviparous animals as you can—for example, hen, crow, other birds, frog, lizard, butterfly. Draw their pictures. Compare their sizes.

**ACTIVITY 3 (Experimental investigation)**

The eggs sold in the market are generally unfertilized ones. To observe a developing embryo in an egg, get a fertilized egg from a poultry farm or a hatchery—one that has been incubated for 2–3 days. Break open the egg. You may be able to see a white disc-like structure on the yolk. This is the developing embryo. Sometimes you may even see a red spot, which shows that the heart and blood vessels have started developing.

## METAMORPHOSIS

Newborn mammals and newly hatched birds have similar shape and structure as their parents. However, this is not so throughout the animal kingdom. A frog, mosquito or butterfly have different stages of development between hatching of the eggs and formation of the individual.

A frog passes through three stages during its development from an egg to an adult frog:

Egg → tadpole (larva) → adult frog

The tadpole that hatches out of the egg looks very different from an adult frog. It undergoes changes to finally become a frog.

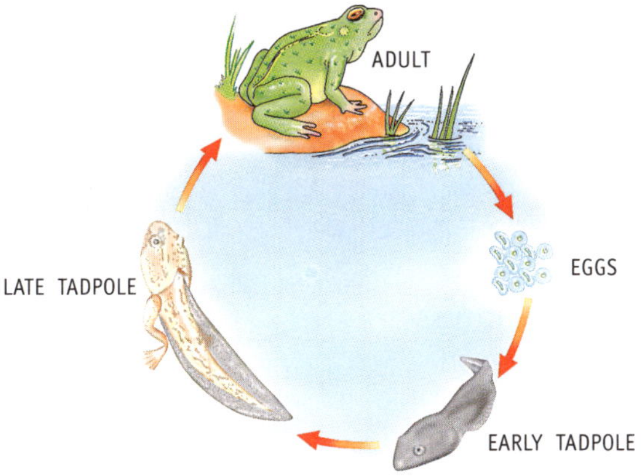


FIG. 9.6 The life cycle of a frog

In mosquito, when the eggs hatch, a worm-like **larva** comes out of each egg. In about two weeks, it changes into an encased form called **pupa** which has the shape of a comma (,). The pupa changes into a mosquito inside the case, and in about a week the mosquito wriggles out of the case.

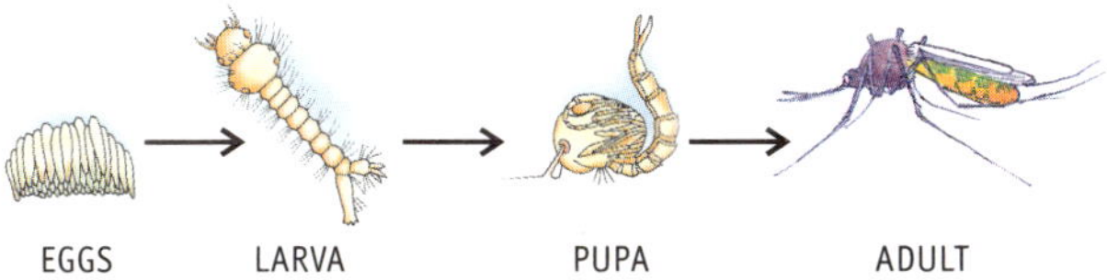


FIG. 9.7 Life cycle of a mosquito

Butterflies and moths also pass through the larva and pupa stages before the winged adult is born:

Egg → caterpillar (larva) → pupa → adult

The transformation of the larva into an adult through drastic changes is called **metamorphosis**.

## ASEXUAL REPRODUCTION

Asexual reproduction involves the production of new organisms by just one parent. It does not require two sexes. There are many forms of asexual reproduction. Some of the asexual reproductions are discussed below.

### Binary Fission

Fission refers to division of a cell into two parts. This is the simplest type of asexual reproduction and is seen in single-celled organisms, such as *Amoeba* (Fig. 9.8) and *Paramecium*. In **binary fission**, the fully grown parent cell splits into two halves, producing two new cells.

In *Amoeba*, the nucleus first divides into two equal parts. The cytoplasm also divides into two parts, each part receiving a nucleus. The two daughter *Amoebae* thus formed grow and attain full size before splitting again.

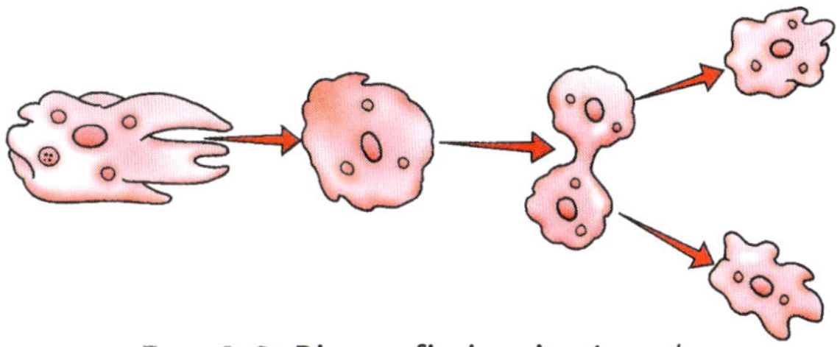

FIG. 9.8 Binary fission in *Amoeba*

### Budding

In budding, a new organism grows in the form of a bulb-like projection called a **bud** from the parent organism. It grows and may eventually break away from the parent.

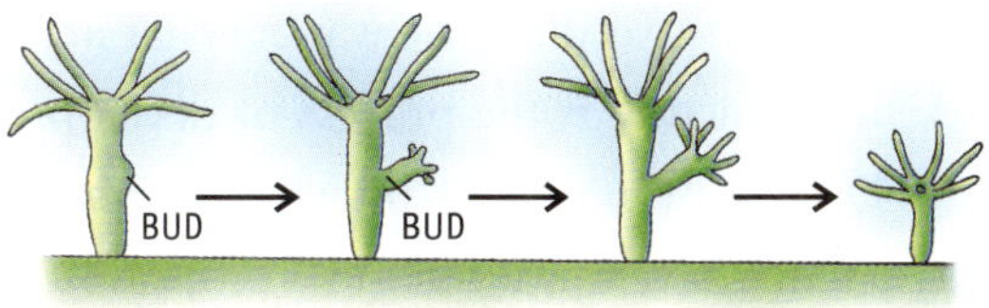


FIG. 9.9 Budding in *Hydra*

Yeast and *Hydra* reproduce by budding. In *Hydra*, a bud appears on the body wall which grows into a full *Hydra* in a day or two and separates from the parent (Fig. 9.9).

In corals and sponges, buds do not separate out but remain attached to the parent organism. They grow to full size and reproduce again and again producing a colony.

### ACTIVITY 4
**(Experimental investigation)**

Observe a slide of *Hydra* with the help of a magnifying lens or a microscope. What do you observe?

Can you spot any bulges of the type shown in Figure 9.9?

## THE STORY OF CLONING

On 27 February 1997, a research article published in the science magazine *Nature* caused a flutter in the scientific world. It talked about the remarkable success achieved by scientist **Dr Ian Wilmut** and his colleagues at the Roslin Institute in Edinburgh, Scotland, in producing a baby sheep without involving the male sperm.

**FIG. 9.10** Dolly and her first-born lamb

The baby sheep **Dolly** was developed from a cell taken from the mammary gland of a female sheep, and an unfertilized egg taken from another female sheep. The nucleus of the unfertilized egg was removed from it. Therefore, no chromosome (and hence no genes) remained in the egg shell.

The two cells were then fused together. The egg cell accepted the nucleus of the mammary gland cell and was 'fooled' into thinking that fertilization had taken place. It started developing into an embryo. The embryo was then put inside the uterus of a third female sheep. It developed into a baby sheep in the uterus and was born in the usual way on 5 July 1996. It took Dr Wilmut 277 attempts to clone Dolly!

Dolly inherited all its genes from the female sheep from whose mammary glands the cells were taken. It was, therefore, an exact copy, or a 'clone' of that sheep. Dolly lived a healthy life for more than 6½ years and produced several offspring through the normal sexual method. She died on 14 February 2003.

Several attempts have been made after the Dolly experiment to clone other animals. However, success has been limited. The cloned animals either die before birth or are born with abnormalities and die soon after.

## ORAL QUESTIONS FOR FORMATIVE ASSESSMENT

1. In animals where fertilization is internal, development of an individual after fertilization can occur in two different ways. What are these two ways?
2. In what way is the process of development of an adult from an egg different in birds and frogs?
3. Describe the process by which *Amoeba* reproduces.
4. *Hydra* develops a bulb-like projection that finally changes into a new individual. What is the projection called?

## NOW YOU KNOW

- Reproduction is the process of producing new individuals of the same kind.
- Sexual reproduction involves two parents—one male which produces the sperm, and one female which produces the ovum. The process of fusion of sperm and ovum to form a zygote is called fertilization.
- External fertilization occurs outside the body of the organism. Internal fertilization occurs inside the body of the organism.
- In humans, the male reproductive organs are the testes which produce sperms. The female reproductive organs are the ovaries which produce the ovum.
- Fertilization in humans occurs in the fallopian tube of the female. The zygote develops into a baby in the uterus before being born.
- In multicellular organisms, development of the embryo occurs by cell division and cell differentiation.
- Viviparous animals give birth to babies; oviparous animals lay eggs.
- In some animals, development of the embryo occurs in stages after the eggs are hatched. The transformation of the larva into an adult through drastic changes is called metamorphosis.
- Asexual reproduction involves the production of new organism by just one parent.
- *Amoeba* reproduces by binary fission, in which the fully grown parent cell splits into two halves, producing two new cells.
- *Hydra* reproduces by budding in which a bud appears on the body wall which grows into a full *Hydra* and separates from the parent.

## NEW WORDS

**EXTERNAL FERTILIZATION**—fertilization that occurs outside the body of the organism

**INTERNAL FERTILIZATION**—fertilization that occurs inside the female's body

**PUBERTY**—onset of sexual maturity

**VIVIPAROUS**—animals that give birth to babies

**OVIPAROUS**—animals that lay eggs

**METAMORPHOSIS**—transformation of the larva into an adult through drastic changes

## FOR FORMATIVE AND SUMMATIVE ASSESSMENT

### A. MULTIPLE-CHOICE QUESTIONS: Choose the most appropriate answer.

1. Which of these are the male reproductive organs in humans?
   a. sperms  b. ova  c. testes  d. ovaries
2. Which of the following is a hermaphrodite animal?
   a. frog  b. cow  c. dog  d. earthworm

3. In __________, the offspring grows out of the parent's body.
   a. *Hydra* b. *Amoeba* c. *Paramecium* d. human
4. In humans, fertilization occurs in
   a. oviduct. b. uterus. c. ovary. d. vagina.
5. In a mosquito, the eggs hatch to produce
   a. pupa. b. larva. c. embryo. d. adult mosquito.
6. Which of the following reproduces by splitting into two?
   a. *Hydra* b. mosquito c. *Amoeba* d. frog
7. The fusion of sperm and egg produces
   a. zygote. b. larva. c. pupa. d. embryo.
8. Humans start becoming sexually mature at the ages of
   a. 10–16. b. 3–5. c. 13–18. d. 25–30.

## B. VERY SHORT-ANSWER QUESTIONS: Give one-word answers.

1. Improper working of the reproductive organs can lead to death. True or false?
2. What is the process of fusion of sperm and ovum called?
3. The fusion product of sperm and ovum is known as __________
4. Organisms in which male and female gametes are present in the same organism are called __________
5. An earthworm, being a hermaphrodite, can reproduce on its own without the need of a partner. True or false?
6. In frogs, is the fertilization external or internal?
7. What is the onset of sexual maturity in animals known as?
8. In humans, which organ produces the ovum?
9. Fertilization in humans takes place in the uterus. True or false?
10. Females of all mammals produce a single ovum at a time. True or false?
11. In mosquito, the life cycle is as follows: egg → pupa → larva → mosquito. True or false?
12. The process of cells changing their size, shape and form to form specialized cells is called __________
13. Is binary fission sexual or asexual?
14. The transformation of the larva into an adult through drastic changes is called __________

## C. SHORT-ANSWER QUESTIONS (TYPE I): Answer in a sentence or two.

1. Why is reproduction important?
2. How is sexual reproduction different from asexual reproduction?
3. What is menstruation?
4. What is cell division?
5. What is metamorphosis?
6. List the various stages in the life cycle of a mosquito.

## D. SHORT-ANSWER QUESTIONS (TYPE II): Answer in about 30 words.

1. Differentiate between external and internal fertilization, giving two examples of each.
2. How does fertilization occur in frogs?
3. How and where does fertilization take place in human beings?
4. What happens in the female body if the ovum is not fertilized by a sperm?
5. How does *Hydra* reproduce?
6. Explain the difference between viviparous and oviparous animals.
7. Explain what happens after a hen lays a fertilized egg.

## E. LONG-ANSWER QUESTIONS: Answer in about 60 words.

1. Give details of two different ways in which a zygote develops in case of animals where fertilization is internal.
2. What is puberty? What is it caused by? What changes occur in boys and girls during puberty?
3. Discuss how a zygote develops into an individual in humans.
4. Explain the life cycle of a frog, with the help of a labelled diagram.

## HOTS QUESTIONS: Think and answer.

1. Can the process of a child changing into an adult be called metamorphosis?
2. Frogs and fishes lay hundreds of eggs at a time. However, their population is very little as compared to the number of eggs they lay. Why?
3. Why do you think it is necessary for frogs and fishes to lay so many eggs?
4. What do you think would have happened if humans also gave birth to a large number of babies at the same time?
5. Can a woman with a blocked fallopian tube give birth to a child? Why?
6. Under what circumstances can twins be born in humans?
7. Why is it that dogs always produce several puppies whereas human beings usually produce only one child at a time?

## FOR FORMATIVE ASSESSMENT*

### In the Library—Research Projects

- Normally, the human female produces one egg at a time so that one child is born at a time. When two babies are born at a time they are called twins. Some twins are of the same sex and are exactly alike. They are called **identical twins**. Others may be of the same or different sex and quite different from each other. They are called non-identical or **fraternal twins**. Find out the difference in the way the two kinds of twins develop.
- Find out about reproduction in the case of honeybees. What is the bee that lays eggs called? Which bees feed the egg-laying bee and look after the young? Which eggs hatch into males and which into females?

*For more tasks see Page 132

## My Virtual Library—Research/Activities on the Internet

- ❐ Visit rsgr.in/lsc-cce-8 and click on LINK 36 to know all about frogs—including their life cycle.
- ❐ Visit rsgr.in/lsc-cce-8 and click on LINK 37 to understand the science of cloning.
- ❐ More than 10 years after Dolly—what now? Visit rsgr.in/lsc-cce-8 and click on LINK 38 to find out.

## In the Laboratory—Experimental Project

**Observe the life cycle of a butterfly** Go on a nature walk. With the help of your teacher, look for eggs of butterfly laid on leaves. Keep them in a large bottle with a lid. Make holes in the lid for air to go in.

The eggs will hatch to produce the larva (caterpillar). Provide lots of leaves for the caterpillars to eat. These should preferably be from the same plant from where the eggs were collected.

Keep a close watch and observe how the pupa is formed, and how it finally changes into a butterfly. Release the butterfly from the bottle and let it fly out.

TEACHER'S NOTES

- Visiting a pond during the rainy season to observe frog's eggs and tadpoles will be instructive. Some tadpoles can be taken to and bred in a makeshift pond in the school to study their metamorphosis. Similarly, study the life cycle of a butterfly (see Experimental Project above).
- Show children models of the reproductive system. Visit the zoological department of a college or a medical college to show them a foetus.

10

# Reaching the Age of Adolescence

### THE ENDOCRINE SYSTEM

You know that processes like breathing and body movements are controlled by the nervous system. There are a number of other slower processes that go on in the body, such as growth. Such processes are primarily controlled by the **endocrine system**. The nervous system and endocrine system often work together to help the body function properly.

The endocrine system controls these processes through chemicals called **hormones**. Hormones are secreted by a number of **glands** that make up the endocrine system, and are released directly into the blood.

Hormones regulate many processes in the body such as growth, development, behaviour and reproduction. Each hormone is required in very small quantity and has its own specific function. Your body has over 30 of these hormones. It is hormones that make you feel hungry or full, determine how you sleep or how you handle stress, and much more.

Glands that produce hormones are located in various parts of the body (Fig. 10.1). These glands do not have ducts and release the hormones directly into the blood stream. They are also called **ductless glands**. Hormones generally do not act at the place where they are produced in the body. They are taken by blood to a particular body part called the **target**

**IN THIS CHAPTER**

THE ENDOCRINE SYSTEM ◆ PUBERTY AND ADOLESCENCE ◆ DETERMINING THE SEX OF THE BABY ◆ HEALTH FOR ADOLESCENTS

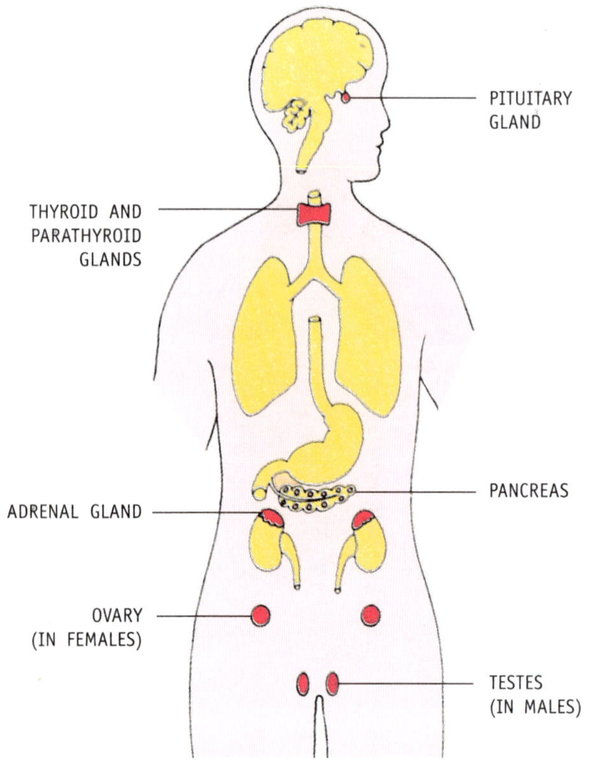


FIG. 10.1 The endocrine system in human beings

site, where they act. Some of the glands and the hormones they produce are mentioned below:

- The **adrenal glands** secrete the hormone **adrenalin** when a person is angry or afraid. It prepares the body to fight or to run away.
- The **pancreas** secretes the hormone **insulin**, which regulates the amount of sugar in the blood.
- The **thyroid gland** produces a hormone called **thyroxine** that affects growth.
- The ovary in females produces the female sex hormone called **oestrogen**. The testes in males produces the male sex hormone called **testosterone**. These hormones control sexual characteristics, as you will read later in this chapter.
- The **pituitary gland** produces several hormones that control water balance, growth and also the release of other hormones. The growth hormone (GH) stimulates growth and development in the body. The thyroid stimulating hormone (TSH) stimulates the thyroid gland to produce thyroxine. Other hormones secreted by the pituitary gland stimulate the testes and ovaries to produce testosterone, oestrogen and progesterone respectively.

The pituitary gland is also called the **master gland** as it influences the functioning of the other glands.

## PUBERTY AND ADOLESCENCE

You have read that humans can reproduce only after achieving sexual maturity. The stage of life when the body becomes capable of reproduction is known as **puberty**. It is normally 11–16 years in boys and 10–15 years in girls. However, the period may vary from person to person.

When a child reaches puberty, he/she becomes an adolescent. The period of transition from a child to an adult is known as **adolescence**. It continues until the age of 18 or 19 years, after which there is no further growth in the body.

During adolescence, the body undergoes several changes. These changes mark the onset of puberty, i.e. the beginning of the body's journey to becoming an adult. Puberty ends with the adolescent reaching reproductive maturity.

### Changes at puberty

At the onset of puberty:

- In boys, the male hormone **testosterone** begins to be released by the testes. This causes the sex organs—testes and penis—to develop completely, and the testes to start producing sperms.
- In girls, the ovaries start producing the female hormones oestrogen and progesterone. As a result, the ovaries enlarge and start releasing eggs.

In addition to the above sex characteristics,

the release of sex hormones brings about the following **secondary sex characteristics**.

### Increase in height

There is a sudden increase in height during adolescence, brought about by elongation of the bones of the arms and legs.

During this period, different parts of the body do not grow at the same rate. For example, the arms and legs often grow faster than other parts, making them appear oversized and awkward. However, this is temporary and soon the body regains its normal proportions.

While the final height an individual attains is primarily controlled by genes, hormones control how the height increases. It is important that the body gets the correct nutrition during adolescence to ensure healthy growth of bones, muscles and other parts.

### Activity 1
### (Information gathering and analysis)

We achieve our full height by about 18–19 years of age. Figure 10.2 shows a typical graph of percentage of full height achieved against age.

You can see that girls grow faster than boys. For example, at the age of 13 years, most girls grow to 95 % of their maximum height whereas boys only achieve 85 % of

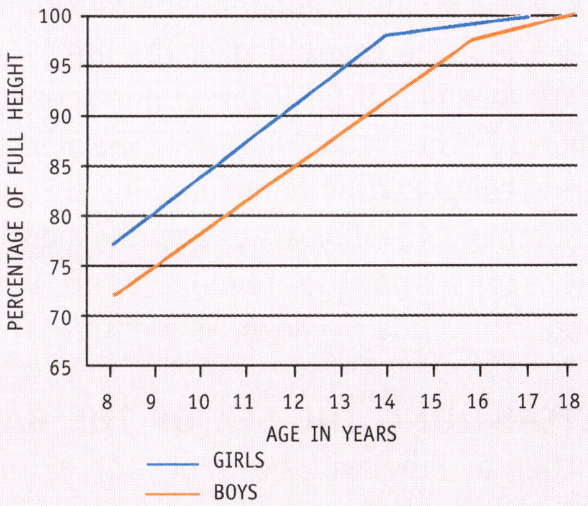


FIG. 10.2 Percentage of full height vs age

their maximum height. But both achieve their maximum heights at 18–19 years of age.

Find out the percentage for your age. Now measure your height and calculate the maximum height you will grow to. An example is worked out below:

Ramesh is 13 years old and has a height of 150 cm.

From the graph, boys achieve 85 % of their maximum height at age of 13 years.

Therefore, Ramesh is likely to grow to (100/85) × 150 = 176.5 cm (approx)

Note, however, that the graph will vary from person to person and these figures are only indicative.

### Changes in body shape

In boys, the shoulders become broader and the chest becomes wider. The muscles grow more than in girls.

In girls, the pelvic region widens, hips broaden, breasts develop and increase in size. Mammary glands (milk secretion glands) develop inside the breasts.

### Development of hair

In both sexes, hair start growing in the armpits and in the pubic area. In boys, facial hair (beard and moustache) develop.

### Voice changes

The voice box or the **larynx** begins to grow. It becomes bigger in boys than in girls. This is why boys develop a deep voice whereas girls

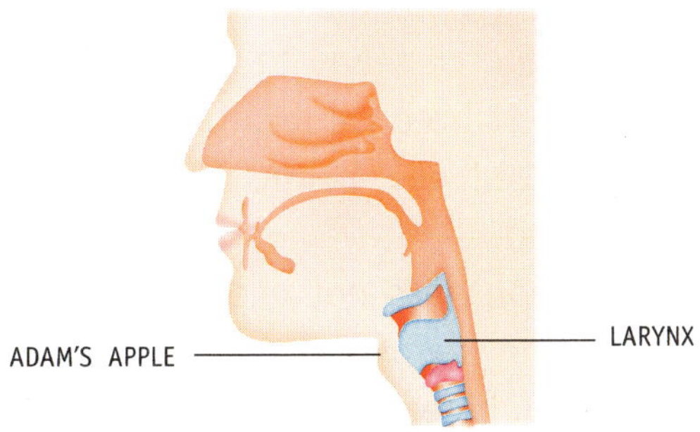


FIG. 10.3 The larynx and the Adam's apple

have a high pitched voice. In boys as the larynx begins to grow, the voice often cracks. Sometimes the voice also becomes hoarse. However, this is temporary and the voice is soon back to normal.

### Activity of sweat and oil glands

There is increase in the activity of sweat and sebaceous (oil) glands. This leads to increased sweating often resulting in body odour. The skin becomes oilier. This often leads to appearance of acne and pimples on the face (Fig. 10.4).

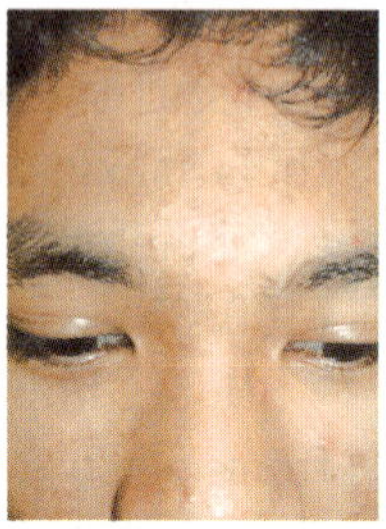

FIG. 10.4

### Changes in behaviour and attitudes

Intellectual development occurs during adolescence to transform the individual from a child to an adult.

As a result of trying to adjust to the changes in the body and mind, adolescents often find themselves feeling confused, insecure and self conscious. This is a natural part of growing up and is experienced by everyone. Therefore, there is no reason to feel insecure.

### Sexual feelings

Sexual maturity causes boys and girls to become interested in and attracted to the opposite sex.

### ORAL QUESTIONS FOR FORMATIVE ASSESSMENT

1. State two processes in the body that are controlled by the nervous system and two that are controlled by the endocrine system.
2. The nervous system controls body processes by sending messages from the brain through the nerves. How does the endocrine system control body processes?
3. At which stage in a child's life does he/she become an adolescent? What marks the end of adolescence?
4. Hormones control the increase in the height of an adolescent and the final height attained. Do you agree? Give reasons.
5. Pimples appear in those adolescents who do not keep their skin clean. Do you agree? Give reasons.

## THE MENSTRUAL CYCLE

In females, the reproductive age starts at puberty and continues to approximately 45–50 years of age. During this period, one of the two ovaries produces an egg (or ovum) every 28–30 days. This process is known as **ovulation**.

During this period, the walls of the uterus become thick and cushiony to receive the egg. If the egg is fertilized, it results in pregnancy and the fertilized egg begins to develop, as you already read.

If fertilization does not occur, the egg and the lining of the uterus are shed, accompanied by blood. The bleeding lasts for 4-6 days and is known as **menstruation** or **period**. The first menstrual flow that begins at puberty is known as **menarche**. The periods may be irregular initially but become regular after some time.

The cycle of producing and releasing a mature egg, the thickening of the uterus wall, and its shedding if fertilization does not occur is known as the **menstrual cycle**. The menstrual cycle is controlled by hormones.

At around 45–50 years of age, the menstrual cycle stops and the female is no longer reproductive. This is known as **menopause**.

## DETERMINING THE SEX OF THE BABY

Whether a baby will be a boy or a girl is determined by the chromosomes present inside the nucleus of the fertilized egg.

You have read that chromosomes in the nucleus occur in matching pairs. There are 23 pairs (i.e. 46 chromosomes) in every normal human cell. In each pair, one chromosome comes from the father and one from the mother.

Two out of these 46 chromosomes are sex chromosomes, called X and Y chromosomes. A female has two X sex-chromosomes and a male has one X and one Y sex-chromosome.

Each gamete has only one chromosome. An egg has an X chromosome. A sperm may have an X or a Y chromosome.

- If a sperm containing an X chromosome fertilizes the egg, the zygote would have two X chromosomes and would develop into a female.
- If a sperm containing a Y chromosome fertilizes the egg, the zygote would have one X and one Y chromosome and would develop into a male.

It can be seen from the above that the sex chromosomes of the father, rather than those of the mother, determine the sex of the child.

### Role of hormones in metamorphosis

You have read about metamorphosis in frogs and insects, such as mosquito and butterfly. In frogs, metamorphosis is controlled by the hormone thyroxine produced by the thyroid gland. In insects, it is controlled by insect hormones. For tadpoles to grow into adults, the water should contain iodine. This is because the production of thyroxine requires the presence of iodine.

**ACTIVITY 2 (Research)**

Look at the packet of salt in your kitchen. Does it say 'iodized salt'? Iodine is added to salt so that we get iodine in sufficient quantities. Iodine has an important effect on the health of the thyroid gland. An unhealthy thyroid can lead to a number of conditions, including goitre, a swelling of the thyroid gland. This appears as a lump in the neck region. Find out what other problems are caused by iodine deficiency.

## HEALTH FOR ADOLESCENTS

During adolescence, there is rapid mental and physical growth. Therefore, looking after physical and mental health at this stage is of utmost importance.

For proper physical health you need:

- A **balanced diet** containing the right amounts of proteins, carbohydrates, fats, vitamins and minerals. The diet should contain adequate amounts of cereals for carbohydrates; milk, meat, nuts and pulses for proteins; controlled amounts of butter/ghee/oils and sugars for energy; and fruits and vegetables for protection against

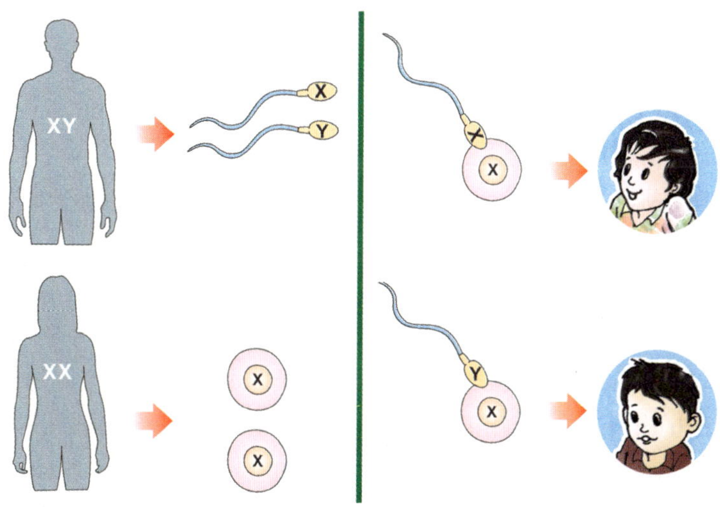


FIG. 10.5 Determination of the sex of a child

diseases. Fast food which is tasty but does not have adequate nutrition, such as chips or aerated drinks, should not be used as substitute for meals.

- **Personal hygiene:** Due to increased activity of sweat and sebaceous glands, proper personal hygiene is very important for adolescents. Taking a bath every day and cleaning all parts of the body is essential, otherwise body odour and bacterial infection may result. Girls should be especially careful about hygiene during menstruation.
- **Physical exercise:** Walking, jogging, aerobics, outdoor games, etc., are good for the growing adolescent body.

Since adolescence is also a stage of insecurity and confusion, it is easy for the adolescent mind to be led astray by wrong company or advice, and fall prey to drug and alcohol abuse. Drugs are very addictive and once taken, there is a tendency to take them again and again. They harm the body in the long run, ruining health and happiness.

### Always say NO to drugs

When confused, confide in parents and teachers and seek their guidance, as they are your well wishers and have passed through the same stage. Books and good Internet sites can also be referred. Seeking advice from only friends is not advisable as they themselves are experiencing the process for the first time.

**IT'S A FACT!**

**Legal age for marriage** The legal age for marriage in India is 18 years for girls and 21 years for boys. Girls are physically not ready for bearing children before 18. They may also not be mentally mature enough to bear the responsibilities of motherhood. Both these factors affect the health of the mother and child. Motherhood at such an early age also binds the woman to the home and stops her from having a career.

## ORAL QUESTIONS FOR FORMATIVE ASSESSMENT

1. The menstrual cycle consists of three processes. What are these?
2. The sex of a baby is determined by which egg gets fertilized—one containing the X chromosome or one containing the Y chromosome. Do you agree? Give reasons.
3. Why is iodine essential for metamorphosis to take place properly?

## NOW YOU KNOW

- The endocrine system consists of a number of ductless glands that secrete hormones.
- The hormones control several processes in the body.
- The pituitary gland produces several hormones that stimulate other glands to secrete their hormones.
- The ovaries in females produce the female sex hormone oestrogen. The testes in males produce the male sex hormone testosterone.
- The stage of life when the body becomes capable of reproduction is known as puberty.
- The period of transition from a child to an adult is known as adolescence. It continues until the age of 18 or 19 years, after which there is no further growth in the body.

- Several changes occur in the body during adolescence due to the release of sex hormones.
- Some of the secondary sex characteristics are sudden increase in height, changes in body shape, development of pubic and facial hair, voice changes, increased activity of sweat and sebaceous glands, changes in behaviour and attitudes, and arousal of sexual feelings towards the opposite sex.
- The cycle of producing and releasing a mature egg, the thickening of the uterus wall, and its shedding if fertilization does not occur is known as the menstrual cycle. The menstrual cycle is controlled by hormones.
- The sex of the baby is determined by which sperm, one containing the X or the Y chromosome, fertilizes the egg.
- Looking after physical and mental health at the adolescent stage is very important due to the rapid physical and mental growth at this stage.

## NEW WORDS

**HORMONES**—chemicals secreted by the glands of the endocrine system that control several processes in the body

**OESTROGEN AND PROGESTERONE**—female sex hormones

**TESTOSTERONE**—male sex hormone

**PUBERTY**—the stage of life when the body becomes capable of reproduction

**ADOLESCENCE**—the period of transition from a child to an adult

**MENARCHE**—the first period that a girl has

**MENOPAUSE**—the stoppage of the menstrual cycle

## FOR FORMATIVE AND SUMMATIVE ASSESSMENT

### A. MULTIPLE-CHOICE QUESTIONS: Choose the most appropriate answer.

1. Which of these processes in the body is controlled by hormones?
   a. blood circulation b. growth c. digestion d. excretion
2. Which of these is not a gland of the endocrine system?
   a. adrenal b. thyroid c. penis d. ovaries
3. Which of these is called the master gland?
   a. pituitary gland b. testes c. thyroid gland d. pancreas
4. Which combination of sex chromosomes is present in a female?
   a. XX b. YY c. XY d. none of these
5. The stage at which the body becomes capable of reproduction is called
   a. puberty. b. menopause. c. menstruation. d. gestation.
6. The pituitary gland is located
   a. above the kidneys. b. in the neck.
   c. at the base of the brain. d. near the sex organs.

7. Which hormone controls metamorphosis in frogs?
   a. thyroxine
   b. adrenaline
   c. growth hormone (GH)
   d. testosterone
8. Which of these is not a secondary sex characteristic?
   a. increase in height
   b. release of testosterone
   c. voice change
   d. hair growth on body

**B. VERY SHORT-ANSWER QUESTIONS: Give one-word answers.**

1. The glands of the __________ system secrete hormones.
2. Glands release hormones into the blood stream through ducts. True or false?
3. Hormones act wherever they are released by the glands. True or false?
4. The hormone __________ released by the __________ gland gives sudden energy to the body to fight or run away when in danger.
5. In males, the hormone __________ controls sexual characteristics.
6. Adolescence is marked by the onset of puberty. True or false?
7. All parts of the body grow at the same rate during adolescence. True or false?
8. The larynx is bigger in __________ (boys/girls).
9. Adolescents normally sweat more than adults. Is that true or is it a myth?
10. Ovulation is the production of an __________ by one of the __________
11. Does a female begin or end her reproductive period at menopause?
12. Every sperm has __________ (one/two) sex chromosomes.

**C. SHORT-ANSWER QUESTIONS (TYPE I): Answer in a sentence or two.**

1. What is the function of the endocrine system? What is it made up of?
2. Name four body processes that hormones control.
3. What hormone does the adrenal glands produce? What is the function of this hormone?
4. Why is the pituitary gland referred to as the 'master gland'?
5. Name four endocrine glands and the hormones they secrete.
6. What do you understand by 'puberty'?
7. Why is looking after physical health more important at the adolescent age?
8. What is the final height achieved by an individual primarily governed by? What is the role of hormones in this process?

**D. SHORT-ANSWER QUESTIONS (TYPE II): Answer in about 30 words.**

1. What are the functions of the pituitary gland? List two hormones it produces and give their functions.
2. Discuss the way height in adolescents increases.
3. What causes pimples to appear in adolescents?
4. What changes occur in the body shapes of boys and girls at adolescence?
5. Why do adolescents often find themselves confused and insecure?

## E. LONG-ANSWER QUESTIONS: Answer in about 60 words.

1. Discuss the changes in the voices of boys and girls during adolescence.
2. Discuss the menstrual cycle.
3. Explain what determines the sex of a baby.
4. How should an adolescent look after his/her physical health?

## HOTS QUESTIONS: Think and answer.

1. Many adolescent boys look awkward and disproportionate. Why is that so?
2. Why do you think the pelvic area in girls broadens at puberty?
3. Drugs are harmful at all ages. Why do we then specially emphasise that adolescents should avoid drugs?

## FOR FORMATIVE ASSESSMENT*

### In the Library—Research Projects

- **Sexually transmitted diseases** Many diseases are caused and spread by sexual contact. These are called sexually transmitted diseases (STDs). The most dangerous of these is AIDS (Acquired Immune Deficiency Syndrome). It results from damage to the human immune system by the HIV (Human Immunodeficiency Virus). In a person having this disease, the effectiveness of the immune system progressively reduces, leaving the individual susceptible to many diseases.

  HIV is most commonly transmitted by infected hypodermic needles and by sexual intercourse with a partner having HIV. Having safe sex using condoms is a safeguard against contracting the disease. Scientists are still trying to find a cure for the disease.

  Find out if any of their efforts have been successful and the vaccine or cure available if any.

- From the latest Census Report of India, find out how many adolescent females are there for every 1000 males. Has this number increased or decreased in the last ten years? What do you think is the reason?

### My Virtual Library—Research/Activities on the Internet

- Visit rsgr.in/lsc-cce-8 and click on LINK 39, LINK 40 and LINK 41 to find out more about adolescence, puberty and health.
- Visit rsgr.in/lsc-cce-8 and click on LINK 42 to learn about acne and pimples.
- Visit rsgr.in/lsc-cce-8 and click on LINK 43 to get information on alcohol and drug use by youth.
- Visit rsgr.in/lsc-cce-8 and click on LINK 44 for information on AIDS.

### In the Laboratory—Experimental Project

Collect data on the height of girls and boys of ages 10–18 in your school. Find their averages. Draw separate age vs average height graphs for boys and girls. Study the increase in height. What conclusions can you draw?

*For more tasks see Page 132

# MORE TASKS for FORMATIVE ASSESSMENT (FA 2)

## for Chapters 6–10

In addition to the activities and projects given in the respective chapters, the following tasks can also be used for formative assessment.

### RESEARCH PROJECTS

❒ **Bt cotton** Cotton crop is very susceptible to pest attacks and requires intensive use of pesticides. Over the past 40 years, many pests have developed resistance to pesticides. Bt cotton was developed by what is known as **genetic engineering** (altering the genes of an organism). Bt cotton contains a foreign gene which gives it the ability to produce a toxin (Bt toxin) on its own. Bt toxin acts against bollworm, a major cotton pest, and protects the plant from it. Because of this, Bt cotton gives greater yield and requires less pesticides than normal varieties of cotton.

However, not all scientists agree to these claims and the use of Bt cotton has become controversial. Find out what arguments against Bt cotton has led to this controversy. Also find out about Bt brinjals and why it has not been allowed in India.

❒ **Biodiversity hotspots** A biodiversity hotspot is a region with a significant reservoir of biodiversity that is under threat from humans. **Conservation International**, a nonprofit environmental organisation based in Washington DC, has identified more than 30 biodiversity hotspots around the world.

The Eastern Himalayas and the Western Ghats are two biodiversity hotspots in India. Find out about these two hotspots and the efforts being made to protect them.

Find out who initiated the concept of biodiversity hotspots. Also find out about other biodiversity hotspots in the world.

### RESEARCH ON SCIENTIST

**M Krishnan** (1912–1996) was a naturalist. For nearly 60 years, he wrote on nature and culture of the Indian subcontinent. His subjects included tigers, elephants, butterflies, reptiles, wetlands, deserts and croplands. Find out more about the life and work of M Krishnan.

### DESIGNING A MODEL

Design a fire extinguisher. Remember the following things while designing the model.

- When dilute acid is mixed with carbonate/bicarbonate of metals, carbon dioxide gas is produced.
- Think of an arrangement by which you will have an option to mix the acid with the carbonate/bicarbonate solution.
- You can also add some liquid soap to the carbonate/bicarbonate solution to make the carbon dioxide gas foamy.

### FIELD TRIP

Visit a poultry farm. Find out about the difference between fertilized and unfertilized eggs from the caretaker. Also observe, what are the different species of poultry reared there?

# TEST PAPER 1 for SUMMATIVE ASSESSMENT (SA 1)

## for Chapters 1–10

**Maximum Time: 2½–3 hours** **Maximum Marks: 70**

### A. Answer in one word only. [5 × 1 mark]

1. Which is the best method of irrigation when there is scarcity of water?
2. When a vaccine is injected into the body, what does the body produces to fight the germs in the vaccine?
3. Can bakelite be repeatedly softened by heating?
4. Metals can be drawn into thin wires. What is this property known as?
5. An animal cell does not have a cell wall. What is it protected by?

### B. Answer in one sentence only. [10 × 2 marks]

1. How is transplanting useful to the farmer?
2. State the rule that governs the displacement of a metal from its salt solution by another metal.
3. What is the main purpose of petroleum refining?
4. Why is the calorific value of a fuel important?
5. Algae are considered to be closer to plants than to animals. Why?
6. What is a polymer?
7. What is an endemic species?
8. What is the main function of the nucleus of a cell?
9. How is a zygote formed?
10. What is the function of hormones in the body?

### C. Answer in about 30 words. [5 × 3 marks]

1. What is pasteurization of milk? How is it useful?
2. Silver is more likely to tarnish near a petroleum refinery that releases hydrogen sulphide into the atmosphere than in a place with unpolluted air. Explain why.
3. Differentiate between renewable and non-renewable resources, giving one example of each.
4. Explain with examples the difference between endangered and extinct species.
5. Why do adolescents commonly suffer from body odour, pimples and acne?

### D. Answer in about 60 words. [4 × 5 marks]

1. Name three plant diseases caused by microorganisms. Name the microorganism each is caused by and how each disease spreads.
2. Discuss the properties of nylon that make it such a useful fibre.
3. What are fossil fuels? Discuss why they are an important source of energy for us today.
4. Explain with the help of a diagram, how binary fission takes place in *Amoeba*.

## E. Choose the most appropriate response out of the given four. [10 × 1 mark]

1. Which of the following nutrients does compost lack?
   a. potassium b. nitrogen c. phosphorous d. all of these
2. Pick the odd one out.
   a. virus b. mammal c. bacterium d. fungus
3. Which of these synthetic fibres can substitute wool?
   a. acrylic b. rayon c. nylon d. polyester
4. An iron pipe coated with which of the following metals is called a galvanized pipe?
   a. silver b. copper c. chromium d. zinc
5. Which of these is not obtained by refining of petroleum?
   a. LPG b. CNG c. diesel d. petrol
6. Which zone in a candle flame gives out the maximum light?
   a. dark zone b. non-luminous zone c. blue zone d. luminous zone
7. The animals found in a particular region are known as
   a. endemic species. b. endangered species. c. flora. d. fauna.
8. Organelles are
   a. small organs in the body of multicellular organisms.
   b. small unicellular living organisms.
   c. small multicellular organisms.
   d. small living structures present inside a cell.
9. After fertilization, the zygote gets implanted in
   a. the vagina. b. an ovary.
   c. the oviduct. d. the wall of the uterus.
10. A woman is no longer reproductive after the occurrence of
    a. menstrual cycle. b. menarche. c. menopause. d. ovulation.

# 11

# Force and Pressure

## FORCE

How many times do you push or pull something every day? When you open a drawer you are pulling. When you close a drawer you are pushing. Lifting your school-bag is pulling.

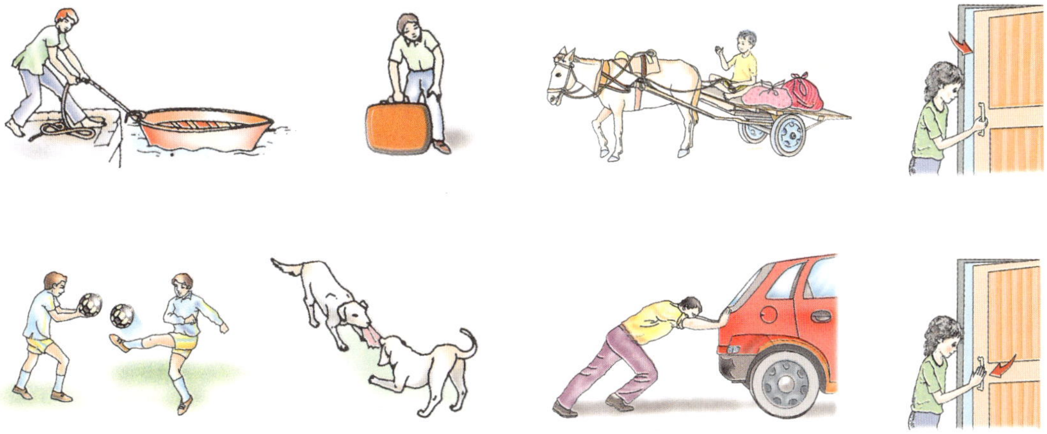

FIG. 11.1 Can these be grouped as pushes or pulls?

**IN THIS CHAPTER**

TYPES OF FORCE AND ITS EFFECTS ◆ PRESSURE AND ITS APPLICATIONS IN DAILY LIFE ◆ PRESSURE EXERTED BY LIQUIDS ◆ ATMOSPHERIC PRESSURE

**ACTIVITY 1 (Critical thinking):**
**To identify any action as push or pull**
Look at the pictures in Figure 11.1. Identify the action in each picture as pushing, pulling, lifting, kicking, stopping, throwing, etc. Then try to see if the action can be grouped as a push or a pull.

You will notice that each of these actions is either a push or a pull.

Pushes and pulls are **forces**. The direction in which an object is pushed or pulled is called the **direction of the force**. We apply force to perform various activities—to lift a glass of water, to ride a bicycle, to push the switch of a TV set to put it on, or to open a car door to get in.

If you stand in front of a door, it will not open by itself. You have to interact with the door by pushing or pulling it, i.e. by applying force on it, to make it open. The two dogs in Figure 11.1 are pulling at each other to apply force. They are also applying force by interacting with each other. What about the other situations in Figure 11.1? Can you say which objects are interacting to apply force?

We therefore conclude that objects must interact with each other for a force to come into play.

**ACTIVITY 2 (Experimental investigation):**
**Net effect of two forces acting on a body**
Push a heavy object to move it. You might be able to move it with some difficulty. Now ask one of your friends to help by pushing with you in the same direction. Can you together push it more easily? Why?

Now push the object again, but ask your friend to push it from the opposite direction. Does the object move now? Why?

a. Forces in the same direction

b. Forces in the opposite directions

FIG. 11.2

These activities suggest that:

- When forces are applied on an object in the same direction, they add up. The net force on the object is a single force whose magnitude is the **sum of the two forces**. The net force acts in the same direction as the two forces.
- When forces are applied on an object in opposite directions, they oppose each other. The net force on the object is the **difference between the two forces**. This net force will act in the direction of the larger force. If the two opposing forces are equal, the net force is zero.

In a tug-of-war match, the rope will move in the direction of the team that applies more force. If the two teams apply the same force, the rope will not move at all.

A force can be described by stating its **magnitude** and the **direction** in which it acts.

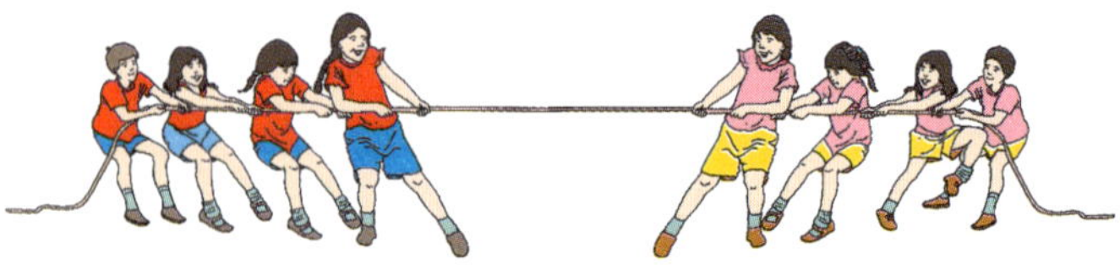
FIG. 11.3 A game of tug-of-war

When two forces act on an object in the same or opposite directions, the effect on the object is due to the net force acting on it. In this case it is the sum or difference of the two forces.

What about a situation where two or more forces act on a body in different directions?

**ACTIVITY 3 (Observation and deduction): Two or more forces acting on a body**

Observe a group of ants trying to pull a dead insect to their anthill. If all ants were to pull in the same direction, the forces would add up and their job would be easy. However, the ants do not know this! Notice that the ants do not pull in one direction—each ant pulls in a different direction. The insect moves in the direction of the net effect of all these forces. If the insect moves in the desired direction, the ants keep on pulling. But if it moves in a different direction, they change their positions and pull again. They keep adjusting their positions until the net force acts in the desired direction and the insect moves towards their anthill!

We conclude that when two or more forces act on an object in different directions, the effect on the object is due to the magnitude and direction of the net force acting on it.

## EFFECTS OF FORCE

What can force do?

1. **Force can make a stationary object move, or can change its position of rest:** When you kick a stationary football, you make it move. When you pick up a glass of water, you change its position of rest.

2. **Force can change the speed of a moving object:** A goalkeeper applies force to stop a football and reduce its speed to zero (Fig. 11.4a). If he is not able to stop the ball

a. To slow down or stop a moving object

b. To make a moving object move faster

FIG. 11.4 Some effects of force

properly, it may only slow down and not come to a position of rest. When a player kicks a moving football, it starts moving faster (Fig. 11.4b).

A goalkeeper slows down or stops a football by applying force in the opposite direction to which the football is moving. On the other hand, to make the ball move faster, the player applies a force in the same direction in which the ball is moving.

3. **Force can change the direction of motion of a moving object:** When a batsman hits a ball with his bat, he applies force to change the direction of the motion of the ball. If you allow a moving ball to hit the palm of your hand, a force is exerted on the ball which changes its direction of motion.

The state of motion of a body is described by its speed and direction of motion. The state of motion of an object at rest is the state of zero speed. A change in the speed of an object, or its direction of motion or both is referred to as change in the state of motion of the object.

Thus, the above three effects of force can be stated as: force brings about a change in the state of motion of a body. However, a force may not always bring about a change in the state of motion of an object. For example, if you push a wall, there is no change in the state of motion of the wall.

4. **Force can change the shape or size of an object:** If you squeeze a sponge, its shape

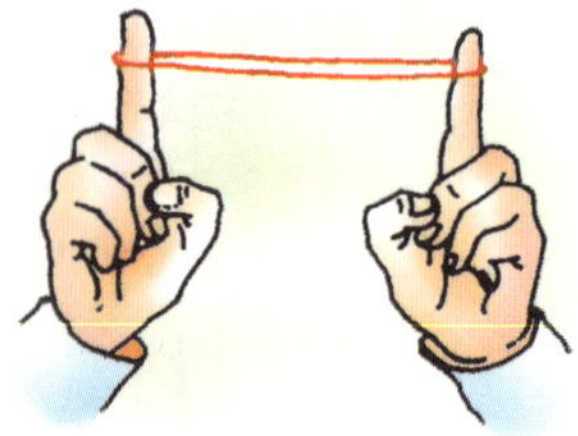

FIG. 11.5 A rubber band on pulling becomes longer.

changes. If you pull a rubber band, it becomes longer (Fig. 11.5). You can use the force of your hand to change the shape of plasticine or an inflated balloon. In the kitchen, force is applied to change the shape of dough to make thin, circular *chapattis*. You can pull a spring to increase its length, and push it to reduce its length.

However, a force acting on an object does not always bring about a change in its shape or size. For example, if you squeeze an iron ball, its shape or size does not change.

## TYPES OF FORCES

Some forces act on bodies only when they are in contact with the body. Examples are muscular force and frictional force. These are known as **contact forces**. Some other forces can also act on bodies which are not in contact. Examples are gravitational force, magnetic force and electrostatic force. These are **non-contact forces**.

### Contact Forces

**Muscular force:** When you lift your school bag, or kick a football, you apply force. This force is exerted by the muscles of your body, and is called **muscular force**. A horse uses muscular force to pull a cart. Your blood gets pushed into your arteries by the muscular force exerted by your heart.

**Frictional force:** What happens when you stop pedalling a bicycle? It slows down and stops after some time. If you kick a small block of wood, it slides for some time and then comes to rest. Why? This happens because of a force called **friction**. Friction is a force that slows things down or prevents things from moving.

Whenever one surface moves or tries to move over another surface, the force of friction starts acting on the surfaces. It always opposes the motion. There is friction between the tyres of a bicycle and the road, and between the block of wood and the floor.

Since the force of friction arises due to contact between surfaces, it is a contact force.

### Non-contact Forces

**Gravitational force:** A force that acts on you and on all objects around you all the time is the force of **gravity**. Gravity is the force with which the earth pulls everything towards itself. It is due to gravity that things on earth fall downwards and not upwards. A ball thrown up slows down and then falls down towards the earth because of the force of gravity.

Gravitational force is the force of attraction between particles of matter. Every object exerts this force on every other object. The magnitude of this force depends on the masses of the two objects and the distance between them. Two cars pull each other with a gravitational force even though it is very small. Because the earth has such a large mass, objects on the earth are pulled towards the earth (due to the force of gravity of the earth) more than they are pulled towards each other. The earth pulls a car towards itself with a force which is about 30,00,00,00,000 times more than the force with which two cars pull each other!

**ACTIVITY 4 (Experimental investigation): Gravitational pull**

Tie a small stone to a rubber band and let it hang. The rubber band gets stretched slightly as the earth pulls the stone towards it. Now tie a bigger stone to it. What do you notice? The rubber band is stretched more. Why?

This is because the earth pulls the bigger stone with greater force. We say that the big stone has more **weight** than the small stone. Thus, weight is a measure of the earth's gravitational pull on an object.

When you weigh an object using a spring balance, you measure the earth's gravitational force on the object (Fig. 11.6). You would weigh less on the moon than on the earth because the moon has less mass than the earth, and hence smaller force of gravity. It, therefore, pulls objects towards itself with lesser force. On the other hand, you would weigh three times more on Jupiter which has greater mass than the earth, and hence greater force of gravity.

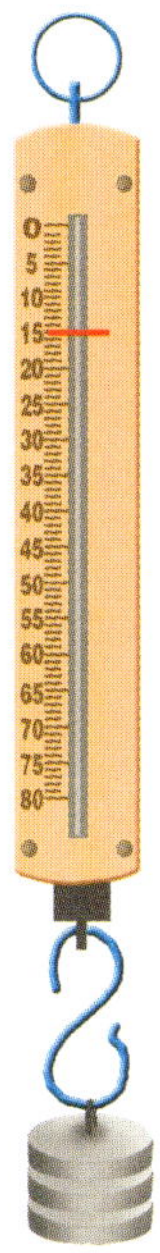

FIG. 11.6 A spring balance

**Magnetic force:** Look at Figure 11.7. A large magnet is being used to pick out scraps of iron from the garbage. It is using force to lift the iron pieces. This force is called **magnetic force** or **magnetism**. Magnetic force is exerted by a magnet on certain metals such as iron.

FIG. 11.7 A magnet being used to pick scraps of iron.

### ACTIVITY 5 (Experimental investigation): Magnetic force I

Put some iron nails on a sheet of paper. Bring a small magnet near these iron nails. You will see that the iron nails are pulled towards the magnet even when they are a little distance away from it (Fig. 11.8). This shows that magnetic force can act from a distance.

FIG. 11.8 Magnetic force acting from a distance

A magnet can act from a distance because it is surrounded by an invisible field of magnetic force. When large scraps of iron from garbage, or small iron pieces get close to that field of force, they are pulled towards the magnet. Thus magnetic force is a non-contact force.

However, what happens when two magnets are brought close together?

### ACTIVITY 6 (Experimental investigation): Magnetic force II

Take two bar magnets. Bring them close together end to end, so that their north poles face each other. What happens? Do they attract or repel each other? Now bring the south pole of one of the magnets near the north pole of the second magnet and try again. What happens now? You will find that their behaviour is opposite to what you observed earlier.

Thus, two magnets attract or repel each other depending on which ends are facing each other. Like poles repel each other, whereas unlike poles attract each other.

**Electrostatic force:** There is another kind of non-contact force, which is observed in the following activity.

**ACTIVITY 7 (Experimental investigation): Electrostatic force**

Rub a comb through your dry hair for some time. Then bring the comb near bits of paper. Are they attracted towards the comb?

When the comb is rubbed in your hair, it acquires a property called **electrostatic charge**.

FIG. 11.9 Electrostatic force acting from a distance

Electrostatic charge can exert a force called electrostatic force. It is because of this force that the bits of paper move towards the comb. Electrostatic force, like magnetic force, also acts from a distance, and is a non-contact force.

Electrostatic force is used to control pollution by separating solid pollutant particles from smoke given out from factories.

## ORAL QUESTIONS FOR FORMATIVE ASSESSMENT

1. A force can move a stationary object. If force is applied to a stationary object, does it always move?
2. Two equal forces act on an object. Is this information enough to say which way the object will move? Give reasons.
3. Name the force that acts on all bodies on the earth at all times.
4. Name a force that always opposes motion.
5. Can a force act on an object even when it is not in contact with the object? Give examples.

## PRESSURE

Consider a force applied on an object. You have already seen the effects that a force can produce on the object. But how do we find out how much effect the force will produce on the object?

The effect that a force produces on an object depends on two factors.

- The magnitude of force applied—the greater the force, the greater is its effect.
- The area over which the force is applied, i.e. the area of contact between the two objects.

When you cut an apple with a knife, the area of contact is the area of the cutting edge of the knife. If the knife has a sharp edge, the area of contact is small. But if the knife has a blunt edge, the area of contact becomes larger. In which case is it easier to cut the apple—when the knife is sharp or when it is blunt? What does this show? This shows that the smaller the area of contact, i.e. the smaller the area over which the force acts, the greater is the effect of the force.

**ACTIVITY 8 (Experimental investigation): Force and area of contact I**

Sharpen a pencil at one end. Hold it between the index fingers of both your hands and press it from both sides (Fig. 11.10). On which finger do you feel pain? On which finger does the pencil leave a deeper mark? Why?

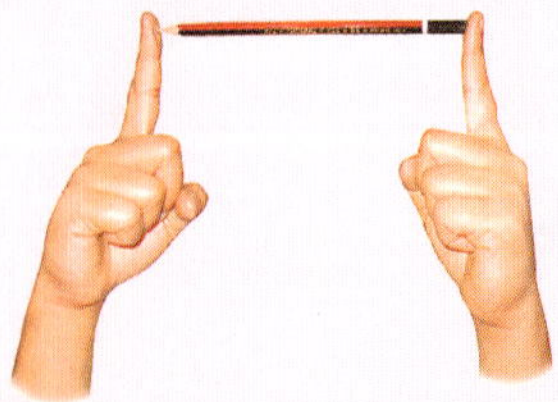

FIG. 11.10 Effect of a force is greater when area of contact is smaller.

You will see that the pencil leaves a deeper mark on the finger pressing the pointed end. This shows that the effect of the force is felt more on the finger pressing the pointed end of the pencil. This is because the area of the pointed end of the pencil is smaller than the area of the head of the pencil.

Another interesting activity to prove this is given below.

**ACTIVITY 9 (Experimental investigation):**
**Force and area of contact II**

Perform this activity in a freshly watered flower bed, where the soil is still soft. First, place one brick upright in the soil (Fig. 11.11a). Remove it to see how deep an impression it has made in the soil. Next, keep two bricks, one on top of the other as shown (Fig. 11.11b). This increases the force exerted on the soil, with the area of contact remaining the same. Is the impression in this case deeper? Why?

Now lay the first brick on the soil on its widest base and note the impression it makes (Fig. 11.11c). Is the impression in this case the shallowest? Why?

a. b. c.

FIG. 11.11 To show that the effect of force depends on the area of contact

### Unit of force

In the SI system, the standard units of length, mass and time are metre, kilogram and second, respectively. In this system, the standard unit of force is **newton (N)**. In the CGS system, the unit of force is **dyne** (1 N = $10^5$ dynes).

To measure and describe the effect of the force acting on a surface, we need a quantity that takes into account the force applied as well as the area over which it is applied. Such a quantity is **pressure**. Pressure is defined as the force exerted per unit area.

$$\text{Pressure} = \frac{\text{Force}}{\text{Area over which the force acts}}$$

It is clear from this that smaller the area over which a force acts, the greater is the pressure, and, therefore, the greater is the effect of the force.

(**NOTE:** The 'force' used in defining pressure is the force acting perpendicular to the area on which it acts.)

### Unit of pressure

In the SI system, the unit of pressure is **newton per sq metre or N/m$^2$**. This unit of pressure is commonly known as **pascal (Pa)** after the French scientist Blaise Pascal. Pressure can also be measured in **kg-wt/m$^2$**.

$$\text{Pressure (in Pa)} = \frac{\text{Force (in newton)}}{\text{Area (in m}^2\text{)}}$$

In the CGS system, the unit of pressure is dyne per square centimetre or **dyne/cm$^2$**.

**EXAMPLE:** Calculate the pressure exerted by a brick, which applies a force of 2.5 N, when (a) it is placed upright on the soil, (b) when it is placed on its widest base. The dimensions of the brick are 25 cm × 10 cm × 5 cm.

**SOLUTION:** (a) When the brick is placed upright:

Area in contact with soil

$$= 10 \text{ cm} \times 5 \text{ cm} = \frac{10}{100} \text{ m} \times \frac{5}{100} \text{ m}$$

$$= 0.005 \text{ m}^2$$

$$\therefore \text{ Pressure exerted} = \frac{F}{A} = \frac{2.5 \text{ N}}{0.005 \text{ m}^2}$$

$$= 500 \text{ Pa}$$

(b) When the brick is placed on its widest base:

Area in contact with soil

$$= 25 \text{ cm} \times 10 \text{ cm} = \frac{25}{100} \text{ m} \times \frac{10}{100} \text{ m}$$

$$= 0.025 \text{ m}^2$$

$$\therefore \text{ Pressure exerted} = \frac{F}{A} = \frac{2.5 \text{ N}}{0.025 \text{ m}^2}$$

$$= 100 \text{ Pa}$$

### Application of force and pressure in daily life

Have you ever tried to run on sand? It is difficult because your feet sink into the sand. A camel is able to move fast on sand because it has flat broad feet. This increases the area of contact with the sand. Hence, the pressure exerted by the camel on the sand is reduced and the camel's feet sink very little in the sand.

Trucks meant to carry heavy loads have eight rather than four tyres to increase the area of contact with the road. Heavy tanks have broad chains called caterpillar tracks which considerably increase the area of contact. The tracks help the tank to distribute its weight more evenly over a larger surface area than wheels can. This prevents it from sinking in areas where wheeled vehicles of the same weight would sink.

Cutting and piercing tools, such as knives, needles and saws, have sharp blades or points to reduce the area of contact so that they exert greater pressure with a comparatively small force. It is easier to hammer a sharp nail into wood than a blunt one. Can you say why?

### Pressure exerted by liquids

Liquids also exert pressure, as we will learn from the activity given below.

**ACTIVITY 10 (Experimental investigation): Liquid pressure**

Take a wide glass tube open at both ends. Tie a rubber balloon to its lower end. Pour water into the tube (Fig. 11.12a). You will notice that the balloon bulges downwards. This shows that liquids exert pressure on the base of the container in which they are kept.

Now take a vessel with a tap-like opening at its side. Tie a balloon to the opening and fill the vessel with water (Fig. 11.12b). You will notice that the balloon bulges outwards. This shows that liquids exert pressure not only on the base of the container but also sideways on the walls of the container. This sideways pressure is exerted by liquids but not by solids.

a. Liquids exert pressure downwards.

b. Liquids exert pressure sideways.

FIG. 11.12 Liquids exert pressure.

**ACTIVITY 11 (Experimental investigation): Variation of liquid pressure with depth**

Take a plastic container and make four holes in it at different heights. Fill the container with water, and let water keep flowing into it from a tap (Fig. 11.13a). Notice the force with which water comes out of the holes.

You will find that water comes out with greater force from the holes at greater depth. Water from the bottom-most hole will be spurted out the farthest from the container. This shows that the pressure in a liquid increases with increasing depth.

a. Water pressure increases with depth.

b. Pressure at the same depth is the same in all directions.

FIG. 11.13

Now take another plastic container and make holes all around it at the same depth, by measuring from the top of the container (Fig. 11.13b).

You will notice that water comes out from all the holes with the same force. This shows that at the same depth, the pressure is the same in all directions.

The pressure at the bottom of the sea is much greater than near the surface. This is the reason why deep-sea divers have to wear special suits to prevent their bodies from being crushed.

### Measuring liquid pressure

An instrument used to measure liquid pressure is called **pressure gauge**. The simplest form of pressure gauge is a **manometer**, which measures pressure difference. You can easily make your own manometer.

#### ACTIVITY 12 (Making a model): Improvised manometer

Take a U-tube made of glass or transparent polythene. Fix it vertically on a stand. Pour coloured water into it so that it is half-full of water. The level in both arms of the U-tube will be the same.

Attach a polythene tube to one end of the U-tube. At the other end of the polythene tube, attach a thistle funnel. Stretch and tie a thin rubber balloon over the mouth of the funnel so that the rubber remains taut. Your manometer is ready to measure pressure.

Take a large glass jar full of water. Slowly lower the funnel into the water. As the funnel goes deeper and deeper into the water, the difference in the liquid level in the U-tube goes on increasing. If you double the depth from 10 cm to 20 cm, does the difference in liquid level also double?

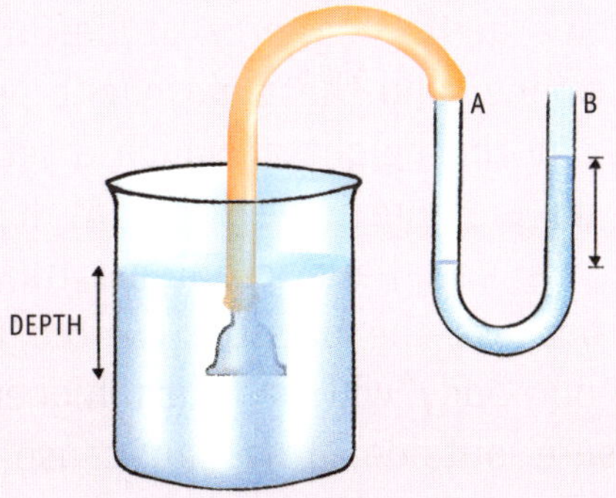


FIG. 11.14 Measuring pressure at different depths

The difference in liquid levels in the U-tube is a measure of the pressure applied by the water.

### Atmospheric pressure

The earth is surrounded by a layer of air called the atmosphere. We live at the bottom of this layer. The air above presses down on us with a force equal to that exerted by a mass of 1 kilogram, on every square centimetre. This is called the **atmospheric pressure**. The reason we are not crushed under this weight is that the pressure exerted by our body is equal (and opposite) to the atmospheric pressure acting on our body, and so cancels the effect of the atmospheric pressure.

Let us understand this phenomenon with a simple example. The area of the palm of your hand is about 100 square centimetres. Thus, a force equal to that exerted by a mass of about 100 kg acts on your palm due to the atmospheric pressure. You cannot feel it because an equal force is acting from within your hand, which balances the force due to the atmospheric pressure, and cancels its effect.

To demonstrate the effect of atmospheric pressure that can act on a surface, we need to remove the air from one side of that surface. This can easily be done, as shown in the activity given below.

**ACTIVITY 13 (Experimental investigation): Air pressure**

Take a rubber sucker. Press it hard against a smooth surface such as a window pane. This expels the air between the sucker and the surface. Now try to pull it away (Fig. 11.15).

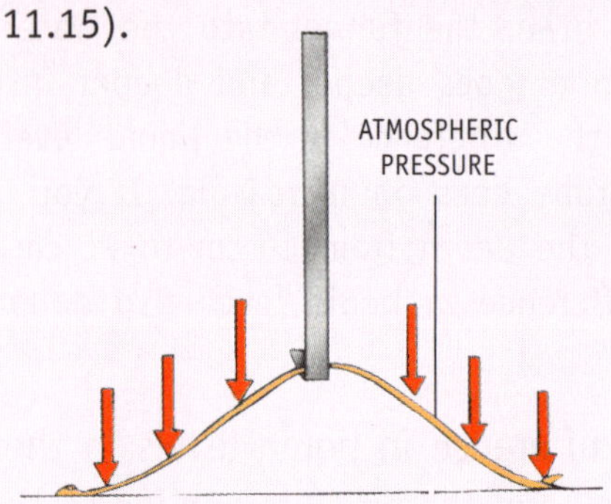


FIG. 11.15 A rubber sucker pressed on a smooth surface

You will have great difficulty in doing so. This can easily be explained. There is very little air between the sucker and the smooth surface of the window pane to push from inside. Therefore, the greater atmospheric pressure from outside pushes the sucker firmly to the window pane.

**IT'S A FACT!**

*We cannot dive more than about 120 m in water. The water pressure below this is enough to crush the human body.*

The following activity also demonstrates how strong atmospheric pressure can be.

**ACTIVITY 14 (Experimental investigation): Atmospheric pressure**

Take a plastic bottle. Put some boiling water in it. The steam coming out of the water will expel most of the air from inside the bottle. After about two minutes, screw the cap tightly on the bottle. Put the bottle in a trough and pour some cold water mixed with ice on it (Fig. 11.16). As the bottle cools down and the steam condenses, what do you observe? Why does the bottle get crushed?

FIG. 11.16 Air exerts pressure in all directions.

Since the steam had expelled most of the air from inside the bottle, and since the steam inside the bottle has also been condensed, the bottle now has very little air inside it. The atmospheric pressure acting on the bottle from outside is, therefore, much larger than the pressure exerted by the air inside it. This causes the bottle to get crushed.

You will see that the bottle gets crushed from all sides. The activity also shows that atmospheric pressure, like the pressure exerted by liquids, acts equally in all directions.

The atmospheric pressure is maximum at sea level. As we go to higher altitudes, the air becomes thinner and the atmospheric pressure decreases. At the height at which a jet plane flies, the air pressure is very low. At such low pressure, we can have problems like nose bleeding because the pressure exerted by the blood in our body will be much higher than the pressure outside. This can cause blood vessels to burst. That is why the pressure inside an aeroplane is maintained at the normal ground level atmospheric pressure.

## ORAL QUESTIONS FOR FORMATIVE ASSESSMENT

1. A force acts perpendicular to a given surface. What is the quantity 'force per unit area' known as?
2. How is pressure related to the area over which a force acts?
3. What is the force of 1 N acting over an area of 1 $m^2$ called?
4. How does the pressure exerted by a liquid vary with a. direction? b. depth?
5. You are put into a room where the air pressure is very low. What effect will this have on your body?

## NOW YOU KNOW

- Pushes and pulls are forces.
- For a force to come into play, objects must interact with each other.
- A force can be described by stating its magnitude and the direction in which it acts.
- When two or more forces act on an object in different directions, the effect on the object is due to the magnitude and direction of the net force acting on it.
- Force can: make a stationary object move or change its position of rest, change the speed of a moving object, change the direction of motion of a moving object, and change the shape or size of an object.
- Muscular force and frictional force are contact forces.
- Friction is the force that slows things down or prevents them from moving.
- Gravitational force, magnetic force and electrostatic force are non-contact forces.
- Gravity is the force with which the earth pulls eyerything towards itself.
- Weight is a measure of the earth's gravitational pull on an object.
- The effect that a contact force has depends on the magnitude of the force and the area over which it acts. The smaller the area of contact, the greater is the effect of the force.
- Pressure is the force exerted per unit area.
- Pressure in a liquid increases with depth, but at the same depth, the pressure exerted is equal in all directions.
- The pressure exerted by air is called atmospheric pressure. It is exerted equally in all directions. It reduces with height above sea level.

## NEW WORDS

**CONTACT FORCE**—a force that acts only when it is in contact with an object

**NON-CONTACT FORCE**—a force that acts on an object without being in contact with it

**MAGNETIC FORCE**—force with which a magnet pulls objects made of certain metals, for example, iron, towards itself

**ELECTROSTATIC FORCE**—force exerted by an object with static electric charge on it

**PRESSURE**—force exerted per unit area

**ATMOSPHERIC PRESSURE**—pressure exerted by the atmosphere on all objects

## FOR FORMATIVE AND SUMMATIVE ASSESSMENT

### A. MULTIPLE-CHOICE QUESTIONS: Choose the most appropriate answer.

1. There is one force which is exerted by all matter on all other matter. Which force is this?
   a. gravitational force
   b. magnetic force
   c. electrostatic force
   d. frictional force
2. Which of these is a contact force?
   a. friction
   b. magnetic force
   c. gravitational force
   d. electrostatic force
3. Which of the following is true for the pressure exerted by a liquid?
   a. Pressure does not depend on depth.
   b. Pressure is only exerted in the downward direction.
   c. Pressure is exerted both downwards and sideways but downwards pressure is greater than sideways pressure.
   d. At the same depth, pressure is same in all directions.
4. The SI unit of pressure is
   a. $kg/m^3$.
   b. $kg/m^2$.
   c. pascal.
   d. newton.
5. Two forces A and B act on an object in opposite directions. A is bigger than B. The net force on the object is
   a. A + B acting in the direction of A.
   b. A – B acting in the direction of A.
   c. A + B acting in the direction of B.
   d. A – B acting in the direction of B.
6. Which of these can a force acting on an object not change?
   a. direction of motion
   b. state of rest
   c. shape
   d. mass
7. The weight of an object is due to
   a. gravitational force.
   b. frictional force.
   c. both gravitational and frictional force.
   d. neither gravitational nor frictional force.
8. A force of 10 N acts on an area of 0.1 $m^2$. The force is kept the same but the area is reduced to half. Which of the following is true?
   a. The pressure does not change.
   b. The pressure reduces to half.
   c. The pressure increases by 1.5 times.
   d. The pressure doubles.

### B. VERY SHORT-ANSWER QUESTIONS: Give one-word answers.

1. All pushes and pulls are forces. True or false?
2. If a force acts on a body it will move in the direction in which the force acts. True or false?
3. A force with magnitude A and another with magnitude B act on an object in the same direction. What is the net force acting on the object?
4. A force with magnitude A and another smaller force with magnitude B act on an object in the opposite directions. What is the net force acting on the object?
5. Does a force acting on a body always cause a change in its state of motion?

6. Only the earth exerts gravitational force on all objects. True or false?
7. What measures the earth's gravitational pull on an object—its weight or mass?
8. This force acts from a distance and affects only objects made of certain metals such as iron. Name the force.
9. Which type of force is exerted by an electrostatic charge?
10. Which force tends to slow down objects or prevent them from moving?
11. The larger the area over which a force acts, the ________ is the pressure.
12. Does pressure exerted by a liquid increase or decrease with depth?
13. Every square centimetre of your body experiences a force equal to the weight of 1 kg due to the atmospheric pressure. True or false?
14. Atmospheric pressure increases with height. True or false?

## C. SHORT-ANSWER QUESTIONS (TYPE I): Answer in a sentence or two.

1. What two things fully describe a force?
2. If several forces act in different directions on a body, in which direction will the body move?
3. If an object is thrown up, it finally comes down. Why?
4. What is the difference between mass and weight?
5. Why can a magnet act from a distance?
6. What is pressure? What does pressure depend on?
7. What is atmospheric pressure? What is it caused by?
8. Why is it difficult to cut vegetables with a blunt knife?

## D. SHORT-ANSWER QUESTIONS (TYPE II): Answer in about 30 words.

1. What is force? What are the four main effects of force?
2. What is the difference between contact and non-contact forces? Explain with the help of one example of each.
3. What is friction? Explain with an example.
4. Why are caterpillar tracks used in battle tanks instead of tyres?
5. How does the pressure exerted by a liquid change with depth? Explain with a diagram.
6. When you press a rubber sucker on a smooth surface, it sticks to the surface. Explain why this happens?

## E. LONG-ANSWER QUESTIONS: Answer in about 60 words.

1. Two forces act on an object. Explain what the net force acting on the object will be in different situations.
2. Explain the effects that a force acting on an object can have on the object.
3. Describe an experiment to show that air exerts pressure in all directions.

## HOTS Questions: Think and answer.

1. If a body is moving with uniform speed in a particular direction on a perfectly smooth surface, then no force is acting on it. True or false? Explain.
2. If you use a stick to push an object, the muscular force acting on the object is a non-contact force since your body is not in contact with the object. True or false? Explain.
3. Gravitational force exists between you and a building. Why are you not pulled towards the building?
4. Why do you think it is necessary to define a separate quantity called pressure? Why is defining only force not enough?
5. Suppose you are going in a jet plane, and one of the windows breaks due to an accident. What problems do you think you will face?
6. If you press a rubber sucker on a rough surface, it does not stick to the surface. Why?

## FOR FORMATIVE ASSESSMENT*

### In the Library—Research Project

A beam of light is also affected by gravity. But the effect is so small that it cannot normally be observed. However, there are certain bodies in outer space which are very dense. Gravity on these bodies is so high that no object, not even light, is able to escape from their surfaces. So these bodies cannot be seen or detected by any scientific instrument since they cannot reflect light. The presence of these bodies can only be detected by the effect of their gravity on nearby stars. For example, if a massive star is seen revolving around with no visible star at the centre of its orbit, then we can assume the presence of this body at the centre of the orbit. Find out the names of these bodies. The presence of these bodies was predicted by an Indian-born scientist. Find out his name.

Visit rsgr.in/lsc-cce-8 and click on LINK 45 to find out more about these objects.

### My Virtual Library—Research/Activities on the Internet

- Visit rsgr.in/lsc-cce-8 and click on LINK 46 to get tutorial on force and pressure.
- Visit rsgr.in/lsc-cce-8 and click on LINK 47 to investigate the difference between weight and mass—find your weight on different planets and stars.
- Visit rsgr.in/lsc-cce-8 and click on LINK 48 to design your own roller coaster using principles used to design actual roller coasters.

### To Meet—Research on Scientist

**Sir Isaac Newton** (1642–1727) was one of the greatest scientists who ever lived. He was a mathematician and physicist. Many theories of modern science are based on the laws that he discovered.

Newton was born in Woolsthorpe in England. In 1669, at the age of 27, he became Professor of Mathematics. In 1686, he published his famous book *The Mathematical Principles of Natural Philosophy* in which he presented his theory of gravitation and the laws of motion. His **theory of gravitation** says that all matter pulls all other matter towards itself. Newton studied moving objects and gave the famous **laws of motion**.

*For more tasks see Page 200

Newton invented the **mirror telescope**, which overcame some defects of telescopes in use at that time. Many of our present-day telescopes are based on his design.

Newton, along with another mathematician Leibniz, is considered to be the father of a very important branch of mathematics called **calculus**.

Find out more about the life and work of Newton.

### Talk to the Class—Presentation

Make a presentation on the life of Sir Isaac Newton and his numerous contributions to the progress of science.

## LIFE SKILL

**Lifting a heavy weight**

A number of back injuries happen when trying to lift heavy loads. Lifting a load causes considerable stress on the muscles and ligaments that support the spine, and exert pressure on the discs. To reduce the danger of injuries to your back, follow these precautions.

- Stand close to the load. Centre yourself and put your feet apart to the same length as your shoulders. Tighten your abdominal muscles. Carefully lift up on one edge of the object to get an idea of how heavy it is. If the object seems too heavy, it is not advisable to lift it yourself.
- Bend your knees and squat down to reach for the load **while keeping your back as straight as possible**. The most common mistake people make is to bend their back while getting hold of the load.
- While lifting the load, maintain a straight back and keep the load close to your body. Begin applying force with your legs and arms. Do this slowly. If you give a sudden hard pull or jerk, you could injure your back.
- While placing the load down, bend through your knees and keep a straight back.

bend your knees, not your back while lifting a heavy object

SKILLS INVOLVED: Thinking skill, Self-preservation

12

# Friction

## WHAT IS FRICTION?

You have already read about the force of friction. Now, we will learn more about this force which we experience in many of our activities in daily life. Roll a ball on the ground. Does it come to rest after some time?

This shows that some force must be acting on the ball, which makes the ball slow down. This force is called the **force of friction**. Hence, it is obvious that this force must be acting in a direction opposite to the direction of motion of the ball. So, force of friction tries to stop a moving object.

What else can the force of friction do? Let us see in the following activity.

### Activity 1 (Experimental investigation)

Push a heavy box and try to move it from left to right. Does it move when you apply

Fig. 12.1 Friction prevents movement until the force applied is greater than the force of friction.

**IN THIS CHAPTER**

WHAT IS FRICTION? ◆ WHAT CAUSES FRICTION? ◆ ADVANTAGES AND DISADVANTAGES OF FRICTION ◆ MINIMIZING AND INCREASING FRICTION ◆ FLUID FRICTION

a small force on it? Now increase the force until it starts moving.

Now push the box from the opposite side and try to move it from right to left. Are your observations the same as before?

What prevents the box from moving initially? It is the force of friction. You have to apply sufficient force to overcome friction before the box starts moving. Here also, the force of friction acts in a direction opposite to the direction in which the object tends to move. If you push from left to right, the force of friction acts from right to left. If you push from right to left, the force of friction acts from left to right.

The above two activities show that the force of friction always opposes the motion of an object.

- It tends to stop a moving object.
- It also tends to prevent a stationary object from moving.

We can therefore define friction as: Friction is a force that slows down moving objects or prevents stationary objects from moving.

## WHAT CAUSES FRICTION?

You have seen that friction is a contact force. It acts when one surface moves or tries to move over another surface.

Observe the surface of a table with a powerful magnifying lens. You will notice that it is rough and has very small irregularities in the form of grooves and ridges. You can see the grooves and ridges more clearly on very rough surfaces such as that of sandpaper. When one surface moves over another, these grooves and ridges get caught up with each other and slow down the motion. This causes friction.

This means that smoother a surface is, the lesser will be the friction on it. To see if this is true, we will need to measure the force of friction. We can easily do this by using a spring balance.

### SPRING BALANCE

Spring balance is a device that measures force. It uses the principle that the greater the force, the greater is the extension that the force produces in a coiled spring. It consists of a coiled spring with a pointer attached to it. As the spring is stretched, the pointer moves on a graduated scale. The reading on the scale gives the magnitude of the force.

### ACTIVITY 2 (Making a model): Friction tester

Tie a strong string around a brick and attach the other end of the brick to a spring balance. Your 'friction tester' is ready.

Keep the brick on a rough surface such as a carpet. Pull the spring balance until the brick just starts to move. Note the reading on the spring balance. This gives an idea of the force of friction between the two surfaces. Now keep the brick on a smooth surface such as a smooth table. Pull the spring balance and take the reading when the brick just starts to move.

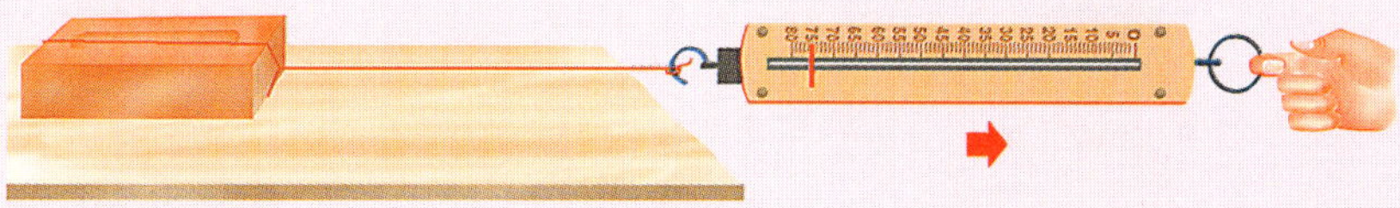

FIG. 12.2 Friction tester

In which case is the reading more? Why?

Test other surfaces with your friction tester. You can also test different materials such as paper or polythene for friction by wrapping the brick in it and then testing it on a smooth surface.

Do you understand now why a ball rolled on a smooth surface will travel a longer distance before coming to rest, than when rolled over a rough surface?

Figure 12.3 a. and b. show microscopic views of contact between two types of surfaces.

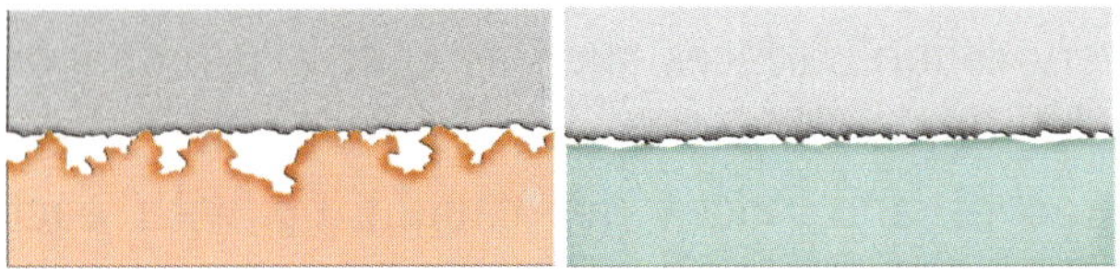

a. Contact between a smooth surface and a rough surface

b. Contact between two smooth surfaces

FIG. 12.3 Microscopic views of surfaces in contact

**ACTIVITY 3 (Experimental investigation): Dependence of friction on how hard the surfaces press together**

Test the friction of the floor in your class using a brick and your friction tester. Now ask a friend to press down on the brick and test again. Do you find now that the friction is more? Why?

The friction is more when you press down because the interlocking of irregularities (between the surfaces of the brick and the floor) increases when you press the two surfaces harder together.

### ORAL QUESTIONS FOR FORMATIVE ASSESSMENT

1. Does friction always oppose motion?
2. A surface is rubbed to make it smoother. What effect will this have on friction? Give reasons.
3. Two surfaces are rubbed together, first with a small force and then with a greater force. In which case will the friction between the surfaces be higher? Give reasons.

## FRICTION IN DAILY LIFE

### Advantages of friction

- It would be impossible for us to walk without friction. It is because of friction between our feet or shoes and the ground that we are able to walk by pushing our feet against the ground. Without friction, we would slip as soon as we tried to walk. It is very difficult to walk on ice or on a very smooth and polished floor. This is because the friction between our shoes and these surfaces is very little.

FIG. 12.4 Walking on a floor with little friction is difficult.

- Cars and buses are able to move safely on the road because of friction between the treaded tyres and the surface of the road.

FIG. 12.5 Treaded tyre of a bus

**IT'S A FACT!**

Tyres of ordinary cars have grooves to increase friction with the road, so that the car does not skid on the road. However, tyres of racing cars are smooth to reduce friction so that they can go faster. Such tyres are called **slicks**.

- Brakes on cycles or cars work because of friction. When brakes are applied, the 'shoes' of the brakes rub against the wheels. The friction between them reduces the speed.
- It would not be possible to light a matchstick by rubbing it against the matchbox if there was no friction.
- You would not be able to write on paper without friction between the pencil or pen and paper. Neither could your teacher write on the blackboard.
- Friction causes nails and screws to hold on to walls.

### Disadvantages of friction

- Friction causes **wastage of energy**. This is because any object that moves, has to overcome the force of friction.
- Friction **wears out the rubbing surfaces**. The soles of your shoes wear out in a few months due to friction. The moving parts of a machine wear out with time because of friction.
- Friction **generates heat**. Sometimes this can be harmful. The heat produced in a fast-moving machine is very high. Proper arrangements have to be made to cool the machine, otherwise it can get damaged. If the cooling arrangement in a car does not work properly, the engine can get jammed.

### Minimizing friction

Since friction is due to roughness of surfaces, any process that makes the contact surfaces smooth will reduce friction.

- **By polishing:** Polishing a rough surface smoothens it and reduces friction.
- **By lubrication:** Friction is decreased by lubricating surfaces with oil, grease or graphite. The sliding surfaces then have a thin layer of the lubricant between them. The friction is then between the surfaces and the lubricant layer which is much less. Graphite is used as a lubricant in machines where the moving parts reach very high temperatures.

  While playing carrom, you put fine talcum powder on the carrom board to reduce friction.
- **By streamlining to reduce fluid friction:** Fluids such as water and air also exert friction on objects moving through them. This frictional force that fluids exert on objects is called **drag**. It depends on the nature of the fluid, the shape of the object and the speed of the object with respect to the fluid. Friction is minimum for a streamlined shape, which is rounded in the front and narrow at the back. Nature has given birds and fish streamlined bodies. The bodies of aeroplanes, missiles, rockets, cars are streamlined to reduce friction with air, called **air resistance**. Ships also have streamlined shapes to reduce friction with water.
- **By using wheels and ball bearings—rolling friction:** When a spherical or cylindrical object rolls on a surface, the resistance it encounters is called **rolling friction**. The resistance that an object encounters when it slides over a surface is called **sliding friction**. It is easier to roll an object than to slide it. Rolling friction is therefore less than sliding friction. That is why vehicles are equipped with wheels. You must have also seen luggage equipped with wheels. It is much easier to roll along the luggage with you than to carry or slide it.

## Activity 4 (Experimental investigation): To show that rolling friction is less than sliding friction

Measure the friction on a table top by using your friction tester as in Activity 2. Now put some round pencils below the brick and test again. What do you find? Has the friction reduced now?

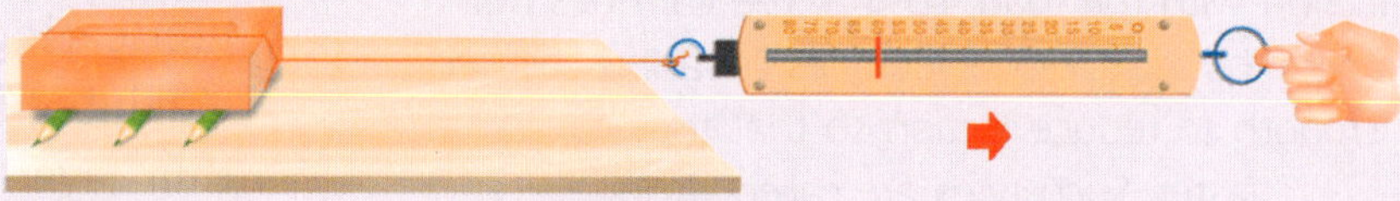

Fig. 12.6 Rolling friction

The principle that rolling friction is less than sliding friction is also made use of in ball bearings which contain steel balls or rollers. Ball bearings used between the wheel and axle of a car reduce friction considerably. Most machines with moving parts use ball bearings.

Fig. 12.7 Ball bearings

However, it is not possible to reduce friction to zero, as no surface is absolutely smooth.

### Increasing friction

It is sometimes desirable to increase friction to avoid slipping. Friction can be increased by making the surfaces rough.

- Tyres have designs and patterns with grooves on the surface to increase friction with the road. This prevents slipping of the tyres on a wet road.
- Sand and gravel is strewn on slippery ground during the rainy season to increase friction. It is then easier to walk on the ground.
- Spikes are provided in the soles of shoes used by players and athletes to increase friction so that they get a firm grip on the ground.
- Gymnasts apply a coarse substance on their hands to improve their grip.

## ORAL QUESTIONS FOR FORMATIVE ASSESSMENT

1. Since friction slows us down, we can run very fast if friction is eliminated. Do you agree? Give reasons.
2. It was found that a machine with moving parts was getting overheated. What was the heat due to? How can the heat generated be reduced?
3. Does air exert friction on an object moving through it?

## NOW YOU KNOW

- Friction is a force that slows things down or prevents things from moving.
- Friction occurs due to interlocking of irregularities in the surfaces.
- Friction is a necessary evil as several activities cannot be done without friction.
- Friction wastes energy, wears out the rubbing surfaces and generates heat.
- Friction is minimised by polishing, lubrication, streamlining, and by using wheels and ball bearings.
- In some cases, it is necessary to increase friction.

## NEW WORDS

**SLIDING FRICTION**—friction encountered by an object when it slides on a surface

**ROLLING FRICTION**—friction encountered by a spherical or cylindrical object rolling on a surface

## FOR FORMATIVE AND SUMMATIVE ASSESSMENT

### A. MULTIPLE-CHOICE QUESTIONS: Choose the most appropriate answer.

1. Friction is
   a. always a disadvantage.
   b. always an advantage.
   c. sometimes a disadvantage and sometimes an advantage.
   d. neither a disadvantage nor an advantage.
2. It is difficult to walk on ice because
   a. pressure is high.
   b. pressure is low.
   c. friction is high.
   d. friction is low.
3. Friction can be increased by
   a. making the surfaces smooth.
   b. lubricating the surfaces.
   c. using ball bearings.
   d. making the surfaces rough.
4. Which of these is true about friction?
   a. It can stop a moving object.
   b. It can change the shape of an object.
   c. It can change the direction of a moving object.
   d. It can make a moving object move faster.
5. In which case is friction a disadvantage?
   a. running a machine
   b. walking
   c. applying brakes
   d. writing
6. Ball bearings are useful because
   a. rolling friction is more than sliding friction.
   b. rolling friction is less than sliding friction.
   c. rolling friction is same as sliding friction.
   d. it is easier to apply grease to ball bearings to reduce friction.

### B. VERY SHORT-ANSWER QUESTIONS: Give one-word answers.

1. Friction always opposes ____________
2. Friction is caused by ____________ on the surfaces in contact.
3. Is friction a contact or a non-contact force?
4. The smoother a surface is, the ____________ (greater / lesser) will be the friction.
5. Brakes on cars will work best if the friction between the brake shoes and wheels is reduced. True or false?

6. Friction causes wastage of energy. True or false?
7. A machine with moving parts will become less hot while running if it is well lubricated. True or false?
8. Friction due to fluids is called __________
9. Rolling friction is __________ (greater / smaller) than sliding friction.
10. To reduce fluid friction, the object should have a __________ shape.

## C. SHORT-ANSWER QUESTIONS (TYPE I): Answer in a sentence or two.

1. What is friction?
2. An object is moving from north to south. What is the direction of the force of friction on the object?
3. On what principle do ball bearings work?
4. How does lubrication reduce friction?
5. Give an example to show the effect of heat generated in a machine due to excessive friction.

## D. SHORT-ANSWER QUESTIONS (TYPE II): Answer in about 30 words.

1. What is the effect of friction on motion?
2. What causes friction between two surfaces in contact?
3. Why does a rough surface have greater friction than a smooth surface?
4. Give two situations where it is desirable to increase friction.
5. What is 'streamlining'? How is it useful?

## E. LONG-ANSWER QUESTIONS: Answer in about 60 words.

1. Discuss three situations in daily life where friction is an advantage?
2. Explain with examples the disadvantages of friction.
3. Explain four methods by which friction between two solid surfaces in contact can be reduced.

## HOTS QUESTIONS: Think and answer.

1. If there was no friction, what would happen to a moving object?
2. When you rub your hands together, they become warm. What is this due to?
3. If you try to hold a glass with oil on your hands, it tends to slip. Why?
4. Why do you think rolling friction is less than sliding friction?
5. Friction is a necessary evil. Explain.

## FOR FORMATIVE ASSESSMENT*

### In the Library—Research Project

Friction produces sound. Some of these sounds are pleasant and some are annoying. Make a list of both these kinds of sounds around you.

*For more tasks see Page 200

## My Virtual Library—Research/Activities on the Internet

- Visit rsgr.in/lsc-cce-8 and click on LINK 49 for a tutorial on friction.
- Visit rsgr.in/lsc-cce-8 and click on LINK 50 to try an activity on friction on different kinds of surfaces.
- Visit rsgr.in/lsc-cce-8 and click on LINK 51 for experiments with friction on a road.

## In the Laboratory—Designing an Experiment

### Investigate friction

**You will need** ◆ a smooth piece of plywood ◆ a wooden block ◆ a protractor ◆ test surfaces such as plastic, metal foil, sandpaper

**Procedure:**

- Keep the plywood piece on a table. Keep the wooden block over one end of the plywood piece. Lift that end slowly, keeping the other end secure with your hand. Lift until the wooden block just starts moving.
- Ask a friend to measure the angle the plywood piece makes with the table surface using a protractor. The angle will give an idea of the friction between the block and the plywood. The greater the friction, the greater will be the angle at which the block starts moving.

- Secure the test surfaces over the plywood piece one by one and note the angles at which the wooden block just starts moving over them. List the surfaces in order of increasing friction.
- To study the effect of lubricants such as oil or grease, smear the plywood surface with the lubricant and repeat the experiments. What do you find?

## LIFE SKILL

### Making cycling easier

You can make cycling easier by reducing the different kinds of friction you encounter while cycling—sliding and rolling friction, and air resistance acting on the bicycle and on you.

- To reduce friction in the bicycle, put oil on the chain and on the gears.
- To reduce air resistance on the bicycle, polish your bicycle so that it has a smoother surface.
- To reduce air resistance on yourself:
  - Bend forward while cycling—this reduces the area of contact between you and the air, and hence reduces air resistance. This is why cyclists in a race are always bent forward.
  - Wear shorts and shirt made of very smooth, slick material—this has the effect of making your body smoother and hence reduces air resistance (note the dress worn by cyclists in races).

SKILLS INVOLVED: Thinking skill, Preservation skill

13

# Sound

You hear sounds of various types around you every day. Some of them, like the sound of thunder, are loud; others, like the rustling of leaves are soft. Some sounds, like those of a whistle are shrill; while others, such as the beating of drums are dull.

Some sounds, such as those produced by a guitar are pleasant; while others, such as the sound produced by a drilling machine are unpleasant.

Each sound has its own characteristics. It is because of these that we can recognize different sounds.

Sound helps us to communicate. It is difficult to communicate with each other without talking. Several animals also communicate with each other through sounds.

## HOW SOUND IS PRODUCED

To understand this, try this simple activity using a rubber band.

**ACTIVITY 1 (Experimental investigation): Sound and vibration I**

Tie one end of a rubber band to a nail in a wall and pull the other end. Now pluck the rubber band, at a point near its middle, with your finger (Fig. 13.1). Does it make a sound? Can you see the rubber band vibrate?

**IN THIS CHAPTER**

HOW SOUND IS PRODUCED AND ITS CHARACTERISTICS ◆ HOW SOUND TRAVELS ◆ FUNCTIONING OF THE HUMAN EAR ◆ REFLECTION AND ABSORPTION OF SOUND ◆ MUSICAL SOUND AND NOISE

FIG. 13.1 The rapid to-and-fro movement of a rubber band produces sound.

FIG. 13.2 Striking a frying pan with a spoon produces a sound.

Notice that the rubber band moves to-and-fro rapidly when plucked. If you stop the to-and-fro movements with your fingers, the sound also stops. These rapid to-and-fro movements are called **vibrations**. This activity suggests that **sound is produced by vibrations**.

In the same way, the wires of a guitar also vibrate when you pluck them. The wires appear hazy while vibrating.

Hang a frying pan from its handle using a string at a convenient place, so that it does not touch the wall. Strike it hard with a spoon so that a sound is emitted (Fig. 13.2). Touch the pan gently with your fingers. Do you feel the vibrations in the pan?

In a laboratory, a tuning fork is used to produce sound for experiments. It has a handle and two prongs (Fig. 13.3a). When one of the prongs is struck, both prongs vibrate to produce sound (Fig. 13.3b). If you touch the surface of water in a bowl with one of the vibrating prongs of the tuning fork, you will see waves produced in the water by the vibrating prong (Fig. 13.3c).

**ACTIVITY 2 (Experimental investigation): Sound and vibration II**

Hang a table-tennis ball by a thread. Wait for a few minutes till it comes to rest. Then touch it with one of the prongs of a vibrating tuning fork (Fig. 13.3d). Does the ball fly away? Why?

Sound is produced not only by vibrations in strings but also by vibrations in stretched skins or membranes, as well as by vibrations in air columns. In a *tabla* or drum, sound is produced when you strike the stretched skin. When you blow over the mouth of an empty bottle, sound is produced due to vibration of the air column in the bottle.

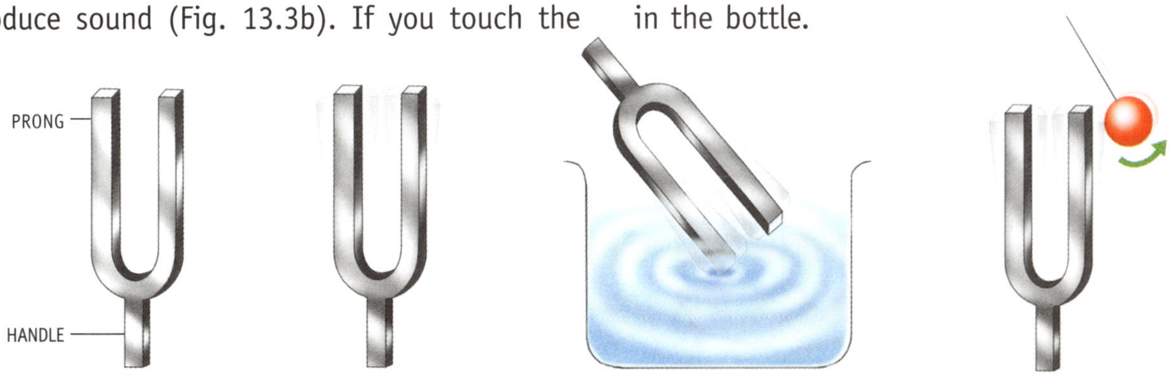


a. A tuning fork

b. Vibrations of prongs

c. The vibrating prongs produce ripples in water.

d. The vibrating prongs cause a table tennis ball to fly away.

FIG. 13.3 Effects of vibrations produced by a tuning fork

### Vibrations or oscillations

In an object producing sound, the vibrations are so rapid that they cannot be observed properly. You can produce slower vibrations, also called **oscillations**, by hanging a ball from a thread. This arrangement is called a **pendulum** (Fig. 13.4). If you give the ball a push, it performs slow to-and-fro movements or oscillations about the central position. These oscillations slowly get reduced and the ball ultimately comes to rest in the central position.

### Amplitude

The oscillations of the ball about the central position are small if you give the ball a small push. If you give the ball a stronger push, the oscillations are larger. The maximum distance by which the ball moves away from its central position is called the amplitude of the oscillation (Fig. 13.4).

### Time period

The time taken for one complete to-and-fro movement, i.e. the distance covered by the ball as it moves from the central position O to the extreme position A, back to O, then to the extreme position B on the other side, and then back to O, is one oscillation of the pendulum (Fig. 13.4).

It is difficult to measure the time for a single oscillation. Therefore, if you measure the time taken for 10 oscillations and divide the total time by 10, it will give you the time taken for one oscillation. Also if you take several readings of the time taken for 10 oscillations for different amplitudes, you will find that the time for one oscillation remains the same, no matter what the amplitudes.

The time taken by the pendulum for one oscillation is called the time period of the pendulum. It remains fixed as long as the length of the pendulum does not change.

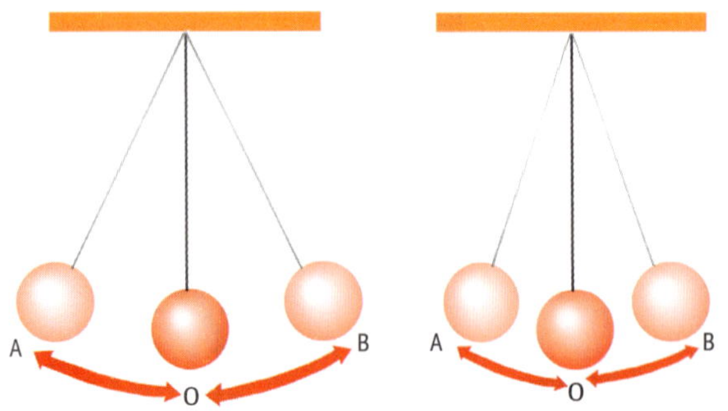


a. Large amplitude    b. Small amplitude

FIG. 13.4 A pendulum oscillates about a central position.

### Frequency

If you count the number of oscillations of a pendulum in, say, 60 seconds and divide the number by 60, it will give you **the number of oscillations per second**. This is called the **frequency of oscillation**. For a pendulum of given length, the frequency remains constant. Frequency is measured in **hertz (Hz)**. If the pendulum makes 5 oscillations every second, its frequency is 5 hertz.

## CHARACTERISTICS OF SOUND

We can recognize most of the sounds without seeing the objects that produce them. This is because all those sounds are different from each other. Have you ever thought what factors make each sound different?

### Loudness and pitch

The factors which make sounds different from each other are called characteristics of sound. Let us study about them further.

#### ACTIVITY 3 (Experimental investigation): Amplitude and loudness of sound

Go back to Activity 1. Pluck the rubber band softly—it produces a soft sound. Pluck it hard—it vibrates with a greater amplitude now and produces a louder sound.

Similarly, if you strike a drum softly, it produces a soft sound. If you strike it hard, its skin vibrates with greater amplitude and a louder sound is produced. This shows that loudness of the sound produced by a vibrating object depends on the amplitude of vibration. Loudness is proportional to the square of the amplitude. This means that if the amplitude is doubled, the loudness increases four times.

**ACTIVITY 4 (Experimental investigation): Frequency of vibration and pitch of sound**

Stretch the rubber band of Activity 1 only slightly and strike it. It will produce a dull sound. Pull it hard and strike it again. A more shrill sound will be produced. Observe the vibrations carefully in the two cases. You may be able to make out that the rubber band vibrates faster when producing a shrill sound than when producing a dull sound.

Thus, the shrillness of sound, called its **pitch**, depends on the frequency of vibration. The higher the frequency, the more shrill is the sound. A shrill sound is said to have a higher pitch than a dull sound.

A woman's voice generally has a higher pitch than a man's voice. This is because the frequency of a woman's voice is higher. The thinner wires of a guitar or *sitar* give out sound of higher pitch than the thicker wires. The thin wires vibrate with greater frequency than the thick wires. Also a guitar wire vibrates with higher frequency if tightened further. This is

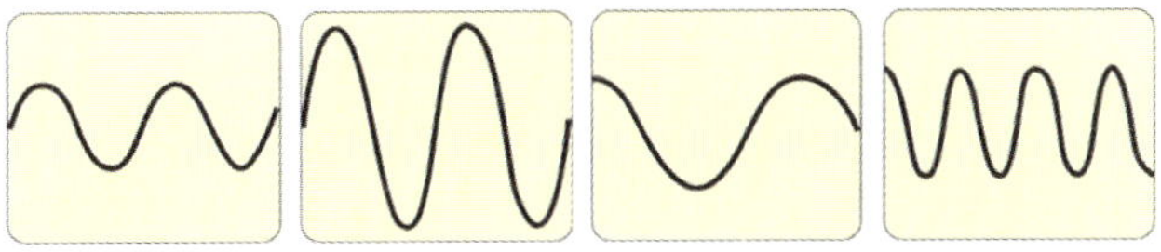

a. Softer sound—low amplitude　b. Louder sound—high amplitude　c. Dull sound—low frequency　d. Shrill sound—high frequency

FIG. 13.5 Representation of sound

true for the skin of a *tabla* also. If you tighten the skin, it produces sound of higher pitch.

### Quality

If the vibrating strings of a *sitar* and a guitar are adjusted to give the same pitch and loudness, we can still distinguish their sound from one another. This is due to another characteristic of sound known as its **quality**. Studies show that most vibrating objects do not generate sound of just one frequency. They also simultaneously generate sounds of other frequencies.

When a note is played on a *sitar*, it produces the 'basic' sound of a certain frequency, called the **fundamental**. Along with it, it produces a mixture of sounds of other frequencies, each differing in loudness. These are called **harmonics**. If the same note is played on a guitar, the fundamental will be the same but the harmonics and their relative loudness will be different. That is why you can distinguish a note played on a *sitar* from the same note played on a guitar.

Thus, the quality of a sound is determined by the frequencies present in it and their relative loudness.

## ORAL QUESTIONS FOR FORMATIVE ASSESSMENT

1. What is the difference between an object vibrating to produce a soft sound and the same object vibrating to produce a loud sound?
2. If you want sound of higher pitch, what characteristic of sound do you have to change?
3. Sound of the same frequency and loudness played on a *sitar* and guitar are different. What causes this difference?

## HOW SOUND TRAVELS

When an object vibrates, it makes the adjacent air molecules vibrate with the same frequency. These, in turn, transfer their vibrations to the neighbouring molecules, and this process goes on (Fig. 13.6a). Thus, vibrations travel all around from the vibrating object. This is similar to the way ripples produced in water by a stone spread in the pond. Just as the ripples die out after some distance, the air vibrations also die out after travelling some distance. The greater the amplitude of vibration, i.e. the louder the sound, the greater is the distance it will travel before dying out.

### How we hear sound

Our ears are sensory organs that help us to hear sound (Fig. 13.6b). Only one of its parts can be seen and felt by you—the outer ear. The rest of the delicate ear is buried deep inside the skull.

- **Outer ear:** It consists of the **pinna** and the **eartube**. The **eardrum** is a tightly stretched membrane that separates the outer ear from the middle ear.
- **Middle ear:** It consists of three very **tiny interlocked bones**. The innermost bone is connected to the inner ear through a tiny window.
- **Inner ear:** It consists of a **coiled organ of hearing**, **semicircular canals**, which are organs of balance, and the **auditory nerve**.

A vibrating object causes air molecules to vibrate. When these vibrations reach our ear, they are collected by the pinna and funnelled into the eartube.

These then strike the eardrum, which starts vibrating with the same frequency. This causes the delicate bones of the middle ear to vibrate. This stimulates tiny hairs in the hearing organ which, in turn, send a signal to the auditory nerve of our nervous system. The auditory nerve takes the signal to the brain and we can then hear the sound.

**ACTIVITY 5 (Making a model): Eardrum**

Take a sturdy plastic glass. Cut off its bottom. Stretch a rubber balloon tightly across this end and tie it with a string.

FIG. 13.7 Eardrum vibrates in the same way

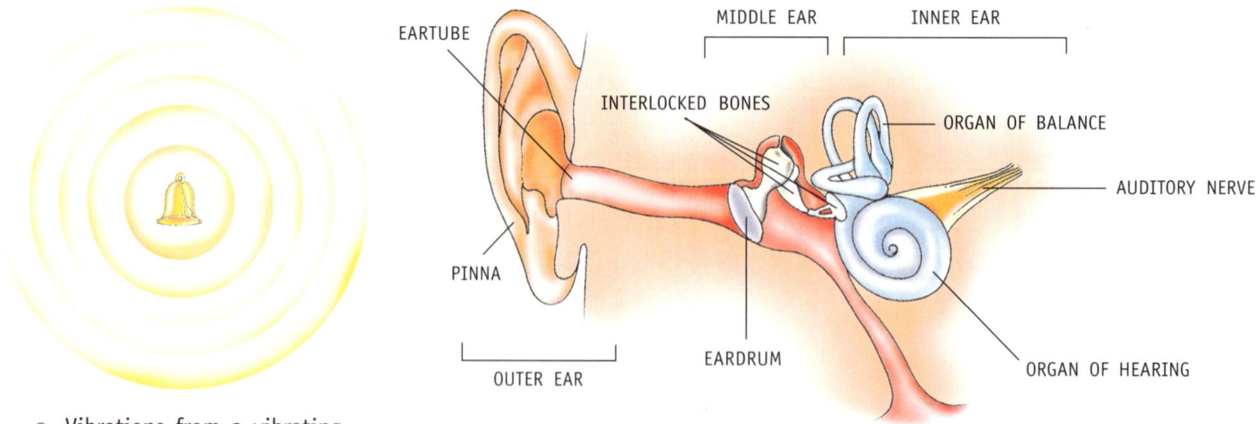


a. Vibrations from a vibrating object travel all around.

b. The human ear

FIG. 13.6 How sound is produced, travels and is heard

Place a few grains of rice on the stretched balloon. Place the glass above a cellphone (Fig 13.7). Call the number of the cellphone so that it rings. Do the rice grains jump up and down when this cellphone rings? This shows that the stretched rubber balloon vibrates when sound falls on it from the ringing cellphone. The eardrum vibrates in the same way.

**IT'S A FACT!**

Never put any hard or sharp thing inside your ear. It can damage your eardrum and affect your hearing.

## Audible and inaudible sounds

Our ears can only hear sounds with frequencies between about 20 hertz and 20,000 hertz. Low frequency sounds which we cannot hear are called **infrasonics**. It is a boon that we cannot hear infrasonics, otherwise we would have heard even the sounds produced by our muscles and by our body movements. Objects that vibrate at frequencies of above 20,000 hertz produce sound which also cannot be heard by us. Such sounds are called **ultrasonics**.

However, some animals, such as dogs, can hear sounds of frequency above 20,000 hertz also.

Technology has made use of ultrasonics in many ways. It is used to form images of organs inside the body. For example, ultrasonics are used to study the growth of the foetus in the uterus of a woman. They are also used to detect flaws in metals and structures.

## Sound requires a medium to travel

We have read that for sound to travel to our ears from a vibrating object, it is necessary to have molecules that can vibrate in the space in between the ear and the object. That is, for sound to travel, it is necessary to have a medium between the vibrating object and the ear.

**ACTIVITY 6 (Experimental investigation): Does sound require a medium to travel?**

Take a container with a tight closing lid. Make a hole at the bottom of the container. Connect a vacuum pump to this hole with a rubber tube. The vacuum pump is used to extract air from the container.

Put a cellphone inside the container and close it with the lid. Call the number of the cellphone so that it rings. You can hear the sound clearly. Now start the vacuum pump and extract the air from the container. Call the number of the cellphone again. Can you hear the sound now?

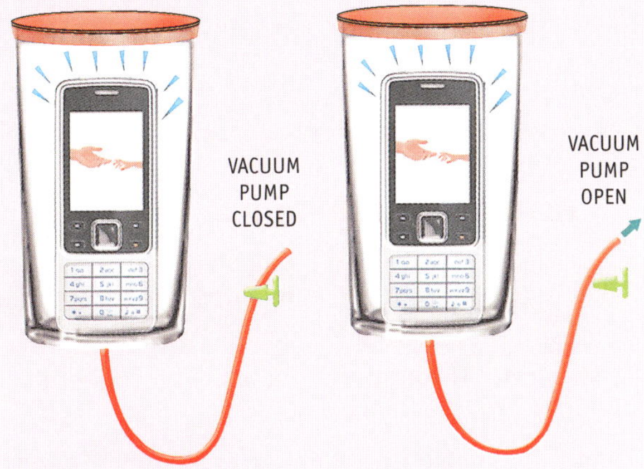


a. Ring heard b. Ring is not heard

FIG. 13.8 Sound requires a medium to travel.

You will notice that as the air gets sucked out from the container by the vacuum pump, the sound reaching you becomes more and more faint.

Ultimately, you may not be able to hear the sound at all. This happens when there is no air present in the container. This shows that sound cannot travel through vacuum. Sound, therefore, requires a medium to travel.

**ACTIVITY 7 (Experimental investigation): Can sound travel through a solid medium?**

Keep one of your ears against one end of your desk. Close the other ear firmly with the palm of your hand. Tell a friend to tap the desk at the other end with his hand (Fig. 13.9). Can your hear the tapping sound? Is it loud or soft?

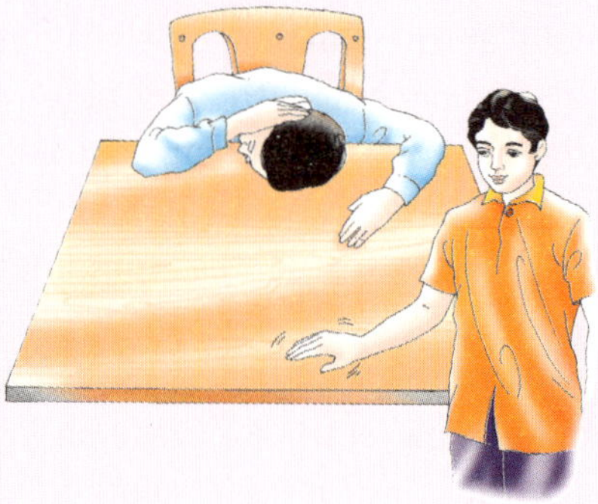

FIG. 13.9 Sound can travel through solids.

You will be able to hear the sound loud and clear. The sound has travelled to your ear through the desk. This shows that sound can travel through solids also.

**ACTIVITY 8 (Making a model): Toy telephone**

Take two empty ice cream cups. Make small holes in the bottom of each. Pass the ends of a string through the holes. Tie the ends to matchsticks to hold them in place. Ask a friend to speak into one of the cups. Stand away so that the string is stretched and put the second cup to your ear. Can you hear your friend through the cup? In this case, sound travels through the string.

FIG. 13.10 Sound can travel through a string.

**ACTIVITY 9: To show that sound can travel through a liquid medium**

Do this experiment in a tub filled with water. Hold a bell in one hand and dip it in water. Keep one of your ears (caution: water should not enter your ear) gently on the surface of water and ring the bell inside the water. Can you hear the bell? What does this show?

FIG. 13.11 Sound can travel through liquids.

You will be able to hear the sound clearly. This shows that sound can travel through liquids also.

We find that sound requires a medium to travel, which can be solid, liquid or gas.

## SPEED OF SOUND

The speed of sound in air at 20 °C is about 340 metres per second. This means that if you shout, your friend standing 340 metres away from you would hear your shout after 1 second.

In solids and liquids, the molecules are closer than they are in air. So, the vibrations are transferred faster to other molecules in solids and liquids than in air. Therefore, the speed of sound is maximum in solids, lesser in liquids and minimum in gases. In fact, sound travels at a speed of about 1500 m/s in water and at 5000 m/s in steel, but as you have already read, at 340 m/s in air.

Compare the speed of sound in air to the speed of light which is 3,00,000 kilometres per second! You will realize that sound takes about

3 seconds to travel 1 km, where light travels that distance in almost no time. Observe a person about 200 metres away from you using a hammer. You will find that the sound of the hammer reaches you a fraction of a second after it strikes.

When a storm is raging, thunder and lightning occur at the same time in the clouds. However, you will hear the thunder a few seconds after you see the lightning.

Both these phenomena happen because light reaches you almost instantly, while sound takes some time to travel and reach to you.

**IT'S A FACT!**

Sound travels faster in water than in air. It also loses its energy much more slowly in water. Therefore, sound can travel much greater distances in water than in air. Whales and dolphins use sound to communicate even when they are hundreds of kilometres away from each other.

## REFLECTION AND ABSORPTION OF SOUND

### The echo

Sound can be reflected or absorbed. These properties of sound have many applications in our daily activities.

You must all be familiar with the echo. It is simply the reflection of sound by a hill or a large building some distance away. Sound is reflected from a surface in the same way as a ball bounces from a wall.

Surfaces reflect sound, whether they are far or near. Why, then, do we hear an echo only from a surface which is far away? This is because if the echo reaches your ears very quickly, then ears are not able to distinguish it as a separate sound. In fact, your ears are able to distinguish two sounds as separate sounds only if the second sound is received after 1/10th of a second or more after the first sound.

The speed of sound in air is about 340 m/s.

FIG. 13.12 The echo of a sound is heard if the reflecting surface is more than 17 m away.

Therefore, distance travelled by sound in $\frac{1}{10}$ second = speed × time

$$= 340 \text{ m/s} \times \left(\frac{1}{10}\right) \text{ s} = 34 \text{ m}$$

Therefore, as shown in Figure 13.12, the echo can be heard by the girl only if she is at a distance of more than 17 m from the wall.

### Sound absorption

Have you ever tried to speak to someone in a completely empty, unfurnished room? Why is it difficult to hear each other's voice clearly? This is because the sound gets reflected again and again by the walls of the room. Therefore, any sound takes a long time to die out. When you speak, the sounds overlap each other and it is difficult to tell them apart. However, this does not happen if the same room has curtains and furniture. Why? Obviously, curtains and furniture absorb sound.

Just like heat or light, when sound falls on a surface, it is partly reflected and partly absorbed. Walls of a room are good reflectors of sound. Wood, carpets, curtains, clothes and even our bodies are poor reflectors of sound, but absorb sound better. In fact, soft surfaces are better absorbers of sound whereas hard surfaces are better reflectors of sound.

Sound absorbing material is used in walls of auditoriums to stop undue reflection. It is also used in offices, aeroplanes, hospitals and factories to cut down noise.

### IT'S A FACT!

Supersonic jets fly faster than sound. So you cannot hear them coming towards you. You will hear the sound only after the jet passes you!

### IT'S A FACT!

How does a loudspeaker make sound louder? The microphone first converts sound into electrical signals. These signals are then amplified by an electronic amplifier. The amplified electrical signals are then converted back to sound by a speaker.

## ORAL QUESTIONS FOR FORMATIVE ASSESSMENT

1. Can sound produced on the moon travel to the earth? Give reasons.
2. Sound is produced when a body undergoes to-and-fro movement. However, no sound is produced when a person waves his/her hand. Why?
3. Sound is produced by vibration. To detect sound, some part in our ear should also vibrate when sound strikes it. Which part of the ear is this?
4. What travels faster—sound or light? Which observation in daily life supports this?
5. In which medium is the speed of sound maximum—air, water or steel?

## SOUNDS PRODUCED BY HUMANS

Put a hand firmly on your throat and sing 'ooooo…'. Can you feel the vibrations in your throat that produce the sound? Sing it low and high. Can you feel the difference in vibrations? We produce sound in the **larynx** of our throats (Fig. 13.13a). The larynx has two **vocal cords**, which are folds of tissue with a slit-like opening between them. When we speak, air passes through the opening and the vocal cords vibrate to produce sound.

### Activity 10 (Making a model): Vocal cords

Take two rubber strips of the same width and length. Put them one above the other. Hold them from both ends and stretch them tight (Fig. 13.13b). Blow air through the slit between them. Is sound produced? The structure of vocal cords is similar.

You can also show this with a piece of paper. Make a round hole in the paper in the centre. Fold it as shown in Figure 13.13b. Hold it between two fingers and blow.

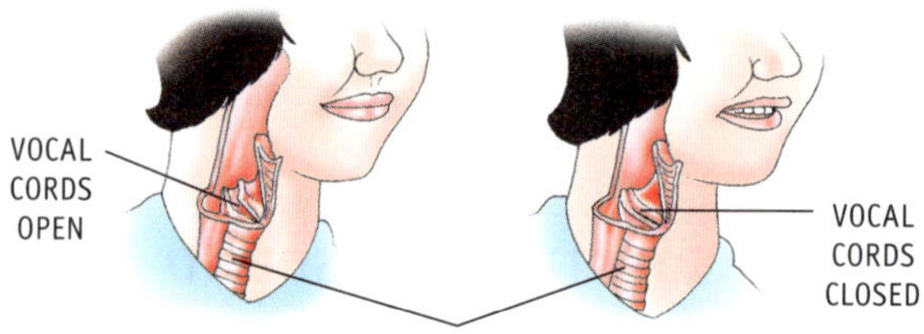


a. Vibrations of the vocal cords produce sound.

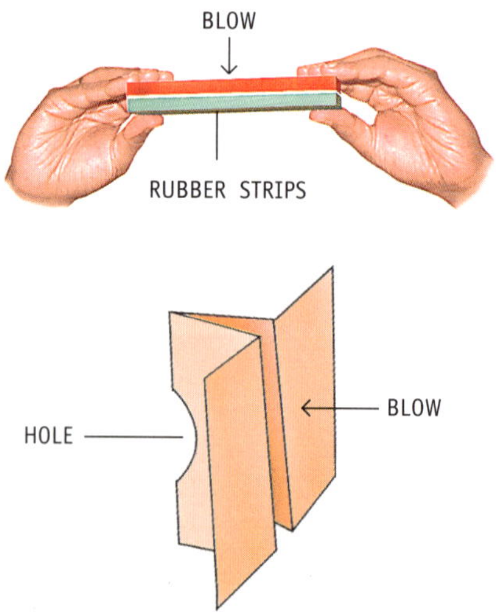


b. Demonstrating how vocal cords work

FIG. 13.13

Women have shorter vocal cords (about 15 mm long) than men (about 20 mm long). Children have very short vocal cords. That is why the frequency of sound produced by women and children is of higher frequency than sound produced by men.

## MUSICAL SOUND

Regular vibrations produce **musical sound** whereas irregular vibrations produce **noise**. However, this is not all. Listen to the sound produced by a tuning fork and the sound of the same fundamental produced by a *sitar*. The tuning fork sounds 'flat' whereas the *sitar* sounds 'rich'. This is because the sound produced by a tuning fork has only one frequency; it has no harmonics. The sound from a *sitar* has a number of harmonics. They arise partly because it is not just the string that is vibrating but the whole instrument. It is the sound of vibration of the whole instrument that we hear.

Thus, harmonics give richness, i.e. musical quality to the sound.

To produce music, the different notes played should have a definite relation to each other. Their frequencies should have a certain ratio to each other. If they do not, the music sounds out of tune (*besura*). In the musical scale, eight notes make up an **octave**. These notes are in order of increasing frequencies.

*sa, re, ga, ma, pa, dha, ni, sa* (Indian)

*do, re, me, pha, so, la, ti, do* (Western)

The first note can be of any frequency, but the other notes must have a definite relation to the first frequency.

### Musical instruments

Musical instruments use vibrations of various kinds to produce music. Depending on the kinds of vibrations produced, they are of three types—stringed, wind and percussion instruments.

**Stringed instruments:** *Sitar*, guitar, violin, *sarod*, etc., are stringed instruments. They use vibrations in metal wires to produce sound. The frequency of sound is varied by varying the length of the vibrating wire. In a *sitar*, for example, the shorter the length of the wire, the higher the pitch it produces.

**Wind instruments:** Flute, *shehnai*, etc., are wind instruments. They use vibrations in air columns to produce sound. Holes in a flute, for example, are opened or closed in order to change the length of the vibrating air column. This changes the pitch of the sound.

**Percussion instruments:** Drum, *tabla*, *mridangam*, etc., are percussion instruments. They have a stretched skin whose vibrations produce sound. Loudness is increased by striking the skin harder. The pitch is increased by stretching the skin more.

## NOISE

We have seen that irregular vibrations produce noise. Too much noise in our surroundings is harmful to us and is referred to as **noise pollution**. Traffic on the road, machines in factories, mixers and grinders, vacuum cleaners, air coolers, etc., cause noise pollution. In fact, even loud music causes noise pollution.

The unit used to measure loudness of sound is called **decibel (dB)**.

The range of loudness in decibels and how it is perceived is given in Table 13.1.

TABLE 13.1 Range of loudness in dB and how it is felt

| RANGE OF LOUDNESS (dB) | FEELING |
|---|---|
| 1 – 10 | just audible |
| 10 – 30 | very quiet |
| 30 – 50 | quiet |
| 50 – 70 | moderately loud |
| 70 – 90 | very loud |
| 90 – 120 | uncomfortable |
| 120 – 180 | painful |

TABLE 13.2 Various sources of sound and their sound levels

| SOURCE | SOUND LEVEL (dB) |
|---|---|
| silence | 0 |
| average sound at home | 30 |
| speech (at 2 ft, normal) | 60 |
| speech (at 2 ft, shouting) | 77 |
| hair dryer | 80 |
| city traffic | 90 |
| truck | 100 |
| car horn (at 1 m) | 110 |
| loud thunder | 120 |
| aircraft taking off | 120 |
| rocket engine | 180 |

### Major sources of noise pollution

**Road traffic:** Road traffic noise is one of the most widespread and growing environmental problems. The main reason is the tremendous increase in traffic in cities. Also roads carrying heavy traffic run close to residential areas, without any buffer zones (e.g. green areas) to absorb the noise. As a result, a large number of people are victim to levels of traffic noise that are harmful to health.

**Air and rail traffic:** In areas close to the airports and railway tracks, the sound of aeroplanes and trains are major sources of noise pollution.

**Neighbourhood and domestic noise:** Barking dogs, car horns, loud music, TVs, loudspeakers, building construction and household noise are some of the major sources of noise pollution.

**Noise from industries:** At many places, industries are located in close proximity of residential areas or within the residential areas. There are many activities related to the industries such as sound of machines, horns that cause noise pollution.

### Harmful effects of noise pollution

Noise can affect human health and well-being in a number of ways.

- Exposure to sudden high noise level (e.g. explosion) can cause permanent hearing loss due to rupture of eardrum.
- Prolonged exposure to noise with a volume more than 70 decibels can cause gradual hearing loss, and can even lead to permanent hearing loss.
- High noise levels can also lead to nervous tension and increase of blood pressure.
- People experiencing high noise levels experience sleep deprivation and increased number of headaches, and therefore show increased reliance on sedatives and sleeping pills.

### How to control noise pollution

Some methods of controlling noise pollution are as follows.

- Planning land use to reduce noise; for example, making tree-lined buffer zones between residential colonies and roads with heavy traffic.
- Reducing noise emissions by developing low-noise products, for example, better silencers for automobiles.
- Measures such as screens and enclosures around machinery to obstruct the path of noise. This will help people working in and living near factories.
- Measures at home such as double glazed glass in windows to keep out noise.
- Control over recreational noise, such as use of loudspeakers.
- Increasing public awareness by providing factual information of the harmful effects of noise from blowing horns, loud music and TV, so that people themselves reduce noise generation.

However, all these measures can succeed only by participation of the public.

## ORAL QUESTIONS FOR FORMATIVE ASSESSMENT

1. Sound is produced in our vocal cords. What is the difference in the vocal cords of men and women?
2. What is the difference between the sound produced by regular and irregular vibrations?
3. Name two of each of the following.
   a. Musical instruments that produce sound by vibration of a stretched string
   b. Musical instruments that produce sound by vibration of a stretched skin
   c. Musical instruments that produce sound by vibration of an air column
4. Only noise produces noise pollution. Do you agree? Give reasons.

## NOW YOU KNOW

- Sound is produced by rapid to-and-fro movements, called vibrations.
- The maximum distance to which an oscillating or vibrating object moves from its central position is called amplitude. The loudness of sound depends on the amplitude of vibration.
- The time taken for one complete vibration or oscillation is called its time period.
- The number of oscillations per second is called frequency. It is measured in hertz.
- The pitch of sound depends on the frequency of vibration.
- The quality of a sound is determined by frequencies present in it and their relative loudness.
- The human ear has three parts—outer, middle and inner. The auditory nerve connects the inner ear to the brain.
- Humans can hear sounds with frequencies between 20 hertz and 20,000 hertz; sound with frequency below 20 hertz is called infrasonic; sound with frequency above 20,000 hertz is called ultrasonic.
- Sound needs a medium to travel. The medium can be solid, liquid or gaseous.
- Sound travels with maximum speed in solids, with lesser speed in liquids, and has minimum speed in gases.
- An echo is the reflection of sound by a hill or a building.
- Soft surfaces are better absorbers of sound.
- Humans produce sound in the larynx due to vibrations in the vocal cords.
- Musical instruments are of three types—stringed, wind and percussion.
- Excess noise in our environment is called noise pollution. It is harmful for our health.

## NEW WORDS

**AMPLITUDE OF AN OSCILLATION**—maximum distance through which an oscillating body moves away from its central position

**TIME PERIOD**—time taken for one oscillation

**FREQUENCY**—number of oscillations per second

**INFRASONICS**—low frequency sounds which we cannot hear

**DECIBEL**—unit for measuring loudness of noise

## FOR FORMATIVE AND SUMMATIVE ASSESSMENT

### A. MULTIPLE-CHOICE QUESTIONS: Choose the most appropriate answer.

1. For an oscillating pendulum of fixed length, which of the following is true?
   a. Frequency depends on amplitude of oscillation.
   b. Frequency and time period are not related.
   c. Time period depends on amplitude of oscillation.
   d. Frequency and time period do not depend on amplitude of oscillation.
2. The quality of sound produced by a tuning fork is different from that produced by a musical instrument because of difference in
   a. amplitude. b. frequency. c. harmonics. d. none of these
3. Sound can travel through
   a. solids only. b. liquids only. c. gases only. d. all of these
4. An object vibrates with a frequency of 15 hertz. Which of the following is true?
   a. It produces sound which we can hear. b. It does not produce sound.
   c. It produces sound which we cannot hear. d. It produces sound which we can hear if we strain our ears.
5. In which medium does sound travel fastest?
   a. air b. water c. steel d. vacuum
6. Which of the following characteristics of sound depends on the amplitude of vibrations?
   a. speed b. pitch c. loudness d. quality
7. Sound of frequency 320 Hz is of lower pitch than sound of frequency
   a. 10 Hz. b. 180 Hz. c. 256 Hz. d. 512 Hz.
8. Sound of which of the following frequency can you hear?
   a. 5 Hz b. 15 Hz c. 500 Hz d. 50,000 Hz
9. Which of these is expected to be the best absorber of sound?
   a. iron b. wood c. wool d. cemented wall

### B. VERY SHORT-ANSWER QUESTIONS: Give one-word answers.

1. Sound is produced by ____________
2. Name the instrument used in the laboratory to produce sound of a fixed frequency.
3. What does loudness of sound depend on?
4. Give the term for 'number of vibrations per second'.
5. Frequency is measured in ____________
6. The pitch of sound depends on time period of vibration. True or false?
7. In general, which sound has greater frequency—a bird singing or a man singing?
8. Most vibrating objects generate sound of several frequencies simultaneously. True or false?
9. The quality of two sounds with the same fundamental frequency differs because of the number and relative loudness of the ____________

10. The sound produced by a tuning fork has no harmonics. True or false?
11. Flute is a __________ type of musical instrument.
12. The pitch of the sound produced in a guitar can be altered by reducing the vibrating length of the wire. True or false?
13. What is the name given to sound produced by irregular vibrations?
14. In our ears, the vibrations in the air are picked up by the __________ ear.
15. What travels faster—light or sound?
16. The two kinds of sounds we cannot hear are __________ and __________
17. A soft board will __________ (reflect / absorb) most of the sound falling on it.
18. What is the unit in which loudness of sound is measured?
19. Prolonged exposure to noise louder than __________ dB can lead to permanent hearing damage.
20. Which surfaces reflect sound better—hard or soft?

## C. SHORT-ANSWER QUESTIONS (TYPE I): Answer in a sentence or two.

1. How is sound produced?
2. Distinguish between infrasonics and ultrasonics.
3. What do you mean by time period of a vibrating object?
4. What is the 'amplitude' of a vibrating object?
5. What is the 'frequency' of a vibrating object? How is it related to shrillness of sound?
6. Why do women have shriller voices than men?

## D. SHORT-ANSWER QUESTIONS (TYPE II): Answer in about 30 words.

1. In what way does loudness of sound depend on amplitude? If the amplitude is increased by three times, by how much does the loudness increase?
2. Ramesh measured the time gap between lightning and thunder, and found that it was 3 seconds. Assuming light covers the distance instantly, what is the distance of the clouds from Ramesh?
3. Why can you not hear the echo if you stand 10 m away from a wall and shout towards it?
4. How is sound produced in our throat?
5. Name the three types of musical instruments. How is sound produced in each type?
6. What do you mean by noise pollution? What are the main causes of noise pollution?
7. List four ill effects that noise pollution has on us.
8. List three methods of controlling noise pollution.

## E. LONG-ANSWER QUESTIONS: Answer in about 60 words.

1. Explain what you mean by quality of sound. What is it determined by?
2. Explain how sound produced by a vibrating object reaches your ears. What happens after it enters the ears?
3. Describe an experiment to show that sound can travel through liquids.
4. Describe an experiment to show that sound cannot travel through vacuum.

## HOTS QUESTIONS: Think and answer.

1. An explosion occurs on the moon. Will it be **a.** seen, **b.** heard on the earth instantly or after some time?
2. In the game hide-and-seek, how can the blind-folded person guess which player is closest to him?

## FOR FORMATIVE ASSESSMENT*

### In the Library—Research Projects

- The principle of reflection of sound is used in an instrument called the SONAR which is used to find the depth of the sea at any place.
  A SONAR produces ultrasonic pulses which are sent down into the sea from a ship. They are received back after being reflected by the bottom of the sea. The depth of the sea is calculated by measuring the time taken by the echo to be received.
  Find out the full form of SONAR.
  Find out how bats use this technique to 'see' at night and to detect and catch insects.
- Find out what is meant by 'surround sound'? Where is this technology generally used?
- The frequency range for hearing of animals is different from ours—for example, dogs can hear sounds above 20,000 Hz. Find the audible frequency range for a dog and a cat.

### My Virtual Library—Research/Activities on the Internet

- Visit rsgr.in/lsc-cce-8 and click on LINK 52 to find out more about sound.
- Visit rsgr.in/lsc-cce-8 and click on LINK 53 to download musical sound simulators (freeware, shareware) to create music on your computer.

### To Meet—Research on Scientist

**Ernst Mach** (1838–1916) This Austrian physicist showed that when an object crosses the speed of sound, there is a loud sound called a sonic boom. Today we know that loud sonic booms are produced when a supersonic jet crosses the speed of sound. To honour the scientist the speed of supersonic aircraft is today given in terms of Mach numbers. These numbers relate the speed to the speed of sound. Thus, an aircraft travelling at Mach 2 has a speed double that of sound.

Find out more about Ernst Mach. Find out what you can about the cause of the sonic boom.

### In the Laboratory—Making a Model

**Make a *jal tarang*** Take 8 glasses of the same size. Fill them with water to different levels. Strike them one by one with a pencil. Do they emit sound of different frequencies? Take the help of your music teacher to adjust the level of water in the glasses so that you can get the notes *sa, re, ga, ma, pa, dha, ni, sa*. Your *jal tarang* is ready to play.

*For more tasks see Page 200

14

# Some Natural Phenomena

## LIGHTNING

You must have observed lightning in the sky during a storm. You would also have seen sparks in an electric gas lighter used to light LPG at home. Have you seen similar sparks in a loose electric plug? All these sparks have similar nature—they arise because of flow of electric current through air. However, you have also read in Class 7 that air is an insulator and that electric current cannot pass through it. So how do the sparks and lightning occur? Let us try to understand the nature of the sparks. For this, let us first understand the nature of electric charges.

## ELECTRICAL CHARGE

Let us perform the following activities to understand the concept of electric charge.

**ACTIVITY 1 (Experimental investigation)**

Rub a plastic comb in your hair several times. Both comb and your hair should be dry. In fact, this experiment works best when the weather is also dry. Now hold the comb above small pieces of paper (Fig. 14.1a). What happens?

You will find that the paper pieces get attracted to the comb.

**IN THIS CHAPTER**

CONCEPT OF CHARGE AND ITS TYPES ◆ ATTRACTION AND REPULSION OF CHARGES ◆ DETECTION AND MEASUREMENT OF CHARGE ◆ FLOW OF CHARGE ◆ LIGHTNING ◆ SAFETY DURING LIGHTNING ◆ RICHTER SCALE ◆ CAUSES AND EFFECTS OF EARTHQUAKES ◆ PROTECTION AGAINST EARTHQUAKES

a. Pieces of paper get attracted to a charged comb. b. Charging a balloon c. Two charged balloons repel each other.

FIG. 14.1 Electrostatic force produced by an electrical charge

**ACTIVITY 2 (Experimental investigation)**

Inflate a balloon and rub it against your dry hair (Fig. 14.1b). Now gently place it against a wall. The balloon will stick to the wall. Now rub another balloon in a similar way. Hang both the balloons close to each other.

You will find that the two balloons push each other away (or repel each other) (Fig. 14.1c).

The comb or balloon are said to be **electrically charged** when they are rubbed against the hair. They acquire **electrical charge**. The electric charges generated by rubbing are **static**—i.e. they do not move. These electric charges produce in them a kind of force which can attract as well as repel objects. We call this **electrostatic force**.

### Positive and negative charges

Let us investigate the nature of these charges.

**ACTIVITY 3 (Experimental investigation)**

Rub an ebonite rod with wool or flannel and hang it with a thread. Rub another ebonite rod in the same way and bring it near the suspended rod. You will find that the two ebonite rods repel each other (Fig. 14.2a).

Now rub a glass rod with silk and bring it near the charged ebonite rod. The glass rod will attract the ebonite rod (Fig. 14.2b).

Repeat the activity by bringing a charged glass rod near another suspended charged glass rod. The two will repel each other (Fig. 14.2c).

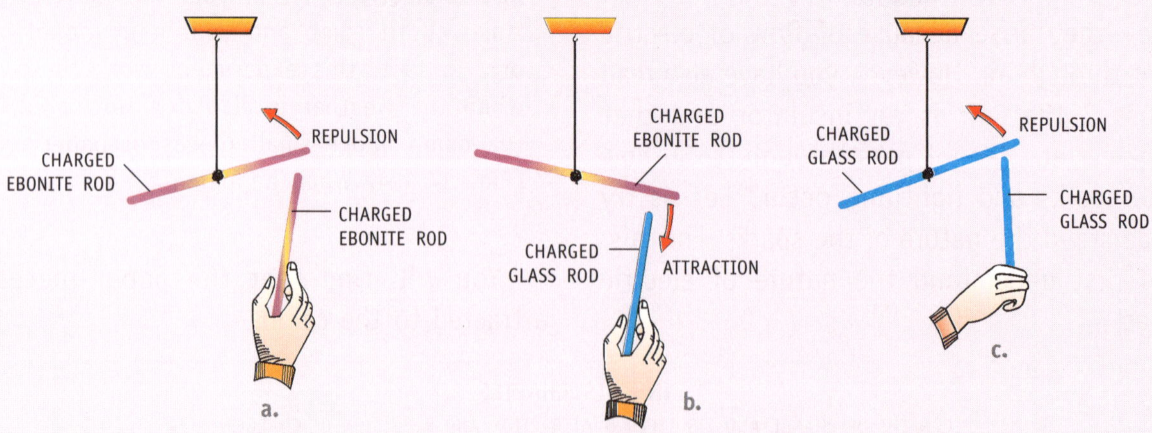


FIG. 14.2 Like charges repel and unlike charges attract each other.

This activity clearly shows that the charges on the ebonite and glass rods are not of the same type. There must be two different kinds of charges—one on the ebonite rod rubbed with wool or flannel, and the other on the glass rod rubbed with silk.

**Benjamin Franklin**, a scientist of the eighteenth century, gave specific names to these charges. The charge on the glass rod was named **positive charge**, and the charge on the ebonite rod was called **negative charge**.

From the above activities we can infer the following:

- two negatively-charged objects (the ebonite rods) repel each other,
- two positively-charged objects (the glass rods) also repel each other, and
- a positively-charged object (glass rod) attracts a negatively-charged object (ebonite rod).

This leads us to the conclusion that like charges repel and unlike charges attract each other.

### Equal and opposite charges

When you rub a glass rod with silk, it acquires a positive charge. At the same time, the silk cloth acquires an equal negative charge. Similarly, when ebonite is rubbed with wool, the ebonite gets a negative charge, whereas the wool gets an equal positive charge.

Thus, when two bodies are charged by rubbing against each other, they acquire equal and opposite charges.

> **IT'S A FACT!**
>
> **William Gilbert** (1540–1563), an English physician and physicist found that gems like diamond, sapphire, spall, carbuncle, jet and ordinary rock crystals, when rubbed, attracted other materials. He named these substances 'electrics'.

### Testing for Charge

We have seen that a charged body attracts another body with an opposite charge. A charged body can also attract an uncharged body, for example, the charged comb can attract pieces of paper which are not charged. Therefore, attraction by a charged body does not indicate whether the other body is also charged or not. However, if the body being tested is repelled by a charged body, you are certain that it is charged. It has the same charge as on the charged body.

Therefore, to test if a body is charged or not, bring near it a positively-charged body and a negatively-charged body, one by one. If it is

- attracted by both, it has no charge.
- repelled by the positively-charged body, it is also positively-charged.
- repelled by the negatively-charged body, it is also negatively-charged.

Thus, repulsion alone is a sure test of whether a body is charged or not.

### Electric charges in atoms

When we rub two bodies together, where do electric charges come from? Electric charges are actually present inside atoms. Every atom contains particles with both positive and negative electric charges. Under normal circumstances, the number of particles with negative charge (called **electrons**) in an atom is equal to the number of particles with positive charge (called **protons**). So the charges **neutralize** or cancel out each other's effect, and the atom is electrically **neutral**. The positively-charged particles are firmly bound in the atom while the negatively-charged particles are more loosely bound. It is possible to remove some of the negatively-charged particles by processes such as rubbing.

- When a glass rod is rubbed with silk cloth, some negatively-charged particles move from the glass rod to the silk cloth. The result is that the glass rod is left with an excess of positively-charged particles, while the silk cloth acquires excess of negatively-charged particles. That is why the glass rod becomes positively-charged and the silk cloth becomes negatively-charged.

- When ebonite is rubbed with wool, negatively-charged particles are transferred from wool to ebonite. Thus, wool acquires positive charge and ebonite acquires negative charge.

This also explains why two bodies rubbed against each other acquire equal and opposite charge.

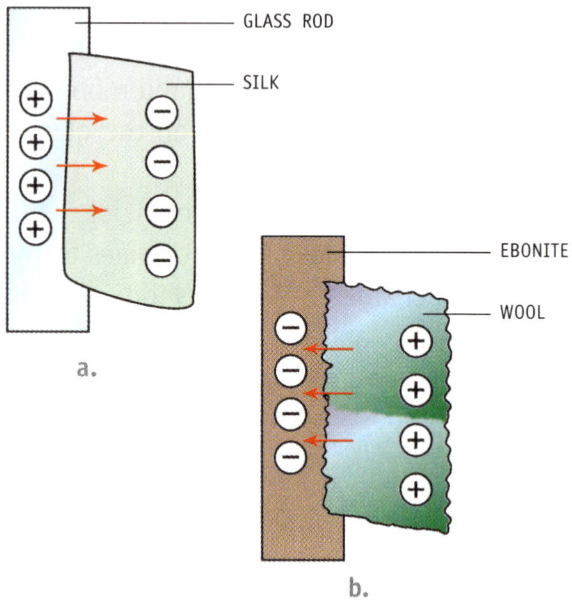


FIG. 14.3 Effect of rubbing
a. Glass with silk b. Ebonite with wool
(Arrows show movement of electrons)

## DIFFERENT WAYS OF CHARGING A BODY

### Charging by friction

You know that when two bodies are rubbed against each other, they acquire equal and opposite charges. When you rub a glass rod with silk, the glass rod acquires a positive charge. The silk cloth acquires a negative charge. When two bodies are rubbed together, there is friction between them. Therefore, a body can be charged by friction. This method of charging a body is called **charging by friction**.

### Charging by conduction

An object can also be charged by touching it to a charged body. This happens because some charge from the charged body gets transferred to the uncharged body. This is called **charging by conduction**. In this case, the body being charged acquires the same charge as that on the charged body.

### Charging by induction

A body can also be charged by bringing a charged body near it, but not touching it. This is called charging by **induction**. In this case, the body being charged acquires an opposite charge to that of the body charging it.

## ORAL QUESTIONS FOR FORMATIVE ASSESSMENT

1. There are two kinds of charges. How do we know this?
2. What effect do the two kinds of charges have on each other?
3. Where do the two kinds of charges come from?
4. Two objects rubbed against each other acquire charge.
   a. What is the relationship between the charges acquired by the two objects?
   b. What action does rubbing cause, because of which the objects acquire charge?

## DETECTING AND MEASURING CHARGE—THE ELECTROSCOPE

You can make your own electroscope to detect if a body is charged or not, and also to measure its charge.

**ACTIVITY 4 (Experimental investigation)**

Take a glass bottle with a wide mouth. Cover it with a piece of cardboard. Make a hole in the cardboard and pass a metal wire through it. Turn both ends of the wire (Fig 14.4). Cut two strips of aluminium foil, about 3 cm by 1 cm each. Hang them on the lower end of the metal wire. Touch a negatively-charged ebonite rod to the upper end of the iron wire. Do the two aluminium strips repel each other?

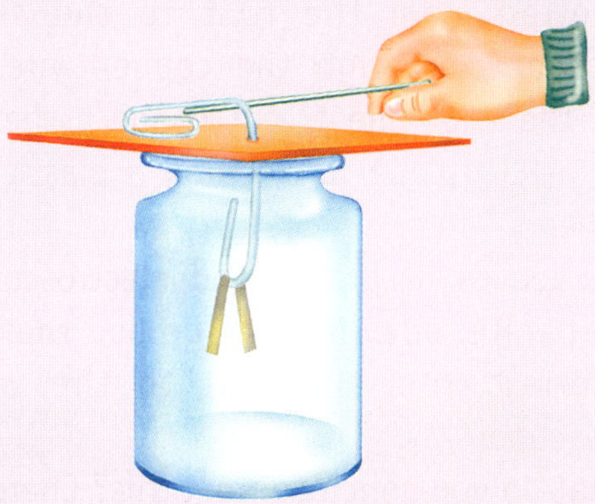

FIG. 14.4 The principle of the electroscope

This happens because the strips get charged negatively by conduction when touched with the ebonite rod. The two strips repel each other and open out. The greater the charge on the ebonite rod, the more the charge it will transfer to the strips, and the greater will be the separation between the strips.

This arrangement can be used to detect if an object is charged, and also to measure its charge by noting the amount of separation it produces in the two strips.

This is the principle used to make the **electroscope**, a device used to detect and measure electric charge.

### The gold-leaf electroscope

The gold-leaf electroscope consists of a metal disc to which a metal rod is attached. The metal rod passes into a bell jar through a tightly-fitted rubber stopper. At the bottom of the metal rod are mounted two thin strips (or leaves) of metal. These can be made of copper, brass or gold. The bell jar rests on a wooden base. Tin foil is attached to the sides of the bell jar.

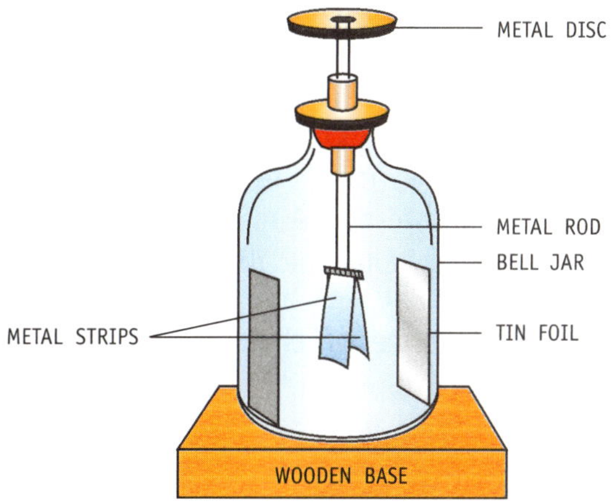


FIG. 14.5 A gold-leaf electroscope

The gold-leaf electroscope is used:

- To detect and measure charge.

**ACTIVITY 5 (Experimental investigation)**

Touch the body to be tested to the metal disc of the gold-leaf electroscope. If the leaves diverge, the body is charged.

The amount of divergence of the leaves is a measure of the amount of charge on the body.

- To find the nature of the charge. To test whether a body has a positive or negative charge, it is necessary to charge the electroscope with a known charge.

**ACTIVITY 6 (Experimental investigation)**

- Touch the disc of the electroscope with a negatively-charged ebonite rod. The leaves get charged negatively and diverge (Fig. 14.6a).

**Fig. 14.6** Testing the nature of charge with an electroscope

- Note the amount of divergence.
- Now bring the body with an unknown charge close to the disc of the electroscope. Note the divergence.

If the divergence of the leaves increases, the body has a similar charge, i.e. it is negatively charged (Fig. 14.6b). If the divergence of the leaves decreases, the body has opposite charge, i.e. it is positively charged (Fig. 14.6c).

**IT'S A FACT!**

Many photocopiers use static electricity to work. The image to be photocopied is first converted into static charges. These charges attract particles of fine black powder called the toner. The toner particles are then transferred to an electrically charged paper to reproduce the image on the paper.

## FLOW OF CHARGE—CONDUCTORS AND INSULATORS

**Activity 7 (Experimental investigation)**

Take two electroscopes. Charge the leaves of one of them using an ebonite rod. Now connect the discs of the two electroscopes using a copper wire. Take care not to touch the discs or the copper wire with your hand.

You will find that the leaves of the second electroscope also diverge. The divergence of the leaves of the first electroscope decreases. This shows that some of the charge has been transferred from the first to the second electroscope, through the copper wire. Now repeat the experiment and connect the discs of the electroscope by keeping a plastic scale over them.

The leaves of the second electroscope do not separate out. No charge is, therefore, transferred from the first to the second electroscope.

What do you conclude from this? Charge can flow through the copper wire, but cannot flow through plastic. Copper is a **conductor** of charge. Plastic is an **insulator** or a **non-conductor** of charge. You can test other materials in the same way. You will find that metals, such as iron and aluminium are conductors. So is the 'lead' of your pencil. The 'lead' is actually a form of carbon called graphite. Rubber, wood, paper, plastic, ebonite, glass, etc., are non-conductors.

When charges move, they constitute an electric current. This electric current or electricity lights up bulbs in our houses, makes our fans work, runs our refrigerators, provides us warmth through room heaters, and helps us in many other ways.

### Earthing

The human body can also conduct charge to some extent. This is why if you touch the disc of a charged electroscope with your fingers, the metal leaves collapse because the charge flows through your body to the earth. This process of transferring of charge from a charged object to the earth is known as earthing. Earthing is used to 'discharge' an electroscope before it can be used for another experiment.

## ELECTRIC CURRENT

We have seen that when a charged electroscope is connected to an uncharged electroscope through a copper wire, charge flows from the charged to the uncharged electroscope. This flow of charge in a conductor is called **electric current**. This is the electric current that we are so used to in our daily life and about which you studied in earlier classes. However, when a charged body is connected to an uncharged body through a conductor, electric current flows for a little time only. It flows until the two bodies are similarly charged (Note that this does not mean that they have the same charge. This point will be clarified in higher classes.). This is like two water tanks, one with water and one with no water, connected together. Water flows from one tank to the other tank until the water level in both tanks is the same.

To make water flow continuously you need to use a water pump. Similarly, to make electric current move continuously in a wire we need an electric cell or a generator.

## ATMOSPHERIC ELECTRICITY

Let us now come back to studying how lightning is produced. **Benjamin Franklin** first proved that clouds build up charge during a storm.

He flew a silk kite into the clouds during a thunderstorm, with a metal key tied to the thread of the kite. He got an **electric shock** when he touched the metal key. This happened because the charge in the clouds flowed down the wet string to the metal key. When the metal key was touched, heavy charge flowed through Franklin's body to the earth, giving him an electric shock (Fig. 14.7).

FIG. 14.7 Benjamin Franklin's famous experiment with a silk kite led to the invention of the lightning conductor.

During a thunderstorm, clouds gather charge. It is not known exactly why this happens. However, some experiments have suggested that charges develop in water droplets present in the clouds. It is seen that lighter droplets acquire positive charge, and being lighter move to the upper regions of the clouds. Bigger droplets acquire negative charge, and being heavier, move to the lower regions of the clouds.

Though air is an insulator, it too allows the passage of current through it if the quantity of charge is large and the distance is small. In such a situation, very heavy charge passes through the air in a very short time. Normally this is accompanied by heat and light. This phenomenon is called **electric discharge**. It can be observed in an electric gas lighter, a loose electric plug or an automobile spark plug.

When two clouds with unlike charges come near each other, there can be a very heavy discharge between them. Huge amount of energy is released in the form of heat, light and sound during such a discharge. This is the lightning we see and the thunder we hear during a storm.

Clouds can charge tall buildings and trees by induction. The buildings and trees thus acquire the opposite charge. If the build up of charge is very heavy, heavy flow of electric charge can occur between the cloud and the tree or building. This can be very dangerous and can result in the building or the tree catching fire because of the huge amount of energy released. In hilly areas, clouds are comparatively closer to the ground than in the plains. Therefore, lightning strikes are more frequent in hilly areas. Thus, **lightning** is a very heavy flow of charge between clouds, or between clouds and earth.

FIG. 14.8 Lightning

While lightning can be dangerous, it is also useful to us in some ways. The heat and light released during lightning enables nitrogen of the air to combine with oxygen to form oxides of nitrogen. These get dissolved in water to form very dilute nitric acid, which comes down with rain. The acid reacts with salts in the soil to form nitrogenous compounds, which are essential for growth of plants. Lightning also enables ozone to be formed from oxygen. As you may have read in earlier classes, the ozone present in air stops the harmful ultraviolet rays of the sun from reaching us.

### The lightning conductor

To protect tall buildings from damage by lightning, a **lightning conductor** is fixed on them (Fig. 14.9). Benjamin Franklin developed the idea of using lightning conductors to protect tall buildings. A lightning conductor consists of a metal rod ending in spikes at the top. The lower end of the rod is attached to a copper plate buried deep in the earth. If lightning does strike the building, it flows harmlessly to the earth through the metal rod, and no damage is done to the building.

### Safety during lightning

A lightning strike is very dangerous. It can destroy an entire building or a tree on which it strikes. It is advisable to take shelter in a safe place when you hear thunder, and not to remain in an open place.

FIG. 14.9 A lightning conductor

- A building, especially one with a lightning conductor is safe.
- A car or bus is also safe. Shut the windows of the vehicle.
- Taking shelter under a tree is not safe as lightning can strike the tree. If you are forced to take shelter under a tree, for example if you are in a forest, choose a short tree.
- An open place is not a safe place to be in, especially if it is elevated. If in an open place, stay away from trees and poles. If you cannot find any shelter, squat low on the ground.

### ORAL QUESTIONS FOR FORMATIVE ASSESSMENT

1. An electroscope is used to detect and measure charges. What happens in an electroscope when its disc is touched with a charged object?
2. To find the nature of charge on an object, will you use a charged electroscope or an uncharged one?
3. Should the rod of the electroscope connecting the disc with the strips be made of a conductor or an insulator? Why?
4. Air is an insulator, but can conduct electricity under certain conditions. What are these conditions? What is conduction of electricity through air called?
5. If lightning strikes a building, it flows harmlessly through the lightning conductor. What property should the material of which the lightning conductor is made have, to make this possible?

## EARTHQUAKES

Any sudden disturbance below the earth's surface may produce vibrations or tremors in the earth's crust. These vibrations or shakings are known as **earthquakes**. In other words, the shaking of the ground caused by sudden movements in Earth's crust is called an earthquake.

The enormous energy released by an earthquake travels through the ground in the form of waves. Some waves can make the ground ripple up and down, while others can shake it from side to side.

Each type of wave travels through the earth at a different speed. The waves generated by an earthquake are called **seismic waves**. These are recorded by an instrument called **seismograph** or **seismometer**. The characteristics of an earthquake waves can be recorded on the screen of a seismograph, and is called a **seismogram**.

The science that deals with the seismic waves is called **seismology** and earthquake scientists are called **seismologists**.

The magnitude or intensity of an earthquake depends on the amount of energy released and is based on the direct measurement of the size of seismic waves.

### IT'S A FACT!

The simplest form of a seismograph is a simple pendulum. When the ground shakes, the base and frame of the seismometer move with it, but the pendulum bob remains in place. Thus, there is relative motion between the bob and the shaking ground. A pen below the bob records this motion on a paper that is moved by a rotating drum. The recording is the seismogram.

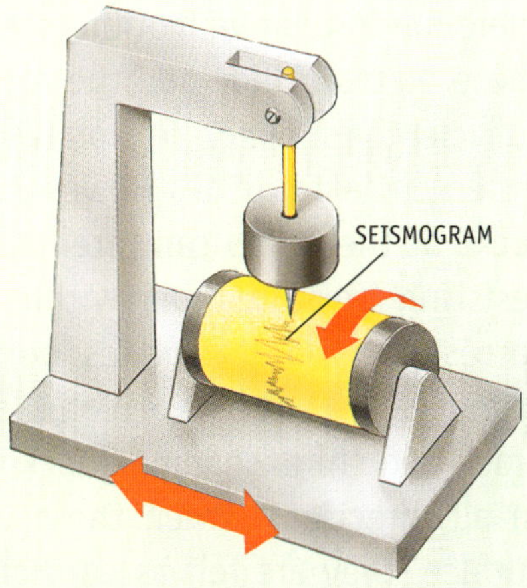


FIG. 14.10 A seismograph

### Richter Scale

The magnitude or intensity of an earthquake is measured by the Richter scale, developed by **Charles F Richter**, a US seismologist, in 1935. The number indicating the magnitude or intensity on Richter scale ranges between 0 and 9. The Richter scale is not a linear scale. On this scale the vibrations of an earthquake with a magnitude of 2 are **10 times** greater in amplitude than those of an earthquake with a magnitude of 1, and the vibrations of an earthquake with a magnitude of 8 are one million times greater in amplitude than those of an earthquake with a magnitude of 2. The severest earthquake ever recorded had a magnitude of 8.7.

Earthquakes measuring 0–3 on the Richter scale are often not even noticed. An earthquake of intensity 4.5 is considered moderate and can disturb loose objects. At intensity 5.5, the earthquake is strong and can cause furniture to move and trees to sway. At intensity 6.5, an earthquake can damage weak structures. An earthquake of intensity 8 or more can be very disastrous and can destroy entire cities.

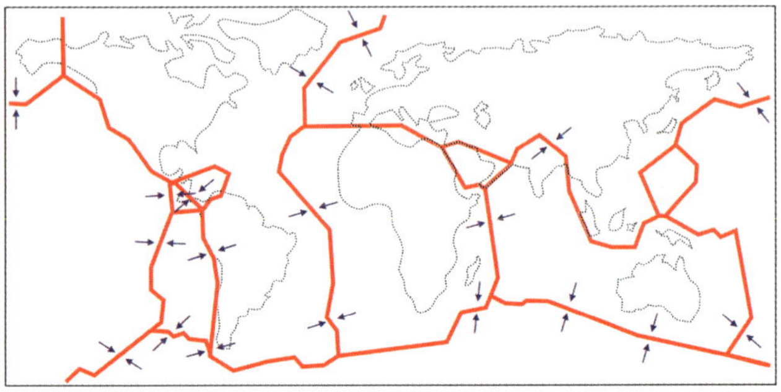

a. The tectonic plates and their movements

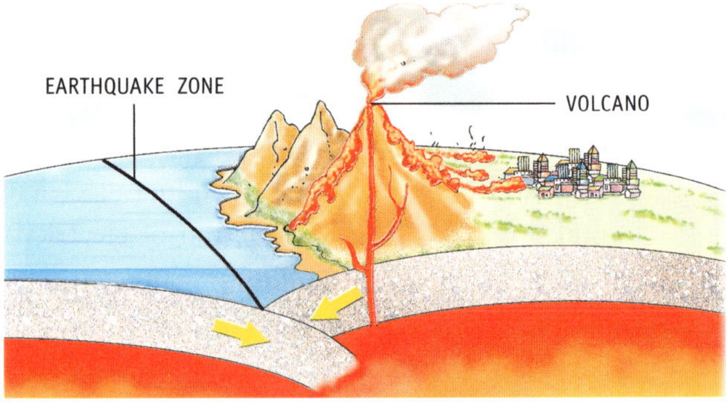


b. The effect of crashing of two plates

FIG. 14.11

## MAIN CAUSES OF EARTHQUAKES

The Earth's lithosphere is divided into about 20 parts called **tectonic plates**. These plates float over the hot magma below, and are therefore in relative motion to each other. When these plates collide and the rock at the joint is sufficiently slippery, the plates slide over each other, little by little. However, sometimes the rocks at the joints can interlock and get stuck, resisting pressure from within. For years, the forces pushing the plates build up until the strain can rip the two plates apart. The rocks crack and shift, sending shock waves of energy in all directions. When these waves reach the surface, they are felt as earthquakes.

The point from which the earthquake waves originate is called the **seismic focus**. It lies within the crust of the earth. The point on the earth's surface vertically above the focus is called the **epicentre** of the earthquake. The intensity of the earthquake is greatest at the epicentre.

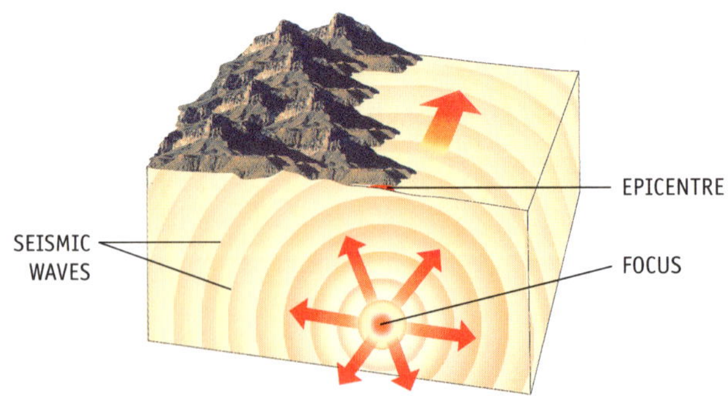


FIG. 14.12 Seismic focus and epicentre of an earthquake

The boundaries of the tectonic plates are the zones where earthquakes are most likely to occur. These are known as **seismic** or **fault**

**zones**. In India, the fault zone at the boundary of the Indian plate and Eurasian plate passes through Kashmir, western and central Himalayas, the whole of North-East, Rann of Kachchh, Rajasthan and the Indo-Gangetic plain. These areas are therefore most threatened.

**GUJARAT EARTHQUAKE**

A severe earthquake struck the Kachchh region of Gujarat at 8.45 AM on 26 January 2001. It shook the region for almost one minute. Under the impact of the earthquake, villages and towns were flattened, high-rise buildings collapsed, communication and power-lines were completely disrupted, transport system was thrown out of gear and settlements became heaps of debris.

Initially, the intensity of this earthquake was measured 6.9 on the Richter scale by the Indian Meteorological Department. It was subsequently upgraded to 8.1. About 50,000 to 1,00,000 people were killed and about 5,00,000 were adversely affected. There was large scale destruction of property in Bhuj, Rajkot and Ahmedabad.

### Volcanic activity

Volcanic activity is considered to be another main cause of earthquakes. Almost each volcanic eruption is followed by earthquakes and many of the severe earthquakes cause volcanic eruptions (Fig 14.11b).

The explosive violent gases during a volcanic eruption try to escape upward. This leads to severe tremors of high magnitude, which depend upon the intensity of the volcanic eruption.

**IT'S A FACT!**

Tsunami is a Japanese word which means 'harbour wave'. Tsunamis are large waves that are generated when the sea floor is deformed by seismic activity, vertically displacing the overlying water in the ocean. A tsunami can be 10 to 20 metres high when it hits the shore. A tsunami is not one giant wave but a series of waves that come ashore at intervals of 10 to 45 minutes.

## EFFECTS OF EARTHQUAKES

The direct and indirect effects of earthquakes include deformation of ground surface, damage and destruction of human-made structures, towns and cities, loss of life, violent devastating fires, landslides, floods, etc.

**Deformed ground surface:** The earthquake tremors and the resultant vibrations result in the deformation of the ground surface.

**Damage to human-made structures:** Human-made structures such as buildings, roads, rails, factories, dams, bridges, etc., get severely damaged.

**Damage to towns and cities:** Towns and cities are the worst affected due to high density of buildings and population. Large buildings collapse and men and women get buried under the debris. Groundwater pipes are damaged and thus water supply is totally disrupted. Electric poles get uprooted, telephone wires are damaged and the collapse of the sewer system causes epidemics.

**Loss of human and animal life:** The Bhuj earthquake of India in 2001 recorded 8.1 on the Richter scale and caused over one lakh human casualties.

**Devastating fires:** The strong vibrations caused by an earthquake can cause fire in houses, mines and factories due to the bursting of gas cylinders and short circuiting of live electric wires. Two oil refineries in Turkey were destroyed by fire caused by an earthquake in 1999.

**Landslides:** The tremors in hilly and mountainous areas can cause instability of rock materials. This ultimately leads to landslides, which damage settlements and transport systems.

## PROTECTION AGAINST EARTHQUAKE

It is very difficult to predict the occurrence of an earthquake, as it occurs suddenly. Violent earthquakes are often destructive. They cause serious damage to life and property. We can take the following precautions against earthquakes while building our houses.

- In highly seismic areas, use of timber is better than bricks and concrete. Roofs should be made as light as possible. Houses made of timber are very popular in Japan which is highly prone to earthquakes.
- Buildings should be made quake-safe by constructing them according to quake-proof norms.
- Fire-fighting equipment should be installed and kept in working order.

The following are some steps you should take if you are caught in an earthquake.

- If trapped in your home or a building, take shelter under a table and do not move till the shaking stops. Protect your head with your arms. Avoid using a lift.
- Do not stay near the windows, bookcases, mirrors, hanging pots, fans during or immediately after an earthquake.
- Leave your home or school building and move to open areas.
- If outdoors, keep away from high-rise buildings, trees, signboards, poles and electric poles and electric wires.
- Do not sit inside a car or a bus.
- Help others according to their needs.

### ORAL QUESTIONS FOR FORMATIVE ASSESSMENT

1. By how many times is an earthquake of magnitude 5 on the Richter scale more powerful than one of magnitude 4?
2. Which of these lies on the earth's surface—seismic focus or epicentre?
3. Earthquakes are most likely to occur in fault zones. Where are these fault zones normally situated?
4. During an earthquake, you should take shelter in high-rise buildings. Do you agree? Give reasons.

## NOW YOU KNOW

- Static electricity consists of electrical charges that do not flow.
- There are two kinds of charges—positive and negative. When two bodies are rubbed together, they acquire equal and opposite charges.
- Like charges repel and unlike charges attract each other.
- Since a charged body can attract an uncharged body, repulsion alone is a sure test of whether a body is charged or not.
- Equal number of particles containing positive and negative charges is present in all atoms. A body acquires a charge when it has excess of positively or negatively charged particles.
- When an uncharged body is touched by a charged body, it acquires a similar charge. This is called charging by conduction.

- A body can be charged by bringing a charged body near it, but not touching it. This is called charging by induction.
- The principle of the electroscope is used to detect, to measure and to find the nature of charge.
- Charges can flow through conductors, but not through non-conductors. Flow of charge in a conductor is called electric current.
- Clouds get charged during a storm. This causes lightning and thunder.
- Lightning can occur between a charged cloud and a tall building or a tall tree.
- A lightning conductor is used to prevent damage caused by lightning to buildings.
- The shaking of the ground by the sudden movements in the Earth's crust is called an earthquake.
- The waves generated by an earthquake are called seismic waves.
- The magnitude of an earthquake is measured on the Richter scale.
- The disastrous effects of earthquake are deformed ground surface, destruction of human-made structures, loss of human and animal life, and landslides.

## NEW WORDS

**CURRENT ELECTRICITY**—charges in motion
**STATIC ELECTRICITY**—charges at rest
**SEISMIC WAVES**—waves generated by an earthquake
**TECTONIC PLATES**—the parts into which the earth's lithosphere is divided
**EPICENTRE**—the point directly above the seismic focus at which the intensity of the earthquake is the maximum

## FOR FORMATIVE AND SUMMATIVE ASSESSMENT

### A. MULTIPLE-CHOICE QUESTIONS: Choose the most appropriate answer.

1. Like charges
   a. always repel each other.
   b. always attract each other.
   c. can repel or attract each other depending on conditions.
   d. can repel or attract each other depending on the quantity of charge.
2. A body can be charged by
   a. rubbing it against another body.
   b. touching it to a charged body.
   c. bringing a charged body near it.
   d. all of the above methods.
3. When two bodies are rubbed against each other,
   a. they acquire equal and similar charges.
   b. they acquire equal and opposite charges.
   c. they acquire unequal and similar charges.
   d. they acquire unequal and opposite charges.

4. The gold-leaf electroscope can be used to
   a. detect charge only.
   b. detect and measure charge only.
   c. detect, measure and find the nature of charge.
   d. none of the above
5. Electric charge can flow through
   a. insulators.
   b. conductors.
   c. both insulators and conductors.
   d. neither insulators nor conductors.
6. A lightning conductor is a
   a. piece of wire with spikes through which current can flow.
   b. substance that can be charged by clouds.
   c. metal rod with spikes, ending in a copper plate buried in the ground, fixed to a building to protect it from lightning.
   d. copper plate buried in the ground below a building to protect it from lightning.
7. To test if a body is charged or not you will use
   a. another uncharged body.
   b. a positively charged body.
   c. a negatively charged body.
   d. a positively and a negatively charged body.
8. You are given an uncharged electroscope and a charged body. No other apparatus is allowed. You can use the electroscope to
   a. only detect the charge.
   b. detect and measure the charge.
   c. detect, measure and find the nature of the charge.
   d. neither of these since the electroscope is uncharged.

**B. VERY SHORT-ANSWER QUESTIONS: Give one-word answers.**

1. When charges of static electricity flow through conductors we get current electricity. True or false?
2. Two combs made of the same material are rubbed against your hair and brought near each other. Will they attract or repel each other?
3. A negatively-charged object will __________ a positively-charged object.
4. What kind of charge is produced in a silk cloth when it is rubbed against a glass rod?
5. Under normal circumstances atoms contain equal number of positive and negative charges. True or false?
6. Which charges in an atom are more free to move about—positive or negative?
7. Charging a body by bringing a charged body near it, but not touching it is called charging by __________
8. Charging a body by touching it with a charged body is called charging by __________
9. Name the instrument used for detecting and measuring charge.
10. To find the nature of charge using a gold-leaf electroscope, should the electroscope be initially charged or uncharged?

11. What is the flow of charge called? Can charge flow through an ebonite rod?
12. The flow of heavy charge through air, accompanied by heat and light is called ________
13. Lightning is due to flow of charge between clouds. True or false?
14. An electroscope is charged by induction using a negatively-charged body. What charge will the electroscope acquire—positive or negative?
15. When charged by conduction a body acquires the ________ (same / opposite) charge as the charging body.
16. The intensity of an earthquake is measured on the ________ scale.
17. A ________ records the waves generated by an earthquake, known as ________ waves.
18. An earthquake is most likely to occur in the centre of the tectonic plates. True or false?
19. Volcanic activity can also cause earthquakes. True or false?

## C. SHORT-ANSWER QUESTIONS (TYPE I): Answer in a sentence or two.

1. Why does a comb rubbed on hair attract pieces of paper?
2. Under what conditions do charges attract or repel each other?
3. Why do we say that only repulsion is a sure test of charge on a body?
4. What do you mean by 'charging by conduction'? What kind of charge does the body acquire?
5. What is 'charging by induction'? What kind of charge does the body acquire?
6. What is the difference between conductors and non-conductors? Give two examples of each.
7. What is an electroscope?
8. What is 'earthing'?

## D. SHORT-ANSWER QUESTIONS (TYPE II): Answer in about 30 words.

1. Explain why, when two bodies, charged by rubbing them together, acquire equal and opposite charge.
2. What is the difference between static and current electricity?
3. What is an electric discharge? Under what conditions does it occur?
4. In what situation can lightning be dangerous? How can the danger to tall buildings be reduced?
5. How does a lightning conductor work?
6. List four precautions you will take to save yourself from a lightning strike during a thunderstorm.
7. What is the Richter scale? Why do we say that it is not a linear scale?
8. List three effects of an earthquake.

## E. LONG-ANSWER QUESTIONS: Answer in about 60 words.

1. Draw a labelled diagram of a gold-leaf electroscope. Describe how you will use it to detect a charge, measure a charge, and find the nature of the charge.
2. Explain how lightning occurs between two clouds during a storm.

3. Explain the process of lightning striking a building or tree.
4. In what ways is lightning useful?
5. Explain how an earthquake occurs.
6. List three things you will do during an earthquake.

## HOTS QUESTIONS: Think and answer.

1. Why are taller buildings in greater danger of being struck by lightning?
2. When a positively-charged body is brought near an uncharged metal rod, the part of the rod near the charged body acquires a negative charge, and the far side a positive charge. Can you say why this happens? Remember that in a body, negative charges are mobile whereas positive charges are fixed.
3. If you hold a plastic comb in your hand and rub it in your hair, it will get charged. However, if you do the same with a metal comb it will not get charged. Why? But if the metal comb has a plastic handle and you hold it from the handle, it will also get charged. Why?
4. Why do you think charging by rubbing happens best in dry weather?
5. The rod of a lightning conductor accidentally broke into two from the middle. What danger will this pose if lightning strikes the building? Why?

## FOR FORMATIVE ASSESSMENT*

### In the Library—Research Projects

❐ We have talked about electric charges in this chapter but where do these charges come from? Actually, the two types of charges—positive and negative—are present in particles that make up the atom. Inside the atom are present:
- Heavy particles with no charge on them in the centre of the atom.
- Heavy particles with positive charge on them in the centre of the atom.
- Light particles with negative charge on them which go around the central portion in orbits.

Find out the names of these particles. Also find out what the heavy central portion of the atom is called.

❐ Find out the latest earthquake resistant building bye-laws according to which architects are required to design your building.

### My Virtual Library—Research/Activities on the Internet

❐ Visit rsgr.in/lsc-cce-8 and click on LINK 54 to read about electric charges and their applications.
❐ Visit rsgr.in/lsc-cce-8 and click on LINK 55 to make your own electroscope.
❐ Visit rsgr.in/lsc-cce-8 and click on LINK 56 to find out a lot more about earthquakes.
❐ Visit rsgr.in/lsc-cce-8 and click on LINK 57 to make your own seismometer.

### In the Laboratory—Making a Model

**Storing static electricity** Static electricity can be stored in a device called a 'Leyden jar'. It was accidentally discovered by **Pieter van Musschenbroek** in 1745 in Holland. Modified versions called 'capacitors' are used nowadays in electric circuits. You can make your own Leyden jar.

**You will need** ◆ a wide-mouthed glass bottle ◆ steel paper clips ◆ aluminium foil ◆ a piece of thick iron wire ◆ an electric wire

*For more tasks see Page 200

**Procedure:**

- Make a hole in the bottle cap and pass the iron wire through it. At the lower end, turn the wire to make a hook. From that hook hang a chain of paper clips. When you put the cap on the bottle, the chain should touch the bottom.
- Make a ball out of aluminium foil and fix it on top of the iron wire.
- Cut out two long lengths of aluminium foil. Cover the lower half of the bottle (both inside and outside) with the foil.
- Now cut out two circular pieces of foil. Fix them on the bottom of the bottle, one inside and the other outside the bottle. These foil pieces should touch the pieces covering the sides of the bottle.
- Put the cap on the bottle and make sure that the paper clip chain touches the aluminium foil at the bottom, inside the bottle. Your Leyden jar is ready for use.
- For charging the jar, rub a plastic comb against a piece of woollen cloth and touch the ball of aluminium foil with it. Do this several times. Each time the charge on the comb gets stored in the jar.
- Now take an electric wire with plastic insulation. Remove the insulation from both ends. Touch one end of the wire to the foil outside the bottle. Bring the other end very close to the ball of aluminium foil. Does an electric spark flash between the ball and the wire? Why does this happen?
- Now charge the Leyden jar double the number of times. Does this cause any change in the intensity of the spark?

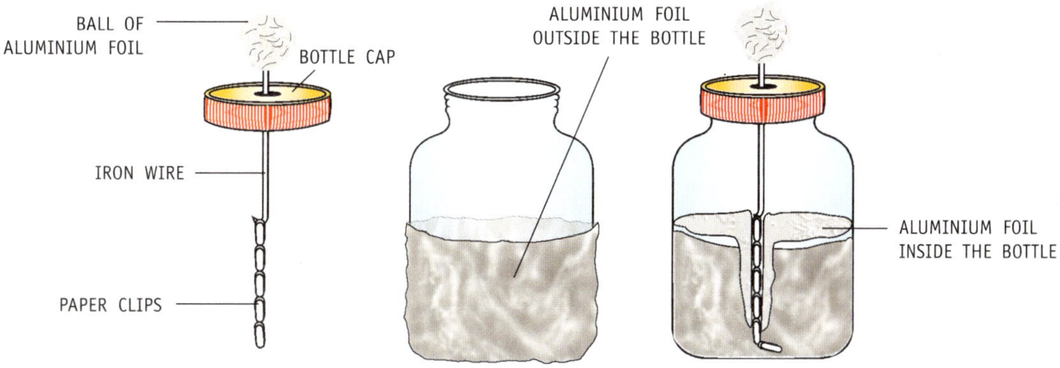


TEACHER'S NOTES

Experiments with static electricity sometimes do not give the required results. Humidity and carelessness in touching a part of the apparatus are some factors responsible. It is advisable for teachers themselves to carry out experiments like charging by conduction/induction several times to understand the pitfalls. Students should be advised to be very careful and patient.

15

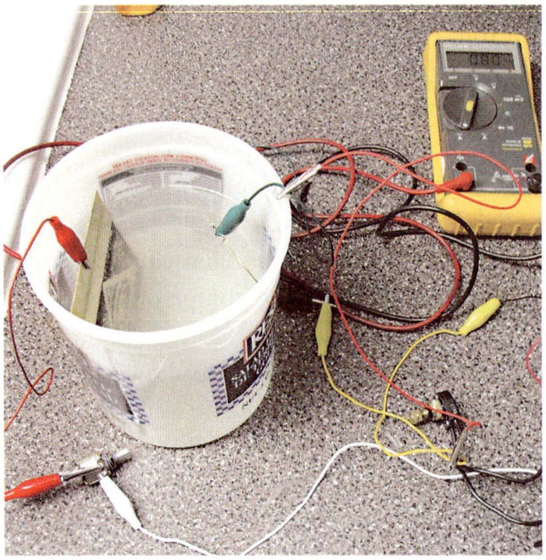

# Chemical Effects of Electric Current

## ELECTRIC CURRENT

You have read that if a charged electroscope is connected to an uncharged electroscope by a metal wire, charges flow through the wire for a short while, till the two electroscopes are similarly charged. It is observed that only negative charges flow through the wire. Positive charges remain fixed and do not flow.

You know that both positively and negatively-charged particles are present inside atoms. The positively-charged particles, called **protons**, are heavy and remain fixed in their positions. The negatively-charged particles, called **electrons**, are lighter and relatively free to move about. Under normal circumstances, the number of positive and negative charges in an atom are equal. The atom as a whole, therefore, shows no charge and is neutral. However, when a glass rod is rubbed with silk, some electrons get ripped off from the glass rod and get transferred to the silk cloth. Thus, the glass rod becomes deficient in electrons and acquires a positive charge. The silk cloth gains excess electrons and acquires an equal negative charge. However, when a plastic comb is rubbed with flannel, electrons are transferred from the flannel to the comb. Thus, the flannel acquires a positive charge and the comb acquires an equal negative charge.

**IN THIS CHAPTER**

ELECTRIC CURRENT ◆ CONDUCTION OF ELECTRICITY THROUGH LIQUIDS ◆ ELECTROLYSIS ◆ ELECTROPLATING

Electrical charge can be made to move in a continuous stream or current. It then becomes much more useful. The movement of electrons constitutes an **electric current**.

To make an electric current flow, two components are necessary. Firstly, a continuous, unbroken path or **circuit** is needed for the current to flow through. For this, a loop of copper wire is generally used as it is a good conductor. A switch is inserted in the circuit to make or break the circuit as required. Secondly, we also need a driving force called **electromotive force** to push the electrons that carry the charge around the circuit. This is provided by an electric cell or a generator.

### Direction of electric current

We know that electrons flow from a body that has an excess of electrons to one that has a deficit of electrons, i.e. from a body that is negatively charged to a body that is positively charged.

Earlier, scientists thought that electric current is the flow of positive charge from a positively-charged body to a negatively-charged body. They, therefore, took this as the direction of flow of current.

Today, we consider the flow of **conventional current** to be from positive to negative and the flow of **electronic current** to be from negative to positive.

## CONDUCTION THROUGH LIQUIDS

As you have read earlier, certain substances such as metals allow electric current to flow through them. They are **conductors** of electric current. Iron, brass, aluminium, copper, graphite etc., are conductors. Air, wood, paper, cloth, rubber or plastic do not allow electric current to flow through them. They are **insulators**. We can test for conductors and insulators in the following way.

**ACTIVITY 1 (Making a model): To make a tester for conductors and insulators**

Make an electric circuit consisting of a cell and a bulb connected through insulating copper wires as shown. Touch the free ends of the wire together for a fraction of a second. If the bulb glows, your tester is ready and working. If it does not glow, check the wires, the connections and the battery one by one to see where the problem lies.

You can test different substances by connecting them to the two free ends of the wire (Fig. 15.1). If the bulb glows, the substance is a conductor. If it does not glow, the substance is an insulator. Try the experiment with a piece of wood, an iron nail, an aluminium spoon, the lead of a pencil, paper, cloth, an eraser and a plastic spoon.

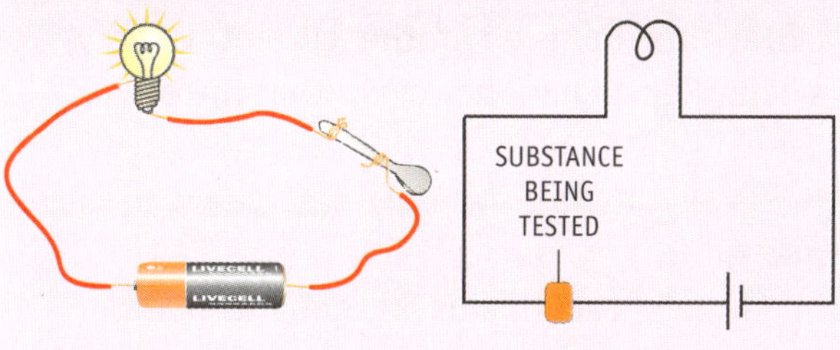


a. A tester for conductors and insulators

b. Circuit diagram for the tester

FIG. 15.1

So far, you have used the tester to test electrical conductivity in solids. Let us now use the tester to see if electricity can also pass through liquids.

**ACTIVITY 2 (Experimental investigation): To observe conduction of electricity through water and other liquids**

You can test different liquids for their electrical conductivity by connecting them to the two free ends of the wires of your tester. If the bulb glows, the liquid conducts electricity. Try this experiment with distilled water, tap water, salt solution, sugar solution, lime juice, vinegar and honey.

An easy way of doing this is by putting a drop of the liquid on a table and touching the two ends of the wire to it. You can also take a small amount of the liquid in the plastic cap of a mineral water bottle. After testing each liquid, remember to wash the ends of the wire in water and dry them before testing another liquid.

While testing liquids, you may find that the bulb does not glow as brightly as with metals. This is because liquids are not such good conductors as metals. Sometimes, the current flowing may be too little for the bulb to glow. For testing conductivities of liquids, we can use an LED (light emitting diode) in the circuit instead of a bulb. The LED lights up even if the current is very small. Remember, however, that in an LED, the **longer lead is connected to the positive end of the cell and the shorter end to the negative end.**

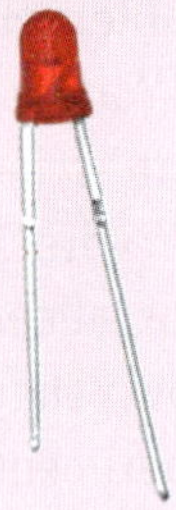

FIG. 15.2 An LED

Classify the liquids as good conductors and poor conductors.

You will find that distilled water is a poor conductor of electricity, but when salt is dissolved in it, it becomes a good conductor. Tap water also conducts electricity. This is because tap water is not pure water and has some salts dissolved in it. But a sugar solution does not conduct electricity.

Lime water also conducts electricity. You know that lime is acidic. Let us see if other acidic and basic solutions also conduct electricity.

### ACTIVITY 3 (Experimental investigation)

Take two small plastic cups. Take some distilled water in them. Add a few drops of dilute sulphuric acid in one cup and sodium hydroxide in another cup. Test them with your tester. What do you find?

You will find that both conduct electricity. In fact, **most liquids that conduct electricity are solutions of acids, bases and salts.**

## ELECTROLYSIS

Let us study further what happens when electric current is passed through water.

### ACTIVITY 4 (Experimental investigation): To demonstrate chemical effect of electric current on water

Take two iron nails. Clean them with sand paper. Wrap one or two rounds of copper wire around them and connect the other ends of the wires to the two terminals of an electric battery. Take water in a beaker and add to it a little salt or a few drops of sulphuric acid to make it conducting. Immerse the nails (called **electrodes**) in the solution. Observe the nails carefully. Can you see small bubbles of gases coming out from the water near the nails?

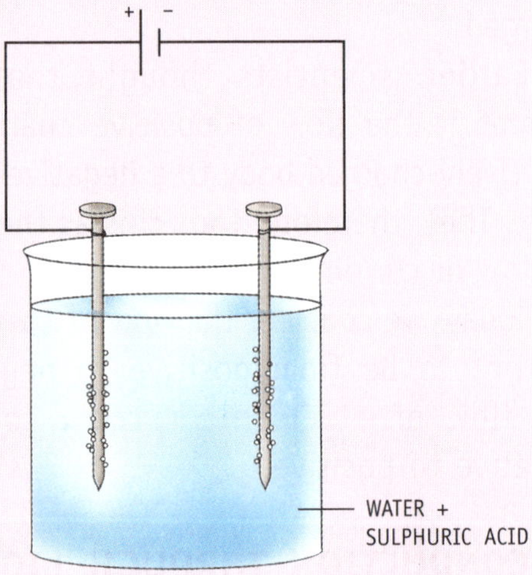


FIG. 15.3 Passing electric current through water

It can be checked that the gases evolved are hydrogen and oxygen. Where did these gases come from? What does this indicate? The gases come from water—electric current breaks up water into its constituent gases, hydrogen and oxygen. This observation, therefore, shows that electric current has a chemical effect on water.

(**NOTE:** The amount of salt added should be very small. If a concentrated solution of salt in water is electrolyzed, hydrogen and chlorine gases are evolved, instead of hydrogen and oxygen.)

This activity shows that **an electric current can bring about a chemical change**.

A substance which conducts electricity in the liquid state or when dissolved in water and breaks up chemically during the process is called an **electrolyte**. The process of breaking up of an electrolyte chemically on passing an electric current through it is called **electrolysis**.

When an electrolyte such as copper sulphate is dissolved in water, it breaks up into positively and negatively-charged particles called **ions**. Positively-charged ions are called **cations** while negatively-charged particles are called **anions**. Ions move about freely in aqueous solution.

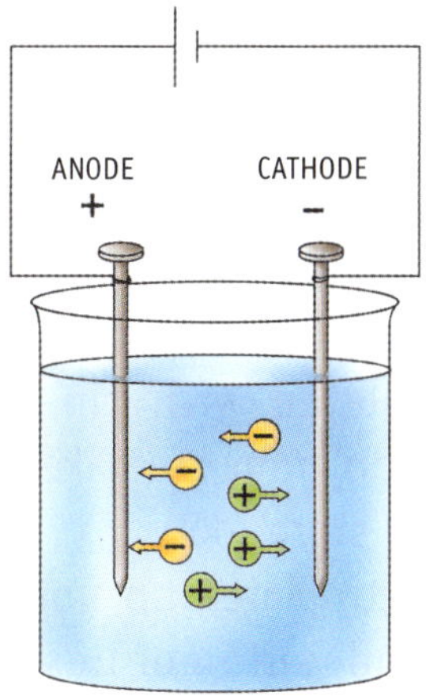


FIG. 15.4 Movement of ions during electrolysis

When electric current is passed through the solution, the cations move towards the negatively-charged electrode (cathode) and anions towards the positively-charged electrode (anode). This results in a chemical change (Fig. 15.4).

## ORAL QUESTIONS FOR FORMATIVE ASSESSMENT

1. Which of these will conduct electricity—tap water or distilled water? Why?
2. Conduction of electricity in liquids occurs through electrons. Do you agree? Give reasons.
3. When a liquid conducts electricity, a process other than conduction also takes place. What process is this?

## ELECTROPLATING

Electrolysis has a number of applications. The most common of these is **electroplating**, i.e. coating a thin layer of a metal, such as gold, silver, chromium, tin or nickel, over another cheaper metal. This is done either to protect the metal, or to make it look attractive.

- Chromium is a shiny metal that does not corrode and resists scratches. It is deposited on other cheaper metals such as iron to make car parts, taps, bicycle handle bars, wheel rims, etc. This makes them look more attractive and also resist corrosion.

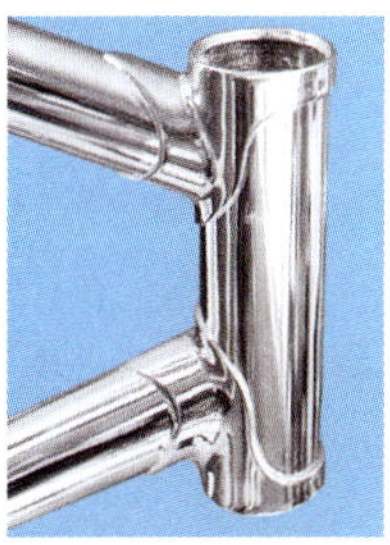

a. chromium-plated handle bar

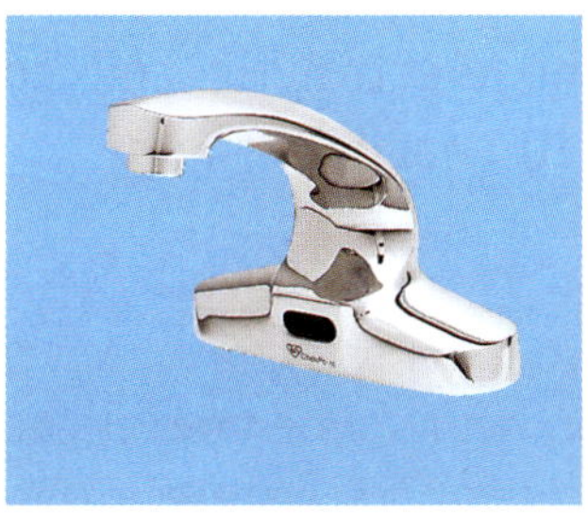

b. chromium-plated tap

c. tin-plated can

d. gold-plated jewellery

FIG. 15.5 Some electroplated items

- Gold or silver is electroplated on jewellery made out of a cheaper metal to make it look attractive.
- Food kept in iron cans gets spoilt because of reaction with iron. To prevent this, iron is electroplated with tin, which is less reactive than iron, to make tin cans. They are used to store food.
- Zinc is electroplated on iron used to make bridges and automobiles. The coating prevents iron from rusting.

You can easily carry out electroplating of copper in the laboratory.

### Activity 5 (Making a model): To electroplate a metal object with copper in the laboratory

You will need a glass beaker, a thick copper wire, a metal spoon, a battery cell, a solution of copper sulphate, connecting wires and a switch.

Fill around three-fourth of the beaker with the copper sulphate solution. Hammer the copper wire to flatten it out and connect it to the positive terminal of the battery. Connect the spoon through a switch to the negative terminal of the battery. Dip both of them in the copper sulphate solution, making sure that they do not touch each other (Fig. 15.6). Put on the switch and let the current pass through the solution for about half an hour. Does a layer of copper get deposited on the spoon?

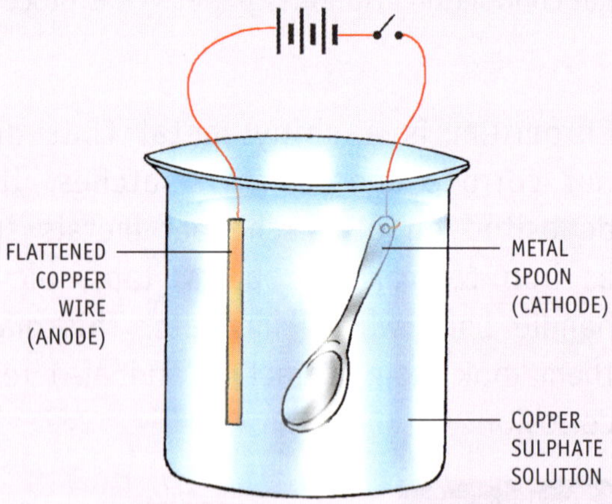


FIG. 15.6 Electroplating of copper

When copper sulphate is dissolved in water, it forms positively-charged copper ions and negatively-charged sulphate ions. When an electric current is passed through the solution:

- The copper ions (cations) move towards the cathode, pick up electrons from there (supplied by the electric current), and get deposited on it as copper atoms.
- At the anode, the copper atoms in the copper plate lose electrons to form copper ions. The ions go into solution. Thus, the copper lost to the cathode is restored by the anode.

Therefore, the anode slowly dissolves into the solution, while a layer of copper gets deposited on the cathode. The sulphate ions do not take part in the chemical reaction. Thus, the net effect is that **copper gets transferred from the anode to the cathode**.

This method can be used to deposit a layer of any metal on another material.

The above arrangement consisting of an electrolyte, two electrodes (anode and cathode) and a source of current is called an **electrolytic cell**. The electrolytic cell converts electrical energy to chemical energy.

### GALVANIC CELL

A galvanic cell does the opposite of an electrolytic cell—it converts chemical energy into electrical energy. It has an electrolyte, and electrodes of different metals. When the electrodes are connected through an external circuit, electric current flows in the circuit.

An example is the **Voltaic cell** in which dilute sulphuric acid is the electrolyte. One electrode is made of copper, and the other of zinc. Electrons flow in the external circuit from the zinc to the copper electrode.

Another example is the **dry cell** that we use in torches and radios. In a dry cell, the electrolyte is a paste of ammonium chloride. One of the electrodes is the carbon rod. The container of the cell is made of zinc and acts as the other electrode. Manganese dioxide present inside improves the performance of the cell by absorbing the hydrogen gas produced.

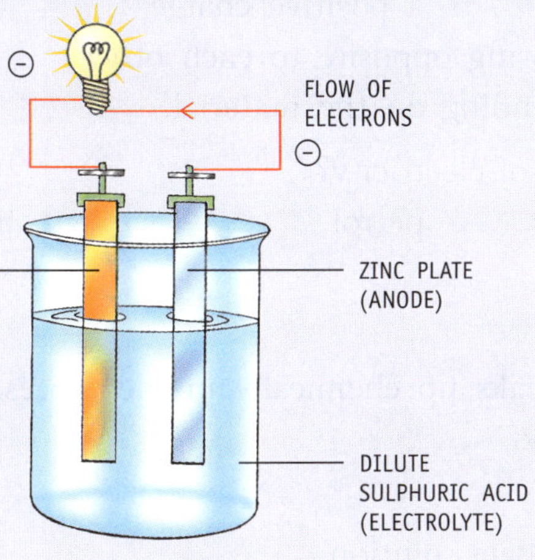

FIG. 15.7 Voltaic cell

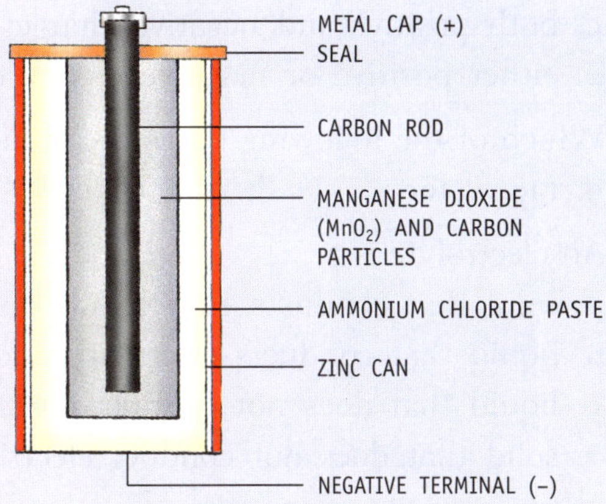

FIG. 15.8 Dry cell

## ORAL QUESTIONS FOR FORMATIVE ASSESSMENT

1. To electroplate copper on a metal object, what will you use as electrolyte, anode and cathode?
2. What is the need to electroplate one metal over another?

## NOW YOU KNOW

- The flow of electrons constitutes an electric current.
- Conventional current flows from positive to negative terminal; electronic current flows from negative to positive terminal.
- Most liquids that conduct electricity are solutions of acids, bases and salts.
- An electric current can bring about a chemical change.
- The process of breaking of an electrolyte chemically on passing an electric current through it is called electrolysis.
- Electrolysis is used for electroplating one metal over another.

## NEW WORDS

**CATIONS**—positively-charged ions
**ANIONS**—negatively-charged ions
**ELECTROLYSIS**—the process of breaking up of an electrolyte chemically on passing an electric current through it
**ELECTROPLATING**—coating a thin layer of a metal over another metal with the help of the process of electrolysis

## FOR FORMATIVE AND SUMMATIVE ASSESSMENT

### A. MULTIPLE-CHOICE QUESTIONS: Choose the most appropriate answer.

1. Electric current is the flow of particles with
   a. a negative charge. b. a positive charge.
   c. both positive and negative charges flowing opposite to each other.
   d. either positive or negative charge depending on the material.
2. Which of the following is not a conductor of electricity?
   a. tap water b. salt water c. petrol d. lime juice
3. An electrolyte is a
   a. solid that conducts electricity.
   b. liquid that conducts electricity and breaks up chemically in the process.
   c. liquid that does not conduct electricity.
   d. solid that does not conduct electricity.
4. On passing electricity through copper sulphate solution,
   a. copper is formed at anode. b. copper is formed at cathode.
   c. oxygen is formed at anode. d. hydrogen is formed at cathode.
5. In which of these is current not conducted by electrons?
   a. copper b. aluminium c. tap water d. mercury
6. Which of these metals will you electroplate on iron to protect it from rusting and to make it shine?
   a. copper b. gold c. zinc d. chromium

### B. VERY SHORT-ANSWER QUESTIONS: Give one-word answers.

1. A positively-charged body has a ________ (deficit / excess) of electrons.
2. Electronic current flows from positive to negative. True or false?
3. A battery is used as a driving force in an electric circuit. True or false?
4. Which of these particles are responsible for the flow of electric current—electrons, protons or neutrons?
5. Metals are conductors of electricity. True or false?
6. Which of these is better for use in a tester for testing conductivity of liquids—electric bulb or LED?
7. Most liquids that conduct electricity are solutions of ________, ________ or ________
8. When electricity is passed through tap water, the gases ________ and ________ are evolved.
9. Ions may be positively charged or negatively charged. True or false?
10. An electric current brings about chemical changes in most conducting ________ (solids / liquids).

11. During electroplating, copper is deposited at the __________ (anode / cathode).
12. Expensive metals are protected by electroplating. True or false?

## C. SHORT-ANSWER QUESTIONS (TYPE I): Answer in a sentence or two.

1. What is electric current?
2. How is electronic current different from conventional current?
3. Differentiate between conductors and insulators.
4. What is an electrolyte?
5. Why is zinc electroplated on iron?

## D. SHORT-ANSWER QUESTIONS (TYPE II): Answer in about 30 words.

1. Draw a circuit diagram showing a dry cell connected to a bulb through a switch. Mark the positive and the negative terminals of the cell, and the direction of flow of **a.** electron, **b.** conventional current.
2. What are the advantages of electroplating iron with chromium?
3. Discuss what happens when an electrolyte is dissolved in water, and then an electric current is passed through it.
4. What happens when electricity is passed through tap water?

## E. LONG-ANSWER QUESTIONS: Answer in about 60 words.

1. How will you show experimentally that an electric current can bring about a chemical change? What is this phenomenon called?
2. What is electroplating? How will you carry out electroplating of copper in the laboratory?
3. List four uses of electroplating, giving the reason for electroplating in each case.

## HOTS QUESTIONS: Think and answer.

1. Which of these do you think uses less electrical energy—electric bulb or LED?
2. Mercury is a liquid and conducts electricity. Do you think it is an electrolyte? (**HINT**: Mercury is a metal that is a liquid at room temperature.)
3. Solid copper sulphate does not conduct electricity, but when it is dissolved in water, it does conduct electricity. Why?
4. Copper conducts electricity through electrons, whereas salt solution conducts electricity through ions. Do you agree?
5. Why should you not touch electrical appliances with wet hands?
6. After doing Activity 5 (electroplating a spoon with copper), a student interchanged the connections of the copper plate and the spoon. What do you think will happen now?
7. We should not try to put out a fire in an electrical appliance by pouring water on it. Why?
8. Instead of taking the trouble of electroplating metals with chromium for making car parts, taps, cycle parts, etc., why are these objects not made of chromium itself?

## FOR FORMATIVE ASSESSMENT*

### In the Library—Research Projects

- You have read about conductors and insulators. There are some materials that are mid-way between conductors and insulators in their ability to pass electricity. They are known as semiconductors. Semiconductors are extremely useful in the field of electronics. Without them, it would not have been possible to produce small transistor-radios, calculators, computers and a number of other electronic equipments.

  Find out the name of the semiconductor that is most commonly used in making electronic devices. Find out how solar cells are made from this semiconductor. Find out how very small electronic components, which have made it possible to produce the small computers used today, are made from it.

- LEDs are made from semiconductors and can be made to emit light of different colours. They are expected to be used more and more for lighting in the future because they are much more efficient than conventional (incandescent) bulbs. This is because conventional bulbs depend on heating of the filament to produce light. The heat energy given out is completely wasted. LEDs generate very little heat, and a much higher percentage of the electrical power goes directly into generating light. Thus, LEDs use up much less electric power to give the same intensity of light. The disadvantage of LEDs is that they are still expensive. However, with advancement of technology, they are expected to become more affordable in future. CFLs (compact fluorescent lightbulbs) are also more efficient than conventional bulbs, but they **contain mercury which is toxic**. Hence, **disposing off CFLs poses a big problem**.

  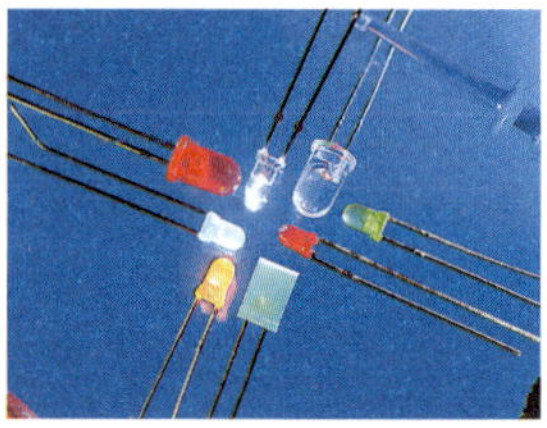

  Find out where LEDs are commonly used today.

### My Virtual Library—Research/Activities on the Internet

- Visit rsgr.in/lsc-cce-8 and click on LINK 58 to find out how LEDs work.
- Why are CFLs more efficient than conventional electric bulbs?
  Visit rsgr.in/lsc-cce-8 and click on LINK 59 to find out.
- Visit rsgr.in/lsc-cce-8 and click on LINK 60 to make hydrogen at home by electrolysis.
- Visit rsgr.in/lsc-cce-8 and click on LINK 61 to get reference for several experiments on electrolysis.

### To Meet—Research on Scientist

**Count Alessandro Volta** (1745–1827) This Italian physicist is known for his pioneering work in electricity. He made the first electric battery, called the voltaic pile. Among his many other contributions to science was the invention of the device known as the **electrophorus** which produced static charges. Napolean made Volta a Count in honour of his work. Volt, the unit of electric voltage, is named after him.

Find out more about the life and work of Volta, and make a presentation on it.

### In the Laboratory—Designing Models

- **Make another current tester** You studied about the magnetic effects of current in the previous class—that a current-carrying wire can deflect a magnetic needle from its north–south position. We can use this effect to make a tester to check if current is flowing in a circuit.

*For more tasks see Page 200

Take a magnetic compass and place it in the tray of an empty matchbox. Wrap a few rounds of copper wire around the box as shown. Place the box on a table. Touch the two ends of the wire momentarily to the two terminals of an electric cell. Does the compass needle show a deflection?

Your tester is ready. You can use it in place of an LED tester.

❐ **Write with electricity—electric pen**

**You will need** ◆ KI (potassium iodide) salt solution ◆ starch solution ◆ a metal sheet ◆ a paper napkin ◆ a battery ◆ copper wire

**Procedure:**

Take KI salt solution in a beaker. Connect the metal sheet to the negative end of the battery. Add a few drops of starch solution to it. Soak a piece of paper napkin in the KI solution in the beaker and place it on the metal sheet. Connect another wire to the positive terminal of the battery. Now write with this positive wire on the paper napkin. You must take help of your teacher.

## LIFE SKILL

### How to prolong the life of your cell phone rechargeable battery

- If you are in an area with no reception, e.g. a basement or remote area, turn the cell phone off since constantly searching for service depletes the battery fairly quickly.
- The vibrate function uses up a lot of battery power. So, switch it off when not needed and use only the ring tone.
- The back light of the phone uses up power—either turn it off or set it reduce the time for which it is on.
- Turn off Bluetooth, Wifi, GPS and infrared capability when not in use—they drain the battery pretty fast.
- High temperature is an enemy of the battery. Keep the battery cool—avoid leaving your phone in a hot car or in direct sunlight.
- Initialize a new battery by charging it fully before its first use to obtain maximum capacity. Nickel-based batteries should be charged for 16 hours initially and run through 2–4 full charge/full discharge cycles. Lithium ion batteries should be charged for about 5–6 hours.
- Charge your battery correctly, in accordance with its type. Most new cell phones have lithium-ion batteries, while older ones generally have nickel-based batteries. A good rule to follow for nickel-battery cell phones is to discharge them completely once every two to three weeks, and then charge them fully. This is not necessary for lithium-ion batteries.
- A battery which is not being used should be stored in a cool place—put it in a 'zip lock' bag and store in a refrigerator. Do not store a battery fully charged—charge it to about 40 % before storage.
- Similar batteries are used in laptops and cameras, so the same rules apply for charging and storage.

SKILLS INVOLVED: Thinking skill, Preservation skill

TEACHER'S NOTES

It should be made very clear to students that the mechanism of conduction of electricity is different in liquids and solids. Explain to them what happens when acids, bases and salts dissolve in water. Once they understand ions, it will be simple to understand why chemical effects of electricity occur in liquids/solutions and not in solids, and why solid salts do not conduct electricity.

# MORE TASKS for FORMATIVE ASSESSMENT (FA 3)

## for Chapters 11–15

In addition to the activities and projects given in the respective chapters, the following tasks can also be used for formative assessment.

### RESEARCH PROJECTS

- You know that X-rays can be used to photograph the bones inside the body. However, it is not advisable to use X-rays to check the progress of a baby developing in its mother's womb. Find out why. The method normally used for this purpose utilizes a special kind of sound to build up a picture of the baby. Find out the name of the technique and the type of sound it uses.
- An aircraft often flies through a storm, and is struck by lightning. However, there is rarely any damage to the aircraft because of this. Find out why. What precautions are taken in designing an aircraft to ensure this?

### RESEARCH ON SCIENTIST

**Charles Augustin Coulomb** (1736–1806) The unit for measuring amount of charge is called 'coulomb' and is named after this French physicist. Coulomb made sensitive instruments to measure the forces between electric charges. He also worked on friction and magnetism.

Find out more about the life and work of Coulomb and make a presentation on it.

### DESIGNING AN EXPERIMENT

Design an experiment to study the effect of dropping two objects of different masses from the same height and to show which of them will exert a greater force on the ground.

### MAKING A MODEL

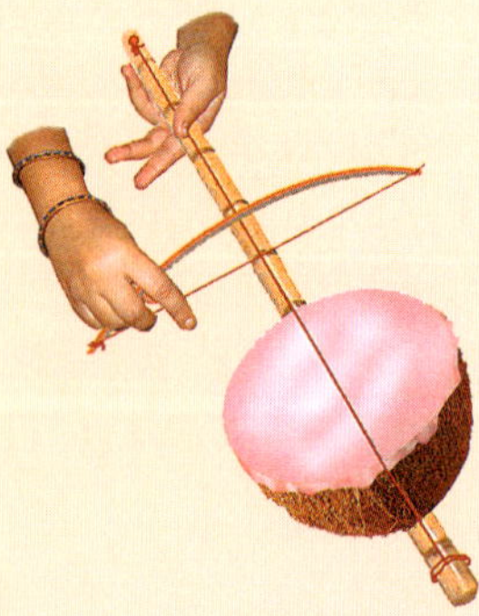

**Make an *ektara*** You will need a hollow coconut shell or a small earthen pot, two pieces of bamboo, metal wire, and a strong piece of string. Make the musical instrument called 'ektara' as shown in the figure. Play the instrument and identify its vibrating part.

### FIELD TRIP

Visit a shoe store. Observe the shoes displayed there for various sports. Do you notice differences in the soles of these shoes?

You will notice that a football shoe has studs on its sole. Since the studs have small area of contact with the ground, the pressure exerted under the studs is high enough to grip the ground.

Find out what spikes and skiis are and what they are used for.

# 16

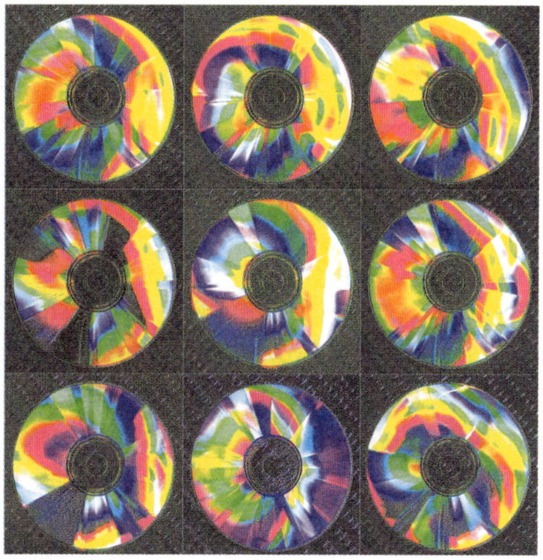

# Light

We are able to see the objects around us because of the light which falls on them and is sent back. When this light reaches our eyes, we are able to see the objects. This sending back of light by objects is called **reflection of light**. Reflection is the phenomenon in which light, on striking a surface, changes its direction and is thrown back into the same medium.

The amount of light that is reflected depends on the material and nature of the surface on which the light falls.

- An **opaque body** absorbs some of the light that falls on it and reflects the remaining light.
- A **transparent body** allows almost all the light to pass through it and reflects very little light.
- A smooth and a **highly polished surface** such as a shiny stainless steel surface or a mirror reflects almost all the light that falls on it.

## REGULAR AND DIFFUSED REFLECTIONS

The surface of a mirror is very smooth. Therefore, if a beam of light falls on it, the entire beam is reflected in only one direction. This is called **regular reflection** (Fig. 16.1a).

However, the surfaces of most objects around us are not so smooth. When the rays in a beam of light fall on an object with an uneven

**IN THIS CHAPTER**

REGULAR AND DIFFUSED REFLECTION ◆ LAWS OF REFLECTION ◆ CHARACTERISTICS OF IMAGE FORMED WITH A PLANE MIRROR ◆ MULTIPLE REFLECTION

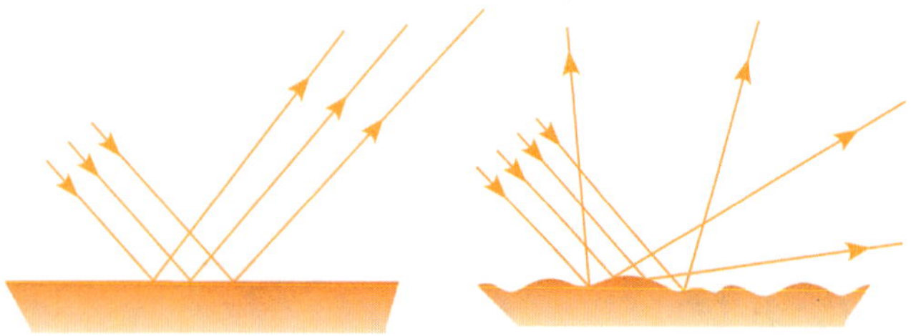

a. Regular reflection   b. Irregular reflection

**Fig. 16.1** Types of reflections

surface, they get reflected in different directions. This is called **irregular** or **diffused reflection** (Fig. 16.1b).

It is because of irregular reflection that we can see objects from every direction. Irregular reflection of sunlight by objects around us enables our room to have light during the day even if sunlight does not directly fall into it.

## LAWS OF REFLECTION

We will now study some properties of light.

**IT'S A FACT!**

A ray of light is an idealization in reality, just like a 'line' in geometry which is not supposed to have breadth. Even the narrowest beam of light that we can get is made up of several rays. For simplicity, we use the term ray for a narrow beam of light.

**Activity 1 (Experimental investigation): To study the first law of reflection**

Fix a sheet of white paper on a table. Cut out a thin slit about 1 mm wide, in a piece of cardboard. Make the cardboard piece stand vertically on the white sheet using supports (Fig. 16.2a). Darken the room. Shine a torch just behind the slit. You can see the path of light on the sheet of paper. Keep a mirror vertically in the path of light.

The light falling on the mirror is called the **incident ray**. You can clearly see the path this ray takes after being reflected by the mirror. After reflection it is called the **reflected ray**. If you rotate the mirror, this reflected ray also rotates.

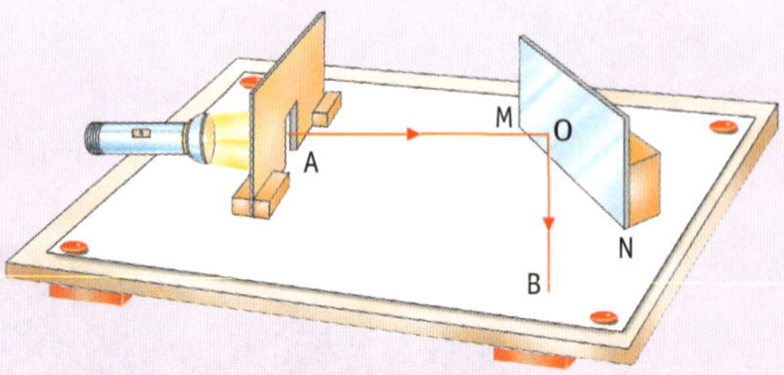


a. Experimental set-up

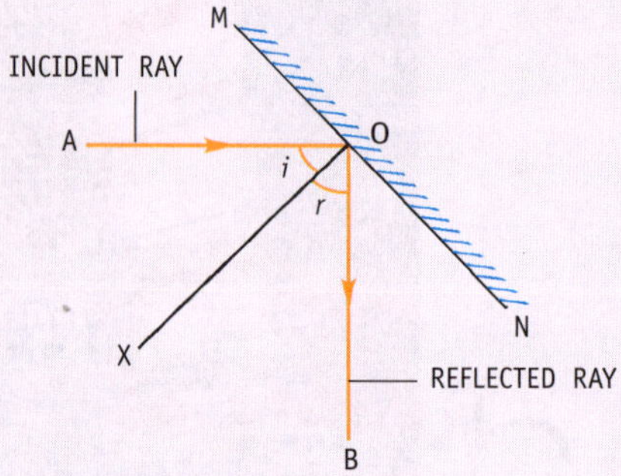


b. Angle of incidence is equal to the angle of reflection.

**Fig. 16.2** To study the first law of reflection

Mark the position of the mirror MN with a straight line. Using a scale and a pencil, mark the path of the incident ray AO and the reflected ray OB (Fig. 16.2b). Measure the angles that the incident and the reflected rays make with the mirror (∠MOA and ∠NOB, respectively).

You will find that these angles are equal. This shows that the reflected ray leaves the mirror at the same angle at which the incident ray strikes it.

Now, let us consider two other angles. At O, called the point of incidence, draw a perpendicular to the mirror, OX. This is called the **normal** at the point of incidence. We call ∠AOX the **angle of incidence**, and ∠BOX the **angle of reflection**. Measure ∠AOX and ∠BOX. You will see that ∠AOX and ∠BOX are equal.

Therefore, angle of incidence = angle of reflection

Or $\angle i = \angle r$

This is the **first law of reflection**.

There is another law of reflection which firmly fixes the reflected ray. Once you have drawn the incident ray and the normal, there is only one plane that can pass through both of these. In this case it is the plane of the paper.

In Activity 1, use a bigger sheet of paper and extend it beyond the edge of the table. Fold the paper downwards at the edge of the table so that it hangs down. Does the reflected ray reach the edge of the paper beyond the table? Now straighten the paper so that it is again in the plane of the table. Does the reflected ray now reach the edge of the paper? This shows that the reflected ray is also in the plane of the paper.

Thus, the second law of reflection states that the incident ray, the normal and the reflected ray all lie in the same plane.

The above activity is, however, too rough to give exact values. In the laboratory, we use pins to mark the incident and reflected rays to get more accurate results, as explained below.

### ACTIVITY 2 (Experimental investigation): To verify the laws of reflection experimentally

Fix a sheet of white paper on a table. Draw a line MN and keep the mirror vertical exactly along this line (Fig. 16.3a).

Draw an incident ray XO which meets the mirror at an angle (say 45°). Fix two pins A and B, about 5 cm apart, on this ray. Now look at the reflections of A and B and fix a pin C in such a way that pin C and the reflections of pins A and B appear to be in

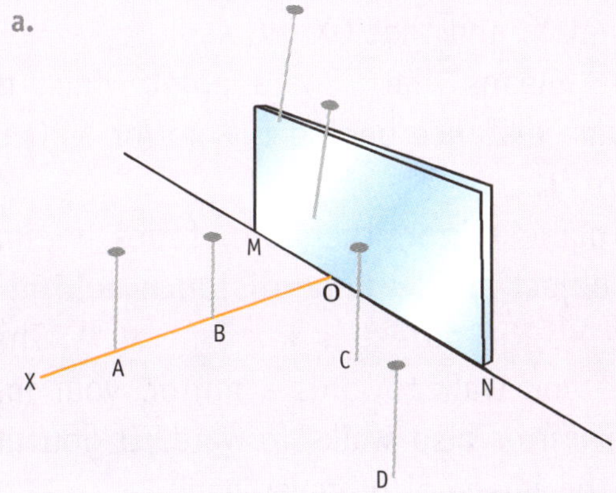


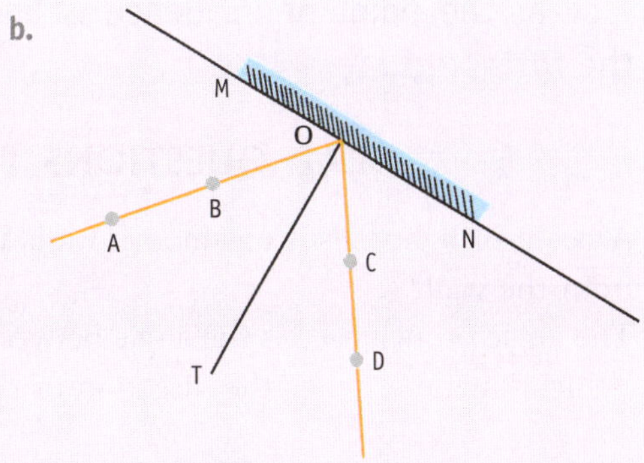


**FIG. 16.3** Experiment to verify the first law of reflection

a straight line. Fix another pin D after C, but nearer your eye, such that D, C and the images of A and B appear to be in a straight line. Then CD is the reflected ray.

Remove the pins and the mirror. Join DC and extend it to meet the mirror. If you have been accurate in your work, this should meet the mirror line exactly at O. Draw the normal OT at O. Measure ∠AOT and ∠DOT. You will find that these angles are equal (Fig. 16.3b).

If you carry out the activity for different positions of the incident ray, you will find that in all cases,

Angle of incidence = Angle of reflection

Also, the incident ray, the reflected ray and the normal all lie in one plane, that is, on the plane of the paper.

This experiment verifies the two laws of reflection.

Let us summarise the definitions of terms you have learnt so far.

- The ray of light from the source that strikes a given surface is called the **incident ray**.
- The point at which the incident ray strikes the surface is called the **point of incidence**.
- The perpendicular to the surface at the point of incidence is called the **normal**.
- The angle between the normal and the incident ray is called the **angle of incidence**.
- The ray of light that gets reflected by the

surface at the point of incidence is known as the **reflected ray**.

- The angle between the reflected ray and the normal is known as the **angle of reflection**.

### ORAL QUESTIONS FOR FORMATIVE ASSESSMENT

1. A beam of light falls on a smooth wall. Will you observe regular reflection or diffused reflection from the wall?
2. The angle of incidence is the angle between a ray of light and the mirror. Do you agree? Give reasons.
3. Which law determines the direction of the reflected ray from a plane mirror?

## LOCATING THE IMAGE FORMED BY A PLANE MIRROR

You have seen that the image formed by a plane mirror is virtual, i.e. the image cannot be obtained on a screen. You cannot, therefore, place your hand at the point where the image is formed.

The formation of images in a plane mirror can be understood by drawing ray diagrams. We will again need the help of Activity 2 to locate the position of the image formed.

### ACTIVITY 3 (Experimental investigation): To locate an image formed by a plane mirror

Keep a plane mirror vertically along the line MN on a sheet of white paper. Place a pin at point O whose image we want to locate (Fig. 16.4a). Draw two incident rays OA and OB.

Place pins C and D on these rays. Locate the reflected ray EF by fixing pins E and F such that E, F and images of O and C are

a.

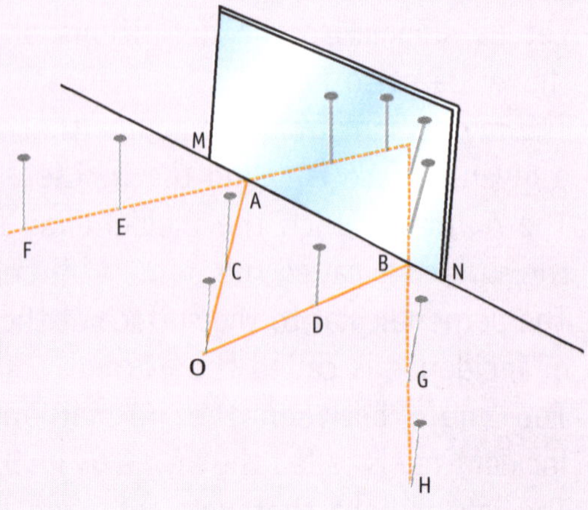


b.

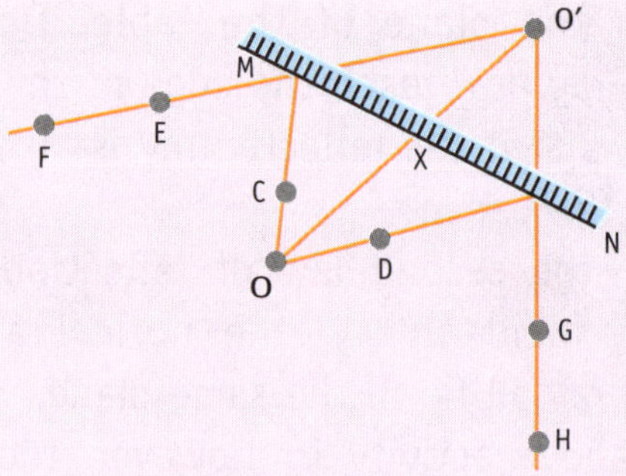


FIG. 16.4 Locating the image formed by a plane mirror

in one straight line; and the reflected ray GH by fixing pins G and H such that G, H and the images of O and D are in one straight line.

Remove the mirror and extend the two reflected rays backwards. They meet at a point O′ (Fig. 16.4b).

Notice that the reflected rays appear to come from O′. Therefore, O′ is the virtual image of O. Join OO′. Measure the angle which OO′ makes with the mirror at point X. Also measure OX and O′X.

You will find OO′ is perpendicular to the mirror at X, and that OX = O′X.

This means that O′ is a point which is at the same distance behind the mirror as O is in front of it.

A plane mirror, therefore, forms an image of an object at **the same distance behind the mirror as the object is in front of it**. This is why, if you walk towards a mirror, your image in the mirror also walks forward. If you move back, the image also moves back.

### Lateral inversion

**ACTIVITY 4 (Observation): To observe lateral inversion in a plane mirror**

Stand in front of a mirror. Raise your right hand. Which hand does your image raise?

FIG. 16.5 Lateral inversion in a plane mirror

It raises its left hand! This shows that, in the image formed by a plane mirror, there is an interchange of left and right. This is called **lateral inversion** and is an important property of the plane mirror image.

### Characteristics of an image formed with a plane mirror

- The image formed is erect.
- The image is of the same size as the object.
- The image is laterally inverted, that is, the right side of the object appears as the left side of the image.
- The image is as far behind the mirror as the object is in front of it.
- The image formed is virtual, that is, it cannot be caught on a screen. There is no actual meeting of the light rays (incident and reflected).

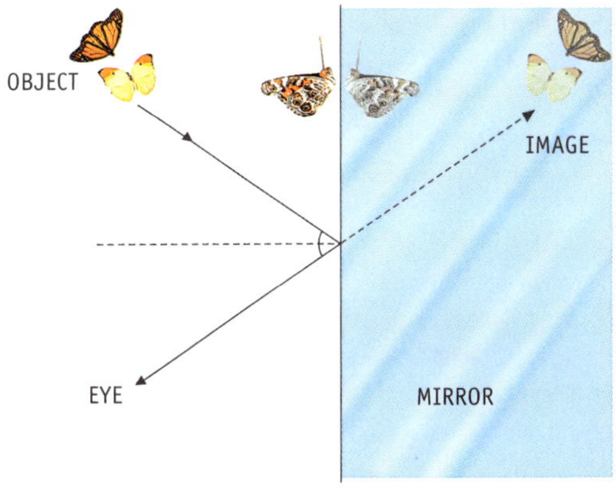


FIG. 16.6 Images formed by a plane mirror

## IMAGES FORMED BY MIRRORS AT AN ANGLE

Have you ever looked at your image in two mirrors fixed parallel to each other on opposite walls in a room, for example, in a barber shop? You can see a large number of images. This is because the image formed by one mirror serves as the object for the other mirror, and so on. Let us see how many images are formed by two mirrors kept at an angle to each other.

FIG. 16.7 Multiple images formed by parallel mirrors facing each other

**ACTIVITY 5 (Experimental investigation): To observe images formed by mirrors at an angle to each other**

Fix a white sheet of paper on a table. Take two plane mirrors and make them stand on the paper such that one of their vertical edges touch each other. Adjust the angle between the mirrors to 90°. Keep a pencil between the mirrors and count the number of images you can see. You will find that there are 3 images. Reduce the angle between the mirrors. Does the number of images increase or decrease? Increase the angle. What happens now?

Change the angle between the mirrors

to 30°, 45°, 60°, 120°, etc. Note down the number of images in each case.

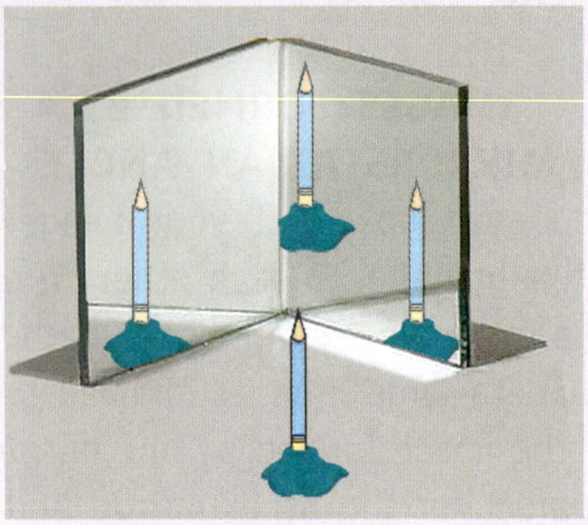

FIG. 16.8 Three images are formed by two mirrors placed at right angles to each other.

We get many images of the object because the image formed by one mirror acts as an object for the second mirror. Further images of an image are also formed. This continues till no more reflection by either mirror is possible. This phenomenon is referred to as **multiple reflection**.

The number of images formed by mirrors at an angle is given by a simple formula. If θ is the angle of inclination between two mirrors, then the number of images formed is given by the formula

$$n = (360/\theta) - 1$$

TABLE 16.1 Multiple images formed by mirrors at an angle

| S.NO. | ANGLE BETWEEN THE MIRRORS, θ | NO. OF IMAGES |
|---|---|---|
| 1 | 90° | 3 |
| 2 | 60° | 5 |
| 3 | 30° | 11 |
| 4 | 0° (mirrors are parallel) | infinite |

## The kaleidoscope

The principle of forming multiple images by mirrors at an angle to each other is used in a toy called **kaleidoscope** which many of you may have played with. It consists of three plane mirrors inclined at an angle of 60° to each other. The arrangement is kept in a cylindrical cardboard box with a few pieces of coloured glass at one end. The mirrors form multiple images of these glass pieces, resulting in beautiful patterns when seen from the other end. On rotating the cylindrical box, the patterns change continuously as the position of the glass pieces shifts.

### ACTIVITY 6 (Making a model): To make a kaleidoscope

Firmly tape three mirror strips together so that they are at an angle of 60° to each other, with the shiny surfaces facing inwards.

Take a piece of cardboard of the same length as the mirror strips. Bend and fit it around the mirror strips. Tape it in place. Cover the two open ends of the cardboard with clear plastic and tape it in place. At one end place some broken pieces of coloured glass bangles on the plastic (be careful while handling the bangle pieces). Tape some tracing paper on top of the plastic, leaving enough space between the plastic and paper for the bangle pieces to move.

Hold your kaleidoscope towards light. Look through the other end and see the beautiful patterns formed as you rotate the tube.

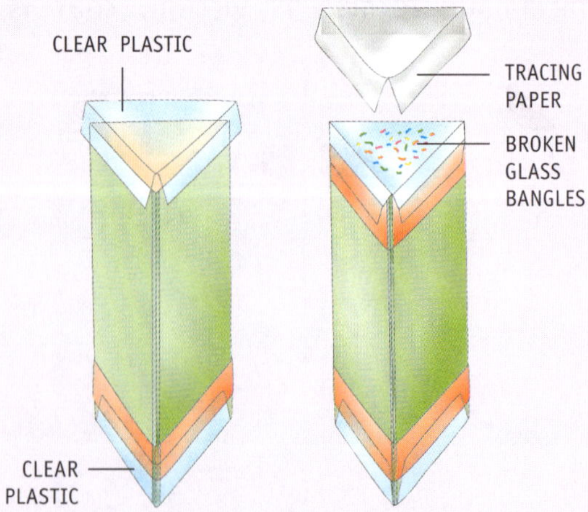


FIG. 16.9 Making a kaleidoscope

### Uses of plane mirrors

- We commonly use plane mirrors in our homes to look at our reflection. In beauty parlours, plane mirrors kept at an angle are used to view the side of the head. Plane mirrors parallel to each other are used to view the back of the head.
- Plane mirrors are used to reflect light on an object. For example, during outdoor shooting of a film, metal sheets are used as plane mirrors to reflect sunlight on the actors.
- They are also used in solar cookers to reflect light on the food being cooked.
- They are used in periscopes. From a submarine under the sea, a sailor can see objects and enemy ships on the surface of the sea by using a periscope.

## ORAL QUESTIONS FOR FORMATIVE ASSESSMENT

1. Why do we say that a plane mirror forms a virtual image of an object?
2. Somebody asks you to count the number of images formed by two mirrors kept parallel to each other. Can you do this? Why?
3. As the angle between two plane mirrors decreases, the number of images increases. Do you agree? If the angle is given, how will you find the number of images without performing an experiment?

## NOW YOU KNOW

- When a beam of light falls on a smooth surface it gets reflected in one direction. This is called regular reflection.
- When a beam of light falls on an uneven surface it gets reflected in different directions. This is called irregular or diffused reflection.
- There are two laws of reflection: ◆ the angle of incidence is equal to the angle of reflection ◆ the incident ray, the normal and the reflected ray all lie in the same plane.
- The image formed by a plane mirror is virtual, erect, of the same size as the object, as much behind the mirror as the object is in front of it, and laterally inverted.
- A number of images are formed if the object is placed between two mirrors at an angle. This principle is used in making a kaleidoscope.
- Plane mirrors are used as looking glass, to reflect light on objects, in solar cookers, in kaleidoscopes and in periscopes.

## NEW WORDS

**OPAQUE BODY**—body which absorbs some light incident on it and reflects the remaining light

**TRANSPARENT BODY**—body which allows almost all the light to pass through it and reflects very little light

## FOR FORMATIVE AND SUMMATIVE ASSESSMENT

### A. MULTIPLE-CHOICE QUESTIONS: Choose the most appropriate answer.

1. The angle of incidence is
   a. the angle that the incident ray makes with the mirror.
   b. the angle that the incident ray makes with the normal at the point of incidence.
   c. 180° minus the angle that the incident ray makes with the mirror.
   d. the angle that the incident ray makes with the reflected ray.
2. If you stand in front of a plane mirror and scratch your left cheek, your image
   a. scratches its left cheek. b. scratches its right cheek.
   c. scratches both cheeks one by one. d. does not scratch at all.
3. The image formed by a plane mirror is
   a. virtual, erect, behind the mirror and smaller than the object.
   b. virtual, erect, behind the mirror and the same size as the object.
   c. virtual, inverted, behind the mirror and the same size as the object.
   d. real, erect, behind the mirror and the same size as the object.
4. If the angle between the mirror and the incident ray is 30°, the angle of reflection is
   a. 30°. b. 60°. c. 15°. d. 90°.
5. The image formed by a plane mirror is formed
   a. on the surface of the mirror. b. just in front of the mirror.
   c. just behind the mirror.
   d. as much behind the mirror as the object is in front of the mirror.
6. Two plane mirrors are kept at the following angles one by one. In which case is the number of images formed the maximum?
   a. 30° b. 60° c. 45° d. 90°

### B. VERY SHORT-ANSWER QUESTIONS: Give one-word answers.

1. Is the reflection of light by the smooth walls of your house regular or irregular?
2. A plane mirror always forms the image of an object exactly on the reflecting surface. True or false?
3. Is the image formed by a plane mirror exactly of the same size as the object?
4. The image formed by a plane mirror is always erect. True or false?
5. If angle of incidence of a ray on a plane mirror is 60°, what is the angle of reflection?
6. The angle of incidence of a ray on a mirror is the angle that the ray makes with the mirror at the point of incidence. True or false?
7. Two plane mirrors kept at 60° form __________ images of an object kept between them.
8. In a kaleidoscope, the mirrors make an angle of __________ with each other.

### C. SHORT-ANSWER QUESTIONS (TYPE I): Answer in a sentence or two.

1. What is reflection of light?

2. What is the second law of reflection?
3. What is lateral inversion?
4. Draw the image of the letter 'B' as formed by a plane mirror placed on the right side of 'B'.
5. What is the function of a periscope in a submarine?

## D. SHORT-ANSWER QUESTIONS (TYPE II): Answer in about 30 words.

1. Differentiate between regular and diffused reflection. Draw diagrams to show the two types of reflections.
2. State the first law of reflection, and show it by a labelled diagram.
3. Why are multiple images formed when two mirrors are placed at right angles to each other?
4. Calculate the number of images formed by plane mirrors kept at an angle of 10° to each other.
5. What is a kaleidoscope? State the principle on which it is based.

## E. LONG-ANSWER QUESTIONS: Answer in about 60 words.

1. List the main characteristics of the image formed by a plane mirror.
2. State three uses of a plane mirror.
3. Two mirrors are kept perpendicular to each other. A ray strikes one mirror at an angle of 45° to the normal. Find the direction of the ray after reflection by the second mirror, by drawing a ray diagram.

## HOTS QUESTIONS: Think and answer.

1. In which direction will a light ray falling along the normal to a mirror be reflected?
2. A ray incident on a plane mirror is reflected in a direction such that the angle between the incident and the reflected ray is 90°. What are the angles of incidence and reflection?
3. If all objects around us were to reflect light in a regular way, what problems might we face?
4. A boy is standing at a distance of 4 m in front of a mirror. He moves 2 m towards the mirror. In which direction will the image move—towards the mirror or away from it?
5. In the figure shown below, MN is a plane mirror. W, X, Y and Z are four children. Mark the positions of the reflections of W, X, Y and Z in the mirror. Answer the following questions.
   a. Which child/children can see their own images in the mirror?
   b. Can child W see the images of X, Y and Z in the mirror?

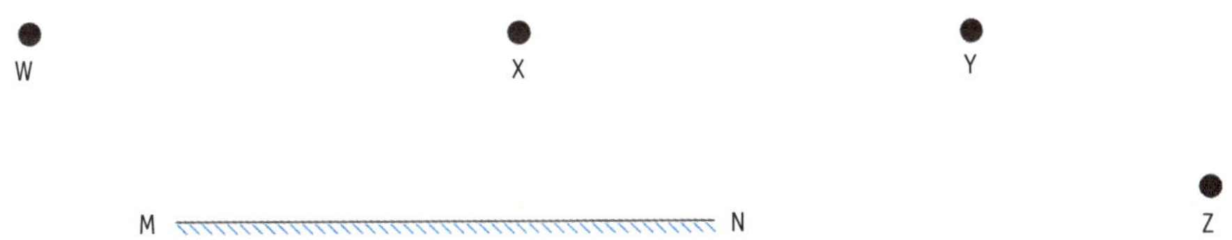


6. Can the image formed by a plane mirror be projected onto a screen?
7. Image of an object is formed by two plane mirrors. One of the mirrors is double the size of the other. In which case will the image be bigger? Why?

## FOR FORMATIVE ASSESSMENT*

### My Virtual Library—Research/Activities on the Internet

- ❐ Visit rsgr.in/lsc-cce-8 and click on LINK 62 to find activities on reflection.
- ❐ Visit rsgr.in/lsc-cce-8 and click on LINK 63 for an interesting activity on lateral inversion.
- ❐ Visit rsgr.in/lsc-cce-8 and click on LINK 64 to make a more professional kaleidoscope.

### In the Laboratory—Making a Model

**Make your own periscope**

**You will need** ◆ two milk or juice cartons ◆ two small mirrors ◆ scissors ◆ tape

**Procedure:**

- ◆ Open the tops of the two cartons. Tape the open parts together to make one long box.
- ◆ Cut two windows—one in the front at the bottom and one on the back at the top.
- ◆ Opposite one window, cut two slots so that when you slide in the mirror into the slots, it is at an angle of 45°. Do the same opposite the other window.
- ◆ Slide the mirrors in the slots. Now look through the bottom window of your periscope. You should be able to see out of the top window. If you can't, adjust the lower mirror till you can.
- ◆ Once your adjustments are done, tape the mirrors in place. Your periscope is ready

## LIFE SKILL

**Caring for your eyes**

Your eyes are your most important sense organ, and you must take all precautions to protect them. Here are some tips.

- ◆ Eat a balanced diet. Foods with vitamin A (for example, carrots) are necessary to prevent night blindness (though they do not improve normal eyesight).
- ◆ Wear protective goggles in a workshop and in the chemistry lab.
- ◆ Ultraviolet rays in sunlight adversely affect your eyes. Make sure that the sunglasses you wear have UV protection.
- ◆ Read in good light. Though reading in dim light does not damage the eyes, it does tire them more quickly.
- ◆ Do not watch television in a dark room. Keep a light on.
- ◆ If you wear glasses, use them. Straining to see without glasses tires the eyes.
- ◆ Use an antiglare filter on your computer monitor.
- ◆ Position the computer monitor at just below eye level and a little farther away than you would hold a book while reading.
- ◆ Take frequent breaks from watching TV, working on a computer or reading, to give your eye muscles a rest. Close your eyes or stare at a distance.
- ◆ At the first sign of a problem with the eyes—irritation, burning or problems in reading or seeing far objects, get a check up done.

SKILLS INVOLVED: Thinking skill, Self-preservation

*For more tasks see Page 257

17

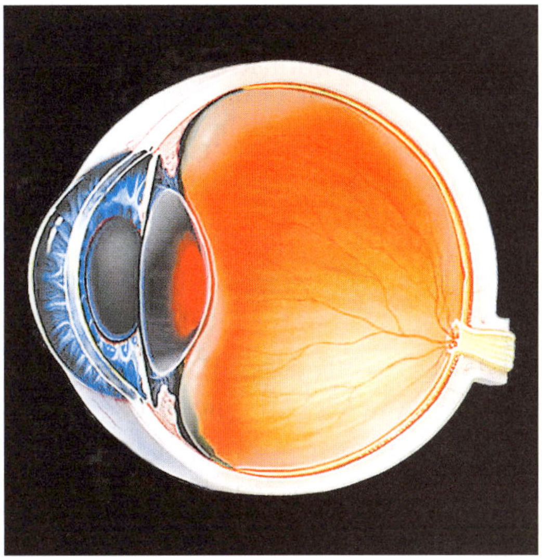

# Refraction and Dispersion of Light

## REFRACTION OF LIGHT

Let us learn about some more properties of light in this chapter.

**Activity 1 (Experimental investigation)**

Take a powerful torch and cover its face with black paper with a small hole in the middle. It will be your point source of light. In a dark room, shine the torch towards the surface of water taken in a glass beaker. You can put a few drops of milk in the water to enable you to clearly see the path of light in water. Observe the path of light as it enters the water. What do you notice?

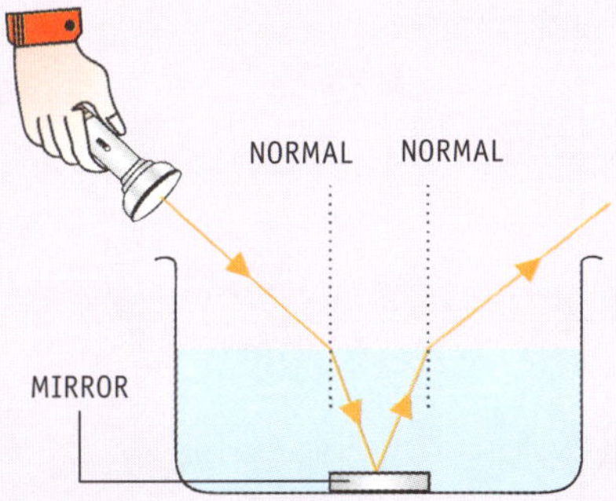


**Fig. 17.1** To observe refraction of light

You will notice that as the light enters the water, it bends at the surface. This bending of light as it passes from one medium to another is called **refraction**. You will see from Figure 17.1 that as light enters from air to water, it bends towards the normal.

Now, keep a mirror at the bottom of the

**IN THIS CHAPTER**

REFRACTION OF LIGHT ◆ DISPERSION OF LIGHT ◆ LENSES ◆ STRUCTURE OF THE EYE ◆ VISUALLY IMPAIRED beaker and observe the path of light as it emerges from water into the air.

You will notice that as light goes from water to air, it bends away from the normal.

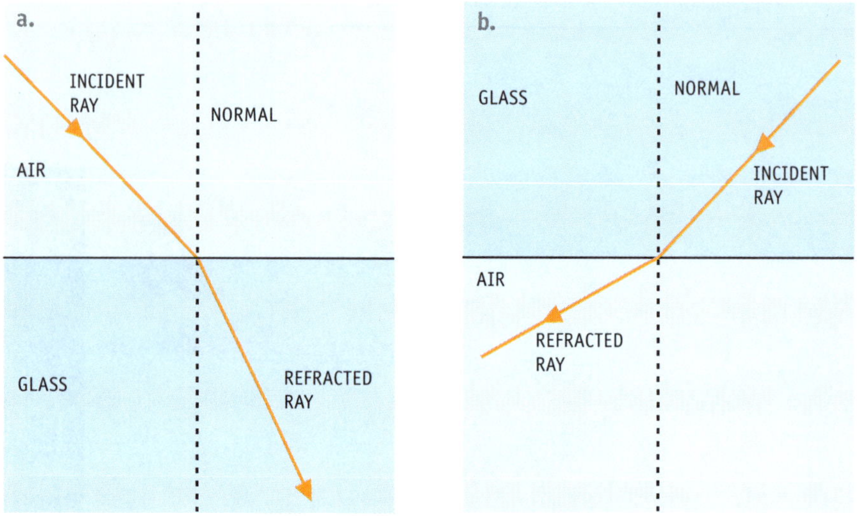


FIG. 17.2 Refraction of light passing through mediums of different optical densities

### Refraction and the speed of light

Light travels at lower speeds in glass and water than in air. We say that glass and water are optically denser than air. **Optical density** is a property of a transparent material. It is a measure of the speed of light through the material.

- A ray of light going from an **optically rarer medium** (e.g. air) **to an optically denser medium** (e.g. glass) slows down and **bends towards the normal** (Fig. 17.2a).
- A ray of light going from an **optically denser medium to an optically rarer medium** speeds up and **bends away from the normal** (Fig. 17.2b).

The speed of light in glass is less than that in water. Therefore, glass is optically denser than water. It can bend light more than water.

### Effects of refraction

You will now learn about the interesting effects of refraction of light.

**Real and apparent depth**: Let us perform the following activity.

**ACTIVITY 2 (Investigation)**

Place a thick glass slab, rectangular in shape, on the printed page of a book. Look at the printed words on the page from the top of the glass slab. Do the words seen through the glass slab appear to be raised up?

Yes, the words would appear to be raised up. Similarly, a swimming pool appears to be less deep than it actually is, when seen from above the surface of water. This shows that any optically denser material, when seen from an optically rarer material, appears less deep than it actually is. Let us see why this happens.

Consider a point D at the bottom of a swimming pool (Fig. 17.3). The real depth of the swimming pool is OD. The ray of light DO along the normal does not bend as it emerges from the water. It, therefore, goes along the path OC. The ray of light DA bends away from the normal and takes the path AB. The two emergent rays appear to come from D′. Hence, D′ is the virtual image of D.

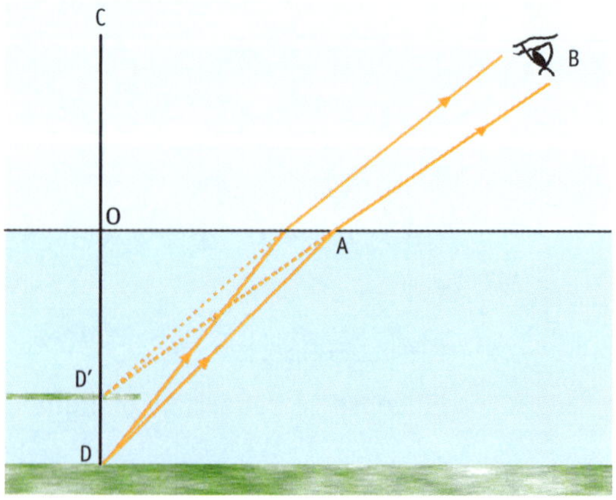


FIG. 17.3 Real and apparent depth

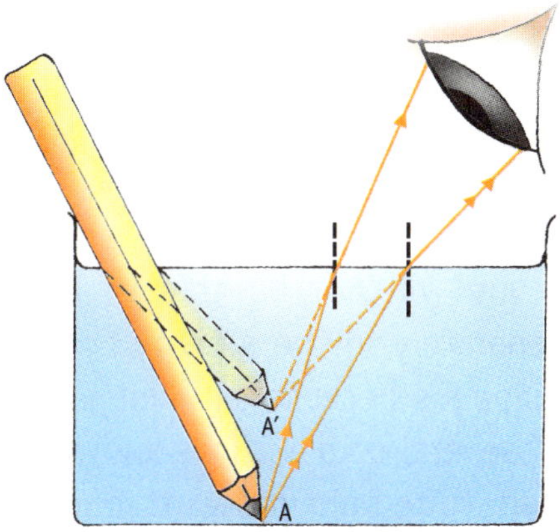


FIG. 17.4 Apparent bending of a pencil

To a person looking into the swimming pool, the bottom of the pool would, therefore, appear to be at depth OD′. This is the **apparent depth** of the pool.

The words of the book in Activity 2 appear to be raised up for the same reason.

**Apparent bending of a pencil:** If you dip a pencil obliquely in water, it appears to be bent at the surface of water. This happens because of refraction.

Rays of light from any point (say A) on the pencil, refract away from the normal as they emerge from water into air. As can be seen from Figure 17.4, the rays appear to come from a point A′ above A. Thus, A′ is the virtual image of A. In the same way, each point on the dipped part of the pencil has a corresponding virtual image above that point. The pencil, therefore, appears bent to our eyes.

### Refraction by a glass slab

As a ray enters a glass slab from air, it bends towards the normal. As it emerges from the slab into air, it bends away from the normal. The net effect is that the **emergent ray is parallel to the incident ray but laterally displaced from it** (Fig 17.5).

This means that the light ray passing through the glass slab is displaced, but its **direction is not changed**. This is because the

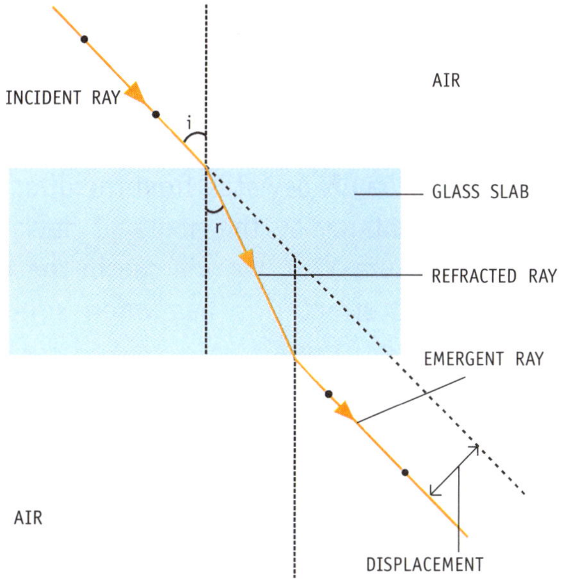


FIG. 17.5 Refraction by a glass slab

two opposite sides of the glass slab are parallel.

### Refraction by a prism

We have seen that in the case of a rectangular glass slab, where the two refracting surfaces of the glass slab are parallel to each other, the emergent ray is parallel to the incident ray. Let us now see what happens when the two refracting surfaces are not parallel to each other. For this we take a triangular glass block called a **prism**.

In the prism PQR, let light be incident on the surface PQ. It bends towards the normal, i.e. towards the base QR. As it emerges from the surface PR, it bends away from the normal. You can see from Fig. 17.6 that because of the structure of the prism, the light ray bends

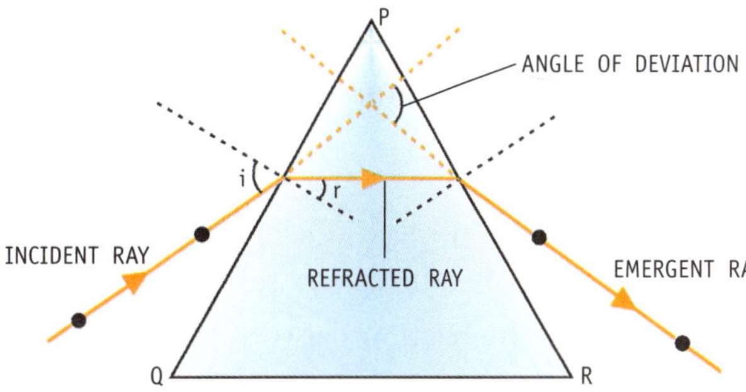


FIG. 17.6 Refraction through a prism

more in the same direction, i.e. towards the base QR.

You will notice that the incident and emergent rays are not parallel to each other. The emergent ray is deviated from the direction of the incident ray by the angle of deviation marked in Figure 17.6. We will see in the next section what effect this has when sunlight passes through a prism.

## DISPERSION

When **Sir Isaac Newton** placed a glass prism in the path of sunlight, he had expected to see a white image of the sun on the screen. But he was surprised when he saw the result. The following activity is similar to Newton's experiment.

**ACTIVITY 3 (Experimental investigation)**

Allow a narrow beam of light from the sun or some other source of white light (not light of any colour) to fall on a prism. Let the emergent beam fall on a white screen. What do you see on the screen (Fig. 17.7)?

FIG. 17.7 Dispersion of light

You will notice that though the incident beam falling on the prism was white light, the emergent beam has spread out into many colours on the screen. The order of colours is the same as that seen in a rainbow, i.e. red, orange, yellow, green, blue, indigo and violet. However, you will not be able to see all the colours separately in the activity.

This happens because sunlight is a mixture of light of several colours. It is known as **white light**. When white light passes through a prism, it is separated into its various constituent colours. The splitting up of light into its constituent colours is called **dispersion**. The patch of coloured light obtained on the screen is known as a **spectrum**.

### Reason for dispersion

The reason for dispersion is that a transparent medium (like a glass prism) bends (or deviates) different colours of light by different amounts. The deviation is maximum for violet and minimum for red. Therefore, when white light passes through a prism, the different colours present in it get deviated by different amounts. Hence, they separate out on emerging from the prism and form a spectrum.

**IT'S A FACT!**

The rainbow is a natural spectrum formed by dispersion of sunlight by tiny droplets of water suspended in the air. It is always formed in a direction opposite to that of the sun.

## ORAL QUESTIONS FOR FORMATIVE ASSESSMENT

1. When light enters water from air, what change is observed in its speed?
2. The change in speed (Q. 1) causes a change in the direction of the light ray. What change is observed when light goes from: **a.** air to water **b.** water to air?
3. What is the relation between the incident ray on a glass slab and the emergent ray?
4. Which is deviated more by a glass prism—red light or violet light?

## LENSES

All of you must have seen a magnifying glass. Feel the surface of a magnifying glass with your hand. Is it straight or curved? Is it thicker in the middle or at the edges?

A transparent medium bounded by two surfaces of which at least one is spherical is called a lens. Lenses are of various shapes and sizes. They can, however, be classified into two types:

- converging (or convex) lens, and
- diverging (or concave) lens.

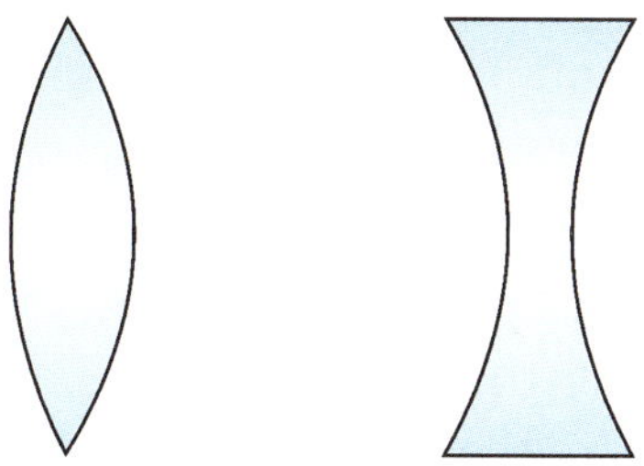


FIG. 17.8 Types of lenses

A converging (convex) lens is thick in the middle and becomes thinner at the edges (Fig. 17.8). A magnifying lens is a converging lens. A converging lens bends a ray of light passing through it inwards.

A diverging (concave) lens is thin in the middle and thicker at the edges (Fig. 17.8). It has the property of bending a ray of light passing through it outwards.

### Terms related to lenses

- **Principal axis:** The line joining the centres of the two spheres $C_1C_2$ of which the lenses form a part is called the principal axis of the lens (Fig. 17.9).
- **Optical centre:** A ray of light passing through the centre O of the lens is not deviated. It does undergo a little displacement. However, since the lens is thin, this displacement is very small and can be neglected. The point O is called the optical centre of the lens (Fig. 17.9). Thus, the optical centre of a lens is a point on the principal axis such that a ray passing through it does not undergo any deviation.
- **Principal focus:** If a beam of light parallel to the principal axis is incident on a converging lens, the rays of light after passing through the lens converge at a point F (Fig. 17.10a). This point is called the **principal focus** or simply the **focus** of the lens. For a diverging lens, the focus is the

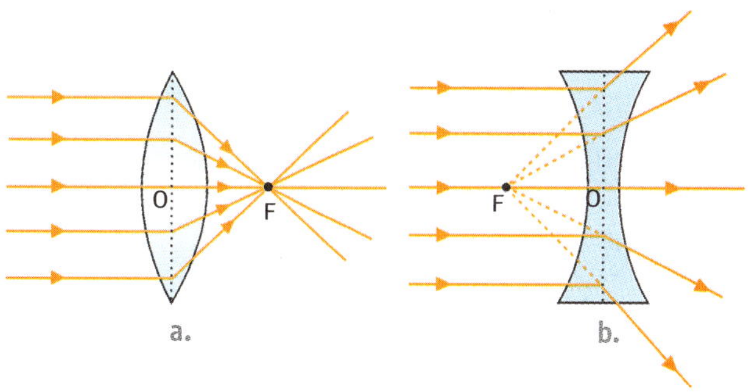


FIG. 17.10 Principal focus of a lens

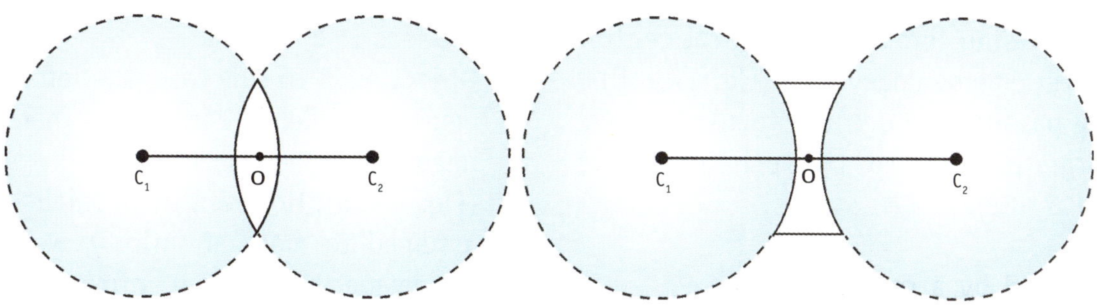


FIG. 17.9 Principal axis of a lens

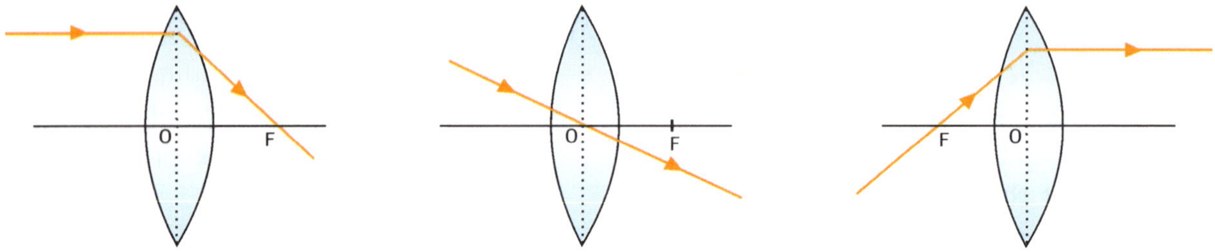


a. Parallel to the principal axis b. Passing through the optical centre c. Passing through the focus

FIG. 17.11 Paths of rays incident at different points on a convex lens

point from where the rays of light appear to come from, after passing through the lens (Fig. 17.10b).

- **Focal length:** The distance between the optical centre and the focus of a lens is called the **focal length** of the lens (OF in Fig. 17.10a and b). The thicker the lens, the more it bends light rays, and the smaller is its focal length.

## Image formed by a lens

To locate the image formed by a lens, we have to trace the paths of any two rays coming from a point on the object after they are refracted by the lens. The point at which the rays meet, or appear to come from, is the image. For convenience, we take any two of the following rays:

- **A ray parallel to the principal axis:** In the case of a converging lens, after refraction, this ray will pass through the focus (Fig. 17.11a). In case of a diverging lens, after refraction, it will appear to come from the focus (Fig. 17.10b).
- **A ray passing through the optical centre:** This will emerge undeviated (Fig. 17.11b).
- **A ray passing through the focus:** This will emerge parallel to the principal axis (Fig. 17.11c).

## Image formed by a convex lens

The image formed by a convex lens varies in size, position and nature (erect or inverted, real or virtual) depending upon the distance of the object from the lens.

- **Object very far off (or at infinity):** The rays of light coming from an object that is very far off (like the sun) are parallel to each other. We have already seen that if the rays are parallel to the principal axis, they meet at the focus. Thus, the image is formed at the focus. If the rays are not parallel to the principal axis (Fig. 17.12), the image is still formed at the focus. It is real, inverted and smaller than the object.
- **Object beyond 2F:** The image formed is between F and 2F on the other side of the lens. It is real, inverted and smaller than the object (Fig. 17.13). Being a real image it can be formed on a screen placed at that point.
- **Object at 2F:** The image is real, inverted and of the same size as the object. It is located at 2F on the other side of the lens (Fig. 17.14).
- **Object between F and 2F:** The image is real, inverted and larger than the object. It is situated beyond 2F on the other side of the lens (Fig. 17.15).
- **Object at F:** In this case, the refracted rays emerge parallel to each other. Therefore, no image is formed as the rays do not meet (Fig. 17.16). However, since parallel rays are assumed to meet at infinity, we say that the image is formed at infinity. The image formed is real and inverted. It is highly enlarged in size than the object.

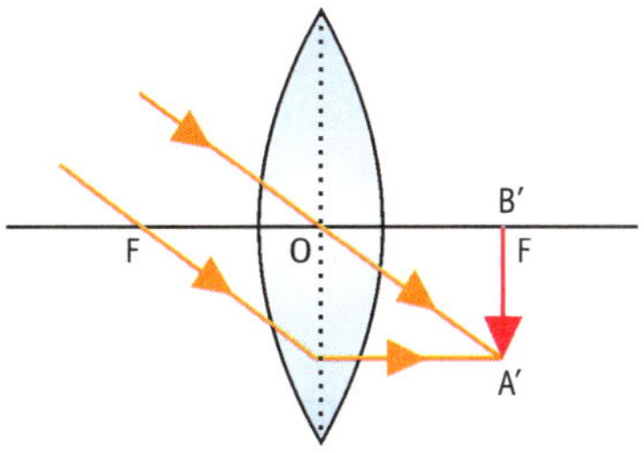


FIG. 17.12 Object very far-off

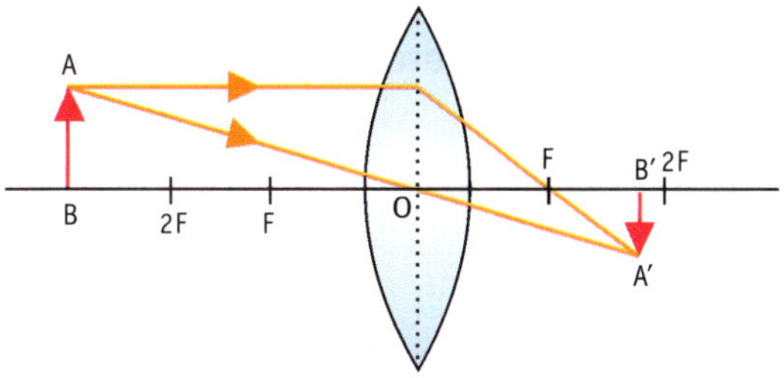


FIG. 17.13 Object beyond 2F

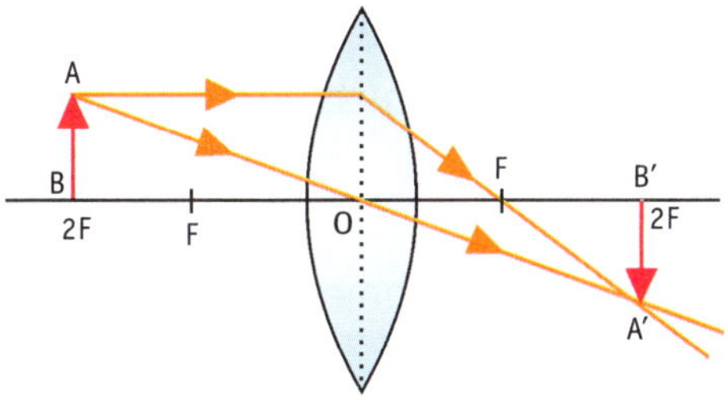


FIG. 17.14 Object at 2F

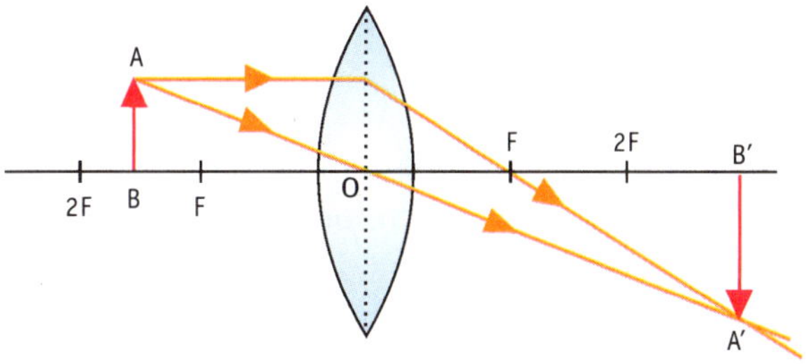


FIG. 17.15 Object between F and 2F

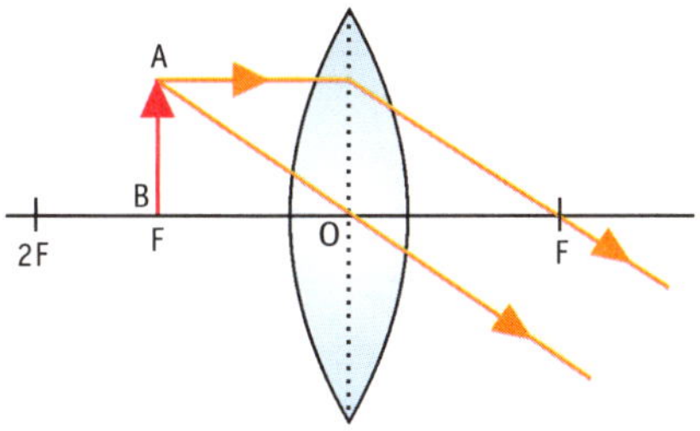


FIG. 17.16 Object at F

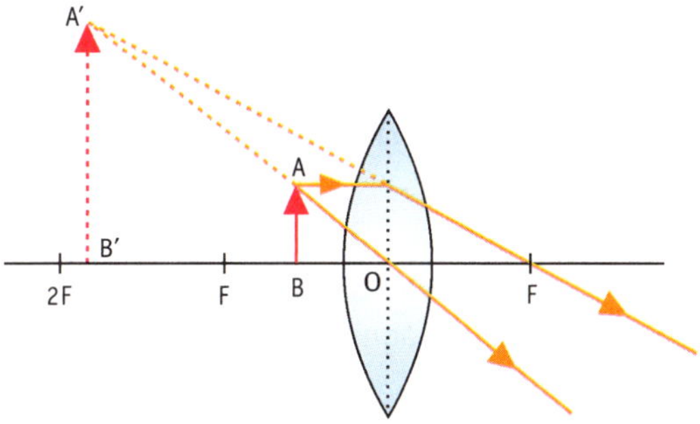


FIG. 17.17 Object between F and O

- **Object between F and O:** In this case, the incident rays diverge after refraction. Thus, a real image is not formed. If the divergent rays are produced backwards they meet at a point. Thus, the rays appear to come from this point. The image is, therefore, virtual. It is erect, bigger than the object and is formed on the same side of the lens as the object (Fig. 17.17). When a convex lens is used as a magnifying glass, we keep the object to be viewed between F and O of the lens.

The nature, size and location of the image formed by a convex lens for different positions of an object are given in Table 17.1.

TABLE 17.1 Position, nature and size of images formed by a convex lens

| POSITION OF THE OBJECT | POSITION OF THE IMAGE | NATURE OF THE IMAGE | SIZE OF THE IMAGE |
|---|---|---|---|
| very far-off | at F | real and inverted | smaller than the object |
| beyond 2F | between F and 2F | real and inverted | smaller than the object |
| at 2F | at 2F | real and inverted | same size as the object |
| between F and 2F | beyond 2F | real and inverted | larger than the object |
| at F | at infinity | real and inverted | much larger than the object |
| between F and O | on the same side as the object | virtual and erect | larger than the object |

**Activity 4 (Experimental investigation)**

Hold a magnifying glass in one hand with one of its convex surfaces facing the sun. Hold a white cardboard sheet in your other hand, and keep it some distance away, on the other side of the lens (Fig. 17.18). You will see sunlight falling on the cardboard after passing through the lens. Move the lens backward and forward, until a small, sharp image of the sun is formed on the cardboard. Recall that the image of a distant object like the sun is formed at the focus of the lens. Therefore, the distance from the lens to the cardboard gives the approximate focal length of the lens.

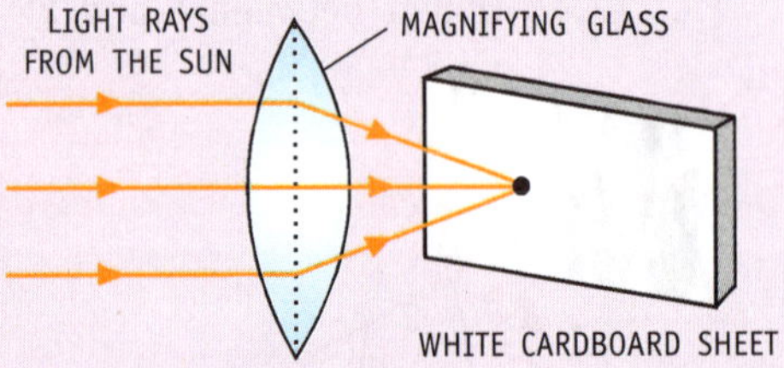


**Fig. 17.18** Finding the approximate focal length of a magnifying lens

At this point, the cardboard may start smouldering after a few seconds. This is because the lens concentrates the rays of the sun over a very small area, making the area very hot.

### Image formed by a concave lens

The rays falling on a concave lens, after refraction, always diverge. Therefore, no matter where the object is kept, a diverging lens always forms a virtual image, which is erect and smaller in size than the object. It is formed between the optical centre and the focus, on the same side of the lens as the object (Fig. 17.19).

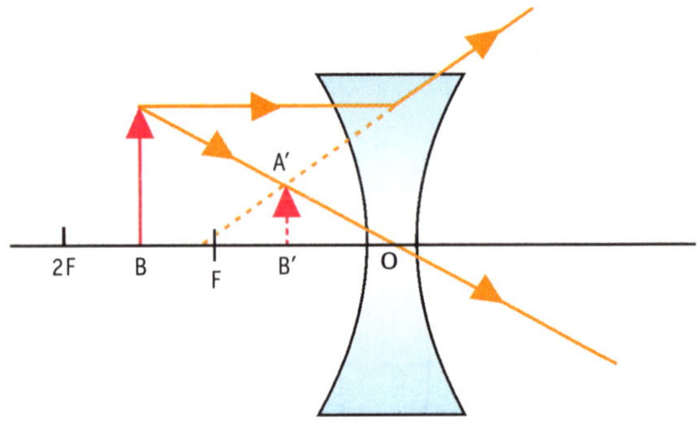


**Fig. 17.19** Image formed by a concave lens

## ORAL QUESTIONS FOR FORMATIVE ASSESSMENT

1. What type of lens is thicker in the middle than at the edges?
2. What effect does a convex lens have on parallel rays of light incident on it? In what way is the effect of a concave lens different?
3. A ray of light passing through a certain point of a lens does not undergo any deviation. What point is this?
4. What kind of lens always forms a virtual image of an object?

## EYE—THE NATURAL OPTICAL INSTRUMENT

The eye is a natural optical instrument. It enables us to see things around us by forming their images on a screen called the **retina**.

The eye consists of the **eyeball** which is nearly spherical in shape. Its front portion, called the **cornea**, is made up of a transparent material. Light enters the eye through the cornea (Fig. 17.20). The cornea not only protects the eyes but also helps in focusing light.

Behind the cornea is the **iris** with a hole in the centre called the **pupil**. This is the small dark circle seen in the centre of the eye. Light goes into the eye through the pupil. It is the iris that gives the eyes their characteristic colour. The amount of light entering into the eye is controlled by the iris. In bright light, it expands and reduces the size of the pupil. In

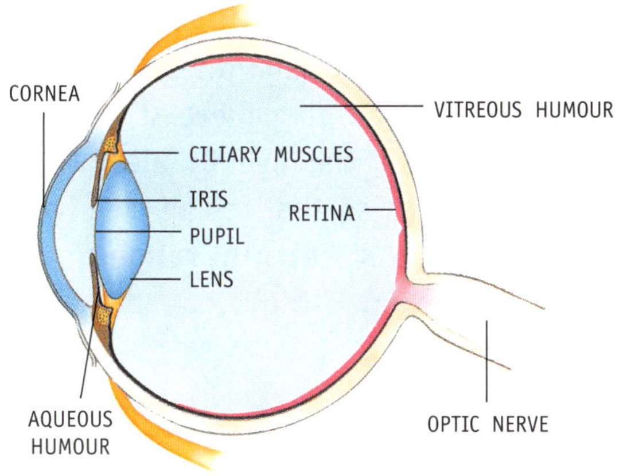


FIG. 17.20 Structure of the eye

dull light, the iris contracts to increase the size of the pupil to admit more light. This is why the pupil appears smaller during the day than at dusk. The pupil appears to be black as all the light falling on it enters the eye and no light is reflected back.

**ACTIVITY 5 (Investigation)**

Stand with a friend in a dimly lit room. Look into your friend's eyes and note the size of the pupils. Now throw light on his eyes with a torch and note if the size of the pupils change. Switch off the light and check the size again. What is your conclusion?

The region between the cornea and the lens is filled with a transparent liquid called the **aqueous humour**.

Behind the pupil is the **lens** which is made of a jelly-like substance. It is a converging lens that forms images of objects on a layer called **retina** located at the back of the eye. The lens is held in place by the **ciliary muscles**, which can change the thickness of the lens and hence its focal length. The region between the lens and retina is filled with a transparent jelly-like substance called the **vitreous humour**.

The retina contains several nerve cells, which sense the image formed on the retina. These cells are of two kinds:

- **cones** which are sensitive to bright light, can detect colour.
- **rods** which are sensitive to dim light.

The image of an object formed on the retina is smaller than the object and is inverted. It is sensed by the nerve cells and then communicated to the brain through the **optic nerve**. The brain interprets the image as erect and of the correct size.

### Blind spot—the area of no vision

Blind spot is the region of the retina at the junction of the optic nerve and the retina. There are no sensory cells at this spot, hence any image formed here cannot be seen.

**ACTIVITY 6 (Investigation): To demonstrate the presence of blind spot in a human eye**

To demonstrate the blind spot, turn the book clockwise through 90° and hold it at arm's length with the two symbols straight in front of your eyes. Close your left eye and concentrate on the cross with your right eye. Bring the book slowly towards you. Keep looking at the cross on the left: eventually, as the image of the dot falls on the blind spot of your right retina, the dot disappears. Repeat this activity by closing your right eye and looking at the dot. Does the cross disappear?

FIG. 17.21

## Accommodation of the eye

A normal eye can see clearly from a distance of 25 cm to infinity. Notice, however, that the distance from the lens to the retina (screen) always remains the same. How is it that the eye always forms the image on the retina of objects at varying distances from the eye?

This is achieved by changing the thickness of the lens and hence its focal length by the action of the ciliary muscles. When the eye is focused at far off objects, such as the moon, the ciliary muscles are relaxed and the eye lens is at its thinnest (maximum focal length) (Fig. 17.22a). As the object comes close, the ciliary muscles make the lens thicker (reducing its focal length). The converging power of the lens increases and it can then focus nearby objects clearly on the retina (Fig. 17.22b).

The action of the ciliary muscles in a normal eye stops when the object is at a distance of about 25 cm. The focal length of the eye lens cannot be reduced further. Therefore, a normal eye cannot clearly see objects closer than 25 cm. Then the image is formed behind the retina and the object appears hazy. This least distance at which the eye can see an object clearly is called the near point of the eye. The far point of the eye is the maximum distance at which it can see clearly. For a normal eye, it is at infinity.

The ability of the eye to alter the focal length of its lens so that it can clearly see all objects within a certain range is called **accommodation of the eye.**

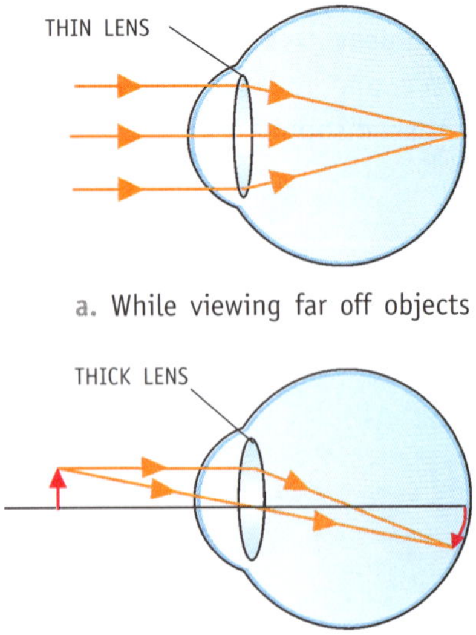


a. While viewing far off objects

b. While viewing nearby objects

FIG. 17.22 Accommodation of the eye

## Defects of vision

There are two main defects the eye suffers from. These are:

- myopia, and
- hypermetropia

**Myopia or short sightedness:** A person suffering from this defect can see nearby objects clearly but distant objects appear blurred. This defect is due to the eye lens being too thick. The ciliary muscles do not relax sufficiently to make the eye lens thin when viewing distant objects. As a result, the image of a distant

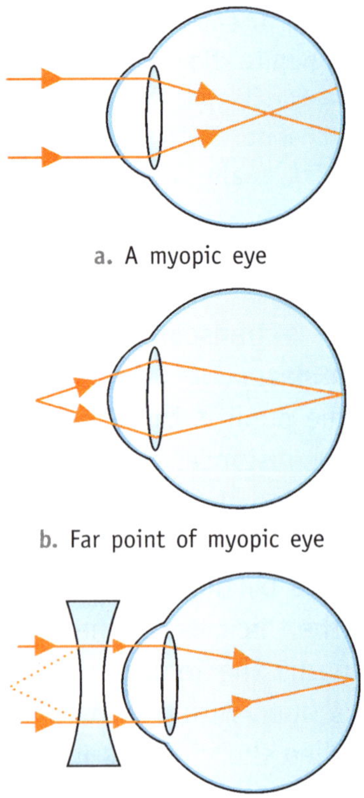

a. A myopic eye

b. Far point of myopic eye

c. Defect corrected by concave lens

FIG. 17.23 Myopia of the eye

object is formed before the retina and cannot be clearly seen (Fig. 17.23a). For a person suffering from myopia the **far point** is at a finite distance and not at infinity (Fig. 17.23b).

To correct this defect, spectacles with concave lenses of the required power are used. The concave lens diverges the parallel rays coming from a distant object in such a way that they appear to come from the far point of the defective eye. In other words, the lens forms a virtual image of a far off object at the far point of the defective eye. The eye can then see the distant object clearly (Fig. 17.23c).

**Hypermetropia or long sightedness:** A person suffering from this defect can see distant objects clearly but nearby objects appear blurred. This defect occurs due to the eye lens being too thin. The ciliary muscles are unable to thicken the eye lens enough to see nearby objects clearly. This defect generally occurs in old age when the ciliary muscles become weak.

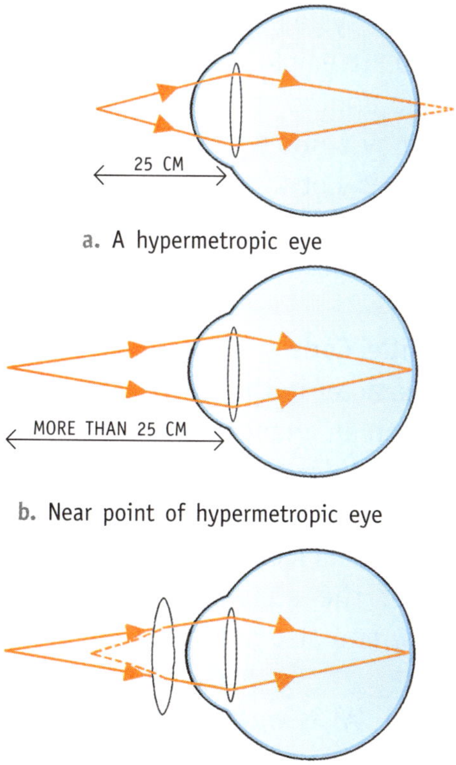


a. A hypermetropic eye

b. Near point of hypermetropic eye

c. Defect corrected by convex lens

FIG. 17.24 Hypermetropia of the eye

The image of a near object is formed behind the retina and, therefore, appears blurred (Fig. 17.24a). For a person suffering from hypermetropia, the **near point** is beyond 25 cm (Fig. 17.24b).

To correct this defect, spectacles with convex lenses of the required power are used. The convex lens converges the rays from a near object in such a way that they appear to come from the near point of the defective eye. That is, the lens forms a virtual image of the object at the near point of the defective eye. The eye then forms a sharp image of the object on the retina (Fig. 17.24c).

**Cataract:** This is another defect of the eye generally occurring at old age. In a person suffering from cataract, the eye lens becomes cloudy leading to loss of vision.

Cataract can be treated by surgically removing the eye lens and inserting in its place a new artificial lens. Due to the use of modern technology, this surgery is now very safe.

## Care of the eyes

We must take proper care of the eyes. We must try to avoid any kind of injury to our eyes. Some simple precautions given below may help in protecting our eyes.

- Wash and clean your eyes with clean cold water at least twice a day.
- Do not work or read in a dim light or very bright light. This tires the eyes.
- Do not look directly at very powerful light sources like the sun or a welding machine.
- Do not read in a moving vehicle. It strains the eyes.
- Never rub your eyes if something gets into it. Wash your eyes with clean cold water. If there is no improvement, consult a doctor.
- Avoid watching TV or working on a computer for long sessions. Take frequent breaks to rest your eyes.

- Always try to read from the normal distance of vision. If you have problems with this, or if you cannot properly see the blackboard in class, there may be a defect in the eyes. Consult a doctor.
- Eat a balanced diet. Vitamin A, which is found in raw carrots, broccoli, green vegetables (like spinach), cod liver oil, eggs, milk, curd and in fruits like papaya and mango, is good for eyes, and can **prevent night blindness**. Vitamins C and E are also beneficial for eyes.

### Persistence of vision

When an image of an object is formed on the retina, it stays for about $^{1}/_{16th}$ of a second. This is called **persistence of vision**. Moving images that you see on the TV or in a cinema depend on this property of the eye. If successive still images of a running dog are flashed before your eyes at the rate of more than 16 images per second, you would see it as a movie of a running dog.

**ACTIVITY 7 (Making a model)**

Cut out a round disc of about 10 cm diameter from a piece of thick white paper board. Punch two holes opposite to each other. Secure a loop of string through each hole. Draw a bird on one side of the disc, and a cage on the other. The two images should be centred on the disc. Hold the string ends one in each hand and twist the strings to make the disc twirl rapidly. Can you see the bird inside the cage?

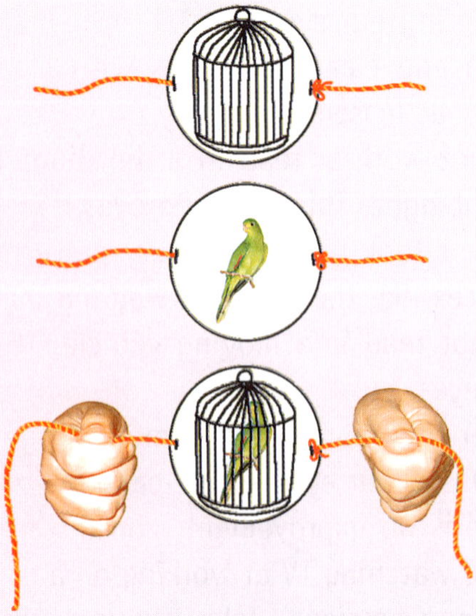

FIG. 17.25 Persistence of vision

## THE VISUALLY-IMPAIRED

There are an estimated 180 million visually-impaired people in the world while the number in India is around 7,00,000. Some of them are born with defects and others lose their eyesight because of diseases such as cataract. Since visually impaired people depend a lot on the senses of feeling and hearing, they often develop a very keen sense of touch and hearing.

### Use of Braille

The Braille system is a method of writing for the blind. It employs groups of raised dots to represent printed letters and numbers. It was invented by **Louis Braille** of France in the early 1800s. It is not a separate language, but just another way to read and write English or any other language.

### The Braille Code

Every character in the Braille code is based on an arrangement of one to six raised dots. Each dot has a numbered position in the Braille cell. These characters make up the letters of the alphabet, punctuation marks, numbers, and also special characters.

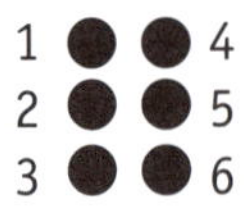


The Braille Cell

The letter "A" is written with only 1 dot. 

The letter "D" has dots 1, 4, and 5. 

The letter "Y" has dots 1, 3, 4, 5, and 6. ⠽

A "Period" is written with dots 2, 5, and 6. ⠲

Table 17.2 shows how the dots are arranged in the Braille cell for each letter of the alphabet. The numbers 0–9 in Braille are as shown in Table 17.3.

**TABLE 17.2** Alphabets A–Z in Braille

| ⠁ | ⠃ | ⠉ | ⠙ | ⠑ | ⠋ | ⠛ | ⠓ | ⠊ | ⠚ |
|---|---|---|---|---|---|---|---|---|---|
| a | b | c | d | e | f | g | h | i | j |

| ⠅ | ⠇ | ⠍ | ⠝ | ⠕ | ⠏ | ⠟ | ⠗ | ⠎ | ⠞ |
|---|---|---|---|---|---|---|---|---|---|
| k | l | m | n | o | p | q | r | s | t |

| ⠥ | ⠧ | ⠺ | ⠭ | ⠽ | ⠵ |
|---|---|---|---|---|---|
| u | v | w | x | y | z |

**TABLE 17.3** Numbers 0–9 in Braille

| ⠼ | ⠚ | ⠁ | ⠃ | ⠉ | ⠙ | ⠑ | ⠋ | ⠛ | ⠓ | ⠊ |
|---|---|---|---|---|---|---|---|---|---|---|
| | 0 | 1 | 2 | 3 | 4 | 5 | 6 | 7 | 8 | 9 |

## THE STORY OF HELEN KELLER

Helen Keller, a woman from a small town in USA taught the world to respect people who are blind and deaf. She was born in 1880 in Alabama. When she was less than two years old, she fell very ill and lost both her vision and hearing. When she was seven, her parents hired a tutor named **Anne Sullivan**. In just a few days, she taught Helen how to spell words with her hands. She used the 'manual alphabet', which is part of the sign language that deaf people use. After teaching her a word such as 'water' she would make her feel water to make her understand. By the time she was 10, Helen learned to speak by feeling her teacher's mouth when she spoke! She learned to read French, German, Greek, and Latin in Braille.

When she was 20, she entered Radcliffe College and graduated with honours. While still in college she started writing her first book *The Story of My Life*. It was published in 1903, and was translated into 50 languages. She wrote ten more books and several articles.

Helen also did research, gave speeches, and helped raise money for many organizations, such as the American Foundation for the Blind and the American Foundation for the Overseas Blind (which is now called Helen Keller Worldwide). She travelled around the world, speaking about the experiences and rights of people who are blind. She died in her sleep in 1968.

**Ved Mehta** (1934– ) is an Indian essayist and author who became blind at the age of four due to an attack of cerebrospinal meningitis. His father, a doctor, gave him an education, so that he could become 'a self-supporting citizen of the world'. Born in Lahore, he was partly educated in the USA and Britain, and as a young man worked for *The New Yorker*, where many of his essays first appeared.

He is well known for his autobiography *Face to Face* that describes his childhood and his early struggle with blindness. His other writings include *Portrait of India*, *Walking the Indian Streets*, *Daddyji*, *Mamaji*, and *Sound Shadows of the World*.

## ORAL QUESTIONS FOR FORMATIVE ASSESSMENT

1. The eye can control the amount of light falling on the retina. Which part of the eye is responsible for this?
2. The eye can change the focal length of its lens. Which part of the eye is responsible for this? How does the changing focal length help us?
3. A person cannot see near objects clearly. What kind of lens should his spectacles have to correct this—convex or concave?
4. What is the farthest distance you can see if you have a normal eye?
5. Braille is a language different from English and other languages. Do you agree? Give reasons.

## NOW YOU KNOW

- The bending of light as it passes from one transparent medium to another is called refraction. It occurs because light travels at lower speed in an optically denser medium.
- Light bends towards the normal at the point of incidence as it passes from an optically rarer to an optically denser medium. It bends away from the normal if it passes from a denser to a rarer medium.
- It is due to refraction that a swimming pool appears less deep than it actually is and a pencil appears bent when dipped obliquely in water.
- A glass slab causes a ray of light to be laterally displaced after refraction through it, while still remaining parallel to the incident ray.
- A prism causes an incident ray to be deviated from its path by an angle called the angle of deviation.
- A prism causes white light to break up into its constituent colours. This is called dispersion.
- Lenses are either converging (convex) or diverging (concave).
- A convex lens forms a real, inverted image of objects kept beyond its focal point. For an object kept between its optical centre and focus, it forms a virtual, erect and magnified image.
- A concave lens forms a virtual, erect and diminished image of all objects irrespective of their distance from the lens.
- The eye contains a lens whose thickness can be varied by the ciliary muscles so that a sharp image of all objects between 25 cm (near point) and infinity (far point) are formed on the retina. This ability of the eye is known as accommodation.

- A person suffering from myopia or short sightedness cannot see far-off objects clearly. The defect is corrected by a suitable concave lens.
- A person suffering from hypermetropia or long sightedness cannot see nearby objects clearly. This defect is corrected by a suitable convex lens.
- The Braille system employs groups of dots to represent printed letters and numbers.

## NEW WORDS

**REFRACTION**—bending of light as it passes from one medium to another

**DISPERSION**—breaking up of light into its constituent colours—for example, on passing through a prism

**CONVERGING**—bending light rays inwards

**DIVERGING**—bending light rays outwards

## FOR FORMATIVE AND SUMMATIVE ASSESSMENT

### A. MULTIPLE-CHOICE QUESTIONS: Choose the most appropriate answer.

1. If medium A is optically denser than medium B, then the speed of light is
   a. the same in both mediums.
   b. higher in medium A than in medium B.
   c. higher in medium B than in medium A.
   d. higher in medium A or B depending on which medium is thicker.
2. When light travels from an optically denser medium to a rarer medium,
   a. it bends away from the normal.
   b. it bends towards the normal.
   c. it is undeviated.
   d. it is laterally displaced.
3. The splitting of white light into its constituent colours is called
   a. refraction. b. dispersion.
   c. deviation. d. displacement.
4. At what position of the object does a convex lens act as a magnifying glass?
   a. between F and 2F b. between F and O
   c. beyond F d. beyond 2F
5. Which of the following is true for a person suffering from myopia?
   a. can see far-off objects clearly but near objects appear blurred
   b. can be corrected using a convex lens
   c. far point is at finite distance, and not at infinity
   d. near point is beyond 25 cm
6. If a person is suffering from hypermetropia, which object is he/she most likely to see blurred?
   a. object 25 cm away b. object 10 m away
   c. object 100 m away d. object at infinity

7. Which one of these controls the amount of light entering the eye?
   a. pupil  b. iris  c. cornea  d. ciliary muscles
8. Myopia is corrected by using spectacles with
   a. convex lenses.  b. concave lenses.  c. glass slabs.  d. prisms.
9. When white light passes through a prism, it is
   a. deviated and dispersed.  b. deviated but not dispersed.
   c. laterally displaced and not dispersed.  d. reflected.
10. How many dots does the Braille system use?
   a. 5  b. 6  c. 10  d. 11

## B. VERY SHORT-ANSWER QUESTIONS: Give one-word answers.

1. Refractive index can be defined for both transparent and opaque objects. True or false?
2. Light bends as it passes from one medium to another. What is this phenomenon called?
3. If light enters from water to air it bends __________ the normal.
4. A pencil dipped obliquely in water appears bent at the surface due to dispersion. True or false?
5. In a prism, the emergent ray is parallel to the incident ray. True or false?
6. A transparent medium bends light by the same amount irrespective of the colour of light. True or false?
7. Which of these has a smaller focal length—a thick lens or a thin lens?
8. If an object is situated at the focal point of a convex lens, where is the image formed?
9. A diverging lens forms a real image of an object, placed beyond F, and a virtual image of an object placed between O and F. True or false?
10. The far point of a hypermetropic eye is at a finite distance from the eye. True or false?
11. Which lens is used to correct myopia—convex or concave?
12. A normal eye cannot clearly see objects closer than __________ cm.
13. In cataract, the lens of the eye becomes cloudy. True or false?
14. Write Braille codes for letters A and Y.

## C. SHORT-ANSWER QUESTIONS (TYPE I): Answer in a sentence or two.

1. What do you mean by refraction of light? In which direction will light bend when travelling from an optically rarer medium to an optically denser medium?
2. Why does refraction occur?
3. What is dispersion?
4. Which medium will bend light more—glass or water? Why?
5. What is 'white light'?
6. What is the order of colours in a spectrum of 'white light'?
7. Distinguish between near point and far point of the eye.
8. What is the 'blind spot' of the eye?

## D. SHORT-ANSWER QUESTIONS (TYPE II): Answer in about 30 words.

1. What is the difference between the displacement produced by a rectangular glass slab in a ray of light and the deviation produced by a glass prism?
2. Explain the term 'spectrum'. Why does a glass prism split white light into its constituent colours?
3. Distinguish between converging and diverging lenses.
4. Define the following terms for a lens:
   a. optical centre b. principal axis c. principal focus d. focal length
5. Why does a concave lens always form a virtual image of an object? Draw a diagram to illustrate this.
6. What do you mean by the accommodation of the eye? What gives the eye the power of accommodation?
7. How are letters written in the Braille system? Give two examples.
8. What is meant by 'persistence of vision'? How is this property of the eye used in movie films?

## E. LONG-ANSWER QUESTIONS: Answer in about 60 words.

1. A coin kept at the bottom of a glass bowl full of water appears to be higher than it actually is. With the help of a labelled diagram, explain why this happens.
2. 'As an object is slowly brought from infinity to the focus of a convex lens, the image travels from the focus to infinity.' Show this with the help of diagrams with five different positions of the object.
3. Draw a labelled diagram of the eye and answer the following questions:
   a. From where does light enter inside the eye?
   b. Which muscles control the focal length of the eye lens?
   c. Where is the image formed?
   d. Which nerve sends the image signals to the brain?
4. Distinguish between myopia and hypermetropia. Draw diagrams to show how these defects can be corrected by using suitable lenses.

## HOTS QUESTIONS: Think and answer.

1. Can a glass slab bend different coloured lights by different amounts?
2. You have seen that a prism splits up light into different colours as it bends different colour lights by different amounts. Why does a glass slab not cause dispersion? (**HINT:** Observe the path of light in a glass slab—especially what happens to it when it emerges from the slab.)
3. Suppose a swimming pool is filled with an imaginary liquid which is optically rarer than air. For a person looking at the pool from outside, will the apparent depth of the pool be less than or greater than the real depth? Give reasons.
4. What type of image is formed when rays of light coming from a point on the object diverge after reflection or refraction—real or virtual?
5. Will a spectrum be formed if blue light falls on a prism? Give reasons.

## FOR FORMATIVE ASSESSMENT*

### In the Library—Research Project

**What is light?** You must have seen waves in water. You probably also know that sound travels in the air in the form of waves. However, do you know that light also travels in the form of waves? These waves are very different from water or sound waves. They do not require any medium to travel. They can, therefore, travel through vacuum also. That is why the light from the sun is able to reach us.

Ordinary light is a mixture of waves of different lengths travelling independently of each other. However, in a certain form of light all waves are of the same length and travel exactly in step with each other. Find out what this kind of light is called and how it is useful to us in our daily life, in industry and in warfare.

### My Virtual Library—Research/Activities on the Internet

- Visit rsgr.in/lsc-cce-8 and click on LINK 65 for experiments in dispersion, and click on LINK 66 for experiments in refraction.
- Visit rsgr.in/lsc-cce-8 and click on LINK 67 for light activities—refraction, dispersion, lenses, and much more!

### In the Laboratory—Designing an Experiment

**To detect 'invisible' light** Carry out this experiment on a day when the sun is shining brightly, preferably during summer.

**You will need** ◆ a large prism ◆ a thermometer ◆ white and black pieces of cardboard

**Procedure:**

- Cover a sunny window with the cardboard having a slit of about 2 cm × 0.3 cm. Allow the narrow beam of light that comes through the slit to fall on a large prism.
- Keep the white cardboard piece on the other side of the prism. A spectrum will be formed on the cardboard.
- Hold the bulb of the thermometer for 2–3 minutes in the blue portion of the spectrum. Note the rise in the temperature. Repeat this in the red portion. Where is the rise in the temperature greater?
- Now keep the thermometer bulb just beyond the red portion. Is there any rise in temperature?

Why is the rise in temperature more here than in the red or blue portion?

Obviously, there is some portion of sunlight beyond the visible red colour which does not create the impression of light in our eyes. However, it possesses more heat. The light rays beyond the red portion of the spectrum are called **infrared rays**. There are light rays beyond the violet portion of the spectrum also. However, they cannot be detected by a thermometer as they have very little heat. They are called **ultraviolet rays**.

*For more tasks see Page 257

18

# The Universe

What can you see in the sky during the day? You can only see the **Sun**. Due to the brightness of the Sun, other heavenly bodies cannot be seen. Look up at the sky on a clear night. You can see the **Moon** and thousands of **stars** twinkling in the sky. Seen over several nights, the stars appear to move across the sky. Some of the bright heavenly bodies do not twinkle. They are the **planets**. In Hindi, planets are called *Grah*. The Sun, Moon, stars, planets and other objects in the sky are known as **celestial objects** or **heavenly bodies**.

## THE UNIVERSE

The universe is everything that exists—stars, planets, moons, other heavenly bodies, everything that exists on these heavenly bodies, such as animals and plants on the Earth, and the vast empty space in between. Nobody knows how big the universe is. It is impossible to even imagine its size. In fact, scientists have shown that the universe is expanding, like a balloon being blown up. The branch of science that deals with the study of celestial objects is called **astronomy**. People who study the universe are called **astronomers**. The most important instrument used by astronomers is the **telescope**.

## GALAXIES

Stars are seen in the sky in groups. Each group

**IN THIS CHAPTER**

THE UNIVERSE, GALAXIES, STARS, PLANETS, SATELLITES AND CONSTELLATIONS ◆ MEASURING DISTANCES IN THE UNIVERSE ◆ THE SOLAR SYSTEM ◆ THE ORIGIN OF THE UNIVERSE

has billions of stars in it. Such a group of stars is called a **galaxy**. The Sun, the Earth and other planets, and all the stars that you can see in the sky belong to a galaxy called the **Milky Way**. It is a spiral-shaped galaxy with a bulge in the centre. The Sun is situated on one of the arms of the spiral. On a clear night, it appears like a band of light shining across the sky.

## STARS

Stars are huge spinning balls of hot luminous gases. All stars give out their own light. Most stars are made up almost entirely of two gases—hydrogen and helium. In the centre of the stars, hydrogen atoms combine to form helium atoms. During this process, huge amounts of energy is released in the form of heat and light. The Sun is also a star. It is a medium-sized star—some stars are smaller while others are bigger than the Sun. The Sun is the star closest to us—that is why it appears to be so big. Other stars appear like points of light as they are millions of times farther away from us than the Sun.

There are about 100 billion ($10^{11}$) galaxies in the universe, containing an average of 100 billion stars each. Thus, the total number of stars in the universe is approximately $10^{22}$. This number is so large that it is difficult to even imagine it!

## PLANETS

Planets are heavenly bodies that revolve around the Sun. They do not have light of their own. Their surface reflects the light of the Sun to us. They are smaller than stars. Our Earth is also a planet. Table 18.1 gives the major differences between stars and planets.

TABLE 18.1 Differences between stars and planets

| STARS | PLANETS |
|---|---|
| Emit their own light | Do not emit their own light |
| Made up of hot gases | Made up of rocks |
| When seen from the Earth, they twinkle | Do not twinkle |
| Massive in size | Smaller than stars |

## MEASURING DISTANCES IN THE UNIVERSE

The distances between heavenly bodies in space are very, very large. Measuring these distances in kilometres would mean dealing with very large numbers. The Sun, which is the star nearest to us, is 15,00,00,000 km away. The next star nearest to us is **Proxima Centauri**, which is 4,00,00,00,00,00,000 km away. This, you will realize, is very inconvenient to write or to make calculations with.

Astronomers, therefore, use special units to measure distances in space. Instead of a kilometre, they use a unit called **light year**. A light year is the distance that light travels in one year.

Light travels at an incredible speed of about 3,00,000 km/s. If a spaceship could travel at this speed, it would reach the Moon in just over 1 second!

So, 1 light year = speed of light in km/s × number of seconds in a year

= 3,00,000 × 365 × 24 × 60 × 60 km

= 95,00,00,00,00,000 km (approximately)

= $9.5 \times 10^{12}$ km

In this respect, Proxima Centauri is 4.3 light years away from us. Light from this star takes over four whole years to reach us. This also means that when you look at Proxima Centauri today, you see it as it was 4.3 years ago!

Time taken for light to reach Earth from Sun

$$= \frac{\text{distance of earth from sun}}{\text{speed of light}}$$

$$= \frac{15{,}00{,}00{,}000 \text{ km}}{3{,}00{,}000 \text{ km/s}} = 500 \text{ s} = 8.3 \text{ min}$$

So we can say distance of Earth from Sun is 8.3 light minutes.

## CONSTELLATIONS

Thousands of years ago, astronomers divided the stars into groups and drew imaginary pictures around them, such as that of a hunter or a bear. This made it easier for them to remember the star patterns. Such a group of stars is called a **constellation**. The shape of a constellation always remains the same. Constellations appear to move from east to west. Today, 88 constellations are recognized by astronomers. Remember, however, that the stars in a constellation are actually unrelated. They are at widely varying distances from the Earth. However, when viewed from the Earth, they appear to be at the same distance and form a group. Some constellations are discussed below.

### Ursa Major (Great Bear)

It contains seven bright stars arranged in the form of a big spoon (Fig. 18.1). It is called the **Big Dipper**. This name is derived from the word 'dipper' which in olden days meant a large spoon used for drinking water. It is also called the Great Bear because, along with several other faint stars, it forms the picture of a bear (Fig. 18.1). Its Indian name is *Saptarishi*.

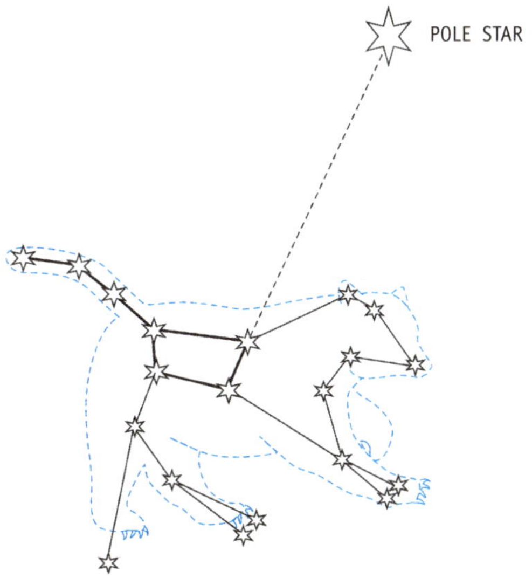


FIG. 18.1 Ursa Major

You can locate the **Pole Star** (*Dhruv Tara*) with the help of Ursa Major. This star is visible towards the north and is the only star that remains stationary in the sky with respect to the Earth (why this happens is discussed in the next section). Before the magnetic compass was invented, sailors used the Pole Star to find the north direction.

**ACTIVITY 1 (Observation)**

Find the constellation Ursa Major in the sky, on a clear night. Imagine a straight line drawn through the two 'pointers' of Ursa Major, and extend it towards the north about 5 times the distance between the two 'pointers'. The line will pass through the Pole Star (Fig. 18.1). The Pole Star is not a very bright star.

**IT'S A FACT!**

The Pole Star is not visible from the southern hemisphere. Some northern constellations like Ursa Major may also not be visible from some points in the southern hemisphere.

### Ursa Minor (Little Bear)

This is also a group of seven bright stars similar to the Ursa Major. The Pole Star is a part of this constellation. Its Indian name is *Laghu Saptarishi*.

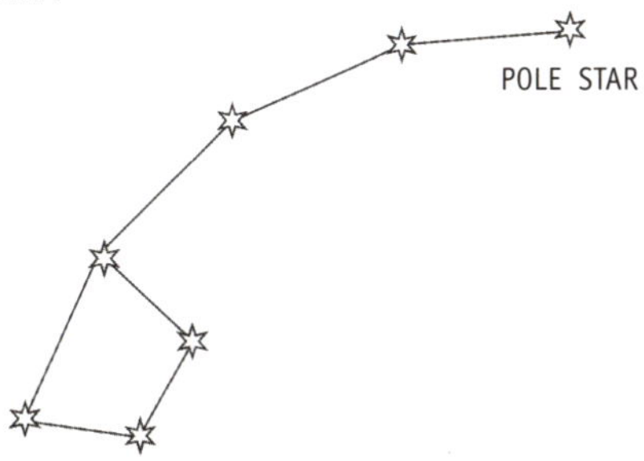


FIG. 18.2 Ursa Minor

### Orion

Orion is also called **The Hunter**. Its Indian name is *Mriga*. It has seven bright stars and several faint ones (Fig. 18.3). Four bright stars mark the shoulder and legs of the hunter and three stars mark its belt. Other faint stars complete the picture. Betelgueuse and Rigel are the two bright stars of this constellation. This constellation is visible in the winter season and is easy to locate.

You can locate **Sirius**, the brightest star in the sky with the help of Orion. A straight line through the three middle stars of Orion leads to Sirius (Fig. 18.3).

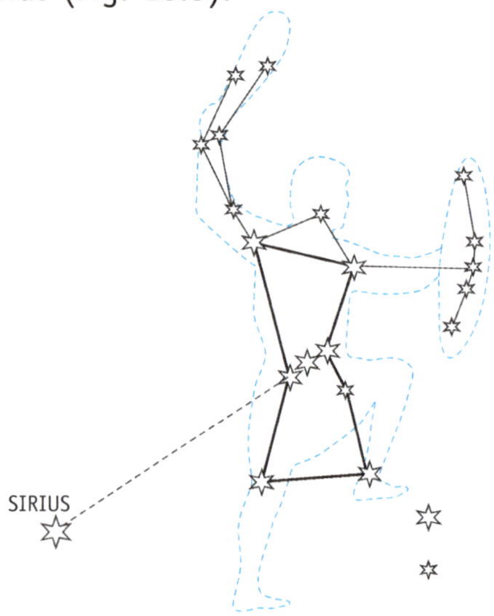


FIG. 18.3 Orion and Sirius

### Scorpius

This constellation contains seven bright stars. **Along with other faint stars, it forms the shape of a scorpion** (Fig. 18.4). It is visible during the summer season.

SCORPIUS

FIG. 18.4

### Cassiopeia

This constellation is visible in the northern sky during winters in the early part of the night. The five prominent stars form a distorted W or M. All the stars in the constellation, are supposed to form an image of the Egyptian queen Cassiopeia. You can read about the associated story in the Internet site given in My Virtual Library section.

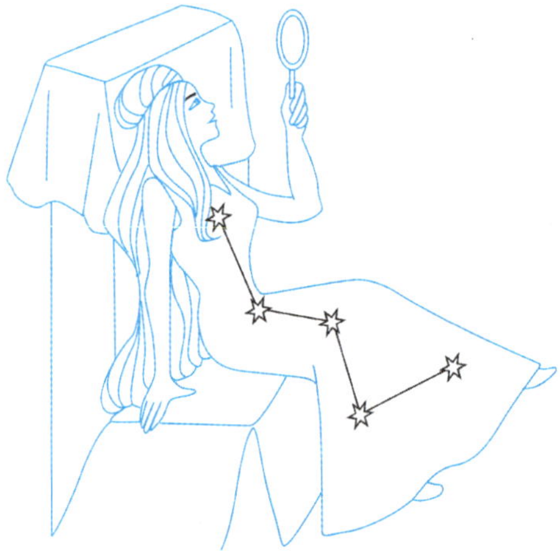

FIG. 18.5 Cassiopeia

## MOVEMENT OF STARS

Let us observe the directions in which stars move.

**ACTIVITY 2 (Observation and analysis):**
**To track the movement of Ursa Major**

For doing this investigation, you will have to stay up till late night. So the first thing that you require is permission from your parents!

- Carry out this investigation on a clear night. Start as soon as the brighter stars in the sky are visible. Stand on a cemented floor—on the roof or a verandah and face towards the north. Use a compass needle to find the direction if you are not sure.
- Find the Pole Star using the Ursa Major constellation.
- Point towards the Pole Star and let your helper mark out the direction of your hand on the floor with a piece of chalk. At the end of the line, make a dot to show the position of the star.
- Now look towards the two pointers of Ursa Major. Point towards them, one by one, and let your friend mark the direction of your hand on the floor in both cases. Mark the position of the stars with dots. Beside the three marks, write the time of observation.

- Go out after every two hours and mark out the directions and positions of the three stars each time. Write the time of the observation next to each mark.
- How do the positions of the three stars change? In which direction do they move?

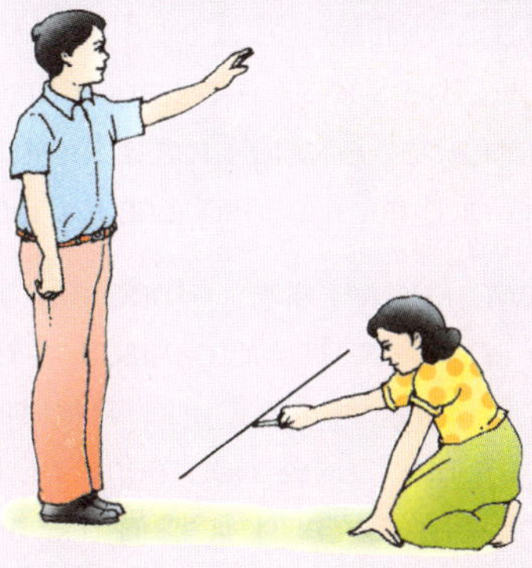

a. Tracking the movement of stars

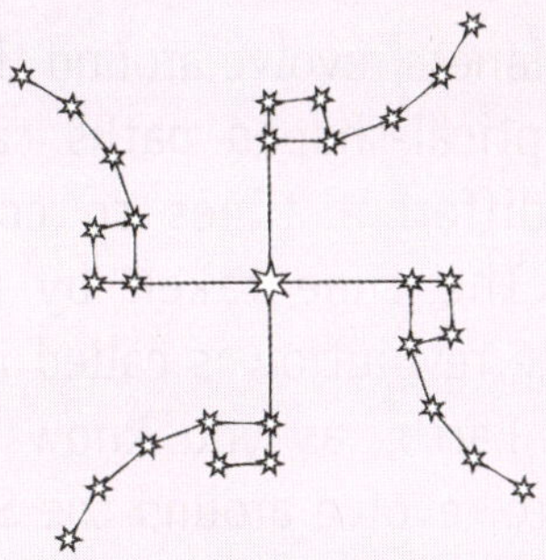

b. Movement of Ursa Major around the Pole Star

FIG. 18.6

The Pole Star appears to be stationary in the sky and all other stars appear to revolve around it from east to west. This happens because of the rotation of the Earth around its axis. As the Earth rotates on its axis from west to east, the stars appear to move from east to west to an observer on the Earth.

**ACTIVITY 3 (Observation)**

Stand outside at a fixed place and rotate in a circle from left to right. In which direction do the trees and buildings around you seem to rotate? You will find that they seem to rotate in the opposite direction—that is from right to left.

But why does the Pole Star appear to be stationary?

**ACTIVITY 4 (Observation)**

Take an umbrella and rotate it with your hands. Observe the different parts of the umbrella. Which part does not rotate at all?

The centre of the umbrella does not rotate at all because it lies on the axis of rotation of the umbrella. In the same way, the Pole Star appears to be stationary as it lies on the axis of rotation of the Earth (Fig. 18.7).

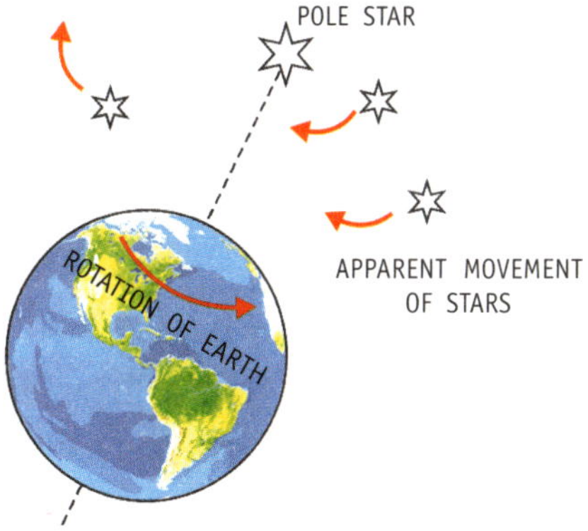


FIG. 18.7 The movement of stars

## ORAL QUESTIONS FOR FORMATIVE ASSESSMENT

1. Most stars are made up of two gases. What are these gases?
2. The Earth is 8.3 light minutes from the Sun. What does this statement mean?
3. A constellation is a group of stars close to each other. Do you agree with this definition of a constellation? Give reasons.
4. Why does the Pole Star seem to be stationary when seen from the Earth?

## THE SOLAR SYSTEM

The Sun, the eight planets, their moons and the other celestial objects that revolve around the Sun form the solar system. (In 2006, scientists decided that Pluto is too small to be called a planet. It is now considered a 'dwarf planet'. The number of planets is therefore reduced to eight.)

### Sun

As you know, the Sun is a star. It is the star closest to the Earth. Its average distance from the Earth is 150 million kilometres. Like all stars, the Sun is a huge ball of hot gases—mostly hydrogen and helium (Fig. 18.8). It is about 1.4 million kilometres in diameter. This is about 110 times the diameter of the Earth. The temperature at its centre is about 14 million degree celsius, while its surface temperature is about 6000 degree celsius. The Sun is the source of almost all energy on the Earth as well as on other planets.

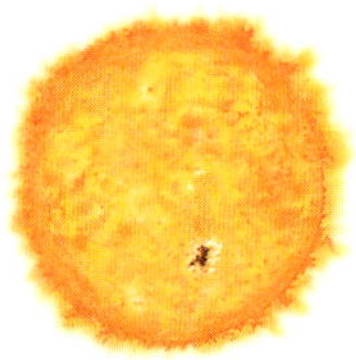

FIG. 18.8 Sun

### The planets

The planets of our solar system in order of their distances from the Sun are **Mercury** (closest to the Sun), **Venus**, **Earth**, **Mars**, **Jupiter**, **Saturn**, **Uranus** and **Neptune** (farthest from the Sun).

**IT'S A FACT!**

**Pluto**, demoted from planet status in 2006, has been reclassified. It and other dwarf planets like it will be called **plutoids**. The International Astronomical Union (IAU) gave a full definition of what counts as a plutoid.

A plutoid is defined as a type of dwarf planet that orbits the Sun at a distance greater than Neptune and has enough mass for its self-gravity to give it a near-spherical shape.

The two known and named plutoids are Pluto and **Eris**. The organization expects more plutoids will be found. Another dwarf planet, Ceres, does not merit the plutoid designation because it is in the asteroid belt between Mars and Jupiter.

All the planets revolve around the Sun along definite elliptical-shaped paths called **orbits**. They take different times to complete one revolution. The time taken by a planet to complete one revolution is called its **period of revolution**. Earth, as you know takes about 365¼ days to revolve around the Sun. Mercury, which is closest to the Sun, takes only 88 days whereas Neptune, being the farthest from the Sun takes 165 years to complete one revolution.

You know that the Earth, besides revolving around the Sun, also rotates about its axis once every 24 hours. The other planets also rotate on their axis. The **period of rotation** is the

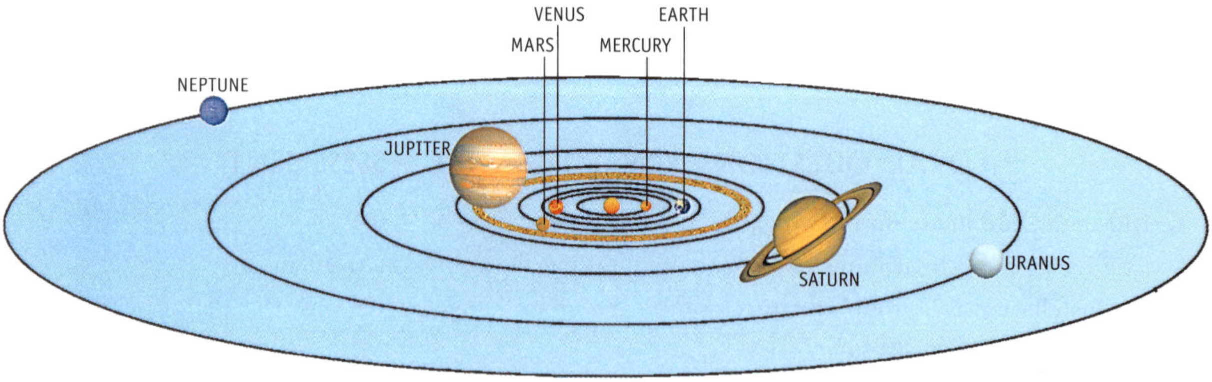


FIG. 18.9 The solar system

TABLE 18.2 Data about planets of the solar system

| PLANET | AVERAGE DISTANCE FROM SUN (MILLION KM) | DIAMETER AT EQUATOR (KM) | MASS IN RELATION TO EARTH (EARTH = 1) | TIME TO ORBIT SUN | TIME OF ROTATION ON AXIS | KNOWN NUMBER OF MOONS* |
|---|---|---|---|---|---|---|
| Mercury | 58 | 4880 | 0.06 | 88 days | 58 days | 0 |
| Venus | 108 | 12100 | 0.82 | 225 days | 243 days | 0 |
| Earth | 150 | 12800 | 1 | 365¼ days | 24 hours | 1 |
| Mars | 228 | 6800 | 0.11 | 687 days | 24 h 37 m | 2 |
| Jupiter | 778 | 142800 | 318 | 12 years | 9 h 55 m | 63 |
| Saturn | 1427 | 120000 | 95 | 29.5 years | 10 h 39 m | 33 |
| Uranus | 2871 | 50800 | 14.5 | 84 years | 10 h 14 m | 27 |
| Neptune | 4497 | 48500 | 17 | 165 years | 16 h 7 m | 13 |

* This number is the number of moons 'reported'. However, not all of them are recognized as 'official' moons by the International Astronomical Union.

time taken by a planet to complete one rotation about its axis. It is the least for Jupiter—only 9 hours 55 minutes, and the most for Venus—243 days. Table 18.2 summarises data about the planets.

Mercury, Venus, Earth and Mars are nearer to the Sun than other planets. They are known as the **inner planets**. They have very few satellites or moons. Jupiter, Saturn, Uranus and Neptune are known as the **outer planets**. They are very far from the Sun. They have rings around them. They have many satellites or moons.

**Mercury (*Budh*):** Mercury is covered with many bowl-shaped holes called **craters** (Fig. 18.10). Being very close to the Sun, Mercury is very hot during the day (about 400 °C). Its gravitational force is not strong enough to hold an atmosphere. Due to the absence of an atmosphere, the heat is quickly lost at night, and it becomes freezing cold (about –200 °C). Mercury can be observed just before sunrise or just after sunset, near the horizon. During the day, it is hidden by the glare of the Sun.

MERCURY

FIG. 18.10

**Venus (*Shukra*):** Venus is about the same size as the Earth, and is the closest planet to the Earth (Fig. 18.11). It is a very hot planet (about 480 °C), even hotter than Mercury, though it is further away from the Sun. This is because of the high percentage of carbon dioxide in its atmosphere, which causes heating due to the greenhouse effect.

VENUS

FIG. 18.11

It appears as the brightest planet in the sky. It appears bright due to its cloudy atmosphere, which reflects almost 75 per cent of the sunlight that falls on it. Sometimes it can be seen in the eastern sky early in the morning before sunrise. At other times, it can be seen in the western sky, after sunset. **Venus is commonly known as the evening and the morning star** (though it is not a star). It appears as an evening star just above the western horizon for 292 days. For the next 292 days, it appears in the eastern sky as morning star.

Unlike the Earth and most other planets, Venus rotates on its axis from east to west, i.e. in the opposite direction. When observed from the Earth, Venus shows phases just like the Moon.

**Earth (*Prithvi*):** Our Earth is the third planet from the Sun. It is the only planet on which life is known to exist. All the factors necessary

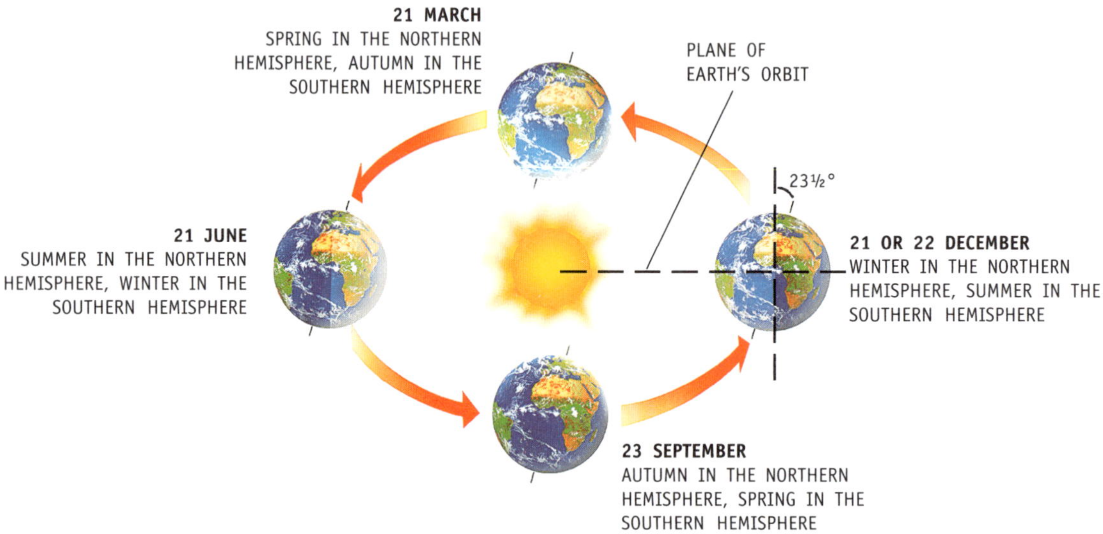


FIG. 18.12 The seasons are caused by the revolution of the tilted Earth around the Sun.

for life are present only on Earth. It has an atmosphere containing the gases, **oxygen** and **carbon dioxide**, which are necessary for life. It has **water** in liquid form, which is essential for life. Being at the right distance from the Sun, it is not as hot as Mercury or Venus, nor is it as cold as the planets which are further away. The right distance of the Earth from the Sun and the suitable atmosphere around it help to maintain the right temperature on the Earth for survival of life. It also has a layer of ozone in its atmosphere which stops harmful ultraviolet rays of the Sun from reaching the Earth. From space, the Earth appears blue-green due to reflection of light from water and landmass on its surface.

The Earth rotates about its imaginary axis. The portion of the Earth facing the Sun at any time has day. The portion facing away has night. As the Earth rotates, day and night follow each other. The Earth also revolves around the Sun in its orbit. The axis of the Earth is not perpendicular to the plane of its orbit but tilted at an angle of 23½°. The Earth completes one revolution around the Sun in 365¼ days. The seasons are caused by the tilt of the Earth's axis and the revolution of the Earth around the Sun. The tilting of the axis of rotation of the Earth always remains in the same direction. When the northern hemisphere is tilted towards the Sun, it is summer in the northern hemisphere, while it is winter in the southern hemisphere (Fig. 18.12).

**Mars (*Mangal*):** Mars is a red, rocky planet about half the size of the Earth (Fig. 18.13). Its surface is covered with craters and mountains. It is seen as a reddish object in the sky. It is commonly known as the red planet. Mars has a very thin atmosphere. It is a cold planet, with temperatures ranging from –120 °C to 25 °C.

MARS

FIG. 18.13

**Jupiter (*Brihaspati*):** Jupiter is the largest planet (Fig. 18.14). Its volume is about 1300 times that of Earth, but its weight is about 318 times that of Earth. It is a cold planet. It has a large red spot on its surface. This spot is actually a giant storm that has been raging for years! It has faint

JUPITER

FIG. 18.14

rings around it. It can be seen as a very bright object for about half the year in the evening sky. Its bright appearance is due to its thick atmosphere which reflects most of the sunlight that falls on it. Four of its large moons can be seen from the Earth with the help of a telescope.

**Saturn (*Shani*):** Saturn is the second largest planet. It is very cold. Three wide rings surround this planet. These rings are not visible with the naked eyes but can be seen only with the help of a telescope. These rings are made of ice and dust. This is the most distinctive feature of Saturn (Fig. 18.15). Saturn has a low density—less than that of water.

SATURN
FIG. 18.15

**Uranus and Neptune:** These are also very cold planets. Being very far away, they can only be seen through a powerful telescope. Uranus, like Venus, rotates from east to west. It has a highly tilted rotational axis because of which it appears to roll along on its orbit.

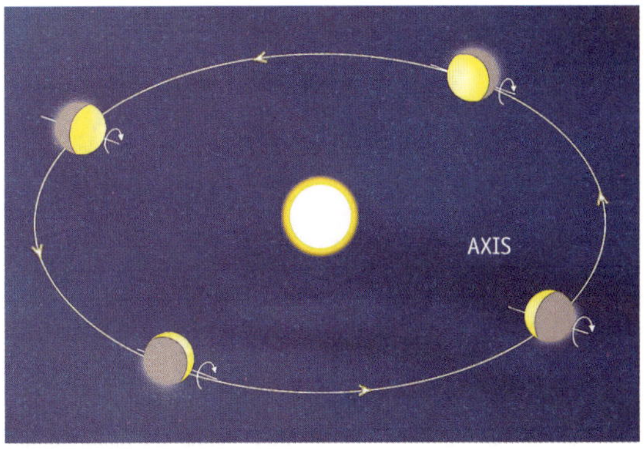


FIG. 18.16 Uranus in its orbit

## ORAL QUESTIONS FOR FORMATIVE ASSESSMENT

1. The Sun is the biggest and brightest star. Do you agree? Give reasons.
2. Mercury does not have an atmosphere. What effect does this have on the temperature of its surface?
3. Suppose the Earth's axis had not been tilted to the plane of its orbit. How would this have affected the annual seasons on the Earth?
4. Does any planet give out its own light?

## THE MOON

A celestial object that revolves around a planet is known as a **natural satellite** or **moon** of the planet. Most planets have moons revolving around them. As you have already seen, the inner planets have fewer moons, while the outer planets have many moons revolving around them.

### The Earth's Moon

The Earth has only one moon. It is held in orbit around the Earth because of the Earth's gravity. It shines because it reflects the light of the Sun. It is dry and barren with no atmosphere. Its surface is covered with several craters and mountains. It has a diameter of about one-fourth that of the Earth. Its mass is about one-hundredth that of the Earth. Its distance from the Earth is about 3,84,400 kilometres.

FIG. 18.17 The surface of the Moon

The Moon completes one revolution around the Earth in 27.3 days. It also rotates once on its axis in the same period of time. Its revolution and rotation are such that **only one**

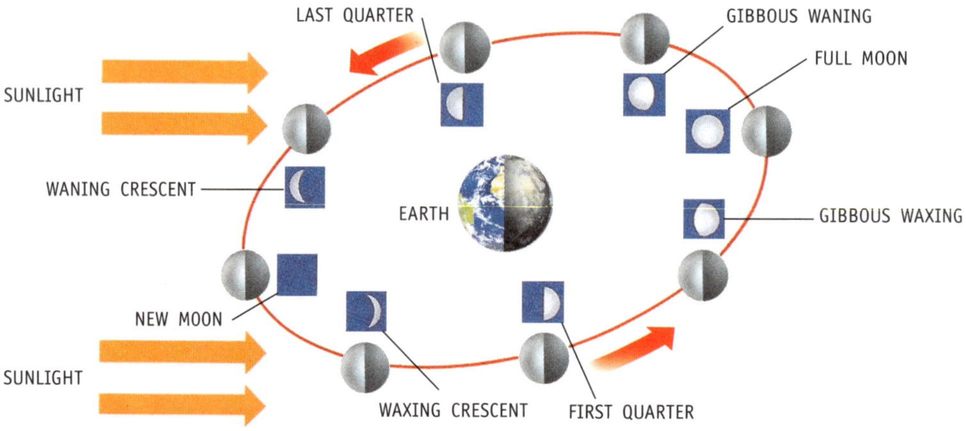


**Fig. 18.18** Phases of the Moon

**side of the Moon always faces us.** The other side is never visible to us.

The side that faces us is also not fully visible all the time. We only see that portion of it which reflects sunlight to us. This changes every day as the relative positions of the Sun, Earth and Moon change every day.

- When the Moon is in between the Earth and the Sun, we do not see the Moon at all. It is called the **new Moon** (*amavasya*).
- Two or three days after this, we see only a part of the Moon. This is called the **crescent Moon**.
- Gradually, the shape of the bright portion of the Moon becomes bigger and bigger. Within a week we see half of the Moon. This is called the **first quarter**.
- When we see more than half of the Moon, it is called the **Gibbous Moon**.
- On the fifteenth day after the new Moon, we see the **full Moon** (*purnima*), when the Earth comes between the Sun and the Moon.
- Thereafter, the bright portion of the Moon reduces, and 15 days after the full Moon, we again have the new Moon.

These shapes of the bright part of the Moon, as seen from the Earth, are known as the **phases of Moon** (Fig. 18.18). The time period between one new Moon and the next (or between one full Moon and the next) is a little over 29 days.

### CHANDRAYAAN

Chandrayaan-1, (चंद्रयान 1 = Moon-vehicle) is India's first mission to the Moon by India's national space agency Indian Space Research Organisation (ISRO). The unmanned lunar exploration mission included a lunar orbiter and an impactor. The spacecraft was launched on 22 October 2008 from Satish Dhawan Space Centre, Sriharikota, Andhra Pradesh at 06:23 IST. The vehicle was successfully inserted into lunar orbit on 8 November 2008. The estimated cost for the project was Rs 386 crore.

The objectives of the mission were:

- To prepare a three-dimensional atlas of both near and far side of the Moon.
- To determine the presence of mineral and chemical elements such as magnesium, aluminium, silicon, calcium, iron, titanium, radon, uranium and thorium on the Moon.
- To land a sub-satellite called the Moon Impact Probe (MIP) on the surface of the Moon as a fore-runner to future soft landing missions.

To find out more about Chandrayaan, visit rsgr.in/lsc-cce-8 and click on **LINK 68**.

Find out how successful Chandrayaan-1 was in its mission.

## ACTIVITY 5 (Experimental investigation)

Light a table lamp in a corner of a dark room. Let it represent the Sun. Paste a white paper on one half of a football. Let it represent the Moon, with the white half being the half that is visible to us from the Earth. Stand at the centre of the room. You are like an observer on the Earth. Let a friend revolve around you very slowly holding the Moon in such a way that the white portion is always towards you. As your friend moves, carefully note the portion of the white half of the football that receives light from the lamp. Compare with the phases of the Moon.

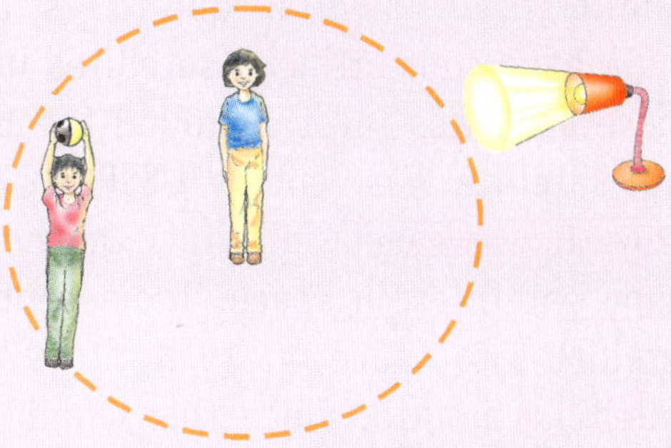

FIG. 18.19

## OTHER CELESTIAL OBJECTS IN THE SOLAR SYSTEM

### Asteroids

There is a large gap between the orbits of Mars and Jupiter. A large number of rocks called asteroids lie in this space. The largest asteroid is **Ceres** (diameter 1003 km). The size of asteroids varies from a kilometre to a few hundred kilometres.

### Comets

Comets are celestial objects that revolve around the Sun in very long periods of revolution. A comet appears like a ball of fire with a long bright 'tail' as it approaches the Sun. The tail always points away from the Sun, and its size increases as it approaches the Sun. The famous **Halley's Comet** appears after every 76 years. It last appeared in 1986.

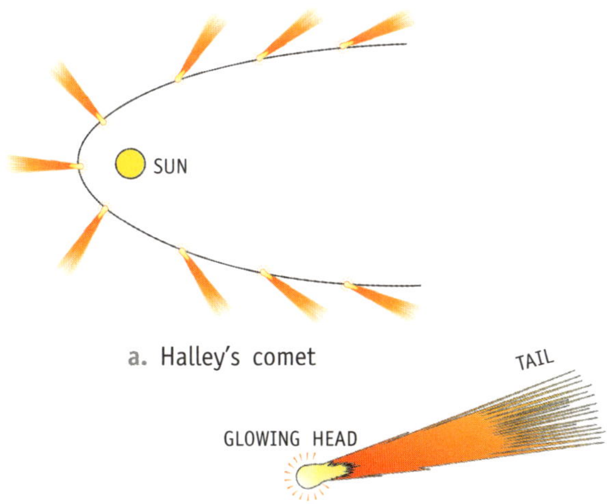


a. Halley's comet

b. A comet in the sky

FIG. 18.20

### Meteors and meteorites

Meteors are small objects made up mainly of stones present in space. They regularly enter the Earth's atmosphere. As a meteor enters the Earth's atmosphere at high speed, it is heated by friction with air, and in most cases it burns to ashes in a very short time. As it heats up and burns, it appears as a glowing streak of light and is called a **shooting star**, though it is not a star at all. You may have seen shooting stars in the sky on a clear night.

If a meteor is large, it may fall on the Earth's surface before being completely burnt out. Such meteors are called **meteorites**. The Barringer Crater in Arizona, USA was formed when a large meteorite struck the Earth (Fig. 18.21).

FIG. 18.21 The Barringer Crater in Arizona

## ARTIFICIAL SATELLITES

Scientists of several countries including India have sent artificial satellites into space. These satellites revolve around the Earth. The first satellite was sent by USSR on 4 October 1957. It was called **Sputnik-I**. Today, there are many satellites in space. India sent her first satellite into space on 19 April 1975. It was called **Aryabhata**. Since then, India has sent many more artificial satellites into space (Table 18.3).

TABLE 18.3 Some artificial satellites sent into space by India

| DATE | SATELLITE |
|---|---|
| 12 July 2010 | STUDSAT |
| 28 April 2008 | CARTOSAT-2A |
| 2 September 2007 | INSAT 4CR |
| 12 March 2007 | INSAT 4B |
| 22 December 2005 | INSAT 4A |
| 20 September 2004 | EDUSAT |
| 17 October 2003 | RESOURCESAT-1 (IRS-P6) |
| 28 September 2003 | INSAT-3E |
| 12 September 2002 | METSAT (KALPANA-1) |
| 26 May 1999 | OCEANSAT (IRS-P4) |
| 7 December 1995 | INSAT-2C |
| 17 March 1988 | IRS-1A |
| 30 August 1983 | INSAT-1B |
| 19 June 1981 | APPLE |
| 18 July 1980 | ROHINI |
| 7 June 1979 | BHASKARA-1 |
| 19 April 1975 | ARYABHATA |

Artificial satellites are very useful to us.

- They help in television and radio transmission.
- They help in telephone communication.
- They help us to study and forecast the weather by sending cloud pictures to the Earth, taken from space.
- They help in locating minerals and studying agricultural yield on the Earth by photographing land from above. This is known as remote sensing, which means, collecting information from a distance.
- They help scientists know more about the universe by collecting information about space.

### ACTIVITY 6 (Investigation)

Draw five or six dots a little apart from each other on a balloon with a sketch pen. Blow air into the balloon. What happens to the dots?

FIG. 18.22 The dots on a balloon move away from each other as the balloon is blown up.

As the balloon is blown up, the dots on it move away from each other.

Scientists have shown that the universe is getting bigger and bigger, like a balloon being blown up. The galaxies are all moving away from each other just as the dots on the balloon move away from each other when it is blown up.

Astronomers found that the universe was expanding. So, they put forward a theory to explain how the universe originated. They believe that about 15 billion years ago, all the matter in the universe was gathered into a single mass. Suddenly the mass exploded, sending particles flying in all directions. These particles formed the galaxies with their stars and planets. These galaxies are still flying away from each other because of the explosion. This is called the **Big Bang Theory**.

## ORAL QUESTIONS FOR FORMATIVE ASSESSMENT

1. For half the year we can see one side of the Moon, and for the other half, the other side of the Moon. Do you agree? Give reasons.
2. Is the Moon a natural or an artificial satellite of the Earth? Why?
3. Is a shooting star actually a star? Explain.
4. A comet is a celestial object that revolves around the Sun like a planet. What is the difference between a comet and a planet?

## NOW YOU KNOW

- The universe comprises everything that exists, which includes stars, planets, moons, other celestial objects, everything that exists on these celestial objects, as well as the vast empty space in between.
- A group of billions of stars make up a galaxy. Our solar system is in the galaxy called the Milky Way.
- Stars are huge spinning balls of luminous gases that give out heat and light. The Sun is a star.
- Planets are celestial objects that revolve around the Sun. They do not give out their own light.
- Distances in space are measured in light years. One light year is the distance travelled by light in one year.
- Constellations are stars that appear to form a pattern when viewed from the Earth. Some important constellations are Ursa Major, Ursa Minor, Orion, Cassiopeia and Scorpius.
- The Sun, the eight planets, their moons and the other celestial objects that revolve around the Sun form the solar system.
- The planets that revolve around the Sun are—Mercury, Venus, Earth, Mars, Jupiter, Saturn, Uranus, and Neptune. The planets also rotate on their axes.
- A celestial object that revolves around a planet is known as a natural satellite or moon of the planet.
- The different shapes of the bright part of the Moon, as seen from the Earth, are known as the phases of the Moon.
- Asteroids, comets and meteors are other heavenly bodies in the solar system.
- Artificial satellites are useful in communication, weather forecasting, studying land and providing information about space.

## NEW WORDS

**GALAXY**—a group of billions of stars
**UNIVERSE**—all the galaxies along with the stars, planets and other heavenly bodies in them, and all the empty space in between
**ASTRONOMER**—person who studies the universe
**LIGHT YEAR**—distance travelled by light in one year

**METEOR**—small object in space made up mainly of stones, which enters the Earth's atmosphere

**METEORITE**—meteor which falls from space on the Earth's surface

## FOR FORMATIVE AND SUMMATIVE ASSESSMENT

### A. MULTIPLE-CHOICE QUESTIONS: Choose the most appropriate answer.

1. A galaxy such as the Milky Way contains
   a. a few thousand stars.
   b. a few million stars.
   c. a few billion stars.
   d. only a few thousand stars but millions of planets.
2. The distance of the star Proxima Centauri from the Earth is
   a. 4.3 million kilometres.
   b. 8¼ light minutes.
   c. 2 million light years.
   d. 4.3 light years.
3. The Pole Star is in the constellation of
   a. Ursa Major.
   b. Ursa Minor.
   c. Orion.
   d. Scorpius.
4. The solar system consists of
   a. the Sun and the planets only.
   b. the Sun, the planets and their moons.
   c. the Sun, the planets, their moons and all other celestial objects that revolve around the Sun.
   d. all the stars in the Milky Way.
5. The hottest planet in the solar system is
   a. Mars.
   b. Sun.
   c. Mercury.
   d. Venus.
6. The large number of rocks that lie between the orbits of Mars and Jupiter are called
   a. comets.
   b. asteroids.
   c. meteors.
   d. meteorites.
7. Artificial satellites are sent in space by scientists because
   a. they look beautiful in the sky.
   b. every country wants to break the record of the largest number of satellites sent.
   c. they serve as stopovers for people going to the Moon.
   d. they are useful in communication, forecasting weather, locating minerals and in studying outer space.
8. The Sun is located at
   a. the centre of the solar system.
   b. the centre of the Milky Way.
   c. the centre of the universe.
   d. none of these

### B. VERY SHORT-ANSWER QUESTIONS: Give one-word answers.

1. What are scientists who study the universe called?
2. Which galaxy do we live in?
3. Stars are made up of rocks. True or false?

4. The Sun is hottest at its outer surface. True or false?
5. What is the distance that light travels in one year called?
6. The stars in a constellation are actually very close to each other. True or false?
7. The constellation Big Dipper is known by another name also. What is it?
8. The stars in which constellation form the shape of a hunting man?
9. Name these:
   a. largest planet  b. planet closest to the Sun
   c. the 'red' planet  d. planet farthest from the Earth
   e. the hottest planet  f. planet with high percentage of carbon dioxide in its atmosphere
10. Name the largest asteroid.
11. Which comet can be seen after every 76 years?
12. Which was the first artificial satellite of the Earth?
13. Which satellite was sent first into space by India?

## C. SHORT-ANSWER QUESTIONS (TYPE I): Answer in a sentence or two.

1. While looking up at the sky, how can you distinguish between a planet and a star?
2. What is the solar system?
3. Why do stars give out heat and light?
4. Which property of the Pole Star makes it very useful for sailors?
5. Why was it necessary to define a new unit to measure distances in the universe? What is this unit?
6. Why is Mercury very hot during the day and very cold at night?
7. What is the most distinctive feature of Saturn?
8. What is the difference between meteors and meteorites?

## D. SHORT-ANSWER QUESTIONS (TYPE II): Answer in about 30 words.

1. Both galaxies and constellations are groups of stars. Give two differences between them.
2. How can you locate the Pole Star with the help of Ursa Major?
3. Explain why the Pole Star appears to be stationary in the sky and all other stars appear to revolve around it from east to west.
4. Show the position of main stars in these constellations: a. Ursa Major b. Orion
5. Why is Venus the hottest planet even though Mercury is closest to the Sun?
6. How is an artificial satellite different from a natural satellite? Give one example of each.
7. Describe the physical features of the Moon.

## E. LONG-ANSWER QUESTIONS: Answer in about 60 words.

1. Give four ways in which stars are different from planets.
2. What major factors have enabled life to evolve and survive on the Earth?
3. Give five ways in which artificial satellites are useful to us.

4. What do you mean by 'phases of the Moon'? Draw a labelled diagram to show the phases of the Moon.

## HOTS QUESTIONS: Think and answer.

1. Why can't we see stars during the day?
2. Suppose a star which is 100 light years away explodes today. It is highly unlikely that you will be able to see the explosion. Why?
3. On the Earth, the Sun rises in the east and sets in the west. Will it be the same on Venus?
4. Since your birth, how many times have you gone around the Sun?
5. Answer the following, giving reasons.
   a. Can you light a fire on the Moon?
   b. If a meteor falls on the Moon, can you hear it fall?
   c. Can you see the meteor falling on the Moon?
   d. Can life exist on the Moon?
6. If the planet Saturn is inserted in water, will it float or sink? Why?

## FOR FORMATIVE ASSESSMENT*

### In the Library—Research Projects

- ❒ GPS is a system of several satellites used for all kinds of navigation—even in a car travelling in a city. It can tell the exact latitude, longitude and altitude of the place a person is located in. Find out the full form of GPS, and how it works. Survey the market for the different car navigation devices based on GPS.
- ❒ On 14 November 2008, the Moon Impact Probe (MIP) with the Indian tricolor painted on it landed on the Moon after ejecting from the Chandrayaan I. India thus became only the fourth nation in the world to land a human-made object on the lunar surface. Find out how successful the mission was and its main findings.
- ❒ You have seen that artificial satellites are used in TV transmission. TV signals from the TV station are sent up to the satellite. Instruments in the satellite receive the signal and send it back to cover large portions of the Earth. The signals are received on the Earth by dish antennas (See the Figure alongside).

  However, you know that satellites revolve around the Earth. If the TV satellite keeps revolving around the Earth, its position changes all the time. It will then not be possible to use it for TV transmission. Find out how this problem is solved.

### My Virtual Library—Research/Activities on the Internet

- ❒ Visit rsgr.in/lsc-cce-8 and click on LINK 69 to get detailed images and information about all constellations.
- ❒ Visit rsgr.in/lsc-cce-8 and click on LINK 70 to read about mythology associated with stars and constellations.

*For more tasks see Page 257

- ❐ Visit rsgr.in/lsc-cce-8 and click on LINK 71 to get lots of information and a number of images of the solar system.
- ❐ View animations:
  - ◆ Phases of the Moon: Visit rsgr.in/lsc-cce-8 and click on LINK 72.
  - ◆ Halley's comet: Visit rsgr.in/lsc-cce-8 and click on LINK 73.
  - ◆ Meteor showers: Visit rsgr.in/lsc-cce-8 and click on LINK 74.
- ❐ Visit rsgr.in/lsc-cce-8 and click on LINK 75 to read about the moons of the planets.
- ❐ Visit rsgr.in/lsc-cce-8 and click on LINK 76 to get details of Chandrayaan-1 mission.

## To Meet—Research on Scientist

**Edmund Halley** (1656–1742) This English astronomer did a great deal of research on comets. He observed a comet in 1682, and showed that it was the same comet which had been seen earlier in 1531 and in 1607. He predicted that it would again be seen in 1759, 1835, 1910, and 1986. This comet is known as Halley's Comet. Perhaps some of you may be able to spot it when it reappears in 2062!

Collect pictures of Halley's comet and make a presentation on it.

## Beyond the Classroom—Field Trip

Visit an observatory or a planetarium if there is one in your town or city. Study the different equipments used.

TEACHER'S NOTES

- It is important to give children the idea of the vastness of the universe. Emphasize that when they look at the sky, they see stars as they appeared several years back. Indicative distances are given below.
  - Sun: 8.3 light minutes
  - Proxima Centauri: 4.3 light years
  - Pole Star: 431 light years
  - Mu Cephei—the most distant star that can be seen without a telescope: About 5000 light years
  - The centre of the Milky Way: About 26,000 light years
  - Andromeda—the nearest large galaxy that can be seen with the naked eye: About 2.5 million light years
- It may be a little difficult for students to visualize why the Pole Star appears stationary while the other stars appear to move around it. Do the umbrella experiment (Activity 4) to clarify this. Point out that the stars are not actually moving, but only seem to be moving in this way because of the rotation of the Earth. In this way, it is very different from the planets moving around the Sun.

19

# Pollution of Water and Air

Living things originated and survived on the earth because:

- All the materials required by living things, such as air, water, soil and minerals are present on the earth. These are the major resources of the earth.
- The earth is at the right distance from the sun and therefore has the right temperature range for life to exist. The light energy received from the sun plays an important role in the survival of life on the earth.

Plants use carbon dioxide from the air, water and minerals from the soil, and sunlight to make food.

Animals need oxygen, water and food to survive. They get oxygen from the air, water from the water bodies such as ponds, lakes and rivers, and food from plants and animals.

## WATER

We need water for drinking, bathing, washing and for various other purposes. Farmers need water for growing crops and raising animals. Factories need water to produce steel, petrol, paper, etc. Many plants and animals live in water. Therefore, clean water is very important for us.

The consumption of water by humans has gone up considerably. This is mainly because of increased population and because industrial

**IN THIS CHAPTER**

POLLUTION AND CONSERVATION OF WATER ◆ POLLUTION AND CONSERVATION OF AIR processes such as production of paper, dyeing of cloth, tanning of leather, etc. use up large amounts of water.

We have learnt earlier that **water is a renewable resource**. This is because **water is recycled naturally in the environment by the water cycle**. Water can be obtained from rivers, lakes, streams, reservoirs and wells. Oceans have a large quantity of water but it cannot be used directly because of its high salt content.

## WATER POLLUTION

Water is said to be polluted if it contains impurities that are harmful to humans, other animals, plants or to the environment. The substances that pollute water are known as **water pollutants**.

Rivers and seas have traditionally been used for the disposal of waste such as sewage and industrial waste. If the amount of waste dumped is not very high, the natural process of decay ensures that water pollution remains within manageable levels. However, with an ever increasing human population and an increasing number of industries, the amount of waste which goes into the water is very high.

The natural process of decay cannot cope with such large amount of waste. The water in rivers and seas is, therefore, becoming more and more polluted. So much so that several rivers in India including the Ganga are 'dead' at many places—the pollution levels are so high that aquatic life cannot survive. Attempts to clean the rivers have not had much success—read the Ganga Action Plan given in the 'news report—Ganga Action Plan' below.

The main causes of water pollution are:

- **Sewage:** Untreated sewage from homes is

### NEWS REPORT—GANGA ACTION PLAN

Ganga Action Plan or GAP was a programme launched by the Government of India in April 1985 to reduce water pollution in the river Ganga. The programme was launched with much fanfare, but it failed to decrease the pollution level in the river.

Given below is an extract from a news item about the Ganga Action Plan published in *The Hindu*, dated 28 August 2004.

NEW DELHI, 27 August 2004. Despite heavy investments towards cleaning the Ganga, pollution levels are just as terrifying as before. This was highlighted during the Clean Ganga Day organized by the Sankat Mochan Foundation, the Asia Foundation and the United States Agency for International Development in the Capital today.

"The Ganga Action Plan was launched by the Government in Varanasi in 1986. Crores have been spent on the project but the pollution levels in the Ganga are as high as ever. Till 1993, the Government said that the project had been successful. But then we started doing water testing and it was clear that sewage was still flowing into the river," said Veer Bhadra Mishra, president of the Sankat Mochan Foundation, Varanasi, at the second Clean Ganga Day.

According to environmentalists, about 90 per cent of pollution into the holy river is caused by sewage generation, while only about 5 to 6 per cent can be blamed on bathing and other activities. "While the real sources of pollution—sewage—continues to flow into the river, we are right now trying to spread awareness among citizens not to pollute the ghats. But 20 years after we started our campaign, I still feel that we have not been able to achieve anything. Our aim is still what it was—to clean the Ganga," Dr Mishra said.

What, in your opinion, can be the causes of the failure of the plan? Find out more about it and have a discussion in class.

often disposed off into rivers. Also, in villages where proper sanitation facilities are not available, people defecate in the open. Rain washes off the human excreta and animal dung into nearby water sources. These wastes contain many harmful microorganisms—bacteria, viruses, fungi and parasites that cause diseases such as diarrhoea, dysentery, cholera, typhoid and jaundice. The treatment of sewage with chemicals such as chlorine can kill many of these organisms. The sewage should be treated before being disposed off.

- **Industrial waste:** Many industries produce waste materials which are often discharged into rivers. Leather, textile and chemical industries, for example, throw out highly poisonous compounds of lead, mercury, arsenic, etc., which pollute the rivers and oceans (Fig. 19.1). Some other polluting industries are oil refineries, paper factories and sugar mills.

The temperature of the waste water from factories that is discharged into rivers is often higher than the temperature of the river water. The resultant increase in the river water temperature is itself a form of pollution as it adversely affects aquatic plants and animals.

To reduce pollution, these waste products must be treated in the factories themselves to convert the poisonous substances into harmless ones before discharging them. While there are rules to prevent dumping of untreated waste in rivers, they are often not followed. The soil also gets affected by impure water. It causes changes in its acidity, growth of worms, etc.

- **Fertilizers and pesticides:** Farmers use chemical fertilizers and pesticides in their fields. These get washed off by rain into water sources. They also seep into the ground to pollute groundwater. Pesticides such as DDT can get into the bodies of fishes through the water. Other animals, including humans, get poisoned if they eat these fish. When fertilizers run off into water sources, they cause an increase in the growth of algae in water which use up the dissolved oxygen from the water. When algae die, they become food for decomposers such as bacteria—these also use the dissolved oxygen, thus reducing oxygen content even further. Their thick growth also stops sunlight from reaching the water. This enrichment of water by nutrients which leads to excessive plant growth and depletion of oxygen is known as **eutrophication**. It adversely affects the water plants and animals (Fig. 19.2).

Chemical fertilizers and pesticides do not decompose by natural methods. Therefore, they

FIG. 19.1 Factories often discharge their wastes into rivers and seas.

FIG. 19.2
An eutrophic pond

go on accumulating and pollution increases. Scientists are now searching for pesticides and fertilizers that will decay naturally, to reduce pollution. Substances that decay naturally are called **biodegradable**. Biodegradable pesticides which use extracts from the neem tree have been tested successfully. Compost, made from natural organic substances, is a biodegradable fertilizer.

## POTABLE WATER

If we drink the polluted water in rivers and lakes we can fall ill. Water also gets polluted at several places underground and becomes unsuitable for drinking. Water has to be treated to make it suitable for drinking. Water that is suitable for drinking is called **potable water**.

**ACTIVITY 1 (Experimental investigation): To filter muddy water**

Take some muddy water in a beaker. Take a circular piece of filter paper and fold it twice as shown in Figure 19.3a. Open it out to make a cone. Place the filter paper cone in a funnel. Keep a beaker below the funnel. Pour the muddy water slowly into the cone, using a glass rod (Fig. 19.3b). Clear water comes out through the funnel and collects in the beaker below. Take out the filter paper cone and open it out. Mud particles are seen on the paper.

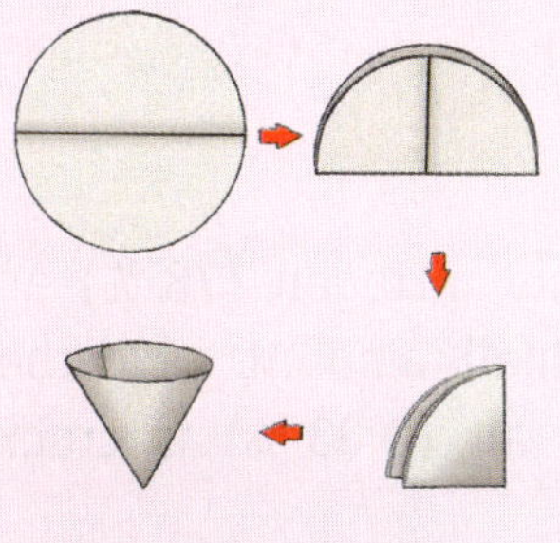

a. Folding a filter paper to form a cone

b. Set up for filtration

FIG. 19.3 The process of filtration

At homes and in offices, special types of filters are used to remove solid impurities from drinking water. In these filters, a porous pot made of ceramic is used as a filter. As the water passes through the fine pores, the solid impurities are filtered out.

However, though the filtered water appears clean as it is free of solid impurities, it may still have germs in it, and is not potable. At home, water can be made potable by killing the germs in the following ways.

- **Boiling** the water for 15–20 minutes kills all germs.
- **Ultraviolet light:** A special type of light called ultraviolet light kills germs—it is used in several water purifiers available in the market today.
- **Reverse osmosis (RO):** Water is passed through a special membrane called a semi-permeable membrane. It has very fine pores through which water can pass through but not the impurities. RO water filters are commonly available in the market—they remove solid impurities as well as germs.
- **Chlorination:** Chlorine added to water in the form of chlorine tablets or bleaching powder kills germs. However, care has to be taken to add the right quantities of chlorine.

### The Water Treatment Plant (the Waterworks)

Tap water supplied to our homes is made potable in the **waterworks**. The processes used are as follows:

- **Sedimentation** and **decantation** is first done to remove larger particles of solid impurities.
- Alum is then added to the water to separate the smaller particles by making them heavier so that they settle down. You have read in earlier classes that this method is known as **loading**.
- The water is then **filtered** by passing it through sand filters.

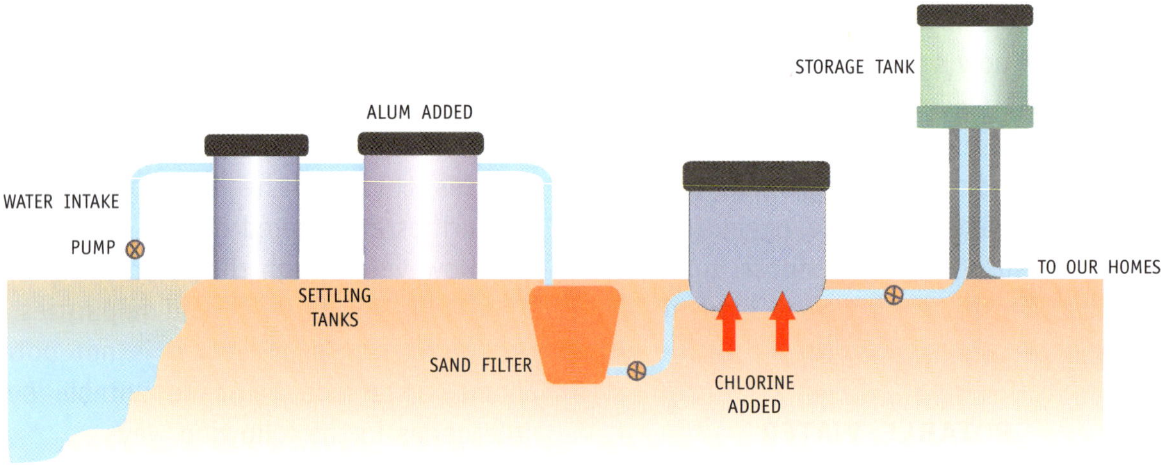


FIG. 19.4 Purification of water in the waterworks

- Germs are killed by adding **chlorine** to the water, i.e. by chlorination.

## WATER CONSERVATION

The purpose of water conservation is to increase the amount of clean water available. Some of the methods of water conservation are as follows:

- Using less water and avoiding wastage at home.
- Using better methods of irrigation, such as drip irrigation, in which water is supplied to the roots of plants drop by drop, instead of filling the entire field with water.
- Recycling of water in factories and using it several times before it is disposed off.
- Effective flood control, specially by building dams and reservoirs.
- Soil conservation methods, such as planting trees increases the level of groundwater.
- Treating sewage and factory wastes before disposing them off so that water sources are not polluted.
- Using biodegradable fertilizers and pesticides.
- Water harvesting of rainwater to raise the groundwater level—you have already read about water harvesting in earlier classes.

## ORAL QUESTIONS FOR FORMATIVE ASSESSMENT

1. Water is said to be a renewable resource because it is naturally recycled. Which natural process is it recycled by?
2. It is understandable that wastes from houses and industries cause water pollution. But how can fertilizers, which are such useful compounds, cause water pollution?
3. Is water that is completely free of all solid and dissolved impurities necessarily potable? Give reasons.
4. How can biodegradable fertilizers and pesticides help in conserving water?

## AIR

All living things need air for breathing. Plants need air for photosynthesis—to make food for the entire living world. Air is also needed for burning. Thus, air is an extremely important natural resource essential for life. As you are aware, air is a mixture of gases, mainly nitrogen (78 %) and oxygen (21 %). The small amount of carbon dioxide present in the air (0.03 %) is crucial for photosynthesis.

Air also contains small quantities of other gases, as well as varying quantities of dust and water vapour.

## AIR POLLUTION

Air is said to be polluted if it contains substances that are harmful to humans, plants and other animals. The harmful substances are called **pollutants**. Air pollution is mainly caused by the burning of fuels in power plants, industries and vehicles, and also burning firewood in homes. This gives off particles of carbon, gases such as carbon monoxide (CO), carbon dioxide ($CO_2$), sulphur dioxide ($SO_2$) and nitrogen dioxide ($NO_2$) and other oxides of nitrogen, and other harmful chemicals containing lead compounds. Pollution of air causes many respiratory problems.

The main causes of air pollution are:

### Suspended particulate matter

Minute solid particles suspended in air are known as suspended particulate matter or SPM. Unburnt carbon particles given out during the burning of fuels or from the exhausts of vehicles, and fine particles of cement given out from a cement factory are examples of SPM. The finer of these particles cannot be filtered by the hair in our noses and hence are a major cause of lung diseases. They also settle on plants and interfere with photosynthesis.

### Carbon monoxide

Carbon monoxide is one of the most dangerous pollutants. It is extremely poisonous. It mixes with the blood and prevents it from carrying oxygen. It can even cause death due to lack of oxygen. Carbon monoxide is odourless and can, therefore, not be detected by its smell.

Carbon monoxide is produced whenever fuels do not burn completely. It is given off when wood, coal or oil are burnt at homes or in factories. Burning of petrol and diesel in automobiles also produces carbon monoxide.

### Excess carbon dioxide—the greenhouse effect

Carbon dioxide is produced whenever any fuel is burnt in homes and factories, or by automobiles. Carbon dioxide itself is not a pollutant. However, since so much fuel is being burnt today, the carbon dioxide content in the air is increasing. Also deforestation reduces the number of trees, which utilize carbon dioxide from air during photosynthesis. This also contributes to increasing the percentage of carbon dioxide in the air.

Excess carbon dioxide in the atmosphere traps the heat of the sun. This is called the **greenhouse effect**. This is believed to cause an increase of the temperature of the earth, called **global warming**. Scientists believe that the average global temperature may rise as much as 2 °C by the end of the century. This can cause large scale melting of ice in the polar regions and also expansion of ocean water. These factors can lead to flooding of coastal areas by sea water. Besides, it is also expected to cause climate changes, affecting rain patterns, agriculture, forests, plants and animals.

Gases such as methane, nitrous oxide and water vapour also contribute towards the greenhouse effect. All such gases are known as **greenhouse gases**.

Several countries have signed the Kyoto Protocol to reduce the emission of greenhouse gases. You can read about the details of the Kyoto Protocol on the Internet site given at the end of the chapter.

### Sulphur dioxide

Sulphur is present in coal as an impurity. Therefore, when coal is burnt in homes, factories or power plants, sulphur dioxide is given off.

Sulphur dioxide is poisonous. It affects our lungs. It combines with the oxygen in the air to form sulphur trioxide ($SO_3$). This reacts with water in the clouds to form sulphuric acid ($H_2SO_4$).

FIG. 19.5 Trees killed by acid rain

Rain mixed with sulphuric acid is called acid rain. It damages buildings and corrodes metal structures. It also reduces the fertility of soil by making the soil acidic. Acid rain also causes harm to plants.

### Nitrogen dioxide

Nitrogen dioxide is given off by exhausts of automobiles, and by some industries. It is poisonous. It irritates the eyes and affects the lungs. Nitrogen dioxide also reacts with water vapour present in the air to form nitric acid ($HNO_3$). This too causes acid rain.

### Chlorofluorocarbons

Chlorofluorocarbons (CFCs) are compounds used in refrigerators, air conditioners and aerosols. They damage the ozone layer in the atmosphere, causing an increase in the amount of ultraviolet rays from the sun reaching the earth. Ultraviolet light causes damage to our eyes and skin and is known to cause skin cancer. Thankfully, CFCs are now being replaced by other compounds and the damage to the ozone layer has been reduced.

**IT'S A FACT!**

The Taj Mahal is losing its white lustre and getting discoloured. Scientists blame pollution from local foundries and the oil refinery at Mathura for this. Efforts by the government have resulted in reduction of air pollutants such as sulphur dioxide and nitrous oxide gases, but suspended particulate matter is still at high levels except during the rainy season. These particles get deposited on the monument's white marble, giving it a yellow tinge.

A report presented to the Parliament suggested that a clay pack treatment that is non-corrosive and non-abrasive be carried out to remove deposits on the marble.

### Lead

A lead compound is added to petrol to prevent engines from '**knocking**'. Lead compounds emitted by exhausts of automobiles are absorbed by our bodies. They cause various problems such as mental disorder and brain damage.

## CONSERVATION OF AIR

Conservation of air means preserving the quality of air by preventing its pollution.

- You are aware that plants clean the air. They absorb excess carbon dioxide and give out oxygen. They also reduce dust particles in the air. Hence, **planting of trees** is important for reducing air pollution.
- Use of efficiently designed **smokeless stoves** for burning coal, kerosene, etc., reduces air pollution.
- Use of **smokeless fuels** such as **LPG (Liquefied Petroleum Gas)** and **CNG (Compressed Natural Gas)** reduces the emission of carbon particles and harmful gases such as carbon monoxide. It has now become compulsory for all commercial vehicles in Delhi to use CNG. This has reduced the pollution in the city.
- To prevent vehicular pollution, new cars are fitted with a special system called **catalytic converter**. It can change harmful exhaust gases like carbon monoxide and nitrogen dioxide into harmless carbon dioxide,

nitrogen and water. The use of **unleaded petrol** also reduces the release of harmful pollutants into the air.

- In factories, powerhouses and petroleum refineries, the gases given off are scrubbed down with water before being released from the chimneys. This removes the poisonous gases such as sulphur dioxide and nitrogen dioxide by dissolving them.
- Some factories use **electrostatic precipitators** to remove particles of solids such as carbon from waste gases before they are let out into the atmosphere.

### VAN MAHOTSAV

Van Mahotsav is an annual tree planting festival celebrated all over India for a week in the month of July. During this festival, millions of trees are planted. It was started in 1950 by K M Munshi who was the Union Minister for Agriculture and Food at that time. Its purpose is to create enthusiasm in the mind of the people for the conservation of forests and planting trees.

## ORAL QUESTIONS FOR FORMATIVE ASSESSMENT

1. What is the single most important cause of air pollution?
2. Carbon dioxide is a pollutant. Do you agree with this statement? Explain.
3. Which two air pollutants can cause acid rain?
4. Which two factors, caused by global warming, can result in flooding of coastal areas in the future?

## NOW YOU KNOW

- Water is renewed continuously in nature through the water cycle.
- Water containing harmful impurities is said to be polluted. Pollution occurs due to dumping of untreated sewage, factory wastes, or due to run off of pesticides and fertilizers into water sources.
- Water can be made potable by filtering and killing germs.
- Water can be conserved by avoiding its wastage, using better methods of irrigation, recycling water in factories, and by other methods.
- Water pollution can be controlled by treating sewage or factory wastes to remove harmful organisms and compounds, and by using biodegradable fertilizers and pesticides.
- Air is mainly polluted by suspended particulate matter, carbon monoxide, excess carbon dioxide, sulphur dioxide, nitrogen dioxide, CFCs and lead.
- Excess carbon dioxide is expected to cause global warming.
- Planting of trees, using smokeless stoves, using smokeless fuels, using catalytic converters in vehicles, and removing pollutants from factory gases before releasing them are some methods of preventing air pollution.

## NEW WORDS

**ACID RAIN**—rain mixed with sulphuric acid

**SPM (SUSPENDED PARTICULATE MATTER)**—minute solid particles suspended in air

**CHLOROFLUOROCARBONS (CFCs)**—compounds used in refrigerators, air conditioners and aerosols that damage the ozone layer in the atmosphere

## FOR FORMATIVE AND SUMMATIVE ASSESSMENT

### A. MULTIPLE-CHOICE QUESTIONS: Choose the most appropriate answer.

1. Which of these causes water pollution?
   a. sewage  b. industrial waste
   c. fertilizers and pesticides  d. all of these
2. Which of these processes cannot remove germs from water?
   a. boiling  b. filtration through porous pot
   c. reverse osmosis  d. exposure to ultraviolet light
3. Which of these methods does not result in conservation of water?
   a. using drip irrigation
   b. recycling of water
   c. cutting vegetation so that less water is lost by transpiration
   d. planting more trees
4. Which of the following is not a pollutant unless present in excess?
   a. sulphur dioxide  b. carbon dioxide
   c. carbon monoxide  d. nitrogen dioxide
5. Which of the following gases combines with the blood and prevents it from carrying oxygen?
   a. carbon monoxide  b. carbon dioxide
   c. nitrogen oxide  d. nitrogen trioxide
6. Which of these can cause acid rain?
   a. carbon monoxide  b. carbon dioxide  c. sulphur dioxide  d. nitrogen

### B. VERY SHORT-ANSWER QUESTIONS: Give one-word answers.

1. Water is a renewable resource. By which process is water recycled in nature?
2. The substances that pollute water or air are called __________
3. Sewage that is __________ (treated/untreated) causes water pollution.
4. Hot water discharge into rivers from factories is also a pollutant. True or false?
5. Give one word for 'enrichment of water of a lake or pond by nutrients that leads to excessive plant growth'.
6. Can you safely drink potable water?
7. Name the kind of light that can kill germs.
8. Using less water and preventing water from getting polluted is called __________ of water.
9. Which polluting gas prevents the blood from carrying oxygen?
10. Carbon dioxide is the only greenhouse gas. True or false?

11. Chlorofluorocarbons damage the __________ layer in the atmosphere.
12. What is rain mixed with sulphuric acid or nitric acid called?
13. Which compound added to petrol to prevent engines from 'knocking' causes pollution of air?
14. Name one fuel that causes very little pollution.

## C. SHORT-ANSWER QUESTIONS (TYPE I): Answer in a sentence or two.

1. What harm can dumping of untreated sewage into a river cause?
2. Why is hot water discharge into rivers also considered as a cause of water pollution?
3. If water is filtered, it becomes free of all suspended impurities and hence potable. Do you agree? Give reasons.
4. Suggest two methods by which water can be made potable at home.
5. What are the main causes of water pollution?
6. The use of CNG instead of diesel is being encouraged these days in vehicles. Why?
7. What is the function of a catalytic converter?
8. Name three greenhouse gases.
9. What should be done to reduce water pollution due to sewage and industrial waste?

## D. SHORT-ANSWER QUESTIONS (TYPE II): Answer in about 30 words.

1. Rivers have always been used to dump waste. How is it that pollution of rivers is becoming more alarming now than it was earlier?
2. What are the cause and effects of eutrophication?
3. Give four methods of conserving water.
4. What is SPM? What harm does SPM pollution cause?
5. Why is carbon monoxide considered to be such a dangerous pollutant?
6. Carbon dioxide in air is essential as plants use it to make food. When does it become a pollutant? What damage does it cause?
7. What is acid rain? What is it caused by?
8. Give four ways in which air can be conserved.

## E. LONG-ANSWER QUESTIONS: Answer in about 60 words.

1. How does the use of excess of fertilizers and pesticides affect water bodies?
2. Discuss the different methods available to us for making water potable by killing germs.
3. How is water treated at the waterworks to make it potable?
4. List the main pollutants of air, and give the ill effects of each.

## HOTS QUESTIONS: Think and answer.

1. Do you think acid rain also affects crops?
2. Air pollution in Delhi improved after CNG was introduced instead of diesel in public transport since CNG gives out less smoke. Introduction of the Metro in Delhi is also expected to reduce pollution. How?

3. What kind of groundwater is more likely to be polluted—that found near the surface of the earth or that found deeper?
4. Afforestation leads to both air and water conservation, as well as soil conservation. How?
5. Does potable water mean pure water without any impurities?

## FOR FORMATIVE ASSESSMENT*

### In the Library—Research Projects

- On 20 April 2010, an explosion on the Deepwater Horizon rig in the Gulf of Mexico caused the largest marine oil spill in the history of the oil industry. The leak was finally stopped by capping the well on 15 July 2010, but not before almost 5 million barrels of oil was released into the sea. Find out about the effects this ecological disaster had on the environment in the region.

  In August 2010, an oil spill occurred near Mumbai. What was the reason? What damage did it cause?

- **Smog** is a combination of smoke and fog. A large part of the gases that form smog is produced by burning of fuels. During the winter, wind speeds are low and cause the smog to stagnate, causing pollution levels to increase near ground level. This makes it more dangerous because it affects the air right at the level at which we breathe. It causes breathing difficulties such as asthma, cough and wheezing in children. It also hampers visibility and harms the environment. At one time London was notorious for its smog which killed thousands of people. Find out when.

### My Virtual Library—Research/Activities on the Internet

- Visit rsgr.in/lsc-cce-8 and click on LINK 77 to learn more about pollution and conservation of water.
- Visit rsgr.in/lsc-cce-8 and click on LINK 78 to learn more about air pollution.
- Visit rsgr.in/lsc-cce-8 and click on LINK 79 to read about the Kyoto Protocol to reduce greenhouse gases.

### To Meet—Research on Scientist

**Frederick Gardner Cottrell** (1877–1948), an American chemist, in 1906 invented the electrostatic precipitator, an electrical device for removing suspended impurities such as dust, fumes or mist from air and other gases. It has proved to be of immense use in removing pollution-causing substances from the exhausts of factories and power plants. It works by charging the molecules of the polluting substances and then separating them by depositing them on oppositely charged electrodes as opposite charges attract each other.

Find out more about the structure of the electrostatic precipitator.

### Beyond the Classroom—Field Trip

Visit a water body like a river, lake or large pond in your city. Observe the water and note the pollutants you can see in the water. What human activities going on near the water body appear to be polluting the water? Collect a sample of the water. Make a slide of a drop of the water and observe under a microscope. Can you see any microorganisms? Try to filter the water in the school lab.

*For more tasks see Page 257

# MORE TASKS for FORMATIVE ASSESSMENT (FA 4)

## for Chapters 16–19

In addition to the activities and projects given in the respective chapters, the following tasks can also be used for formative assessment.

### RESEARCH PROJECTS

- **Sight in animals and birds** Compared to humans, most animals cannot see things in as much detail. Also most animals cannot see colour. However, in many animals, the sense of sight is much more developed than in humans.
  - Nocturnal animals such as cats and mice have eyes that can see in very faint light. Find out why?
  - A fly can even see what is behind it, because of its different eye structure. Find out how the structure is different.
  - A chameleon can see in two different directions at the same time. Why?
  - Birds have a very keen sense of sight. An eagle can see from 20 feet what most humans can see from 5 feet. Find out why? This helps them detect food on the ground even when they are flying high up.
  - Nocturnal birds like owls have big eyes. They can see better at night but not so well during the day. Find out why?
- **Lonar** lake is a saltwater lake at Lonar in Buldana district in Maharashtra. The crater that forms the lake is believed to be formed by the impact of a meteorite. Find out the estimated size of the meteorite, the estimated speed at which it impacted the earth, and when this happened.
  If possible arrange a trip to Lonar.

### INTERNET-LINKED RESEARCH/ACTIVITY

- Visit rsgr.in/lsc-cce-8 and click on LINK 80 and LINK 81 to read about the Ganga Action Plan to clean up the Ganga River.
- Visit rsgr.in/lsc-cce-8 and click on LINK 82 to read an article that analyses the reasons for the failure of the Ganga Action Plan.

### MAKING A MODEL

**Smoke box to observe light rays** Obtain or construct a wooden box about 30 cm high and wide, and about 60 cm in length. Fit panes of window glass on the top and one side of the box. Leave the back open and cover with two pieces of loosely hung black cloth that hang like curtains and can be opened from the centre (like curtains on a stage). Cut a window in the front to let in the light. Make three holes of 4–5 mm diameter on a black cardboard and pin it over the window. Paint the inside black.

Create smoke by burning an incense stick in one corner of the box. Shine a torch as shown. You can now see the light rays inside the box. You can keep a mirror, a glass slab, a prism or a lens in the path of the light rays and study how they are reflected/refracted/dispersed.

# TEST PAPER 2 for SUMMATIVE ASSESSMENT (SA 2)

## for Chapters 11–19

**Maximum Time: 2½–3 hours** **Maximum Marks: 70**

### A. Answer in one word only. [5 × 1 mark]

1. Which friction is smaller—sliding friction or rolling friction?
2. To increase loudness of sound by four times, by how much should the amplitude of vibration be changed?
3. Sound above which frequency is called ultrasonic?
4. Which of these are sensitive to colour—rods or cones?
5. How long does light from the sun take to reach the earth?

### B. Answer in one sentence only. [10 × 2 marks]

1. If you wear pointed heel in the left leg and flat shoe on the right leg, which leg would exert greater pressure on the ground? Why?
2. Why does polishing a surface reduce friction?
3. What is noise pollution?
4. State the rule regarding attraction and repulsion of charges.
5. What do you mean by the 'chemical effect' of electric current?
6. What is the function of a periscope in a submarine?
7. State the first law of reflection.
8. Why is light dispersed by a glass prism?
9. Why does the Pole Star appear to be stationary in the sky?
10. Name four methods by which germs can be killed in water at home.

### C. Answer in about 30 words. [5 × 3 marks]

1. What is the difference between contact and non-contact forces? Explain with the help of one example of each.
2. Is friction between two surfaces dependent on how hard they press against each other? Why?
3. Why is electroplating of one metal on another done? Give one example for each.
4. Calculate the number of images seen when two plane mirrors are placed inclined at an angle of 10° to each other.
5. What can be the consequences of excess greenhouse gases in the earth's atmosphere?

### D. Answer in about 60 words. [4 × 5 marks]

1. What are the effects that a force can have on an object?
2. How can you electroplate an iron nail with copper? Explain with the help of a diagram.

3. Explain why a swimming pool full of water appears less deep than it actually is.
4. What are the uses of artificial satellites?

## E. Choose the most appropriate response out of the given four. [10 × 1 mark]

1. Tyres of heavy vehicles are broad so that
   a. friction with the ground increases.
   b. pressure on the ground increases.
   c. friction with the ground decreases.
   d. pressure on the ground decreases.
2. The pressure exerted by a liquid
   a. does not change with depth.
   b. decreases with depth.
   c. increases with depth.
   d. is different in different directions at the same depth.
3. Friction can be increased by
   a. using ball bearings between the two surfaces.
   b. making the surfaces rough.
   c. lubricating the surfaces.
   d. using streamlined shapes.
4. Noise is produced by
   a. high frequency vibrations.
   b. low frequency vibrations.
   c. regular vibrations.
   d. irregular vibrations.
5. An earthquake measuring 5 on the Richter scale is more powerful than another of magnitude 4 by
   a. 1.25 times.
   b. 100 times.
   c. 0.80 times.
   d. 10 times.
6. Which of these is plated on iron to prevent it from reacting chemically with food?
   a. chromium
   b. tin
   c. silver
   d. gold
7. A plane mirror produces a
   a. virtual inverted image.
   b. virtual erect image.
   c. real erect image.
   d. virtual or real erect image depending on the distance of the object from the mirror.
8. When light travels from an optically rarer medium to a denser medium,
   a. it bends away from the normal.
   b. it bends towards the normal.
   c. it remains undeviated.
   d. it is laterally displaced.
9. A group of a few stars that appear to be close together in the sky when viewed from the earth is called
   a. galaxy.
   b. constellation.
   c. solar system.
   d. universe.
10. Which of these is a greenhouse gas?
    a. carbon dioxide
    b. methane
    c. water vapour
    d. all of these

## NCERT SYLLABUS—CLASS VIII

| Questions | Key Concepts | Resources | Activities/Processes |
|---|---|---|---|
| 1. Food | | | **(Periods–22)** |
| **Crop production**<br>Crop production: How are different food crops produced? What are the various foods we get from animal sources? | Crop production: Soil preparation, selection of seeds, sowing, applying fertilizers, irrigation, weeding, harvesting and storage; nitrogen fixation, nitrogen cycle. | Interaction and discussion with local men and women farmers about farming and farm practices; visit to cold storage, go- downs; visit to any farm/nursery/garden. | Preparing herbarium specimens of some crop plants; collection of some seeds etc; preparing a table/ chart on different irrigation practices and sources of water in different parts of India; looking at roots of any legume crop for nodules, hand section of nodules. |
| **Micro-organisms**<br>What living organisms do we see under a microscope in a drop of water? What helps make curd? How does food go bad? How do we preserve food? | Micro organisms—useful and harmful. | Microscope, kit materials; information about techniques of food preservation. | Making a lens with a bulb; Observation of drop of water, curd, other sources, bread mould, orange mould under the microscope; experiment showing fermentation of dough—increase in volume (using yeast)—collect gas in balloon, test in lime water. |
| 2. Materials | | | **(Periods–26)** |
| **Materials in daily life**<br>Are some of our clothes synthetic? How are they made? Where do the raw materials come from?<br>Do we use other materials that are synthetic? | Synthetic clothing materials. Other synthetic materials, especially plastics; usefulness of plastics and problems associated with their excessive use. | Sharing of prior knowledge, source materials on petroleum products. | Survey on use of synthetic materials.<br>Discussion. |
| Do we use cloth (fabric) for purposes other than making clothes to wear? What kind of fabric do we see around us? What are they used for? | There are a variety of fibrous materials in use. A material is chosen based on desired property. | Collection of material from neighbourhood or should be part of the kit. | Testing various materials—for action of water, reaction on heating, effect of flame, electrical conductivity, thermal conductivity, tensile strength. |
| **Different kinds of materials and their reactions.**<br>Can a wire be drawn out of wood?<br>Do copper or aluminium also rust like iron?<br>What is the black material inside a pencil?<br>Why are electrical wires made of aluminium or copper? | Metals and non-metals. | Kit items. | Simple observations relating to physical properties of metals and non-metals, displacement reactions, experiments involving reactions with acids and bases.<br>Introduction of word equations. |

| Questions | Key Concepts | Resources | Activities/Processes |
|---|---|---|---|
| **How things change/ react with one another**<br>What happens to the wax when a candle is burnt? Is it possible to get this wax back? | Combustion, flame | "The Chemical History of a Candle", by M. Faraday, 1860. | Experiments with candles. |
| What happens to kerosene/ natural gas when it is burnt? Which fuel is the best? Why? | All fuels release heat on burning. Fuels differ in efficiency, cost etc. Natural resources are limited. Burning of fuels leads to harmful by products. | Collecting information from home and other sources. | Collecting information. Discussions involving whole class. |
| 3. The World of the Living | | | **(Periods–44)** |
| **Why conserve**<br>What are reserve forests/ sanctuaries etc? How do we keep track of our plants and animals? How do we know that some species are in danger of disappearing? What would happen if you continuously cut trees? | Conservation of biodiversity/ wild life/plants; zoos, sanctuaries, forest reserves etc. flora, fauna endangered species, red data book; endemic species, migration. | Films on wild life, TV programmes, visit to zoo/ forest area/sanctuaries etc.; case study with information on disappearing tigers; data on endemic and endangered species from MEF, Govt. of India, NGOs. | Discussion on whether we find as many diverse plants/ animals in a 'well kept area' like a park or cultivated land, as compared to any area left alone. Discussion on depletion of wild life, why it happens, on poaching, economics. |
| **The cell**<br>What is the internal structure of a plant—what will we see if we look under the microscope? Which cells from our bodies can be easily seen? Are all cells similar? | Cell structure, plant and animal cells, use of stain to observe, cell organelles—nucleus, vacuole, chloroplast, cell membrane, cell wall. | Microscope, onion peels, epidermal peels of any leaves, petals etc, buccal cavity cells, *Spirogyra;* permanent slides of animal cells. | Use of a microscope, preparation of a slide, observation of onion peel and cheek cells, other cells from plants e.g. *Hydrilla* leaf, permanent slides showing different cells, tissues, blood smear; observation of T.S. stem to see tissues; observing diverse types of cells from plants and animals (some permanent slides). |
| **How babies are formed**<br>How do babies develop inside the mother? Why does our body change when we reach our teens? How is the sex of the child determined? Who looks after the babies in your homes? Do all animals give birth to young ones? | Sexual reproduction and endocrine system in animals, secondary sexual characters, reproductive health; internal and external fertilisation. | Counsellors, films, lectures. | Discussion with counsellors on secondary sexual characters, on how sex of the child is determined, safe sex, reproductive health; observation on eggs, young ones, life cycles.<br>Discussion on Gender issues and social taboo's. |
| 4. Moving Things, People and Ideas | | | |
| **Idea of force**<br>What happens when we push or pull anything? How can we change the speed, direction of a moving object?<br>How can we shape the shape of an object? | Idea of force-push or pull; change in speed, direction of moving objects and shape of objects by applying force; contact and non-contact forces. | Daily-life experience, kit items. | Observing and analysing the relation between force and motion in a variety of daily-life situations.<br>Demonstrating change in speed of a moving object, its direction of motion and shape by applying force. Measuring the weight of an object, as a force (pull) by the earth using a spring balance. |

| Questions | Key Concepts | Resources | Activities/Processes |
|---|---|---|---|
| **Friction**<br>What makes a ball rolling on the ground slow down? | Friction—factors affecting friction, sliding and rolling friction, moving; advantages and disadvantages of friction for the movement of automobiles, airplanes and boats/ships; increasing and reducing friction. | Various rough and smooth surfaces, ball bearings. | Demonstrating friction between rough/smooth surfaces of moving objects in contact, and wear and tear of moving objects by rubbing (eraser on paper, card board, sand paper).<br>Activities on static, sliding and rolling friction.<br>Studying ball bearings.<br>Discussion on other methods of reducing friction and ways of increasing friction. |
| **Pressure**<br>Why are needles made pointed? Why does a balloon burst if too much air is blown into it? Why does an inverted glass/bottle/pitcher resist being pushed down into water? How can air/ liquids exert pressure? | Idea of pressure; pressure exerted by air/liquid; atmospheric pressure. | Daily-life experiences; Experimentation—improvised manometer and improvised pressure detector. | Observing the dependence of pressure exerted by a force on surface area of an object.<br>Demonstrating that air exerts pressure in a variety of situations.<br>Demonstrating that liquids exert pressure.<br>Designing an improvised manometer and measuring pressure exerted by liquids.<br>Designing improvised pressure detector and demonstrating increase in pressure exerted by a liquid at greater depths. |
| **Sound**<br>How do we communicate through sound? How is sound produced? What characterises different sounds? | Various types of sound; sources of sound; vibration as a cause of sound; frequency; medium for propagation of sound; idea of noise as unpleasant and unwanted sound and need to minimise noise. | Daily-life experiences; kit items; musical instruments. | Demonstrating and distinguishing different types (loud and feeble, pleasant/ musical and unpleasant/ noise, audible and inaudible) of sound. Producing different types of sounds. using the same source. Making a *'Jal Tarang'*. Demonstrating that vibration is the cause of sound.<br>Designing a toy telephone.<br>Identifying various sources of noise. (unpleasant and unwanted sound) in the locality and thinking of measures to minimise noise and its hazards (noise-pollution). |

| Questions | Key Concepts | Resources | Activities/Processes |
|---|---|---|---|
| **5. How Things Work** | | | **(Periods–14)** |
| **Electric current and circuits** | | | |
| Why do we get a shock when we touch an electric appliance with wet hands? | Water conducts electricity depending on presence/ absence of salt in it. Other liquids may or may not conduct electricity. | Rubber cap, pins, water, bulb or LED, cells, various liquids. | Activity to study whether current flows through various liquid samples (tap water, salt solution, lemon juice, kerosene, distilled water if available). |
| What happens to a conducting solution when electric current flows through it? | Chemical effects of current. | Carbon rods, beaker, water, bulb, battery. | Emission of gases from salt solution. Deposition of Cu from copper sulphate solution. Electric pen using KI and starch solution. |
| How can we coat an object with a layer of metal? | Basic idea of electroplating. | Improvised electrolytical cell, $CuSO_4$ | Simple experiment to show electroplating. |
| **6. Natural Phenomena** | | | **(Periods–26)** |
| **Rain, thunder and lightning** | | | |
| What is lightning? What safety measures should we take against lightning strikes? | Clouds carry electric charge. Positive and negative charges, attraction and repulsion. Principle of lightning conductor. | Articles on clouds and lightning; kit items. | Discussion on sparks. Experiments with comb and paper to show positive and negative charge. Discussion on lightning conductor. |
| **Light** | | | |
| What are the differences between the images formed on a new utensil and an old one? Why is there this difference? | Laws of reflection. | Mirror, source of light, ray source (mirror covered with black paper with a thin slit). | Exploring laws of reflection using ray source and another mirror. |
| When you see your image in the mirror it appears as if the left is on the right—why? | Characteristics of image formed with a plane mirror. | Plane glass, candle, scale. | Locating the reflected image using glass sheet and candles. |
| Why don't we see images on all surfaces around us? | Regular and diffused reflection. | | Discussion with various examples. |
| What makes things visible? | Reflection of light from an object to the eye. | Experience. | Activity of observing an object through an object through a straight and bent tube; and discussion. |
| How do we see images of our back in a mirror? | Multiple reflection. | Mirrors and objects to be seen. | Observing multiple images formed by mirrors placed at angles to each other. Making a kaleidoscope. |
| Why do we sometimes see colours on oil films on water? | Dispersion of light. | Plane mirror, water. | Observing spectrum obtained on a white sheet of paper/ wall using a plane mirror inclined on a water surface at an angle of 45°. |
| What is inside our eye that enables us to see? | Structure of the eye. | Model or chart of the human eye. | Observing reaction of pupil to a shining torch. Demonstration of blind spot. |
| Why are some people unable to see? | Lens becomes opaque, light not reaching the eye. Visually challenged use other senses to make sense of the world around. Alternative technology available. Role of nutrition in relation to blindness | Experiences of children; case histories. Samples of Braille sheets. | Description of case histories of visually challenged people who have been doing well in their studies and careers. Activities with Braille sheet. |

| Questions | Key Concepts | Resources | Activities/Processes |
|---|---|---|---|
| **Night sky**<br>What do we see in the sky at night? How can we identify stars and planets? | Idea about heavenly bodies/ celestial objects and their classification—moon, planets, stars, constellations.<br>Motion of celestial objects in space; the solar system. | Observation of motion of objects in the sky during the day and at night; models, charts, role-play and games, planetarium. | Observing and identifying the objects moving in the sky during the day and at night.<br>Observing and identifying some prominent stars and constellations.<br>Observing and identifying some prominent planets, visible to the naked eye, (Venus, Mars, Jupiter ) in the night sky and their movement.<br>Design and preparing models and charts of the solar system, constellations, etc.<br>Role-play and games for understanding movement of planets, stars etc. |
| **Earthquakes**<br>What happens during an earthquake? What can we do to minimise its effects? | Phenomena related to earthquakes. | Earthquake data; visit to seismographic centre. | Looking at structures/large objects and guessing what will happen to them in the event of an earthquake; activities to explore stable and unstable structures. |
| 7. Natural Resources<br>**Man's intervention in phenomena of nature**<br>What do we do with wood? What if we had no wood? What will happen if we go on cutting trees/grass without limit? | Consequences of deforestation: scarcity of products for humans and other living beings, change in physical properties of soil, reduced rainfall.<br>Reforestation; recycling of paper. | Data and narratives on deforestation and on movements to protect forests. | Narration and discussions.<br>Project—Recycling of paper. |
| What do we do with coal and petroleum?<br>Can we create coal and petroleum artificially? | Formation of coal and petroleum in nature. (fossil fuels?).<br>Consequences of over extraction of coal and petroleum. | Background materials, charts etc. | Discussion. |
| **Pollution of air and water**<br>What are the various activities by human beings that make air impure? Does clear, transparent water indicate purity? | Water and air are increasingly getting polluted and therefore become scarce for use.<br>Biological and chemical contamination of water; effect of impure water on soil and living beings; effect of soil containing excess of fertilisers and insecticides on water resources. Potable water. | Description of some specific examples of extremely polluted rivers. | Case study and discussion.<br>Purification of water by physical and chemical methods including using sunlight.<br>Discussion on other methods of water purification. |

# LIVING SCIENCE 8

## VALUE-BASED QUESTIONS, PROBLEM-SOLVING ASSESSMENT, OUR HERITAGE, OPEN TEXT-BASED ASSESSMENT (OTBA)

### CHAPTER 1: CROP PRODUCTION

**VALUE-BASED QUESTION**

Mohan and Sohan are farmers in Rajasthan, where there is shortage of water. Mohan waters his crops through irrigation channels connected to a tube well. Sohan uses drip irrigation. Which of them shows greater concern for the environment?

**PROBLEM-SOLVING ASSESSMENT**

An experiment was conducted to study the effect of a new fertilizer on the growth of two varieties of wheat. The data for growth of the plants from germination to next 10 days is shown below.

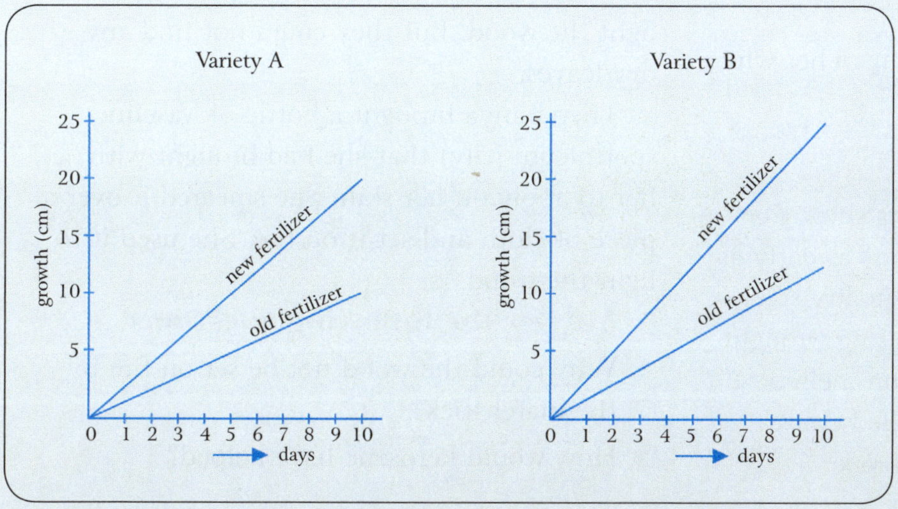


All other growing conditions such as water and sunlight were kept the same for both the varieties.

**Which of the following is the most reasonable conclusion you can draw from the data?**

1. The new fertilizer causes faster growth in both varieties than other fertilizers.
2. The new fertilizer causes faster growth in both varieties in the first ten days only.
3. The new fertilizer influences the growth of both varieties.
4. The new fertilizer causes faster growth in Variety B than in Variety A.

### CHAPTER 2: MICROORGANISMS

**PROBLEM-SOLVING ASSESSMENT**

Ancient Egyptians applied mouldy bread on infected cuts and wounds to heal them. Why do you think this helped in healing the wounds? Nowadays we do not use mouldy bread to cure infection. What do we use instead?

**OUR HERITAGE**

The traditional system of medicine in India called developed in the first **Ayurveda** millennium BCE (years from 1000 BCE to 1 BCE). Two books *Charakasamhita* and *Sushrutasamhita* describe how to protect the healthy and to prolong life. They include details of the examination, diagnosis and treatment of numerous diseases.

## CHAPTER 3: SYNTHETIC FIBRES AND PLASTICS

**VALUE-BASED QUESTION**

Lata always prefers to buy things from the market that use fewer plastics in packaging. Why does Lata do this?

## CHAPTER 4: METALS AND NON-METALS

**PROBLEM-SOLVING ASSESSMENT**

Aluminium is higher than iron in the reactivity series. To see if this was true, Ayesha took similar sized pieces of aluminium and iron in test tubes. She added the same volume of dilute hydrochloric acid to each. She noticed that:

1. Initially there is more vigorous evolution of gas from the test tube having iron.
2. After a couple of minutes, aluminium starts reacting much faster than iron and evolution of gas is much more vigorous.

She was confused. Can you explain to her why this happened?

**OUR HERITAGE**

Recent excavations by archaeologists show that Indians were making iron implements as early as 1800 BCE. Around 200 BCE, high quality steel was being produced in India by heating wrought iron, charcoal and glass until the iron melted and absorbed the carbon. It was called *faulad.* It was exported to parts of Asia and Europe.

## CHAPTER 5: COAL AND PETROLEUM

**VALUE-BASED QUESTION**

Salma always switches off electrical appliances such as lights, fans, air conditioners, heaters etc. when not in use. She says it saves coal and petroleum and helps the environment. Do you agree? Explain.

## CHAPTER 6: COMBUSTION AND FLAME

**VALUE-BASED QUESTION**

Namita noticed that the LPG gas stove in her kitchen was giving out yellow flame and blackening the utensils. She cleaned the stove burners. The flame then became blue and stopped blackening the utensils. She explained to her parents that the stove was not burning efficiently and wasting fuel because it was dirty. What values did Namita show?

**PROBLEM-SOLVING ASSESSMENT**

Students of a school had gone for an overnight camp. They gathered some wood and wanted to light a fire. They tried to light the fire with a matchstick but the wood would not catch fire. Someone suggested pouring kerosene over the wood, but no kerosene was available. Someone else suggested setting dry leaves on fire first with the matchstick and using it to light the wood. But they could not find any dry leaves.

Then Tanya brought a bottle of Vaseline (petroleum jelly) that she had brought with her to apply on her skin. She smeared it over a piece of cloth and set it on fire. She used it to light the wood.

**Answer the following questions.**

1. Why could the wood not be set on fire by the matchstick?
2. How would kerosene have helped?

3. Why were dry leaves suggested and not green leaves?
4. Which two properties of petroleum jelly were used to light the fire?

## CHAPTER 7: CONSERVATION OF PLANTS AND ANIMALS

**VALUE-BASED QUESTION**

Salma is fond of plants and animals. She has a bird house at her home where she puts some grain and water every day. She enjoys looking at the birds feeding and drinking at the bird house.

What values does Salma show?

**PROBLEM-SOLVING ASSESSMENT**

It is often said that by protecting the tiger, we actually protect all other forms of flora and fauna. Is that true? Why?

Suppose the project of protecting the tiger went off so well that the population of tigers increased tremendously. Would that be desirable? Why?

**OUR HERITAGE**

History shows that conservation of natural resources including plants and animals has been considered to be very important in India. For example, **Emperor Ashoka** had a clear policy on protection and use of natural resources. Officials were appointed to oversee the protection. Many rulers followed similar policies. In addition, various tribes have also been practising conservation in different ways.

## CHAPTER 8: CELL—STRUCTURE AND FUNCTIONS

**PROBLEM-SOLVING ASSESSMENT**

Study the diagram. Label the structures A, B and C. What is the function of C? Is this a plant cell or an animal cell?

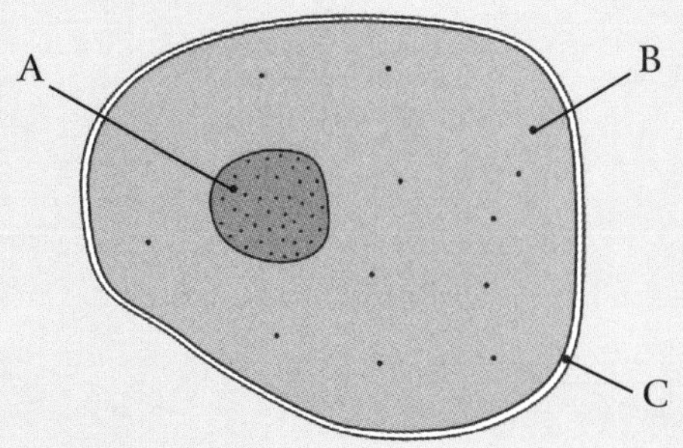


Draw and label 3 extra structures that would change this cell into:

1. a plant cell if it is an animal cell
2. an animal cell if it is a plant cell.

## CHAPTER 9: REPRODUCTION

**VALUE-BASED QUESTION**

Mr Sinha is 65 years old. He was sitting on the seat meant for senior citizens in the metro train. He saw a pregnant lady standing. He immediately got up and offered his seat to the lady. Why did Mr Sinha do this even though the seat was meant for senior citizens?

**PROBLEM-SOLVING ASSESSMENT**

Kamlesh thinks that to produce test tube babies, an egg and a sperm are placed in a test tube and then allowed to fuse under controlled conditions. The baby then develops in the test tube.

Is Kamlesh correct? Which part of his thinking is incorrect?

## CHAPTER 10: REACHING THE AGE OF ADOLESCENCE

**VALUE-BASED QUESTION**

Ramesh studies in Class 10. He says he would like to try alcohol and drugs just to see what they are like. Is he correct in doing this? What advice would you give him?

**PROBLEM-SOLVING ASSESSMENT**

The graph given below shows how the lining of the uterus in a female who has achieved puberty varies with time.

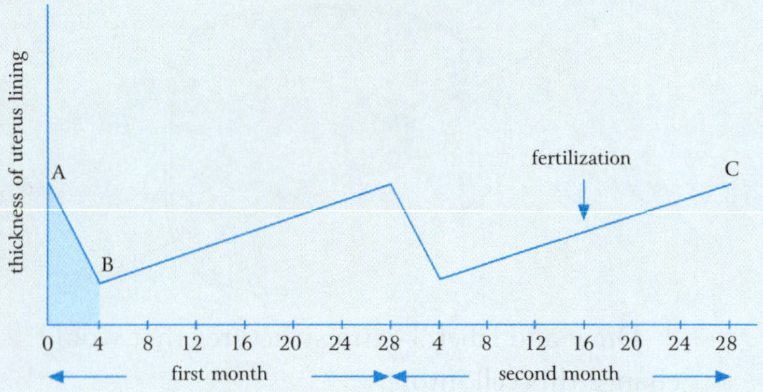


**Examine the graph and answer the following questions.**

1. What is happening between A and B?
2. Mark the corresponding points in the second menstrual cycle when the same happens.
3. Fertilization occurs on day 16 of the second menstrual cycle. How do you expect the graph to behave after point C? Will the pattern of the first and second months be followed?

## CHAPTER 11: FORCE AND PRESSURE

### PROBLEM-SOLVING ASSESSMENT

Pallavi is a weightlifter. The first picture shows her on the earth and the second on the moon.

Can you answer the question that is troubling Pallavi?

## CHAPTER 12: FRICTION

### VALUE-BASED QUESTION

Akash noticed that someone had carelessly thrown a banana peel on the footpath. He thought, "If someone steps on the banana peel, he or she is likely to slip and fall." So he picked it up and threw it in the dustbin.

1. Is Akash right in thinking that people can slip on a banana peel? Why?
2. Which two values did Akash show?

### PROBLEM-SOLVING ASSESSMENT

A businessman went to see a Formula 1 car race. It was raining and several cars skidded on the road. There were a couple of major accidents and some drivers sustained serious injuries.

He decided to do something about it. He designed a racing car tyre with increased friction that would not slip on wet roads. He advertised it as: "Now a racing car tyre that keeps you safe."

However nobody bought the tyres. Where do you think the businessman went wrong?

## CHAPTER 13: SOUND

**VALUE-BASED QUESTION**

Maninder and his friends are having a party with loud music. Sheila who lives in the neighbourhood has an exam the next day and is getting disturbed by the music. She requests Maninder to tone down the music but he refuses. Do you think this is correct?

Mention some considerations you show towards your neighbours.

**PROBLEM-SOLVING ASSESSMENT**

The diagram shows a graph of the sound wave given out by a tuning fork.

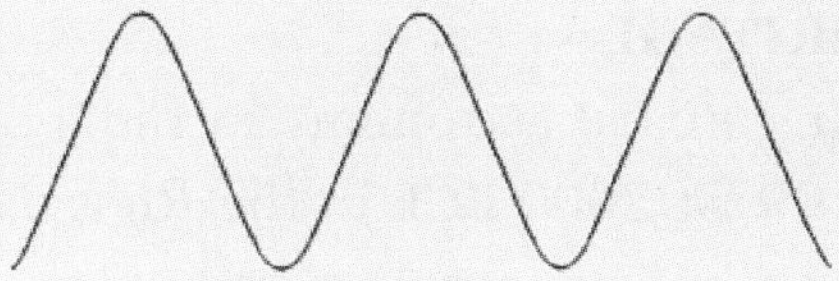

Trace it on a graph paper and draw graphs to show:

1. Louder sound of the same pitch
2. Sound of the same loudness but greater pitch
3. Sound that is louder and also has greater pitch

**OUR HERITAGE**

is the huge mausoleum of **Gol Gumbaj** Mohammed Adil Shah, who was the ruler of Bijapur in Karnataka. It was built in the 17th century. It has a whispering gallery underneath the dome. Even a whisper in the gallery can be heard nearly 40 m away on the other side of the gallery.

## CHAPTER 14: SOME NATURAL PHENOMENA

**VALUE-BASED QUESTION**

When an earthquake suddenly struck Rani's village, she shouted to tell the people that they should come out of their houses and go into the fields, since there were no trees, electric poles or buildings nearby.

Later she went about organizing help for the injured and people who had been rendered homeless.

What values did Rani show?

**PROBLEM-SOLVING ASSESSMENT**

An aircraft flies just below a negatively charged thundercloud.

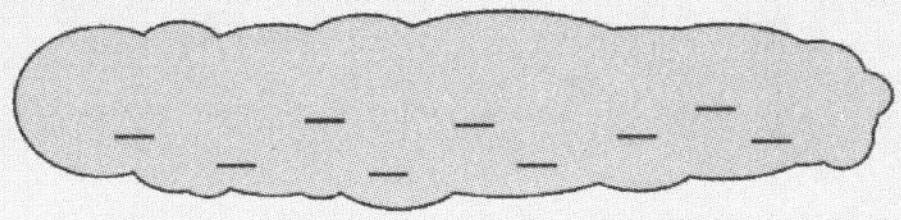

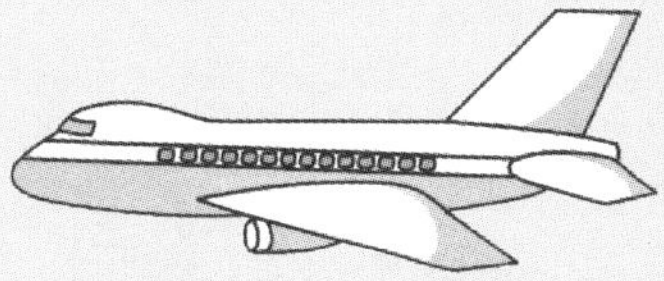

**Answer these questions.**

1. Will any electrostatic charges be induced on the aircraft?
2. If so, draw the signs and positions of the induced charges on the aircraft.
3. Explain the distribution of the charges that you have shown on the basis of movement of electrons.
4. Draw a diagram to show the charges after the aircraft has flown away from the cloud.
5. Explain the distribution of charges you have shown in Ans. 4 on the basis of movement of electrons.

## CHAPTER 17: REFRACTION AND DISPERSION OF LIGHT

**VALUE-BASED QUESTION**

While walking to school, you see a visually-challenged person want to cross a busy road.

But the traffic is very heavy and nobody is willing to stop for him. What will you do?

**PROBLEM-SOLVING ASSESSMENT**

The diagram shows three different light rays falling on prisms. Complete each diagram to show the refracted and emergent rays. What difference will there be between the three?

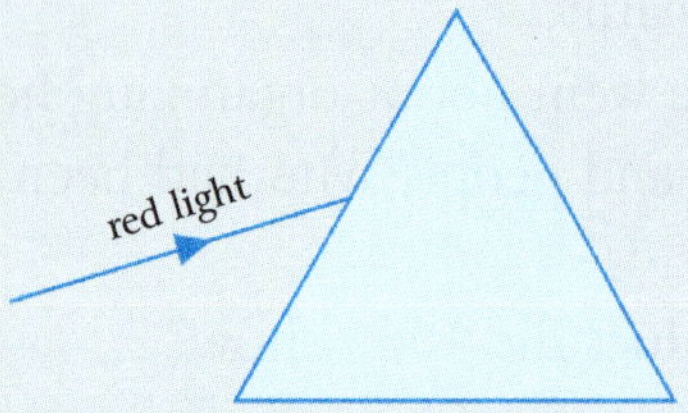


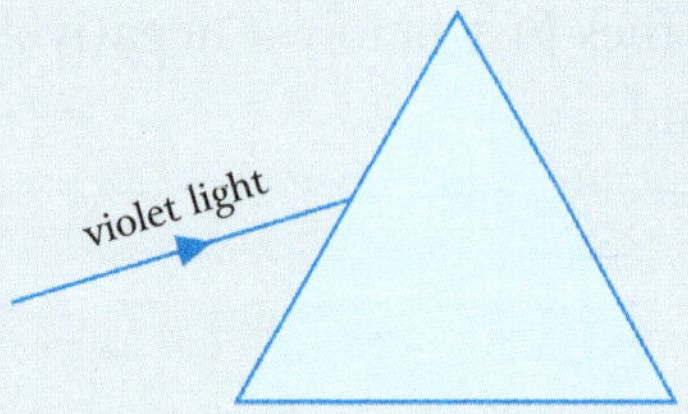


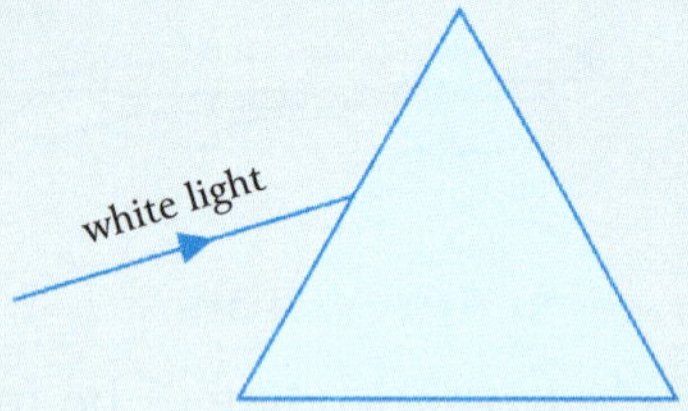


## CHAPTER 18: THE UNIVERSE

**VALUE-BASED QUESTION**

Manish is interested in astronomy and wants to learn more about it. Manish's sister Kamla saved her pocket money to buy Manish a telescope on his 13th birthday. Manish is very happy now, studying the moon and planets with his telescope.

What value did Kamla show?

**PROBLEM-SOLVING ASSESSMENT**

An astronomer discovered a new planet rotating on its axis and revolving around a star. He discovered that the star was about the same size as the sun. He studied the planet and discovered the following.

- Average distance from the star: 145 million km
- Time to orbit the star: 256 days
- Time of rotation on axis: 10 hours
- Axis of rotation: Perpendicular to the plane of its orbit
- Water: Strong possibility of presence of water

**Compare the planet with the earth on the following points.**

1. Length of an year
2. Length of 1 day and 1 night
3. Seasons
4. Whether there is possibility of life

**OUR HERITAGE**

The first records of astronomy in India date back to at least 2000 BCE in the *Rigveda*. The ancient Indian astronomers used the stars and the planets to create astrological charts.

In the 5th Century CE, the Indian astronomer adopted a mathematical **Aryabhata** approach to astronomy. Aryabhata proposed that the moon reflects the light of the sun. He also proposed that the earth rotates rather than the sky. His idea included mathematical models about how to forecast eclipses. He wrote the *Aryabhatia* in CE 499.

## CHAPTER 19: POLLUTION OF WATER AND AIR

**PROBLEM-SOLVING ASSESSMENT**

A scientist analysing pollution caused by discharge of factory waste into a rain-fed river of south India found that pollution is:

1. severe during summer
2. least during the monsoon months
3. keeps increasing during the months after the monsoon months.

Can you explain his observations?

## OPEN TEXT-BASED ASSESSMENT (OTBA)

### WHAT IS OTBA?

In keeping with its recommendation that multiple modes of assessment should be used to assess the varied abilities and individual strengths of learners, the CBSE has introduced an Open Text-Based Assessment (OTBA) for Classes IX and XI from 2014. We have included OTBA in the Class 8 book to develop in students the necessary skills and to give them a feel of what to expect in Class 9, so that they are better equipped.

The textual material may be in the form of an article, a case study, a diagram, a concept/mind map, a picture or a cartoon, or problem/situation. It will be related to concepts included in the syllabus.

OTBA will have questions of higher order thinking skills. Some of these may be subjective, creative and open ended. The students may not find the answers at one place in the text, and may require a clear understanding of many concepts and an ability to integrate them.

The aim is to move away from memorization of facts or data and assess clarity of concepts, and ability to:

- find and use relevant information from the text
- apply concepts to situations
- analyse, integrate and apply more than one concept to reach conclusions
- evaluate and give innovative suggestions to open ended problems/situations.

### PREPARING FOR OTBA

1. Study the text thoroughly so that you understand all concepts well, and can quickly locate each concept in the text.
2. Prepare concise notes on the concepts in the text.
3. Highlight important terms and write down the important formulae.

### TAKING THE TEST

1. Read the questions carefully to understand what is expected, and allocate time for each question.
2. Do the questions that are simpler (for example fact-based) first.
3. Write concise answers backed by evidence given in the text.
4. Use your own words to answerthis shows clear understanding.

## OTBA PRACTICE PAPER 1: IN VITRO FERTILIZATION

Some couples are unable to have children. This may be because the reproductive system of the man is unable to make enough sperms. Another reason is that the fallopian tube of the woman may be blocked, thus preventing the sperm and ... meeting. Such couples can be helped ...tilization ('in vitro' means 'in ... consists of fertilization ... of the woman. Earlier, ... were called

...ith a hormone ... (FSH) which makes her produce eggs. The doctor then makes a small incision in her body and sucks out the eggs using a thin tube. The eggs are kept in a solution of food and oxygen, to keep them alive. Some semen from the man is then mixed with the solution. Fertilization of one or more eggs may occur in the solution. The fertilized eggs are observed through microscope as they develop into embryos. The doctor then selects an embryo and places it in the woman's uterus. The embryo develops into a baby and is born in the usual way.

### QUESTIONS

1. A number of people tend to blame the woman

if the couple is not able to have children. Is this justified? Explain.

2. Some people believe that test-tube babies are completely made outside the woman's body. Is that belief correct?
3. FSH is injected in even those women who are able to normally produce an egg every month. What can be the possible reason for this?
4. Why are the eggs placed in a solution of food and oxygen?
5. Sometimes more than one embryos form. Some people think it is wrong to destroy the extra embryos. What do you think?

## OTBA PRACTICE PAPER 2: ULTRASOUND

X-rays are used to see inside the body, for example when someone has a fracture. But X-rays can be dangerous and cannot be used in all situations. A safer method is to use ultrasonic (or ultrasound). When a sound wave travels from one substance to another, for example from the skin to the muscle and bone, part of it is reflected back to give echoes. An ultrasonic transmitter/receiver is a machine that produces ultrasound and uses the echoes to build a picture on a screen.

Unborn babies can be seen by moving an ultrasonic transmitter/receiver across the mother's stomach. To see fine details, ultrasound of very high frequency (15,00,000 Hz) is used. The same method is used to investigate heart and liver problems and look for tumours in the body.

As people get older, stones sometimes build up inside their kidneys. They are very painful. They can be removed by surgery. However ultrasound offers a method of removing the stones without surgery. High energy shock waves produced by a powerful ultrasound machine is used to smash the stones into tiny pieces. The tiny pieces can then come out with urine.

Ultrasound finds many other medical and industrial uses. A dentist uses ultrasound to shake the dirt and plaque off teeth. The same idea is used to clean spectacles, jewellery and clothes.

### QUESTIONS

1. Why are X-rays not used to see unborn babies in the mother's uterus?
2. Will you be able to hear the sound produced by an ultrasound machine?
3. Which ultrasound will have greater amplitude—one used to see inside the body or one used to smash kidney stones?
4. Ultrasound can be used to determine the sex of the unborn baby. However this is banned in India. Can you say why?
5. Which sound waves can transfer more energy—audible sound or ultrasound?